Psychological Interventions and Cultural Diversity

Related Titles of Interest

Cognitive and Behavioral Interventions: An Empirical Approach to Mental Health Problems
Linda W. Craighead, W. Edward Craighead, Alan E. Kazdin, and Michael J. Mahoney (Editors)
ISBN: 0-205-14586-8

Multicultural Assessment Perspectives for Professional Psychology
Richard H. Dana
ISBN: 0-205-14092-0

Counseling and Psychotherapy: A Multicultural Perspective, Third Edition
Allen E. Ivey, Mary Bradford Ivey, and Lynn Simek-Morgan
ISBN: 0-205-14226-5

Counseling for Diversity: A Guide for School Counselors and Related Professionals
Courtland C. Lee (Editor)
ISBN: 0-205-15321-6

The Clinician's Handbook: Integrated Diagnostics, Assessment, and Intervention in Adult and Adolescent Psychopathology, Fourth Edition
Robert G. Meyer
ISBN: 0-205-17181-8

Psychotherapy and Counseling with Minorities: A Cognitive Approach to Individual and Cultural Differences
Manuel Ramirez III
ISBN: 0-205-14461-6

Psychological Interventions and Cultural Diversity

Edited by
Joseph F. Aponte
University of Louisville

Robin Young Rivers
Young-Rivers Associates
Louisville, KY

Julian Wohl
University of Toledo

Allyn and Bacon
Boston · London · Toronto · Sydney · Tokyo · Singapore

This book is dedicated to those family members who have been instrumental in our professional development and careers

Copyright © 1995 by Allyn & Bacon
A Simon & Schuster Company
Needham Heights, Massachusetts 02194

Library of Congress Cataloging-in-Publication Data
Psychological interventions and cultural diversity / Joseph F. Aponte,
    Robin Young Rivers, Julian Wohl, editors
        p. cm.
    Includes bibliographical references and index.
    ISBN 0-205-14668-6
    1. Minorities—Mental health services—United States. 2. Cultural psychiatry—United States. 3. Psychiatry, Transcultural—United States. 4. Cross-cultural counseling—United States. I. Aponte, Joseph F. II. Rivers, Robin Young. III. Wohl, Julian.
    RC451.5.A2P79 1995
    362.2'08'693—dc20

94-44704
CIP

Printed in the United States of America
10 9 8 7 6 5 4 3 2 1   99 98 97 96 95

Contents

Preface

Historically, America has been viewed as a melting pot in which people from many different cultural and national backgrounds would be immersed. Emerging from this pot with those differences gone, they would be assimilated Americans. Any residues of cultural values and traditions typically were ignored or suppressed in the interest of furthering the process of Americanization. The result was to be a universally shared American value system. For the past five decades, the media have also depicted a normative life-style and values as those of an upper-middle-class White family, usually of mixed and unidentified European background. Despite the fact that this image was true for only a small percentage of the population, it was the stereotype that was presented as the norm.

Mental health professionals, no less than others, are products of their cultures. They too functioned for the most part as if there existed a "normal" American family and individuals against which their clientele could be compared. With that world view, mental health professionals were under no pressure to examine and reconsider the implicit assumption that their theories and methods were universally applicable, despite the fact that their clients were frequently culturally different from themselves. The source of difficulties in those intercultural relationships was more often seen as problems within the client in accepting or cooperating with the treatment. Undoubtedly some professionals modified their treatments so that they could work effectively with culturally different clients, but without necessarily identifying the issues as "cultural." Many others did not.

In the past three decades, the melting pot has been turned upside down and its contents poured out to create the pluralistic society of today. Ethnic groups constitute an increasingly large portion of the American population, a trend that we know will accelerate into the next century because of high immigration and birth rates in those groups. Practitioners are compelled to acknowledge and confront practical problems in working with increasing numbers of culturally different people. These demographic and professional realities have provoked moral sensibility, political consciousness, and social action within the mental health professions. To note that the practitioner must take into account clients' social, ethnic, racial, linguistic, and other culturally defining characteristics has become almost a banality of the trade. Developing the particular skills and sensibilities necessary to make that axiom not just a cliché but a vital part of clinical training and practice is imperative.

Before proceeding, we need to clarify what we mean by the phrase "ethnic minority," designate which ethnic groups we refer to as being at risk, and comment on the terms *ethnic* or *ethnicity, culture,* and *race* as they are used in this field. North American society includes many different groups of people that can claim legitimately to be ethnic minorities. With so many ethnic groups present, any single one must necessarily constitute a minority when compared with the total population. No single ethnic group constitutes anywhere near 50 percent of the overall population, as it would have to do to achieve majority status. It is in this statistical sense and in no other that the term *minority* is used in this book. This point is made because of the complaint occasionally heard that the term *minority* should not be coupled with *ethnic* because it has a pejorative connotation of inferiority or powerlessness. Unfortunately, such interpretations are sometimes made, but we urge readers to keep in mind a politically neutral, nonemotive definiton.

Who are the minority groups that are "at risk"? The literature in this field is noteworthy in its failure to acknowledge that the ethnic minority groups that are the main subject of concern do not exhaust the supply of ethnic groups in North America. Psychological services are difficult to provide to members of many ethnic groups because of differences in cultural backgrounds. This is true, for example, of many individuals of East European and Middle Eastern family origins, who may find the idea of revealing their personal lives to strangers, expressing negative attitudes about family members, or discussing sexual matters with someone much younger or of the opposite sex almost intolerable. But these groups are rarely the focus in discussions of American ethnic minorities, nor will they be here.

In the world of the 1990s, the groups that are the focal point of clinical and human service interest are those that historically and currently have suffered most blatantly and severely from being both underserved and badly served. They have experienced neglect, discrimination, and unequal treatment. A disproportionately large number of them are among the most economically, educationally, and vocationally impoverished members of North American society. Even those who are middle class and upper middle class have suffered the abuse associated with racial discrimination and the effects of racism in the larger society. Four broad groups fulfill these criteria and are included as the focus of this book: African Americans (Blacks), Hispanics (Latinos), Asian Americans, and Native Americans (American Indians). The terms used here to refer to these groups are not the only ones in use. Regional and political differences within these groups exist, and no term used to refer to any particular group will escape some criticism. As much as possible, the terms used in this book reflect prevailing usage.

The concepts of *ethnicity, race,* and *culture* are not used with any great care or precision in this field. Yet it is clear that members of the same ethnic group can differ substantially from one another in their cultural framework. *Ethnicity* refers to a group within a larger group distinguished by nationality (national origins), language, or other distinctive characteristics. *Race* is a biological concept, defined sometimes by a phenotype (hair texture, skin color) and sometimes by the genotype (the frequency of certain genes), which has acquired many unscientific connotations. Often, race is replaced by *ethnicity* in professional communications. Indeed, within the mental health professions, differentiation among the terms *race, ethnicity,* and *culture* is infrequent.

All human behavior is conditioned by and is a reflection of the cultural context in which it is nurtured. *Culture* includes such features as attitudes, forms of emotional expression, patterns of relating to others, and ways of thought. It is patterned, organized, and integrated, not just a collection of traits or characteristics. Members of an ethnic group, by definition, are part of a larger social structure. They may share a common cultural identity to varying degrees, but they also will reflect the larger culture of which their subculture is a part. It is important to allow for both the separateness and the intimate relationship with the larger group of which the ethnic person is a part. From the perspective of clinical understanding of ethnic persons, this is important because it ensures that differing degrees of assimilation of the subculture to the larger culture are considered.

In the broadest sense, the goal of this book is to contribute to the education and training process of psychologists and other mental health workers. It is intended to fill a curriculum gap and a service need, a gap that will widen in the 1990s as training programs expand their teaching on psychological intervention with ethnic groups and as service providers and practitioners increase their contacts with these groups. This book is being created for the use of students in the early stages of their graduate training in the mental health fields. It is designed to be used as a primary text in courses focused on intervention with ethnic groups or as a secondary text for more general courses in intervention. The book is designed in such a fashion that it can also be useful to more advanced practitioners as they confront changes in the cultural makeup of their clientele.

All the chapters are new and appear here in print for the first time. They represent a synthesis of the scholarship and clinical experience of their authors and are designed to stand on their own as well as complement each other. We hope that readers will find useful information and stimulating ideas that can propel them to advance further the development of this youthful, yet rapidly growing, important domain. The ethnic population continues to grow, as does the need for addressing an array of problems faced by ethnic groups. The challenge to mental health professionals is to develop the knowledge and skills to address these needs and problems, and to learn to organize mental health services and treat ethnic groups in a sensitive, timely, and effective manner.

Acknowledgments

The co-editors of this book would like to express their appreciation to Margaret L. Biegert, Normal Jean Ralston, and Carolyn A. Mask for their contributions to various aspects of this book. We want to thank the reviewers of this manuscript for their helpful comments: Evelyn Diaz of the Miami Institute of Psychology, Barry Perlmutter of the California School of Professional Psychology in Fresno, and Sharon Rae Jenkins of the University of North Texas. In addition, the ideas and editorial comments of Catherine E. Aponte and Katherine Todd were particularly helpful on a number of chapters. Finally, we would like to thank our students, who have stimulated our thinking on the topic of diversity and who will find themselves working with diverse populations in one capacity or another.

About the Editors

Joseph F. Aponte is vice-chair and professor of psychology at the University of Louisville. He served as director of clinical psychology training at the University of Louisville for ten years. He is Puerto Rican and has been active in the Minority Post-Doctoral Fellows Program, National Research Council; he has chaired or served as a member of American Psychological Association commitees focusing on the education, training, and delivery of mental health services to ethnic populations. He has presented and published a number of papers on the education and training of ethnic persons and on the education and training of majority students and service providers to work with ethnic populations.

Robin Young Rivers is the president of Young-Rivers Associates, a psychological services and consulting firm in Louisville, Kentucky. She was formerly an assistant professor of psychology at Spaulding University, where she taught undergraduate, master's-, and doctoral-level students for five years. She is an African-American, licensed clinical psychologist whose interests include multicultural awareness/cultural diversity training, stress management training for African Americans, mental health issues of ethnic minority women and children, and treating emotional and behavioral problems of children and adolescents. She has made numerous presentations on cultural diversity issues in psychology.

Julian Wohl is Professor Emeritus of Psychology at the University of Toledo, where he served at different times as chair of the Psychology Department and director of the Clinical Psychology Training Program. For many years he taught a variety of graduate and undergraduate courses, and supervised clinical psychology graduate students in psychotherapy. He is a Diplomate in Clinical Psychology of the American Board of Professional Psychology. His intercultural experience includes Fulbright Lectureships in Burma (Myanmar) and Thailand. Dr. Wohl has taught in Hong Kong and participated in the founding of the Association of Psychological and Educational Counselors in Asia (APECA). He has lectured, written, and published on intercultural psychology.

List of Contributors

Joseph F. Aponte, Ph.D.
Department of Psychology
University of Louisville
Louisville, Kentucky

Jon M. Barnes, M.A.
Department of Psychology
University of Louisville
Louisville, Kentucky

Dana Cherry, M.A.
Behavioral Sciences and Human Services
University of Alaska
Fairbanks, Alaska

Chi-Ah Chun, M.A.
National Research Center on Asian American
   Mental Health
Department of Psychology
University of California
Los Angeles, California

James P. Clifford
Department of Psychology
University of Louisville
Lousiville, Kentucky

Ronald T. Crouch, M.S.W.
Center for Urban and Economic Research

University of Louisville
Louisville, Kentucky

Carol M. Cummings, Ph.D.
Department of Pan-African Studies and De-
   partment of Psychology
University of Louisville
Louisville, Kentucky

Terrlyn L. Curry, M.A.
Department of Psychology
Hofstra University
Hempstead, New York

Judith A. Curry-El, M.A.
Department of Psychology
University of Virginia
Charlottesville, Virginia

Richard H. Dana, Ph.D.
Regional Research Institute
Portland State University
Portland, Oregon

Dana D. DeHart, M.A.
Department of Psychology
University of Louisville
Louisville, Kentucky

xvii

Norman G. Dinges, Ph.D.
Behavioral Sciences and Human Services
University of Alaska
Fairbanks, Alaska

Kenneth Gee, M.D.
Department of Psychiatry
School of Medicine
University of California
San Francisco, California

Ay Ling Han, Ed.S.
Smith College Student Counseling Service
Northampton, Massachusetts

Robert T. Grant, Ph.D.
Department of Psychiatry and Behavioral
    Sciences
School of Medicine
University of Louisville
Louisville, Kentucky

Laura P. Kohn, M.A.
Department of Psychology
University of Virginia
Charlottesville, Virginia

Joan D. Koss-Chioino, Ph.D.
Department of Anthropology
Arizona State University
Tempe, Arizona

Norweeta G. Milburn, Ph.D.
Department of Psychology
Hofstra University
Hempstead, New York

Catherine A. Morrow, M.A.
Department of Psychology
University of Louisville
Louisville, Kentucky

Di-Ann Garnett Phillip, M.A.
Department of Psychology

University of Virginia
Charlottesville, Virginia

Barbara Plested, M.A.
Tri-Ethnic Center for Prevention Research
Department of Psychology
Colorado State University
Fort Collins, Colorado

Robin Young Rivers, Ph.D.
Young-Rivers Associates
Louisville, Kentucky

Stanley Sue, Ph.D.
National Research Center on Asian
    American Mental Health
Department of Psychology
University of California
Los Angeles, California

Randal Swaim, Ph.D.
Tri-Ethnic Center for Prevention Research
Department of Psychology
Colorado State University
Fort Collins, Colorado

Pamela Jumper Thurman, Ph.D.
Tri-Ethnic Center for Prevention Research
Department of Psychology
Colorado State University
Fort Collins, Colorado

Melba J. T. Vasquez, Ph.D.
Vasquez & Associates
Austin, Texas

Melvin N. Wilson, Ph.D.
Department of Psychology
University of Virginia
Charlottesville, Virginia

Julian Wohl, Ph.D.
Department of Psychology
University of Toledo
Toledo, Ohio

Chapter 1

The Changing Ethnic Profile of the United States

JOSEPH F. APONTE
RONALD T. CROUCH

Over the last several decades, census data have revealed significant changes in the number and distribution of culturally diverse populations, changes in immigration and migration patterns, and changes in ethnic group population characteristics (O'Hare, 1989; O'Hare & Felt, 1991; O'Hare, Pollard, Mann, & Kent, 1991; Valdivieso & Davis, 1988). This chapter will identify and describe these changes among African Americans, Hispanics, Asian Americans, and Native Americans, as well as within each of these groups. From this discussion will emerge a portrait of cultural diversity that will provide a context for assessment of the current mental health status and needs of these groups, and for the organization and delivery of mental health services and treatment of ethnic groups in this country.

Although it can be argued that American "racial" categories are too constrictive, illogical, and confusing, and may have adverse effects on ethnic group members (Betancourt & López, 1993; Spickard, 1992; Yee, Fairchild, Weizmann, & Wyatt, 1993), categorization is required for heuristic purposes. Several standard categories for classifying ethnic groups will be used in this chapter. These categories are limited to those used by the U.S. Bureau of the Census and include Blacks, Hispanics, Asian Americans and Pacific Islanders, and American Indians, Eskimos, and Aleuts (U.S. Bureau of Census, 1990a, 1990b). Use of these categories is meant to communicate that these individuals have similar histories, traditions, and personal experiences. However, the rich diversity in individual differences that exists within each of these groups, as well as across groups, must be recognized.

More specifically, for purposes of this chapter, African Americans (this term will be used interchangeably with Blacks) are considered to be those individuals who identify their heritage as being of African descent (O'Hare, 1992). Hispanics are those individuals who trace their cultural heritage to Spanish-speaking countries in Latin America and the Caribbean, to Spain or Mexico, or to the southwestern region of the United States, once under Spanish or Mexican control (Valdivieso & Davis, 1988). Asian Americans include those individuals who identify their ancestry or country of origin as Asian (e.g., China, Japan, Korea, Vietnam, Thailand, or Cambodia) or are from the Pacific Island region (e.g., Phillippines, Samoa, Guam) (O'Hare & Felt, 1991). The last U.S. Bureau of the Census category includes those individuals who can trace their ancestry to Native American, Eskimo, or Aleutian backgrounds.

Over the years, the racial and ethnic categories used in the decennial census have been refined, reflecting the changing social climate and demographic profile of this country (O'Hare, 1992). However, the increasing numbers of persons of mixed racial parentage present a problem. Race is self-reported on the census survey, so a person can identify his or her racial background as being that of either parent, but not of both. Further inaccuracies in census data can occur in the undercounting of racial or ethnic groups, particularly African Americans, Hispanics, and Native Americans who were missed between 4.4 and 5.0 percent of the time in the 1990 census (O'Hare, 1992). Young African Americans, illegal immigrants, Indians living on reservations, and non-English-speaking persons were among the groups most likely to be missed by the census.

The following sections of this chapter will provide information on the changing population base, background variations, place of residence, demographic characteristics, family structure and living arrangements, and socioeconomic status of the ethnic groups that are the focus of this book. It is important to recognize and understand the diversity that exists both across and within these groups. Such diversity will be present regardless of the projections into the twenty-first century and will provide the context for providing mental health services to these populations.

Changes in the Number of Ethnic Persons in the United States

According to the 1990 Census of Population and Housing, there are 29,986,060 Blacks; 22,354,059 persons of Hispanic origin (of any race); 7,273,662 Asian and Pacific Islanders; and 1,959,234 American Indians, Eskimos, and Aleuts (U.S. Bureau of Census, 1992b). A total of 9,804,847 individuals classified themselves as "other race," the vast majority of whom are of Hispanic origin. Of the total 1990 U.S. population of 248,709,873, 24.8 percent fall into the major ethnic categories just identified. Analysis by specific groups yields the following percentages of the total population: African Americans—12.3 percent, Hispanics—9.0 percent, Asian/Pacific Islanders—3.0 percent, and Indians/Eskimos/Aleuts—0.8 percent (see Figure 1-1).

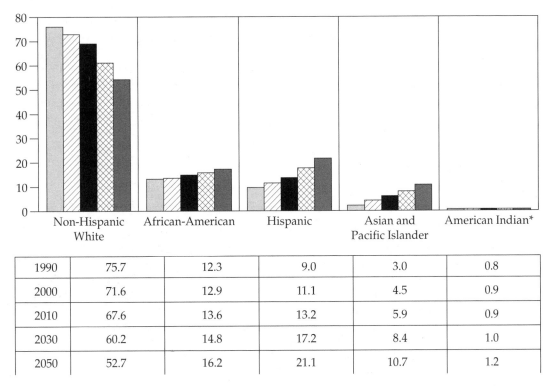

1990	75.7	12.3	9.0	3.0	0.8
2000	71.6	12.9	11.1	4.5	0.9
2010	67.6	13.6	13.2	5.9	0.9
2030	60.2	14.8	17.2	8.4	1.0
2050	52.7	16.2	21.1	10.7	1.2

FIGURE 1-1   Percentage distribution of the United States population by race and Hispanic origin.

Rapid increases in the number and percentage of these ethnic groups over the last several decades have been noted by a number of scholars and researchers (O'Hare, 1989; O'Hare & Felt, 1991; O'Hare et al., 1991; Neighbors, 1989). These changes have only served as a precursor for the dramatic changes that are anticipated by the year 2050 (see Figure 1-1). It is projected that the non-Hispanic White population will grow slowly until 2029, then slowly decline by 2050 (U.S. Bureau of Census, 1992a). The non-Hispanic White share of the population will steadily fall from 75 percent in 1992 to 60 percent in 2030, then to 53 percent in 2050.

Of particular significance are the changes that are projected in the next century for the different ethnic groups (O'Hare, 1992). It is projected that by the year 2000 12.9 percent of the population will be African American, 11.1 percent Hispanic, 4.5 percent Asian/Pacific Islander, and 0.9 percent American Indian/Eskimo/Aleut (U.S. Bureau of Census, 1992a). By 2050, African Americans, Hispanics, Asian Americans/Pacific Islanders, and American Indians/Eskimos/Aleuts will make up 16.2, 21.1, 10.7, and 1.2 percent of the population, respectively. The largest percentage change in population will be in the Hispanic and Asian/Pacific Islander groups, with the Asian/Pacific Islander groups growing at a slightly higher rate than Hispanics.

Immigration accounted for most of the ethnic population growth during the last several decades (O'Hare, 1992). During the last three decades, over 75 percent of all immigrants were either Black, Hispanic, or Asian (Passel & Edmonston, 1992). Immigration accounted for about half of the growth among Hispanics and nearly three-quarters of the growth among Asian Americans (O'Hare, 1992). Changing immigration laws and policies, unstable economic and political conditions, interracial marriages, and wars have accounted for the increased immigration (Thornton, 1992). It is projected that these trends will level off in the next century.

Variations within Ethnic Groups

Many people view all African Americans as being very similar. This view overlooks differences in cultural heritage (Baker, 1988), ethnic identity (Dana, 1993; McGoldrick, Pearce, & Giordano, 1982), family structure (Boyd-Franklin, 1990; Hardy, 1990; Fullilove, 1985), religious affiliation and spirituality (Dana, 1993; Gary, 1987), socioeconomic status (Bass, 1982), and geographical residence (O'Hare et al., 1991). Chapter 2 in this book identifies in detail the variables on which African Americans and other ethnic groups can vary. African Americans, however, are bound together by ancestral heritage and by their experiences with slavery, racism, discrimination, and oppression in this country (Atkinson, Morten, & Sue, 1989; Fleming, 1992; Howard & Scott, 1981).

Hispanics come from different countries and reflect a variety of migratory waves. Hispanics of Mexican ancestry account for 62 percent of Hispanic Americans, followed by Puerto Ricans (13 percent), Central and South Americans (12 percent), and Cubans (5 percent) (Valdivieso & Davis, 1988). Another 9 percent fall into the "Other Hispanic" category in the 1990 census (U.S. Bureau of Census, 1990a). Some Hispanics of Mexican ancestry can trace their origins prior to the settlement of the Southwest and the establishment of this country. Puerto Ricans have a special status because the island is a commonwealth of the United States and this group is free to travel back and forth between Puerto Rico and the mainland United States.

Asian Americans are among the most diverse of the ethnic groups. Some segments of this population have been in this country for many generations, whereas others are recent arrivals (O'Hare & Felt, 1991). The largest percentage of Asian Americans are Chinese (22 percent), followed by Filipinos (21 percent), Japanese (19 percent), Koreans (10 percent), and Asian Indian (10 percent) (U.S. Bureau of Census, 1990a). These groups, as well as more recent arrivals such as Vietnamese, Cambodians, and Laotians, vary in age and have different cultural backgrounds, languages, religions, and socioeconomic status. The forces that have led many of these individuals to migrate to this country also vary from seeking economic opportunities to fleeing political oppression.

The Native American population is markedly diverse. There are more than 200 tribes in the United States alone, speaking one or more of 200 tribal languages

(LaFromboise, 1988). According to Manson and Trimble (1982), there are 511 federally recognized native entities and an additional 365 state-recognized American Indian tribes. Despite these differences, there is a common ethnic background that ties American Indians together that is a product of historical experiences and political ideology more than racial and cultural similarities (Deloria, 1992). Eskimos and Aleutians are more homogeneous groups residing primarily in distinct geographical regions—the Alaskan Peninsula and the Aleutian Islands. These groups are closely related in language, race, and culture.

Where Ethnic Groups Live

At the beginning of the twentieth century approximately 90 percent of African Americans lived in the South (O'Hare, 1992; O'Hare et al., 1991). Difficult economic times in this region lead to an exodus of African Americans to the Northeast and Midwest. From 1970 to 1990, this trend reversed itself, with African Americans moving back to the South. Today approximately 53 percent of African Americans reside in the South, 9 percent in the West, and the remaining 38 percent evenly split between the Midwest and the Northeast (see Figure 1-2). The immigration of Blacks from outside the United States has been negligible. Between 1980 and 1990 an estimated 100,000 individuals of African ancestry migrated to this country from other countries.

Most African Americans live in metropolitan areas and tend to be concentrated

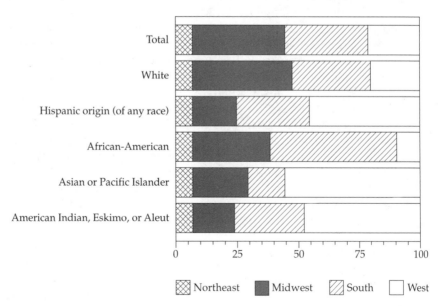

FIGURE 1-2   **Percentage distribution of race and Hispanic origin groups, by region, 1990.**

in the central parts of cities. According to the 1990 census, 31 cities have Black populations of 100,000 or greater (O'Hare et al., 1991). Eight cities (Atlanta, Baltimore, Birmingham, Detroit, Memphis, New Orleans, Newark, and Washington) have populations that are greater than 50 percent African American. African Americans tend to reside in segregated neighborhoods within cities and suburbs (O'Hare et al., 1991). Although they have experienced a decline in residential segregation over the last two decades, they still remain more segregated than Hispanics and Asian Americans (Massey & Denton, 1987).

The various Hispanic groups' geographical distribution has been determined primarily by their historical origins and point of entry into the United States. Mexican Americans are concentrated in the Southwest, particularly in California and Texas (O'Hare, 1992; U.S. Bureau of Census, 1991; Valdivieso & Davis, 1988). California has 7,687,938 persons (25.8 percent of the population) of Hispanic origin, and Texas has 4,339,905 (25.5 percent of its population) (U.S. Bureau of Census, 1990a). Puerto Ricans, the second largest Hispanic group, are concentrated primarily in the Northeast, particularly in the New York metropolitan area. Central and South Americans, though entering the United States typically through California, are found primarily in the Northeast, whereas Cubans are concentrated primarily in southern Florida.

Asian Americans historically, and at the present, are concentrated in the western region of the United States (O'Hare, 1992; U.S. Bureau of Census, 1991). According to O'Hare and Felt (1991), 67 percent of the Asian population resides in five states. The largest concentration of Asian Americans is found in California (40 percent), followed by Hawaii (11 percent); the remaining 16 percent reside in New York, Illinois, and New Jersey. Most Asian Americans are concentrated in metropolitan areas, with almost half of them living in one of six metropolitan areas (Honolulu, Los Angeles–Long Beach, San Francisco–Oakland, New York, Chicago, and San Jose). Approximately equal numbers of Asian Americans live in central cities and suburban areas, and only 6 percent live outside metropolitan areas.

Native Americans, Eskimos, and Aleuts are found primarily in the southern and western regions of the United States (O'Hare, 1992; U.S. Bureau of Census, 1991; 1992c). Of the 1,959,234 people constituting these groups, 28.7 percent are in the southern region and 47.6 percent are in the western region. Within the southern region, most Native Americans are located in Oklahoma (12.9 percent), and within the western region most American Indians are located in California (12.4 percent), Arizona (10.4 percent), and New Mexico (6.8 percent). Although most Eskimos and Aleuts reside in the Alaskan Peninsula and Aleutian Islands, the groups can also be found in the sub-Arctic regions of Canada, Greenland, and Siberia.

Characteristics of the Ethnic Population

African Americans are younger than the United States population as a whole and Whites in particular. According to the 1990 census, the median age of Blacks was

28.4 years, whereas Whites had a median age of 34.4 years (U.S. Bureau of Census, 1992b). It is anticipated that these differences will continue to increase in the future. By the year 2000, it is projected that the median ages of Blacks and Whites will be 29.8 and 37.0 years, respectively. By 2050, the median age of Blacks and White will be 32.8 and 41.5 years, respectively (U.S. Bureau of Census 1992a). As the Black population ages in the future, however, the White population will age at a faster rate.

The Hispanic age structure is similar to that of African Americans. The median age of Hispanics is 26.0 years, which is less than the median ages for both Blacks and Whites (U.S. Bureau of Census, 1992b). Future population projections indicate that differences between Hispanics and Blacks will diminish. It is projected that by the year 2000 the median age of Hispanics will be 27.8 years, in comparison to the 29.8 and 37.0 years of Blacks and Whites respectively. By 2050 it is projected that the median age of Hispanics will be 33.3 years whereas that of Blacks and Whites will be 32.8 and 41.5 years, respectively (U.S. Bureau of Census, 1992a). Thus, as the Hispanic population ages, it will begin to look like the Black population but will still be much younger than the White population.

Asian/Pacific Islanders fall between Blacks and Whites in age. According to the 1990 census, the median age of this group was 29.9 years in comparison to those of Blacks and Whites, which were 28.4 and 34.4 years, respectively (U.S. Bureau of Census, 1992b). Asian/Pacific Islanders will age at a more rapid rate than both Blacks and Whites, so that by the year 2000 the median age for Asian/Pacific Islanders is projected to be 31.2 years, in comparison to 29.8 and 37.0 years for Blacks and Whites, respectively, and by 2050 the median age for Asian/Pacific Islanders is projected to be 36.1 years, in comparison to 32.8 and 41.5 years for Blacks and Whites, respectively (U.S. Bureau of Census, 1992a).

American Indians/Eskimos/Aleuts also tend to be younger than Whites. Their median age is 26.3 years, almost identical to that of Hispanics (U.S. Bureau of Census, 1992b). Future projections for American Indians/Eskimos/Aleuts are also similar to those for Hispanics. According to U.S. Census population projections, by the year 2000 the median age of these groups will be 27.4 years. By 2050, however, these groups will have a median age of 29.2, which is lower than the Hispanic median age of 33.3 years (U.S. Bureau of Census, 1992a). Few changes in age between American Indians/Eskimos/Aleuts are projected for either 2000 or 2050.

To obtain a better understanding of the age population characteristics of the various ethnic groups, the 1990 census data were clustered into eight categories: (1) 0–4 years (Preschool), (2) 5–13 years (Childhood), (3) 14–18 years (Adolescence), (4) 19–24 years (Young Adulthood), (5) 25–44 years (Young Families), (6) 45–64 (Older Families), (7) 65–74 years (Young Elderly), and (8) 75 years and above (Elderly). These categories correspond to well-established age categories and reflect periods during which major life changes, milestones, and a variety of stressful life events and experiences occur.

Table 1-1 indicates that all of the ethnic groups are younger than Whites. American Indians/Eskimos/Aleuts are the youngest, with 37.4 percent being 18 years of age or younger (Preschool, Childhood, and Adolescence categories), fol-

TABLE 1-1   Percentage of Total, Age by Race and Hispanic Origin for
United States, 1990

Age Category	White	African American	Hispanic	Asian/ Pacific Islander	American Indian[a]
0–4 years	6.8	9.3	10.7	8.1	10.3
5–13 years	12.0	16.0	17.1	14.3	18.0
14–18 years	6.3	8.5	8.9	8.0	9.1
19–13 years	8.8	10.6	12.3	10.5	10.3
25–44 years	32.0	32.0	32.9	36.6	31.8
45–64 years	19.7	15.3	13.0	16.3	14.6
65–74 years	8.0	5.0	3.2	4.1	3.7
75+ years	5.9	3.4	2.0	2.1	2.2

[a]Includes Eskimos and Aleutian Islanders.

lowed by Hispanics (36.7 percent), Blacks (33.8 percent) and Asian/Pacific Islanders (30.4 percent). At the other end of the continuum, Whites are clearly older than the other ethnic groups, with 13.9 percent of this population being at least 65 years old (Young Elderly and Elderly categories). Of particular note is the large White cohort (19.7 percent) in the 45–64 group, who will be moving into the Young Elderly category. Blacks are the only group that comes close to the rates for older Whites.

Ethnic Group Birth Rates

Although birth rates (number of live births per 1,000 population) for both Blacks and Whites have declined over the last several decades, the rate for Blacks is still significantly higher than that for Whites (Ahlburg & De Vita, 1992; O'Hare, 1989). Differences in birth rates between African Americans and Whites can be accounted for primarily by socioeconomic status. Comparison of cohorts of the same socioeconomic status reveals few differences between the groups (O'Hare, 1989; O'Hare et al., 1991). The birth rate for Blacks is projected to increase slightly by the year 2000 and then decline to its present level by 2050. Whites, by contrast, will experience a less rapid decrease in birth rate through 2050 (U.S. Bureau of Census, 1992a).

Hispanics currently have the second highest birth rate of all ethnic minority groups (Ahlburg & De Vita, 1992). It is projected, however, that this group's rate will decline to two-thirds of its current rate by 2050. In fact, according to the U.S. Bureau of the Census, by 2025 this group's rate drops below that of Blacks and that of American Indians/Eskimos/Aleuts (U.S. Bureau of Census, 1992a). Such changes are primarily reflective of the age structure of the different groups and the decreasing number of Hispanic women of childbearing age as this group gets older. Variations in birth rate do exist within Hispanic groups, with Cubans having the lowest fertility rates and Puerto Ricans and Mexican Americans having relatively higher rates.

The birth rate for Asian Americans/Pacific Islanders is the lowest of all the ethnic minority groups, although it is higher than that of Whites. As previously mentioned, the rapid population growth that will continue in the future for this group is due primarily to immigration into the United States from Asia and the Pacific Islands (O'Hare & Felt, 1991). Future projections indicate that the birth rate for Asians/Pacific Islanders will decline as 2050 approaches but will continue to be greater than that of Whites (U.S. Bureau of Census, 1992a). Within the Asian groups there is some variation, with the Vietnamese, Laotians, and Cambodians having higher birth rates than the other groups.

American Indians/Eskimos/Aleuts have the highest birth rates of all the ethnic groups. The birth rate by 2050 for this group is projected to be very similar to the current rate (U.S. Bureau of Census, 1992a). Thus, the differences in birth rate between this group and Whites and other ethnic groups will continue to increase as we move into the twenty-first century and the birth rates for these other groups level off. Few differences in birth rate exist between Native Americans, Eskimos, and Aleuts. There are insufficient data to predict whether these similarities will continue in the future.

Ethnic Group Mortality Rates

Life expectancy for both African Americans and Whites has increased over the last several decades, and the gap in life expectancy between these two groups has decreased during this same period (O'Hare et al., 1991; Soldo & Agree, 1988). Whites, however, continue to have a longer life expectancy than Blacks (76.0 vs. 70.0 years) (Soldo & Agree, 1988; U.S. Bureau of Census, 1992d). Closer inspection of available health statistics data yields important gender differences. The differences between Whites and Blacks become even more striking when male and female comparisons are made. White males have a life expectancy of 72.6 years, compared with 66.0 years for Black males, a difference of 6.6 years. White females have a life expectancy of 79.3 years, whereas Black females have a life expectancy of 74.5 years, a difference of 4.8 years.

What accounts for these sharp differences between Black and White life expectancy? One major factor is the high infant mortality rate for Blacks (17.6 infant deaths per 1,000 live births) in comparison to Whites (8.5) (National Center for Health Statistics, 1990). Blacks have higher death rates for a number of illnesses. They are 3.4 times more likely than Whites to die of AIDS, 2.8 times more likely to die of kidney diseases, and 2.4 times more likely to die of diabetes. Another important contributor to the difference in life expectancy is homicide, the leading cause of death for young Black males, who are 7.6 times more likely to die by homicide than are their White counterparts (Hammond & Yung, 1993; O'Hare et al., 1991).

Projections indicate that the rates of change (rates per 1,000 population) for ethnic groups will level off by 2050 and will continue to be significantly different than those for Whites. For the year 2000, the net change (death rate subtracted from birth rate and net migration) for Whites, Blacks, Hispanics, Asian/Pacific Islanders, and American Indians/Eskimos/Aleuts will be 5.9, 13.3, 27.1, 40.7, and 13.9, respectively (U.S. Bureau of Census, 1992a). By 2050, these rates will be 2.2, 9.6, 13.6, 14.8, and 12.4, respectively. The most dramatic change will be for Asian/Pacific Islanders and Hispanics, with net migration rates decreasing dramatically, birth rates decreasing slightly, and death rates increasing slightly for both groups.

Family Structure and Living Arrangements

Household size varies among these ethnic groups. African-American households are larger than White households but not as large as Hispanic households. The average Black household contained 2.9 persons in 1990, in comparison to 2.5 persons for Whites and 3.6 persons for Hispanics (O'Hare, 1992). Asian/Pacific Islander households contained an average of 3.4 persons, and American Indian/Eskimo/Aleutian households contained 3.1 persons. The households of all of the ethnic groups were more likely to include other adults in addition to a married couple. Asian families in particular are more than twice as likely as Whites to live in extended families (O'Hare & Felt, 1991).

Marriage patterns for these ethnic groups are significantly different from those of Whites (Ahlburg & De Vita, 1992). Although divorce rates for both ethnic groups and Whites have increased since the 1960s, the percentage of ethnic women who had never married increased dramatically in comparison to the figure for White women (O'Hare, 1989; O'Hare et al., 1991). In 1990, 17.0 percent of White females, 33.0 percent of Black females, and 23.0 percent of Hispanic females 15 years and older had never married (U.S. Bureau of Census, 1990a). Data are not currently available for Asian/Pacific Islanders and American Indians/Eskimos/Aleuts. These patterns are also reflected in households with children that were headed by females with no husband present (Bianchi, 1990). The percentages were 14.0, 47.0, 22.2, 10.1, and 28.7, respectively, for Whites, Blacks, Hispanics, Asian/Pacific Islanders, and American Indians/Eskimos/Aleuts (U.S. Bureau of Census, 1990b).

Socioeconomic Status of Ethnic Groups

The socioeconomic status (SES) of ethnic groups has a direct impact on the goods, services, opportunities, and power available to individuals from these groups. Although the SES status of most ethnic groups has improved over the last several decades, there remains a significant gap between these groups and Whites (O'Hare et al., 1991, Valdivieso & Davis, 1988). It is also important to recognize the differences in socioeconomic status that exist both across and within ethnic groups (O'Hare & Felt, 1991; O'Hare et al., 1991). For example, although some groups, such as Asian Americans, have prospered, there are subgroups such as Laotians and Vietnamese who have not but have remained at the low-SES end.

Several key variables can be viewed as constituting socioeconomic status: occupational status, income, and education (Adler et al., 1994). Each of these variables can be viewed as important in its own right. Gains have been made by almost all of the ethnic groups in each of these areas, yet many African Americans, Hispanics, Asian Americans, and American Indians still lag behind Whites in the types of jobs they have, the income they earn, and the educational levels they have achieved (O'Hare & Felt, 1991; O'Hare et al., 1991; Valdivieso & Davis, 1988). In addition, some of the gains experienced by these groups in these areas in the 1970s appear either to have leveled off or, in some cases, to have been reversed in the 1980s.

Occupational Status

Although African Americans are one of the groups that made occupational strides in the 1970s, a comparison between this group and Whites indicates that clear disparities remain between the two groups (O'Hare et al., 1991). According to the 1990 census, whereas 27.1 percent of Whites were in managerial and professional positions, only 16.5 percent of Blacks were in such positions (U.S. Bureau of Census, 1990b). At the other end of the continuum, 22.9 percent of Blacks were in semiskilled labor positions, in comparison to 14.2 percent of Whites. Occupational patterns for Black women were similar to those for men, although the disparities were less pronounced.

Hispanics have not fared as well as African Americans at the higher occupational levels (O'Hare, 1992). Only 13.1 percent of Hispanics can be found in managerial and professional occupations (U.S. Bureau of Census, 1990b). As with African Americans, there tend to be high concentrations of Hispanics in semiskilled and service positions. There is also a relatively high concentration of Hispanics in the farming, fishing, and forestry category because of the large number of Hispanic migrant farmworkers. Limited command of English and limited economic opportunities account in part for the high concentration of Hispanics in these occupations.

The distribution of occupations for Asian/Pacific Islanders is similar to that of Whites, but they are more likely to be in managerial or professional positions or manufacturing and trade jobs (O'Hare & Felt, 1991). Asian/Pacific Islanders also are less likely than Whites to be in blue-collar positions and are unlikely to be employed on farms. Interesting age differences are found when the younger and older age cohorts are examined. Young (16–24 years) Asian/Pacific Islanders in comparison to Whites are underrepresented in the job market and are more likely to be in school. At the other end of the continuum (55 years of age and above), Asian/Pacific Islanders tend to be overrepresented in the job market. Members of this ethnic group do not retire at the same rate as Whites.

American Indians/Eskimos/Aleuts resemble African Americans at the higher occupational levels and Hispanics at the lower levels (O'Hare, 1992). Of particular importance is their concentration in semiskilled and service positions, with 38.7 percent having occupations in these categories. Almost 4 percent are engaged in farming and related occupations, which is reflective of the rural backgrounds of many members of this group. The high concentration of ethnic group members in these lower level occupations have a direct bearing on the quality of career opportunities available to them and on individual and family income.

Levels of Income

Striking disparities can be found across ethnic groups in income (O'Hare, 1992). According to the 1990 census, Asian/Pacific Islanders had the highest mean household income ($46,695), followed by Whites ($40,308), Hispanics ($30,301), American Indians/Eskimos/Aleuts ($26,206), and Blacks ($25,872) (U.S. Bureau of Census, 1992c). Such figures are misleading in that Asian/Pacific Islanders and Hispanics tend to have more persons per household than the other groups (O'Hare & Felt, 1991). Per capita income provides a more accurate picture of income. Whites had a mean per capita income of $15,687, followed by Asian/Pacific Islanders ($13,638), Blacks ($8,859), Hispanics ($8,400) and American Indians/Eskimos/Aleuts ($8,328). The last three groups had a per capita income almost half that of Whites.

The relative economic well-being of Asian/Pacific Islanders taken as a group does not reflect the subgroup differences within this broad ethnic group. For example, according to O'Hare and Felt (1991), the median family income of Chinese Americans was four times that of Laotians. Income levels for Asian Americans appear to be driven by residence and immigration status. Those Asian Americans living in high-cost areas (e.g., Los Angeles, San Francisco, Honolulu) may have higher salaries than other Asian Americans, but their living expenses would also be very high. Recent immigrants from China, Laos, Thailand, and Cambodia would tend to earn lower incomes than those Asian Americans who were born in the United States.

Reference to Figure 1-3 indicates that the poverty rates reflect the previously noted income differences. All ethnic groups had higher poverty rates than Whites (Bianchi, 1990; O'Hare, 1992; U.S. Bureau of Census, 1990b). These differences become even more dramatic when one focuses on persons under 18 years of age. Whites in this age group had a poverty rate of 12.5, whereas Blacks, Hispanics, Asian/Pacific Islanders, and American Indians/Eskimos/Aleuts had rates of 39.8, 32.2, 17.1, and 38.8, respectively. The Asian/Pacific Islander group was the only ethnic group that came close to Whites. High poverty rates for Blacks tended to occur outside the West region, particularly in the Northeast and Midwest, and for Hispanics in the Northeast (Massey & Eggers, 1990).

Educational Status

Educational levels can serve as another indicator of socioeconomic status, because education provides access to income and economic opportunity in this country. Inspection of the 1990 census data indicates that Blacks, Hispanics, and American Indians/Eskimos/Aleuts are more likely than Whites to have less than a high school education (see Figure 1-4). Hispanics are the least likely of all the groups to have a high school education, whereas Asian/Pacific Islanders are almost identical to Whites (O'Hare, 1992). At the other end of the continuum, Blacks, Hispanics, and American Indians/Eskimos/Aleuts are less likely to have a bachelor's degree or to have done graduate and professional work. The highest percentage of college graduates are Asian/Pacific Islanders.

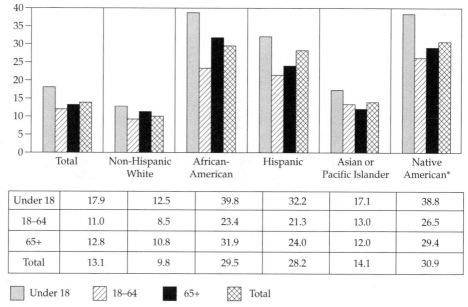

	Total	Non-Hispanic White	African-American	Hispanic	Asian or Pacific Islander	Native American*
Under 18	17.9	12.5	39.8	32.2	17.1	38.8
18–64	11.0	8.5	23.4	21.3	13.0	26.5
65+	12.8	10.8	31.9	24.0	12.0	29.4
Total	13.1	9.8	29.5	28.2	14.1	30.9

▨ Under 18   ▨ 18–64   ■ 65+   ▨ Total

*Includes Eskimo and Aleutian Islanders.

FIGURE 1-3   Percentage distribution in poverty by age for United States by race and Hispanic origin, 1990.

Ethnic youth present a number of problems in the occupational, economic, and educational domains. African-American, Hispanic, and American Indian youth are likely to be unemployed or underemployed. Since individuals from these groups tend to drop out of school early, they find themselves in the job market with limited skills. The positions they do find tend to be in the service sector, with wages at or close to minimum wage. African-American youth are particularly at risk, with unemployment rates over twice that of their White counterparts (U.S. Bureau of Census, 1992d). Patterns are thus in place at a very early age that prevent these individuals from obtaining education and skills that will allow them to escape from poverty.

Implications for Mental Health Status and Delivery of Services to Ethnic Groups

What are the mental health status and service delivery implications of the changing ethnic group profile in this country? It is clear that the absolute number of African Americans, Hispanics, Asian Americans/Pacific Islanders, and American Indians/Eskimos/Aleuts is increasing and that these groups will represent a larger percentage of the total population. According to Cheung and Snowden (1990) the

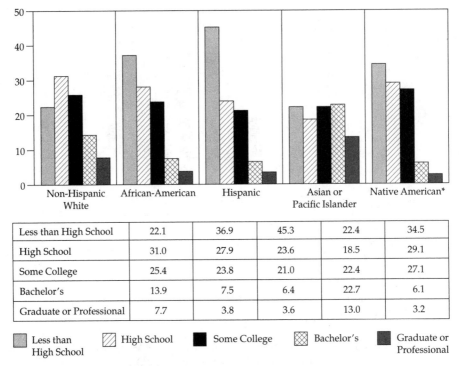

	Non-Hispanic White	African-American	Hispanic	Asian or Pacific Islander	Native American*
Less than High School	22.1	36.9	45.3	22.4	34.5
High School	31.0	27.9	23.6	18.5	29.1
Some College	25.4	23.8	21.0	22.4	27.1
Bachelor's	13.9	7.5	6.4	22.7	6.1
Graduate or Professional	7.7	3.8	3.6	13.0	3.2

Less than High School High School Some College Bachelor's Graduate or Professional

*Includes Eskimo and Aleutian Islanders.

FIGURE 1-4 **Percentage distribution of United States educational levels by race and Hispanic origin, 1990.**

utilization rates of mental health centers and some state hospitals have increased for ethnic groups as a whole. Such changes will further tax the mental health system in this country, which many believe is underfunded, as members of these ethnic groups find their way into the public-sector mental health care delivery system.

These population changes and the resulting pressures on the mental health care delivery system will force mental health planners, administrators, and frontline workers to look more closely at how individuals from various ethnic groups present for treatment and are misdiagnosed (see Chapter 3 of this book). Standard types of psychological assessment devices also will need to be critically evaluated for their appropriateness and adequacy for use with ethnic individuals (see Chapter 4). Finally, the premature termination and unsuccessful treatment outcomes that ethnic persons experience in the mental health system will need to be examined closely in order for the system to be more responsive and effective with these persons (see Chapter 16).

Although ethnic groups are not evenly distributed throughout the United States, the sheer increase in their numbers means that, as time goes by, mental health service providers will be increasingly likely to come into contact with clients from these groups in either the public or the private mental health sector. These contracts will increase as the number of ethnic group members continues to grow dramatically after the year 2000. Therefore, it will be incumbent upon graduate and professional mental health training programs to embed content and training experiences relevant to these groups into their programs in order to train service providers who are competent to work with these groups (American Psychological Association, 1993; see Chapter 17).

The increasing number of recent immigrants will also tax mental health services in a number of ways. Some of the issues for this group are generic to all ethnic groups, whereas others are unique to recent immigrants. Those immigrants who come from impoverished, politically volatile, and wartorn countries present with a number of economic, social, and psychological issues that pose difficult challenges for mental health service providers (see Root, 1992; Takaki, 1994, for more detailed discussions). Recent changes in public attitudes and policies will exacerbate such difficulties as attempts are made to slow immigration and limit access to social services, health care, and education.

Changing ethnic population characteristics (age, fertility rates, and mortality rates) will also have a profound impact on the need for mental health services and on the types of services to be provided to these groups. Ethnic persons tend to be young and will experience problems that are common to all young populations, as well as other issues that are unique to them such as struggles around their ethnic identity, discrimination, oppression, and experiences with war (see Chapters 2 and 10). Members of these groups are also aging and will begin to experience more frequently some of the same problems faced by the White elderly as well as some problems that are unique to the ethnic elderly, such as poverty (see Chapter 12).

There are a number of social, health, and psychological problems that have a greater impact on ethnic group members than on Whites (National Center for Health Statistics, 1991a, 1991b). Members of these groups are more susceptible to acts of violence directed against them. High rates of alcohol and drug abuse are also found among African Americans, Hispanics, and Native Americans, and high rates of AIDS are found in both African-American and Hispanic men and women (see Chapters 13 and 14). Specialized services may be needed to address these problems. The importance of addressing these issues will increase as the ethnic population grows, particularly within the younger age cohorts, which are more susceptible to these problems (see Chapter 10).

Family structure and marriage patterns for these ethnic groups are significantly different from those of Whites (see Chapter 6). Ethnic households tend to be larger than White households. African-American, Hispanic, and Native American households are also more likely than White households to be headed by females, a high percentage of whom have never married (see Chapter 11). Although extended families and flexibility of roles within some ethnic groups can provide social support and serve as a rich resource, the pressures faced and limited resources available to group members can take their toll, leading to the development of a variety of social and psychological problems.

Socioeconomic status and those components that are subsumed under this rubric (occupational status, income, and education) have a direct impact on a number of issues faced by ethnic groups. The relationship between SES and health and mental health functioning is well established (Adler et al., 1994; Dohrenwend & Dohrenwend, 1969; Lorion & Felner, 1986). Ethnic groups, particularly African Americans, Hispanics, and Native Americans, tend to be overrepresented in the lower SES strata. Socioecomomic status is also linked to the availability and utilization of mental health services, with low-SES persons having fewer services available to them, having less experienced clinicians assigned to treat them, being placed on medication more frequently, and finding themselves in the least desirable service setting.

In addition, the existence of barriers to desirable occupations, the high rates of poverty, and the limited educational opportunities and early dropout rates of ethnic students all have a demoralizing and debilitating effect on members of these ethnic groups. Such forces, which limit upward mobility and keep these ethnic groups oppressed, can be viewed as "economic trauma" leading to stress (Herzberg, 1990). Ethnic children, especially when they grow up in single-parent households without the support of extended families, are particularly at risk to perform poorly in school and also to develop psychological problems. The economic forces and limited opportunities experienced by ethnic persons can also lead to families becoming homeless (see Chapter 15).

The increasing need for mental health services resulting from the changing ethnic profile of the United States is obvious. Such a statement was made over a decade ago by the President's Commission on Mental Health (1978). These services need to target high-risk ethnic populations such as children, adolescents, single-parent females, and the elderly. In addition to individual therapeutic intervention strategies, other intervention strategies such as family approaches, group treatments, and community interventions are called for (see Chapters 5, 6, 7, and 8). These approaches will need to be altered, when appropriate, and new intervention approaches and strategies developed in order to ensure their effectiveness with ethnic clients and community residents.

References

Adler, N. E., Boyce, T., Chesney, M. A., Cohen, S., Folkman, S., Kahn, R. L., & Syme, S. L. (1994). Socioeconomic status and health: The challenge of the gradient. *American Psychologist, 49,* 15–24.

Ahlburg, D. A., & De Vita, C. J. (1992). New realities of the American family. *Population Bulletin,* 47(2), 1–44.

American Psychological Association. (1993). Guidelines for providers of psychological services to ethnic, linguistic, and culturally diverse populations. *American Psychologist, 48,* 45–48.

Atkinson, D. R., Morten, G., & Sue, D. W. (Eds.). (1989). *Counseling American minorities: A cross cultural perspective* (3rd ed.). Dubuque, IA: Brown.

Baker, F. M. (1988). Afro-Americans. In L. Comas-Díaz & E. E. H. Griffith (Eds.), *Clinical guidelines in cross-cultural mental health* (pp. 151–181). New York: Wiley.

Bass, B. A. (1982). The validity of socioeconomic factors in the assessment and treatment of Afro-Americans. In B. A. Bass, G. E. Wyatt, & G. J. Powell (Eds.), *The Afro-American family: Assessment, treatment, and research issues* (pp. 69–83). New York: Grune & Stratton.

Betancourt, H., & López, S. R. (1993). The study of culture, ethnicity, and race in American psychology. *American Psychologist, 48,* 629–637.

Bianchi, S. M. (1990). America's children: Mixed prospects. *Population Bulletin, 45,* 1–43.

Boyd-Franklin, N. (1990). Five key factors in the treatment of Black families. In G. W. Saba, B. M. Karrer, & K. V. Hardy (Eds.), *Minorities and family therapy* (pp. 53–69). New York: Haworth.

Cheung, F. K., & Snowden, L. R. (1990). Community mental health and ethnic minority populations. *Community Mental Health Journal, 26,* 277–291.

Dana, R. H. (1993). *Multicultural assessment perspectives for professional psychology.* Boston: Allyn and Bacon.

Deloria, V., Jr. (1992). American Indians. In J. D. Buenker & L. A. Ratner (Eds.), *Multiculturalism in the United States: A comparative guide to acculturation and ethnicity* (pp. 31–52). New York: Greenwood.

Dohrenwend, B. P., & Dohrenwend, B. S. (1969). *Social status and psychological disorder: A casual inquiry.* New York: Wiley.

Fleming, C. G. (1992). African-Americans. In J. D. Buenker & L. A. Ratner (Eds.), *Multiculturalism in the United States: A comparative guide to acculturation and ethnicity* (pp. 9–29). New York: Greenwood.

Fullilove, M. T. (Ed.). (1985). *The Black family: Mental health perspectives.* San Francisco: Rosenberg Foundation.

Gary, L. E. (1987). Religion and mental health in an urban Black community. *Urban Research Review, 7,* 5–7.

Hammond, W. R., & Yung, B. (1993). Psychology's role in the public health response to assaultive violence among young African-American men. *American Psychologist, 48,* 142–154.

Hardy, K. V. (1990). The theoretical myth of sameness: A critical issue in family therapy training and treatment. In G. W. Saba, B. M. Karrer, & K. V. Hardy (Eds.), *Minorities and family therapy* (pp. 17–33). New York: Haworth.

Herzberg, J. H. (1990). Economic trauma: A public health problem. In J. D. Noshpitz & R. D. Coddington (Eds.), *Stressors and the adjustment disorders* (pp. 447–454). New York: Wiley.

Howard, A., & Scott, R. A. (1981). The study of minority groups in complex societies. In R. H. Munroe & B. B. Whiting (Eds.), *Handbook of cross-cultural development* (pp. 113–152). New York: Garland Stem.

LaFromboise, T. D. (1988). American Indian mental health policy. *American Psychologist, 43,* 388–397.

Lorion, R. P., & Felner, R. D. (1986). Research on psychotherapy with the disadvantaged. In S. L. Garfield & A. E. Bergin (Eds.), *Handbook of psychotherapy and behavior change* (3rd ed.) (pp. 739–775), New York: Wiley.

Manson, S. M., & Trimble, J. E. (1982). American Indian and Alaska Native communities: Past efforts, future inquiries. In R. L. Snowden (Ed.), *Reaching the underserved: Mental health needs of neglected populations* (pp. 143–163). Beverly Hills, CA: Sage.

Massey, D., & Denton, N. (1987). Trends in the residential segregation of Blacks, Hispanics, and Asians: 1970–1980. *American Sociological Review, 52,* 802–825.

Massey, D., & Eggers, M. L. (1990). The ecology of inequality: Minorities and the concentration of poverty, 1970–1980. *American Journal of Sociology, 95,* 1153–1188.

McGoldrick, M., Pearce, J. K., & Giordano, J. (1982). (Eds.), *Ethnicity and family therapy.* New York: Guilford.

National Center for Health Statistics. (1990). *Monthly vital statistics report 39,* No. 7. Supplement. Washington, DC: U.S. Government Printing Office.

National Center for Health Statistics. (1991a). *Life tables, Volume 2 of vital health statistics of the United States, 1988.* Washington, DC: U.S. Government Printing Office.

National Center for Health Statistics. (1991b). *Vital and health statistics. Family structure and children's health: United States, 1988.* Washington, DC: U.S. Government Printing Office.

Neighbors, H. W. (1989). Improving the mental health of Black Americans: Lessons from the community mental health movement. In D. P. Willis (Ed.), *Health policies and Black Americans* (pp. 348–380). New Brunswick, NJ: Transaction.

O'Hare, W. P. (1989). Black demographic trends in the 1980s. In D. P. Willis (Ed.), *Health policies and Black Americans* (pp. 37–55). New Brunswick, NJ: Transaction.

O'Hare, W. P. (1992). America's minorities—The demographics of diversity. *Population Bulletin, 47*(4), 1–47.

O'Hare, W. P., & Felt, J. C. (1991). *Asian Americans: America's fastest growing minority group.* Washington, DC: Population Reference Bureau.

O'Hare, W. P., Pollard, K. M., Mann, T. L., & Kent, K. M. (1991). African Americans in the 1990s. *Population Bulletin, 46,* 1–40.

Passel, J. S., & Edmonston, B. (1992). *Immigration and race: Trends in immigration to the United States.* Washington, DC: Urban Institute.

President's Commission on Mental Health. (1978). *Volume 2: Task panel reports: The nature and scope of the problem.* Washington, DC: U.S. Government Printing Office.

Root, M. P. P. (Ed.). (1992). *Racially mixed people in America.* Newbury Park, CA: Sage.

Soldo, B. J., & Agree, E. M. (1988). America's elderly. *Population Bulletin, 43,* 1–51.

Spickard, P. R. (1992). The illogic of American racial categories. In M. P. P. Root (Ed.), *Racially mixed people in America* (pp. 12–23). Newbury Park, CA: Sage.

Takaki, R. (Ed.). (1994). *From different shores: Perspectives on race and ethnicity in America.* New York: Oxford University Press.

Thornton, M. C. (1992). The quiet immigration: Foreign spouses of U.S. citizens, 1945–1985. In M. P. P. Root (Ed.), *Racially mixed people in America* (pp. 64–76). Newbury Park, CA: Sage.

U.S. Bureau of Census. (1990a). *1990 Census of population and housing—Summary tape file 1: Summary population and housing characteristics.* Washington, DC: U.S. Government Printing Office.

U.S. Bureau of Census. (1990b). *1990 Census of population and housing—Summary tape file 3. Summary social, economic, and housing characteristics.* Washington, DC: U.S. Government Printing Office.

U.S. Bureau of Census. (1991). Race and Hispanic origin. *1990 Census Profile,* No. 2, 1–8.

U.S. Bureau of Census. (1992a), *Current population reports, P25-1092, Population projections of the United States by age, sex, race, and Hispanic origin: 1992–2050.* Washington, DC: U.S. Government Printing Office.

U.S. Bureau of Census. (1992b). *1990 Census of population, 1990 CP-1-4, General population characteristics.* Washington, DC: U.S. Government Printing Office.

U.S. Bureau of Census. (1992c), *1990 Census of population and housing, 1990 CPH-1-1, Summary population and housing characteristics.* Washington, DC: U.S. Government Printing Office.

U.S. Bureau of Census. (1992d). *Statistical abstract of the United States: The national data book* (112th ed.). Washington, DC: U.S. Government Printing Office.

Valdivieso, R., & Davis, C. (1988). *U.S. Hispanics: Challenging issues for the 1990s.* Washington, DC: Population Reference Bureau.

Yee, A. H., Fairchild, H. H., Weizmann, F., & Wyatt, G. E. (1993). Addressing psychology's problems with race. *American Psychologist, 48,* 1132–1140.

Chapter 2

Impact of Acculturation and Moderator Variables on the Intervention and Treatment of Ethnic Groups

JOSEPH F. APONTE
JON M. BARNES

The beliefs, values, attitudes, feelings, and behavior of ethnic group members have a direct impact on their psychological functioning, their concept of illness, and their expression of symptoms. These factors also affect their entry into the mental health system, the types of services provided, the processes involved in working with them, and the outcome of the interventions or treatments given. These psychological phenomena are in turn influenced by a number of variables that are the result both of unique individual characteristics and of those unique experiences of ethnic group members resulting from their cultural background, their degree of acculturation, and their experiences with the majority culture (Dana, 1993; Jalali, 1988).

The overall approach taken in this chapter is that the cultural background, degree of acculturation, and experiences within the majority culture provide a framework through which current experiences and information are processed and behavior is produced (Hughes, 1993). A variety of factors will be identified and discussed that have direct impact on four major ethnic groups (African Americans, Hispanics, Asian Americans, and Native Americans). These factors will be subsumed under five major headings: (1) process of acculturation, (2) outcome of the acculturation process, (3) language usage and fluency, (4) characteristics of the ethnic group and their moderating effects, and (5) the moderating effects of the larger society or majority group.

    This chapter utilizes the cross-cultural acculturation model developed by Berry and his associates (Berry, 1980; Berry & Kim, 1988; Berry, Kim, Minde, & Mok, 1987) in which acculturation is viewed as consisting of a number of phases or different forms of contact between the ethnic group and the majority group. Figure 2-1 presents a modified version of the model. The mode or type of acculturation and

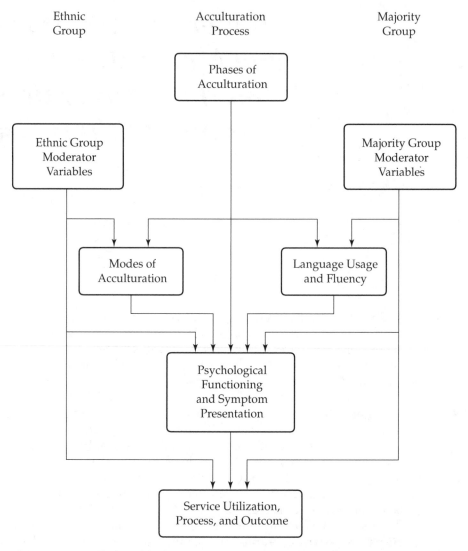

FIGURE 2-1   Relationship between acculturation, moderator variables, and treatment.

language usage and fluency that results from the acculturation process will vary across individuals. Both of these acculturation variables can directly influence psychological functioning and symptom presentation, as well as service utilization, process, and outcome. A series of ethnic group and majority group moderator variables can also have a direct effect on the acculturation process and on the person and treatment components.

Process of Acculturation

The determination of an ethnic person's degree of acculturation is important for several reasons:

1. It leads to a fuller understanding of the person by providing a picture of the person's view of him- or herself, view of others of the same or different ethnic groups, and view of the dominant or majority culture.
2. It can lead to stress and to the development of psychopathology in the person (Berry & Kim, 1988; Berry et al., 1987).
3. It influences how ethnic persons present their problems (see Chapter 3 of this book).
4. It is related to the utilization of mental health services.
5. It is of crucial importance in guiding the treatment of ethnic persons and determining the success of therapeutic interventions.

Acculturation has been traditionally viewed as a unidirectional process of assimilation by which a person relinquishes his or her ethnic values, beliefs, customs, and behaviors for those of the majority culture (Garcia & Lega, 1979; Sodowsky, Lai, & Plake, 1991). Others have argued that acculturation is a bidirectional process in which the ethnic person is assimilated by the majority culture but also retains his or her ethnic culture and identity (Berry, 1980; LeVine & Padilla, 1980; Mendoza & Martinez, 1981; Sanchez & Atkinson, 1983). The majority culture can also be affected and changed by the ethnic person or group. Both the assimilated and retained components need to be assessed in order to obtain an accurate picture of an individual's level of acculturation (Sodowsky et al., 1991).

According to Berry and his associates (Berry, 1980; Berry & Kim, 1988) acculturation can be broken down into a series of phases (see Table 2-1):

1. *Precontact phase,* during which each independent cultural group has its own characteristics
2. *Contact phase,* in which the groups interact with each other
3. *Conflict phase,* in which pressure is exerted on the nondominant group to change in order to fit with the majority group
4. *Crisis phase,* during which the conflict comes to a head

TABLE 2-1 Description of Acculturation and Moderator Variables

Acculturation Variables	Moderator Variables
Phases of Acculturation • *Precontact:* No contact between groups • *Contact:* Interaction between groups • *Conflict:* Differences between groups emerge • *Crisis:* Conflict comes to a head • *Adaptation:* Stability reached between groups *Modes of Acculturation* • *Assimilation*: Relinquish ethnic and assume majority identity • *Integration:* Maintain ethnic and incorporate majority identity • *Separation:* Withdrawal from majority society • *Segregation:* Forced separation by larger society • *Marginalization:* Lack of identification with both ethnic and majority group *Language Usage and Fluency* • *Language usage:* Use of nonstandard English, language switching • *Language fluency:* Monolingual (English), bilingual, monolingual (ethnic language)	*Ethnic Group Moderator Variables* • *Type of acculturating group:* Immigrant, refugee, native people, ethnic group, sojourners • *Cultural characteristics:* World view (values, beliefs, attitudes and behaviors) • *Social characteristics:* Socioeconomic status, familial and social network structure • *Individual characteristics:* Personality characteristics, coping skills *Majority Group Moderator Variables* • Oppression and legal constraints on ethnic groups • Racism, prejudice, and discrimination

5. *Adaptation phase,* in which relations between the two groups are stabilized into one of several modes of acculturation

The amount of stress experienced and the psychological functioning of the ethnic person will vary according to the acculturation phase (Berry & Kim, 1988; Berry et al., 1987).

Outcome of the Acculturation Process

Acculturation can be viewed as an adaptation process in which the ethnic person embraces different modes of acculturation (Berry, 1980; Berry & Kim, 1988). Five modes have been described by Berry and his associates: *assimilation, integration, separation, segregation,* and *marginalization* (see Table 2-1). Which mode is assumed by the ethnic person will depend on how he or she deals with two fundamental questions (Berry & Kim, 1988):

• How much of one's cultural identity is valued and retained?
• To what degree are positive relations with the majority (dominant) culture to be sought?

Assimilation involves the ethnic person relinquishing his or her cultural identity and assuming the beliefs, values, attitudes, and behaviors of the majority group (Berry & Kim, 1988). *Integration* involves maintaining one's cultural identity while also incorporating components of the majority group. *Separation* involves self-imposed withdrawal from the larger society, as opposed to *segregation*, which entails forced separation of ethnic groups by the larger society. Finally, *marginalization* occurs when the ethnic person can identify with neither his or her traditional culture nor with the majority culture. These modes (like the previously mentioned phases) are not static, nor do they have to be sequenced, so that it is possible for an individual to move in and out of a given acculturation phase or mode.

Acculturation is a complex, multifaceted, and multidimensional process (Cuellar, Harris, & Jasso, 1980; Olmedo, 1979; Sodowsky et al., 1991). It is situation-driven in that the ethnic person may adopt different acculturation options in different interpersonal or social situations (Mendoza, 1984; Sodowsky & Carey, 1987). The acculturation status and options available to and used by ethnic persons are influenced by a number of moderator variables such as socioeconomic status, residence (including years of residence in the United States and ethnic density of the person's neighborhood), immigration status, and familial and social network structure (Garcia & Lega, 1979; Sodowsky & Carey, 1987).

Over the past two decades, a number of scholars and researchers have attempted to conceptualize and measure the extent and nature of acculturation of individuals from different ethnic groups (Atkinson, Morten, & Sue, 1989; 1994; Ruiz, 1990). These efforts have employed the terms *cultural* or *ethnic identity*, or *acculturation* models and measures. Acculturation and ethnic identity should not be viewed as synonymous but as separate conceptual elements (Kitano, 1989). Whereas acculturation focuses on the person's values, beliefs, and behaviors, ethnic identity is the process and outcome of integrating a person's racial/ethnic aspects into his or her overall self-concept and identity (Helms, 1990a).

The classification of ethnic persons according to different ethnic identity stages or acculturation categories has recently come under criticism (Atkinson et al., 1989, 1994). Critics have noted that such groupings suggest that these individuals have immutable characteristics and that they move through a linear course of ethnic/cultural development (Helms, 1985; Ponterotto & Wise, 1987). These groupings do not recognize the dynamic interplay and the intrapersonal and interpersonal variations in the ethnic persons' behavior. Such ethnic/cultural identity systems can be useful in understanding an ethnic person, but they should not be used rigidly to classify a person or an ethnic group in the treatment process.

Some of the earlier ethnic identity models described the transformation in values, attitudes, and behaviors that African Americans went through in becoming more aware of their own ethnic identity (Cross, 1972; Hall, Cross, & Freedle, 1972; Jackson, 1975). Jackson (1975), for example, identified the following four stages in his Black Identity Developmental Model: Passive Acceptance, Active Resistance, Redirection, and Internalization. The person moves from acceptance of White values and standards, to rejection of these influences, to viewing White values and standards as irrelevant to Black culture, and finally to both acceptance of Black culture and acceptance of selected aspects of White culture on their own merits.

Many of the African-American experiences identified in these earlier models have been noted in other ethnic groups, and more recent ethnic identity models have been developed that are applicable to other ethnic groups. A prime example is the Minority Identity Development (MID) model developed by Atkinson and his associates (Atkinson et al., 1989; 1994). This model identifies five stages (Conformity, Dissonance, Resistance and Immersion, Introspection, and Synergetic Articulation and Awareness) of the struggles of ethnic persons to understand themselves, their culture, other cultures, and the majority culture. These stages are not rigid boundaries, and it is assumed that ethnic persons will experience each stage at some time in their lives.

A number of other acculturation and ethnic identity measures have been developed for each of the major ethnic groups. Among these are the Developmental Inventory of Black Consciousness (Milliones, 1980); the Hispanic Acculturation Scale (Marin, Sabogal, Marin, Otero-Sabogal, & Perez-Stable, 1987); the Ethnic Identity Questionnaire (Masuda, Matsumoto, & Meredith, 1970); the Rosebud Personal Opinion Survey (Hoffman, Dana, & Bolton, 1985) for American Indians; and the Suinn-Lew Asian Self Identity Acculturation Scale (Suinn, Richard-Figuero, Lew, & Vigil, 1987; see Dana, 1993, and Helms, 1990b for a more detailed description of ethnic identity models and instruments). Instruments such as these can provide important information on the ethnic person's background and on current level of acculturation and ethnic identity.

Language Usage and Fluency

Language usage and fluency can be viewed as both a component and an outcome of the acculturation process. Although language usage and fluency are critical factors in all human interactions, they take on added importance in the therapeutic process with members of ethnic groups such as African Americans, who may not use standard English, and Hispanics and Asians, who may not be fluent in English (Russell, 1988; Sciarra & Ponterotto, 1991). Russell (1988) argues that language not only communicates the content of the message but also provides information on the context of the message and the background of the messenger. This background information can include the messenger's place of origin, group membership, status in the group, and relationship to the person with whom he or she is communicating.

Language Usage

There are a variety of Nonstandard English (NE) language patterns in use in this country, including Louisiana Cajun, Hawaiian pidgin, Southern, New England, and New York dialects (Russell, 1988). The NE that has been most researched and written about is Black Nonstandard English (BNE) (Dillard, 1972). The terms *code switching* (Straker, 1980) and *diglossia* (Giglioli, 1976) are sometimes used inter-changeably to refer to individuals changing into NE in the course of conversations. Under these circumstances the content, grammar, and intonation of the message may change, leading to different interpretations of values, attitudes, and behavior by the listener.

Black Nonstandard English is usually learned from family and peers in informal settings. It is associated with and used to convey intimacy, is used spontaneously, and reflects a feeling of solidarity with others who share its use (Russell, 1988). Standard English is typically used in public and formal settings. The use of BNE and SE can have an impact both on the ethnic person who is receiving services or is being treated by an ethnic therapist, and on the White service provider or therapist working with the ethnic client. This impact can be in the area of perceived credibility and similarity and in the quality of communication between the participants in the treatment process.

The use of NE or BNE may be present at the initial stage of contact between the client and the therapist, or it may emerge during the course of treatment. When present initially, it may lead the therapist to misdiagnose clients or assign them to an inappropriate treatment. Some clients may not be viewed as credible candidates for treatment by the therapist, and the therapist may not be viewed as a credible helping person by some clients. Differences between client and therapist may be heightened and the similarities between the two minimized. Such factors have been found to be linked to premature termination of clients from treatment (Beutler & Clarkin, 1990).

Language Fluency

According to the 1990 census, there were 17,405,064 persons five years of age or older who spoke Spanish (U.S. Bureau of Census, 1990). Of these individuals, 26.2 percent are reported to speak English "not well" or "not at all." Another 4,471,621 individuals used an Asian or Pacific Island language, with 23.8 percent of this group having minimal or no ability to speak English. In both groups, those speaking little or no English were concentrated primarily in cohorts that would use the mental health system (i.e., ages 18–64 years). For these individuals, communication be-tween client and therapist would be hampered, affecting not only entry into the system but also the process and outcome of treatment (Flaskerud & Liu, 1991).

Bilingual clients enter into the treatment process at a disadvantage in compari-son to those who use SE because most clinicians are White and use SE. Marcos (1976), for example, has found that clients who spoke primarily Spanish were rated as having more pathology, having less connection with the interviewer, and being more emotionally withdrawn when interviewed in English as compared to Spanish. These findings were attributed to the disruptive speech patterns and reduced expression of affect that emerge when a person is required to speak in a nondomi-nant language (Marcos & Urcuyo, 1979). The disrupted speech and reduced affect can be interpreted as signs of psychological disturbance and pathology and have a negative impact on the interactions between client and therapist.

It is imperative that practitioners identify the dominant language in their bilingual clients. This is easy to determine when the person does not speak English well or does not speak English at all but is more difficult when the client is completely bilingual. Under these circumstances, it is necessary to determine the client's degree of acculturation. This is done by getting information about the person's use of language with family and friends and on the ethnic moderator variables described in this chapter, such as the nature and extent of the person's social networks and the degree to which he or she embraces and practices ethnic rituals and customs.

Working with monolingual or bilingual clients may call for the use of translators within the assessment and treatment processes. These translators need to be aware of the verbal and nonverbal nuances within the language they are translating and also should have a mental health background (Sabin, 1975; Westermeyer, 1990; 1993). It is also imperative that the clinician be aware of the clinical and linguistic differences in expression in various languages for emotional and psychological experiences (Westermeyer, 1993), the differential importance assigned to psychological symptoms (Kinzie & Manson, 1987), and the connotations that may be present in expressing psychological symptoms.

Characteristics of Ethnic Groups and Their Moderator Variables

A number of variables can interact with and have a moderating effect on acculturation (Berry & Kim, 1988; Sodowsky et al., 1991). This section will focus on the following variables: (1) type of acculturating group (e.g., immigrant, native people); (2) cultural characteristics, as reflected in the world view of African Americans, Hispanics, Asian Americans, and Native Americans; (3) social characteristics of the acculturating group, including socioeconomic status and familial and social network structure; and (4) individual characteristics, including personality characteristics and coping skills. These variables can also have a direct impact on psychological functioning and on the use and effectiveness of mental health services independent of acculturation.

Type of Acculturating Group

A critical element affecting the process and outcome of acculturation is whether or not the acculturation is voluntary or forced (Berry & Kim, 1988). African Americans were forced through slavery to come to this country. Some Hispanic and Asian groups departed their countries for political reasons, whereas others came to the United States voluntarily in search of educational and economic opportunities or may be joining family members already living in this country. Native Americans have experienced the effects of a majority culture that forced its values, beliefs, and practices on them and actively removed them from their ancestral lands in the early history of the United States (LaFromboise, 1988).

These aspects of acculturation are reflected in the different types of acculturating groups described by Berry and Kim (1988): (1) *immigrants,* who are migratory and relatively voluntary; (2) *refugees,* who are migratory and relatively involuntary; (3) *native people,* who are indigenous, nonmigratory, and involuntary; (4) *ethnic groups,* who are nonmigratory and are more or less willingly interacting with the larger society of their own choosing; and (5) *sojourners,* who have temporary cultural contact with the society (e.g., foreign students, diplomats, international workers).

Each of these groups corresponds to ethnic populations found in this country. The groups are at differential risk of developing psychological problems. High rates of anxiety, depression, and adjustment problems, for example, have been found among recent immigrants and refugees (Mollica & Lavelle, 1988; Westermeyer, 1993). This can be attributed to the tumultuous circumstances under which some of the refugees left their country and to the lack of traditional resources and social supports that some immigrants and refugees experience in this country. Native peoples, particularly Native Americans, have also experienced a great many social and psychological problems that can be traced to their earlier experiences with White culture and their current status in this country (LaFromboise, 1988).

Cultural Characteristics of Ethnic Groups

World view constitutes part of the cultural characteristics of ethnic groups. It consists of those values, beliefs, and attitudes that serve to organize and shape perceptions, expectations, and behavior. It also consists of a number of components, including cultural heritage as reflected in values, beliefs, language, group identity, and individual identity or self-concept (Dana, 1993; Landrine, 1992). The world views of members of ethnic groups in the United States are also, to some extent, necessarily shaped and modified by variables related to dealing with the majority culture—that is, by the experience of racism, prejudice, discrimination, and oppression.

Culture-specific elements of world view can have an impact on entry into treatment and its subsequent course and outcome. A representative sample of ethnic culture-specific components of world view might include the individual's beliefs about mental illness and emotional difficulties, beliefs about the appropriate expression of emotion, and attitudes toward authority figures. Once treatment has begun, any or all of these elements might prove to be significantly discrepant from the therapist's conceptualization and treatment of psychological distress. A therapist's failure to appreciate such discrepancies, how these elements may have differently shaped a client's approach to life in general and to therapy in particular, can result in early termination and impaired treatment effectiveness (Atkinson et al., 1989).

To identify this discrepancy, one must first have a context. Sue (1981) presents a generic model of Western psychotherapy that consists of language variables, class-bound values, and culture-bound values. The latter involve seeing therapy as (1) centered on the individual; (2) encouraging verbal, emotional, and behavioral openness and intimacy between client and therapist; (3) employing an analytic, linear, and cause-and-effect approach to problem definition and solution; and (4) making a clear distinction between physical and mental functioning. Disparities between this model of the therapeutic enterprise and the world views of ethnic group members can be found on all of these dimensions.

Western individualism is a value not shared by all other cultures (Draguns, 1988). An emphasis on anonymity, humility, and submission of the self to the welfare of the tribe, for example, is characteristic of Native American culture (Foster, 1988; Heinrich, Corbine, & Thomas, 1990). Among Asian Americans, the group (both family and community) is also valued above the individual (Bemak, 1989; Lee, 1988). The intense focus on the individual typical of Western therapy is alien to these world views, and a lack of sensitivity to the discomfort engendered in an ethnic client by such a focus can lead to ineffective treatment and early termination.

In Western treatment, a premium is placed on verbal communication and overt expression of emotions. In contrast, verbal expression and communication may be lacking or may take different forms in other non-Western groups (see the section on language usage and fluency in this chapter). In addition, suppression, reserve, and caution in the display of emotions when dealing with Whites or people in authority and power who represent the majority culture occur among African Americans (Ridley, 1984), in Hispanic culture (particularly with the male machismo norm) (Ghali, 1977), and in Asian culture (Lee, 1988).

Western patterns of thinking involve linearity, analytical and deductive reasoning, and abstract verbal conceptualization. For most Native Americans, however, a more holistic processing style, utilizing metaphor, intuition, and visual representation, is characteristic (Foster, 1988). Lee (1988) contrasts Western logic of the mind with traditional Asian logic of the heart. A linear cause-and-effect approach to framing and solving such clients' problems is likely to be conceptually alien, leading clients to perceive a lack of therapist understanding and thus prompting early termination from treatment.

Other world view differences between Western and ethnic groups that have an impact on the therapeutic endeavor include (1) the emphasis placed on traditional practices by African Americans (Wilson & Stith, 1991), Hispanics (Ramos-McKay, Comas-Díaz, & Rivera, 1988), Asian Americans (Lee, 1988), and Native Americans (Heinrich, Corbine, & Thomas, 1990), and (2) the perceived relationship of the person to nature and the attribution of causality to internal and external events, with groups such as Asian Americans and Native Americans taking a more fatalistic approach than White majority persons to the experiencing of psychological problems (Atkinson et al., 1989).

Social Characteristics

Social characteristics as moderator variables can be conceptualized as consisting of socioeconomic status and family and social network structure. Although a substantive body of literature exists in each of these areas, this section will focus only on the relationship of ethnicity to these variables. Although these areas are necessarily interrelated, they will be discussed separately. Of particular interest is how these variables affect the acculturation process; the psychological functioning and symptom presentation of ethnic persons; and the mental health service utilization, process, and outcome.

Socioeconomic status (SES) lacks a clear operational definition in the mental health literature (Lorion & Felner, 1986). Classification into SES categories ranging from low SES to high SES is sometimes done on the basis of either education, occupation, or income (Adler et al., 1994). However, reliance on any single factor for classifying an ethnic person's SES is problematic inasmuch as he or she may be well educated but earning little income, or may have limited education yet have a reasonable income through the pooling of familial financial resources. Any operational definition of SES needs to be multidimensional and involve consideration of the individual's economic resources, social prestige, and social influence (Lorion & Felner, 1986). The latter two factors are particularly important for ethnic groups.

Using one or more of the previously identified factors to determine an ethnic person's SES would lead to an inescapable conclusion that a disproportionately high number of ethnic persons, particularly African Americans, Hispanics, and Native Americans, are in the low-SES stratum (see Chapter 1). Even among Asian Americans, who more closely approximate Whites in SES, there is variability such that a number of groups (e.g., Vietnamese, Laotians, and Cambodians) are disproportionately represented in the low-SES stratum because they have only recently arrived in this country and/or come from impoverished backgrounds in their country of origin.

Research across a variety of community and clinical samples indicates a strong relationship between SES and rates of psychopathology, utilization of mental health services, and effectiveness of these services (Atkinson et al., 1989; Comas-Díaz & Griffith, 1988; Gaw, 1993a; Wierzbicki & Pekarik, 1993). The general finding of such research is that persons from low-SES backgrounds exhibit more psychopathology, utilize mental health services less, and have less successful treatment outcomes than do middle-class and upper-class persons. It becomes important, then, to tease out the role that SES plays in each of these arenas. Does SES or ethnicity account for the differential outcomes between ethnic groups and Whites in psychological functioning and service effectiveness?

The research findings have been mixed. Some investigators have found that when SES is controlled, differences in psychopathology, mental health service utilization, and treatment outcomes between ethnic groups and Whites continue to exist (Dohrenwend & Dohrenwend, 1981a). When such differences have been found, a Social Causation Model, as opposed to a Social Selection Model, has been used to explain the results (Dohrenwend & Dohrenwend, 1981a). Other researchers have found that when SES is controlled, differences between ethnic groups and Whites on standard measures of psychological functioning disappear, mental health service utilization rates are similar, and little difference in treatment outcome is found (Briones et al., 1990).

Despite these mixed results, it can be argued that coming from a low-SES background can lead to more stresses than are found in middle- and upper-SES experiences. Low-SES ethnic persons can experience more *victimization* (stressful life experience), be more *vulnerable* (have fewer personal resources and less social supports), experience more *additive burdens* (combined effects of stressful events, limited personal resources, and limited social support), and be subject to more *chronic burdens* (long-term personal and situational stressors) than are persons from other social classes (Dohrenwend & Dohrenwend, 1981b; Lorion & Felner, 1986). Despite these factors, it is possible for low-SES ethnic persons to function well in society and to be "resilient." The question, then, is what accounts for this resiliency?

Familial and social network structure constitutes another important moderator variable that accounts for some of resiliency found in ethnic groups. This is reflected in the area of social support, which has been extensively researched and has been found to be linked to physical and psychological well-being in the general population (Sarason, Sarason, & Pierce, 1990; Schradle & Dougher, 1985). Social support can be viewed as consisting of social interactions or relationships that provide aid to a person and embed that person within a social system that offers love, care, and a sense of attachment. Two broad categories of social support have been identified in the literature: structural support or social embeddedness, and perceived or functional support (Barrera, 1986).

A number of explanations have been posited to account for the relationship between social support and physical and psychological well-being, including the Main Effects Model (Cohen, 1988), the Stress Buffering Model (Cohen & Willis, 1985), and the Stress Deterioration Model (Lin & Ensel, 1989). Although conflicting findings have emerged in the literature, it is apparent that the source of the social support (Dakoff & Taylor, 1990), the strength of the social ties and similarity with the person's social network (Lin, Woelfel, & Light, 1985), and the nature and severity of the stressor (Cohen & Willis, 1985) have important effects on physical and psychological well-being.

Ethnic groups have traditionally relied heavily on their immediate and extended families for social supports, a factor which may account in part for the "resiliency" found in some individuals. African Americans have complex networks involving immediate kin, several generations of relatives, and close friends residing in the same household (Boyd-Franklin, 1990; Miller, 1992). Hispanics and Asian Americans also rely heavily on immediate and extended family members, particularly grandparents (Kitano, 1989; Martinez, 1988). Some groups have a formal system such as the *compadrazgo* (godparents and co-parents) of Puerto Ricans that is built into the extended network (Ramos-McKay, Comas-Díaz, & Rivera, 1988). Native Americans utilize immediate family, extended family, tribal elders, and community for social support (Thompson, Walker, & Silk-Walker, 1993).

Such supports can have a moderating or mediating effect on the stress and difficulties experienced by ethnic persons. Several factors, however, can place ethnic persons at risk of having their social supports diminished or lost. Immigration policies that discourage the entrance of intact families into the United States have historically contributed to the fragmentation of African-American and Asian families. Social and economic policies, such as Aid for Dependent Children, encourage the maintenance of single-parent households. The acculturation of younger generations of Hispanics, Asians, and Native Americans can also lead to tensions and discord between children and their parents, who may be minimally acculturated (Martinez, 1993; Yamamoto, Silva, Justice, Chang, & Leong, 1993).

The extended support system of ethnic persons can also be put at risk through a variety of other factors. Requiring African-American and Hispanic children to attend nonneighborhood schools for purposes of desegregation can strain neighborhood ties. Some Native American children have also been sent to boarding schools away from their tribes. Because of harsh economic conditions on the reservations, some adults have been forced to seek economic opportunities in urban areas where community support may not be present. Immigration and resettlement policies that encourage Hispanics and Asians to reside in parts of the country where there is a low density of these groups may lead to isolation and feeling disconnected from one's group.

Individual Characteristics

A number of authors have attempted to sort out the importance of culture and personality in the development of psychopathology and its treatment (Draguns, 1988; Marsella, Tharp, & Ciborowski, 1979; Odejide, 1979; Smither, 1982). Implicit in their writings is the identification of cause–effect relations between socialization experiences and personality characteristics for different ethnic groups. Two positions have subsequently emerged: the *culturalistic position,* which argues for identifying individual differences that are linked to one's cultural background and experiences (Marsella et al., 1979), and the *universalistic perspective,* which argues that cultural and ethnic differences are of secondary importance (Odejide, 1979). Such positions closely correspond to the *emic* (indigenous/unique) and *etic* (external/universal) positions found in the cross-cultural literature.

Juris Draguns (1988) makes a persuasive argument for the importance of personality in the development and expression of psychopathology. Within any given culture, normal and abnormal persons share common personality characteristics. Yet, people's values, cognitions, locus of control, ego identity, valued behavior within the culture, and sense of belongingness can vary as a by-product of their culture and socialization experiences. In addition, variations exist in what and how thoughts, feelings, and behaviors get expressed publicly. These variations need to be identified and addressed in treatment interventions directed at ethnic persons.

Coping is part of the array of behaviors available to all people, regardless of their origins, for dealing with stress. Coping serves two functions: to protect the individual and to promote human growth and development. Coping strategies are part of a person's culture, particularly as internally represented by the ethnic person's values, beliefs, attitudes, cognitive styles, and behavior (Marsella, De Vos, & Hsu, 1985). Thus, coping cannot be understood apart from a person's basic orientation or world view (Marsella & Dash-Scheuer, 1988), nor without considering the person's experiences with the larger society.

A number of scholars and researchers have described coping as a process that involves eliminating or modifying the conditions that give rise to stress and the individual's reactions to the stress (Folkman & Lazarus, 1984; Pearlin & Schooler, 1978). More specifically, two major types of coping have been identified in the literature: problem-focused coping and emotion-focused coping (Folkman & Lazarus, 1984; Lazarus & Folkman, 1984). Problem-focused coping refers to engaging in problem solving to cope with a stressor, whereas emotion-focused coping involves ameliorating the emotional responses associated with a stressor.

Ethnic groups in the United States face a number of stressors, including those centering around education, employment, housing, family life, marriage, child rearing, security, safety, and health. They continually have to deal with racism, prejudice, and oppression. Many of these forces are external to the individual and beyond his or her control. Ethnic persons often must turn to emotion-focused coping strategies, particularly when difficult situations are chronic and require them to endure. The specific types of coping strategies will vary, given that there is evidence from cross-cultural research that members of different cultures use different coping strategies when confronted with similar stressors (Marsella & Dash-Scheuer, 1988).

Majority Group Moderator Variables

A variety of moderator variables emanating from the larger society or majority group have a direct impact on the acculturation process (see Figure 2-1). This section will focus on two such variables: (1) oppression and legal constraints on ethnic groups and (2) racism, prejudice, and discrimination. Although these factors may not be as blatant and explicit as they once were, they still exist in a variety of implicit and subtle forms, and within the past decade have begun to be expressed more openly. These moderator variables can have a direct effect on the ethnic person's psychological functioning and on the use and effectiveness of mental health services.

Oppression and Legal Constraints on Ethnic Groups

African-American experiences with racism have taken the form of oppression during different periods in United States history. First, Africans were forcibly removed from their homelands to be slaves. This era was followed by Emancipation, Reconstruction, and Black Codes or Jim Crow during the nineteenth century (Dana, 1993). Terrorism in the form of physical violence, lynchings, and property damage has been part of African-American history in this country. African Americans continue to experience limited opportunities and difficulties as reflected in their levels of health, education, occupations, and poverty (see Chapters 1 and 14). More recently, they have experienced the effects of the resurgence of political conservatism as civil rights legislation and affirmative action gains have been reversed (Griffith & Baker, 1993).

The experience of Hispanics has been quite varied. Oppression for Mexican

Americans has taken the form of job discrimination, immigration restrictions, school segregation, and electoral disenfranchisement (Martinez, 1993; Montejano, 1987). Puerto Ricans have experienced job discrimination but arrive in this country as citizens and have easily accessible transportation back to their place of birth (Ramos & Morales, 1985). The Cuban experience has been primarily a politically linked migration, with services such as the Cuban Refugee Program being in place for them (Bernal & Gutierrez, 1988) until the recent changes in 1994 by the Clinton administration. However, all Hispanic groups have experienced discrimination as reflected in the national opposition to bilingualism in this country (Padilla et al., 1991).

Asian Americans comprise a variety of groups with different experiences with oppression in this country. The Chinese and Japanese have the longest history in the United States. They migrated here in the nineteenth century seeking employment and economic opportunities. The Vietnamese, Cambodians, and Laotians are the most recent immigrants. The Chinese, Japanese, Koreans, and Filipinos were subjected to restrictive immigration laws, limited rights to own property, and segregated schooling. During World War II, mainland Japanese, in addition, were incarcerated in internment camps even though they were American citizens. The Exclusion Laws limiting immigration of Asians to this country was not repealed until 1965 (Gaw, 1993b; Fujii, Fukushima, & Yamamoto, 1993).

Like other ethnic groups, Native Americans are not a homogeneous group (LaFromboise, 1988; Thompson et al., 1993). The over 500 native entities that exist, share common experiences of oppression. These experiences have been described as that of a conquered people who have been displaced from their land, had children removed from their families, had the roles of males in their family and community undermined, and had their language eliminated (Dana, 1993; Trimble, 1987). Oppression has also been reflected in the contentious and distrusting relationship with federal government agencies such as the Bureau of Indian Affairs and the Indian Health Service.

Racism, Prejudice, and Discrimination

Another important majority group moderator variable is prejudice and discrimination. When directed at ethnic groups, it is referred to as *racism* and is similar to the many other "isms" encountered in our society, including sexism, classism, and ageism (Adams, 1990). Racism can take two forms—attitudinal (McConahay & Hough, 1976) and structural (Kluegel & Smith, 1983). It can be viewed as a psychosocial stressor that affects the daily lives of ethnic group members and subsequently interferes with the psychological functioning, adjustment, and social adaptation of these groups in the larger society.

At the individual level, *attitudinal racism* can mean that the majority group behaves toward ethnic groups in the following manners: (1) teasing, belittling, ridiculing, and disparaging; (2) labeling, stereotyping, stigmatizing, and derogating; (3) scapegoating and dehumanizing; (4) ignoring, neglecting, and locking away; and (5) denying equal opportunity and equal rights (Adams, 1990). At the broader level, *institutional racism* refers to patterns of rules, regulations, and behaviors that are exclusionary and exploitive and are part of an organization or social system. Such institutional racism typically has an ideology, set of procedures or practices, and physical apparatus supporting it (Adams, 1990).

Racism, prejudice, and discrimination have been viewed as affecting the ethnic person's work, self-regard, interpersonal relationships, and broader social environment. Impaired self-esteem is frequently cited as a psychological consequence of racism (Asamen & Berry, 1987; Brantley, 1983; Hughes & Demo, 1989). Racism has also been cited as a key contributor to psychological problems in ethnic groups, including substance abuse among African Americans, Hispanics, and American Indians (Harper, 1988; Lopez-Bushnell, Tyer, & Futrell, 1992; Oetting, Edwards, & Beauvais, 1988), child abuse and suicide among Native Americans (Hurejsi, Craig, & Pablo, 1992; McIntosh, 1984), and domestic violence among Asian Americans (Ho, 1990).

In addition to contributing to the development of psychological distress, these forces have a negative impact on entry into the mental health system and on the subsequent treatment process. A "healthy cultural paranoia" engendered in African Americans as a consequence of experience with racism and prejudice has been identified (Di-Angi, 1976; Jones, 1990). This distrust of majority institutions combined with the stigmatization associated with entering treatment may prevent the seeking of services (Priest, 1991). Having overcome this initial barrier, ethnic help-seekers may find themselves misdiagnosed, channeled away from needed services, assigned to inappropriate treatments, and serviced by the least experienced practitioners because of racist attitudes (Adams, 1990; Jones, 1990; Sabshin, Diesenhaus, & Wilkerson, 1970).

Ethnic group members may carry the hostility and suspicion resulting from discriminatory experiences into treatment. Barbarin (1984) held that many African Americans have "highly refined sensors capable of detecting racially based slurs in the most innocent of acts" (p. 14). When this "cultural paranoia" (Jones, 1990) combines with inadequate training, inexperience, and perhaps outright racism and prejudice on the therapist's part (thus confirming the client's suspicions), grossly impaired treatment process and attenuated outcome are likely to result (Barbarin, 1984; Jones, 1990; Sook Wha Ahn Toupin, 1980).

Summary

This chapter has pointed out the complexities of the interactions between ethnic and majority groups. The process of acculturation, which is a by-product of this interaction, involves several potential phases (e.g., *precontact, contact, conflict, crisis,* and *adaptation*), which can lead to several modes of adaptation (e.g., *assimilation, integration, separation, segregation,* and *marginalization*) and several patterns of language usage and fluency (Berry, 1980; Berry & Kim, 1988). This process of acculturation is in turn affected by several ethnic group moderator variables (e.g., type of acculturation group; cultural, social, and individual characteristics) and majority group moderator variables (e.g., oppression and legal constraints; racism, prejudice, and discrimination).

Viewing an ethnic person from this perspective can be overwhelming, for it means collecting information on these variables, incorporating these factors in one's conceptualization of the person, and engaging the individual on these issues, since they will be directly related to the person's psychological functioning, symptom presentation, service utilization, treatment process, and outcome. Despite the complexity of the task, this information is vital for the purpose of securing a comprehensive understanding and appreciation of the ethnic person and his or her relationship to others, to the broader community, and to society as a whole. Such information will have a direct impact on the process and outcome of treatment.

References

Adams, P. L. (1990). Prejudice and exclusion as social traumata. In J. D. Noshpitz & R. D. Coddington (Eds.), *Stressors and the adjustment disorders* (pp. 362–391), New York: Wiley.

Adler, N. E., Boyce, T., Chesney, M. A., Cohen, S., Folkman, S., Kahn, R. L., & Syme, S. L. (1994). Socioeconomic status and health: The challenge of the gradient. *American Psychologist, 49*, 15–24.

Asamen, J. K., & Berry, G. L. (1987). Self-concept, alienation, and perceived prejudice: Implications for counseling Asian Americans. *Journal of Multicultural Counseling and Development, 15*, 146–160.

Atkinson, D. R., Morten, G., & Sue, D. W. (1989). *Counseling American minorities: A cross cultural perspective* (3rd ed.). Dubuque, IA: Brown.

Atkinson, D. R., Morton, G., & Sue, D. W. (1994). *Counseling American minorities: A cross cultural perspective* (4th ed.). Dubuque, IA: Brown.

Barbarin, O. A. (1984). Racial themes in psychotherapy with Blacks: Effects of training on the attitudes of Black and White psychiatrists. *American Journal of Social Psychiatry, 4*, 13–20.

Barrera, M. (1986). Distinctions between social support concepts, measures, and models. *American Journal of Community Psychology, 14*, 413–445.

Bemak, F. (1989). Cross-cultural family therapy with Southeast Asian refugees. *Journal of Strategic and Systemic Therapies, 8*, 22–27.

Bernal, G., & Gutierrez, M. (1988). Cubans. In I. Comas-Díaz & E. E. H. Griffith (Eds.), *Clinical guidelines in cross-cultural mental health* (pp. 233–361). New York: Wiley.

Berry, J. W. (1980). Acculturation as varieties of adaptation. In A. M. Padilla (Ed.), *Acculturation: Theory, model, and some new findings* (pp. 9–25). Boulder, CO: Westview.

Berry, J. W., & Kim, U. (1988). Acculturation and mental health. In P. R. Dasen, J. W. Berry, & N. Sartorius (Eds.), *Health and cross-cultural psychology: Toward applications* (pp. 207–236). Newbury Park, CA: Sage.

Berry, J. W., Kim, U., Minde, T., & Mok, D. (1987). Comparative studies of acculturative stress. *International Migration Review, 21*, 491–511.

Beutler, L. E., & Clarkin, J. F. (1990). *Systematic treat selection: Toward targeted therapeutic interventions.* New York: Brunner/Mazel.

Boyd-Franklin, N. (1990). Five key factors in the treatment of Black families. In G. W. Saba, B. M. Karrer, & K. V. Hardy (Eds.), *Minorities and family therapy* (pp. 53–69). New York: Haworth.

Brantley, T. (1983). Racism and its impact on psychotherapy. *American Journal of Psychiatry, 140*, 1605–1608.

Briones, D. F., Heller, P. L., Chalfant, H. P., Roberts, A. E., Aaguirre-Hauchbaum, S. F., & Farr, W. F., Jr. (1990). Socioeconomic status, ethnicity, psychological distress, and readiness to utilize a mental health facility. *American Journal of Psychiatry, 147*, 1333–1340.

Cohen, S. (1988). Psychosocial models of the role of

social support in the etiology of physical disease. *Health Psychology, 7,* 269–297.

Cohen, S., & Willis, T. A. (1985). Stress, social support, and the buffering hypothesis. *Psychological Bulletin, 98,* 310–357.

Comas-Díaz, L., & Griffith, E. E. H. (Eds.). (1988). *Clinical guidelines in cross-cultural mental health.* New York: Wiley.

Cross, W. E. (1972). The Negro-to-Black conversion experience. *Black World, 20,* 13–27.

Cuellar, I., Harris, L. C., & Jasso, R. (1980). An acculturation scale for Mexican American normal and clinical populations. *Hispanic Journal of Behavioral Sciences, 2,* 199–217.

Dakoff, G. A., & Taylor, S. E. (1990). Victims' perception of social support: What is helpful from whom? *Journal of Personality and Social Psychology, 58,* 80–89.

Dana, R. H. (1993). *Multicultural assessment perspectives for professional psychology.* Boston: Allyn and Bacon.

Di-Angi, P. (1976). Barriers to the Black and White therapeutic relationship. *Perspectives in Psychiatric Care, 14,* 180–183.

Dillard, J. L. (1972). *Black English: Its history and usage in the United States.* New York: Random House.

Dohrenwend, B. P., & Dohrenwend, B. S. (1981a). Quasi-experimental evidence on the social-causation-social-selection issue posed by class differences. *American Journal of Community Psychology, 9,* 128–146.

Dohrenwend, B. S., & Dohrenwend, B. P. (1981b). Hypotheses about stress processes linking social class to various types of psychopathology. *American Journal of Community Psychology, 9,* 146–159.

Draguns, J. G. (1988). Personality and culture: Are they relevant for the enhancement of quality of mental life? In P. R. Dasen, J. W. Berry, & N. Sartorius (Eds.), *Health and cross-cultural psychology: Toward applications* (pp. 141–161). Newbury Park, CA: Sage.

Flaskerud, J. H., & Liu, P. Y. (1991). Effects of an Asian client–therapist language, ethnicity, and gender match on utilization and outcome of therapy. *Community Mental Health Journal, 27,* 31–42.

Folkman, S., & Lazarus, R. S. (1984). If it changes it must be a process: Study of emotions and coping during three studies of a college examination. *Journal of Personality and Social Psychology, 48,* 150–170.

Foster, D. V. (1988). Consideration of treatment issues with American Indians detained in the Federal Bureau of Prisons. *Psychiatric Annals, 18,* 698–701.

Fujii, J. S., Fukushima, S. N., & Yamamoto, J. (1993). Psychiatric care of Japanese Americans. In A. C. Gaw (Ed.), *Culture, ethnicity, and mental illness* (pp. 305–345). Washington, DC: American Psychiatric Press.

Garcia, M., & Lega, L. T. (1979). Development of a Cuban ethnic identity questionnaire. *Hispanic Journal of Behavioral Sciences, 1,* 247–261.

Gaw, A. C. (Ed.). (1993a). *Culture, ethnicity, and mental illness.* Washington, DC: American Psychiatric Press.

Gaw, A. C. (1993b). Psychiatric care of Chinese Americans. In A. C. Gaw (Ed.), *Culture, ethnicity, and mental illness* (pp. 245–280). Washington, DC: American Psychiatric Press.

Ghali, S. B. (1977). Cultural sensitivity and the Puerto Rican client. *Social Casework, 58,* 459–468.

Giglioli, P. P. (Ed.). (1976). *Language and social context.* Baltimore: Penguin.

Griffith, E. E. H., & Baker, F. M. (1993). Psychiatric care of African Americans. In A. C. Gaw (Ed.), *Culture, ethnicity, and mental illness* (pp. 147–173). Washington, DC: American Psychiatric Press.

Hall, W. S., Cross, W. E., & Freedle, R. (1972). Stages in the development of Black awareness: An exploratory investigation. In R. I. Jones (Ed.), *Black psychology* (pp. 156–165). New York: Harper & Row.

Harper, F. D. (1988). Alcohol and Black youth: An overview. *Journal of Drug Issues, 18,* 15–20.

Heinrich, R. K., Corbine, J. L., & Thomas, K. R. (1990). Counseling Native Americans. *Journal of Counseling & Development, 69,* 128–133.

Helms, J. E. (1985). Cultural identity in the treatment process. In P. Pederson (Ed.), *Handbook of cross-cultural counseling and therapy* (pp. 239–245). Westport, CT: Greenwood.

Helms, J. E. (1990a). Three perspectives on counseling and psychotherapy with visible racial/ethnic group clients. In F. C. Serafica, A. I. Schwebel, R. K. Russell, P. D. Isaac, & L. B.

Myers (Eds.), *Mental health of ethnic minorities* (pp. 171–201). New York: Praeger.

Helms, J. E. (Ed.). (1990b). *Black and White racial identity: Theory, research and practice.* Westport, CT: Greenwood.

Ho, C. K. (1990). An analysis of domestic violence in Asian American communities: A multicultural approach to counseling. *Women & Therapy, 9,* 129–150.

Hoffmann, T., Dana, R. H., & Bolton, B. (1985). Measured acculturation and MMPI-168 performance of Native American adults. *Journal of Cross-Cultural Psychology, 16,* 243–256.

Hughes, C. C. (1993). Culture in clinical psychiatry. In A. C. Gaw (Ed.), *Culture, ethnicity, and mental illness* (pp. 3–41). Washington, DC: American Psychiatric Press.

Hughes, M., & Demo, D. H. (1989). Self-perceptions of Black Americans: Self-esteem and personal efficacy. *American Journal of Sociology, 95,* 132–159.

Hurejsi, C., Craig, B., & Pablo, J. (1992). Reactions by Native Americans to child protection agencies: Cultural and community factors. *Child Welfare, 71,* 329–342.

Jackson, B. (1975). Black identity development. *ME-FORM: Journal of Educational Diversity & Innovation, 2,* 19–25.

Jalali, B. (1988). Ethnicity, cultural adjustment, and behavior: Implications for family therapy. In L. Comas-Díaz & E. E. H. Griffith (Eds.), *Clinical guidelines in cross-cultural mental health* (pp. 9–32). New York: Wiley.

Jones, N. S. (1990). Black/White issues in psychotherapy: A framework for clinical practice. *Journal of Social Behavior and Personality, 5,* 305–322.

Kinzie, J. D., & Manson, S. M. (1987). The use of self-rating scales in cross cultural psychiatry. *Hospital and Community Psychiatry, 38,* 190–196.

Kitano, H. H. L. (1989). A model for counseling Asian Americans. In P. B. Pedersen, J. G. Draguns, W. J. Lonner, & J. E. Trimble (Eds.), *Counseling across cultures* (3rd ed.) (pp. 139–151). Honolulu: University of Hawaii Press.

Kluegel, J. R., & Smith, E. R. (1983). Affirmative action attitudes: Effects of self-interest, racial affect, and stratification beliefs on Whites' views. *Social Forces, 61,* 797–824.

LaFromboise, T. D. (1988). American Indian mental health policy. *American Psychologist, 43,* 388–397.

Landrine, H. (1992). Clinical implications of cultural differences: The referential versus the indexical self. *Clinical Psychology Review, 12,* 401–415.

Lazarus, R. S., & Folkman, S. (1984). *Stress, appraisal, and coping.* New York: Springer.

Lee, E. (1988). Cultural factors in working with Southeastern Asian refugee adolescents. *Journal of Adolescence, 11,* 167–179.

LeVine, E., & Padilla, A. (1980). *Crossing cultures in therapy: Pluralistic counseling for the Hispanic.* Belmont, CA: Wadsworth.

Lin, N., & Ensel, W. (1989). Life stress and health: Stressors and outcomes. *American Sociological Review, 54,* 382–399.

Lin, N., Woelfel, M. W., & Light, S. C. (1985). The buffering effect of social support subsequent to an important life event. *Journal of Social and Health Behavior, 26,* 247–263.

Lopez-Bushnell, F. K., Tyre, P., & Futrell, M. (1992). Alcoholism and the Hispanic older adult. *Clinical Gerontologist, 11,* 123–130.

Lorion, R. P., & Felner, R. D. (1986). Research on mental health interventions with the disadvantaged. In S. L. Garfield & A. E. Bergin (Eds.), *Handbook of psychotherapy and behavior change* (3rd ed.) (pp. 739–775). New York: Wiley.

Marcos, L. R. (1976). Bilinguals in psychotherapy: Language as an emotional barrier. *American Journal of Psychotherapy, 30,* 552–560.

Marcos, L. R., & Urcuyo, L. (1979). Dynamic psychotherapy with the bilingual patient. *American Journal of Psychotherapy, 33,* 331–338.

Marin, G., Sabogal, F., Marin, B. V., Otero-Sabogal, R., & Perez-Stable, E. (1987). Development of a short acculturation scale for Hispanics. *Hispanic Journal of Behavioral Sciences, 9,* 183–205.

Marsella, A. J., & Dash-Scheuer, A. (1988). Coping, culture, and healthy human development: A research and conceptual overview. In P. R. Dasen, J. W. Berry, & N. Sartorius (Eds.), *Health and cross-cultural psychology: Toward applications* (pp. 162–178). Newbury Park, CA: Sage.

Marsella, A. J., DeVos, G., & Hsu, F. (Eds.). (1985). *Culture and self: Asian and Western perspectives.* New York/London: Tavistock.

Marsella, A. J., Tharp, R. G., & Ciborowski, T. J. (Eds.). (1979). *Perspectives on cross-cultural psychology*. New York: Academic Press.

Martinez, C., Jr. (1988). Mexican-Americans. In L. Comas-Díaz & E. E. H. Griffith (Eds.), *Clinical guidelines in cross-cultural mental health* (pp. 182–232). New York: Wiley.

Martinez, C., Jr. (1993). Psychiatric care of Mexican Americans. In A. C. Gaw (Ed.), *Culture, ethnicity, and mental illness* (pp. 431–466). Washington, DC: American Psychiatric Press.

Masuda, M., Matsumoto, G. H., & Meredith, G. M. (1970). Ethnic identity in three generations of Japanese Americans. *Journal of Social Psychology, 81*, 199–207.

McConahay, J. B., & Hough, J. C. (1976). Symbolic racism. *Journal of Social Issues, 32*, 23–45.

McIntosh, J. L. (1984). Suicide among Native Americans: Further tribal data and considerations. *Omega: The Journal of Death and Dying, 14*, 215–229.

Mendoza, R. H. (1984). Acculturation and sociocultural variability. In J. L. Martinez, Jr., & R. H. Mendoza (Eds.), *Chicano psychology* (2nd ed.) (pp. 61–75). Orlando, FL: Academic Press.

Mendoza, R. H., & Martinez, J. L. (1981). The measurement of acculturation. In A. Baron, Jr. (Ed.), *Explorations in Chicano psychology* (pp. 71–82). New York: Praeger.

Miller, F. S. (1992). Network structural support: Its relationship to the psychosocial development of Black females. In A. K. H. Burlew, W. C. Banks, H. P. McAdoo, & D. A. Azibo (Eds.), *African American psychology: Theory, research, and practice* (pp. 105–126). Newbury Park, CA: Sage.

Milliones, J. (1980). Construction of a Black consciousness measure: Psychotherapeutic implications. *Psychotherapy: Theory, Research and Practice, 17*, 175–182.

Mollica, R. F., & Lavelle, J. (1988). Southeast Asia refugees. In L. Comas-Díaz & E. E. H. Griffith (Eds.), *Clinical guidelines in cross-cultural mental health* (pp. 262–293). New York: Wiley.

Montejano, D. (1987). *Anglos and Mexicans in the making of Texas, 1836–1986*. Austin: University of Texas Press.

Odejide, A. O. (1979). Cross-cultural psychiatry: A myth or reality? *Comprehensive Psychiatry, 20*, 103–108.

Oetting, E. R., Edwards, R. W., & Beauvais, F. (1988). Drugs and Native American youth. *Drugs and Society, 3*, 1–34.

Olmedo, E. (1979). Acculturation: A psychometric perspective. *American Psychologist, 34*, 1061–1070.

Padilla, A. M., Lindholm, K. J., Chen, A., Duran, R., Hakuta, K., Lambert, W., & Tucker, G. R. (1991). The English-only movement: Myths, reality, and implications for psychology. *American Psychologist, 46*, 120–130.

Pearlin, L., & Schooler, C. (1978). The structure of coping. *Journal of Health and Social Behavior, 19*, 2–21.

Ponterotto, J. G., & Wise, S. L. (1987). Construct validity study of the Racial Identity Attitude Scale. *Journal of Counseling Psychology, 34*, 218–223.

Priest, R. (1991). Racism and prejudice as negative impacts on African American clients in therapy. *Journal of Counseling and Development, 70*, 213–215.

Ramos-McKay, J. M., Comas-Díaz, L., & Rivera, L. A. (1988). Puerto Ricans. In L. Comas-Díaz & E. E. H. Griffith (Eds.), *Clinical guidelines in cross-cultural mental health* (pp. 204–232). New York: Wiley.

Ramos, H. A., & Morales, M. M. (1985). U.S. immigration and the Hispanic community: A historical overview and sociological perspective. *Journal of Hispanic Politics, 1*, 1–17.

Ridley, C. R. (1984). Clinical treatment of the nondisclosing Black client: A therapeutic paradox. *American Psychologist, 39*, 1234–1244.

Ruiz, A. S. (1990). Ethnic identity: Crisis and resolution. *Journal of Multicultural Counseling and Development, 18*, 29–40.

Russell, D. M. (1988). Language and psychotherapy: The influence of nonstandard English in clinical practice. In L. Comas-Díaz & E. E. H. Griffith (Eds.), *Clinical guidelines in cross-cultural mental health* (pp. 33–68). New York: Wiley.

Sabin, J. E. (1975). Translating despair. *American Journal of Psychiatry, 132*, 197–199.

Sabshin, M., Diesenhaus, H., & Wilkerson, R. (1970). Dimensions of institutionalized racism in psychiatry. *American Journal of Psychiatry, 127*, 787–793.

Sanchez, A. R., & Atkinson, D. R. (1983). Mexican-

American cultural commitment, preferences for counselor ethnicity, and willingness to use counseling. *Journal of Counseling Psychology, 30,* 215–220.

Sarason, B. R., Sarason, I. G., & Pierce, G. R. (Eds.). (1990). *Social support: An interactional view.* New York: Wiley.

Schradle, S. B., & Dougher, M. J. (1985). Social support as a mediator of stress: Theoretical and empirical issues. *Clinical Psychology Review, 5,* 641–661.

Sciarra, D. T., & Ponterotto, J. G. (1991). Counseling the Hispanic bilingual family: Challenges to the therapeutic process. *Psychotherapy, 28,* 473–479.

Smither, R. (1982). Human migration and the acculturation of minorities. *Human Relations, 35,* 57–68.

Sodowsky, G. R., & Carey, J. C. (1987). Asian Indian immigrants in America: Factors related to adjustment. *Journal of Multicultural Counseling and Development, 15,* 129–141.

Sodowsky, G. R., Lai, E. W., & Plake, B. S. (1991). Moderating effects of socio-cultural variables on acculturation attitudes of Hispanics and Asian Americans. *Journal of Counseling & Development, 70,* 194–204.

Sook Wha Ahn Toupin, E. (1980). Counseling Asians: Psychotherapy in the context of racism and Asian-American history. *American Journal of Orthopsychiatry, 50,* 76–86.

Straker, D. (1980). *Attitudes toward English vernaculars.* Urbana-Champaign: University of Illinois (ERIC Document Reproduction Service No Ed 195 619).

Sue, D. W. (1981). *Counseling the culturally different: Theory and practice.* New York: Wiley.

Suinn, R. M., Richard-Figueroa, K., Lew, S., & Vigil, S. (1987). The Suinn-Lew Asian Self-Identity Acculturation Scale: An initial report. *Educational and Psychological Measurement, 47,* 401–407.

Thompson, J. W., Walker, R. D., & Silk-Walker, P. (1993). Psychiatric care of American Indians and Alaska Natives. In A. C. Gaw (Ed.), *Culture, ethnicity, and mental illness* (pp. 189–243). Washington, DC: American Psychiatric Press.

Trimble, J. E. (1987). Self-perception and perceived alienation among American Indians. *Journal of Community Psychology, 15,* 316–333.

U.S. Bureau of Census. (1990). *1990 census of population and housing Summary tape file: Summary population and housing characteristics.* Washington, DC: U.S. Government Printing Office.

Westermeyer, J. J. (1990). Working with an interpreter in psychiatric assessment and treatment. *Journal of Nervous and Mental Diseases, 178,* 745–749.

Westermeyer, J. J. (1993). Cross-cultural psychiatric assessment. In A. C. Gaw (Ed.) *Culture, ethnicity, and mental illness* (pp. 125–144). Washington, DC: American Psychiatric Press.

Wierzbicki, M., & Pekarik, G. (1993). A meta-analysis of psychotherapy dropout. *Professional Psychology: Research and Practice, 24,* 190–195.

Wilson, L. L., & Stith, S. M. (1991). Culturally sensitive therapy with Black clients. *Journal of Multicultural Counseling and Development, 19,* 32–43.

Yamamoto, J., Silva, J. A., Justice, L. R., Chang, C. Y., & Leong, G. B. (1993). Cross-cultural psychotherapy. In A. C. Gaw (Ed.), *Culture, ethnicity, and mental illness* (pp. 101–124). Washington, DC: American Psychiatric Press.

Chapter *3*

Symptom Expression and the Use of Mental Health Services among American Ethnic Minorities

NORMAN G. DINGES
DANA CHERRY

This chapter will attempt to integrate several interrelated aspects of symptom expression and the use of mental health services among ethnic minorities. A primary focus will be on similarities and differences in psychological symptom expression within and across the following ethnic minorities in the United States: Black, Hispanic, Asian American, and Native American. Each of these general ethnic categories contains numerous important distinctions of subgroup identity and acculturation status that need to be considered in working with members of these groups (see Chapter 2).

In this chapter, we attempt to describe symptom expression for anxiety disorders, mood disorders, and schizophrenia. The clinical research literature does not contain systematic coverage of each of these disorders for each of the major ethnic groups, with the exception of the National Institutes of Mental Health (NIMH) Epidemiological Catchment Area (ECA) studies, whose findings are limited. Therefore, cautious generalization and interpretation of the existing clinical knowledge are required. A closely related topic concerns the impact of symptom expression on the client's clinical presentation, particularly as it may influence pathways to treatment for different ethnic minorities. Here we draw on the broader literature concerning culture and psychopathology in an attempt to provide differing conceptual frameworks within which the service provider and the clinician can understand the influence of ethnicity on behaviors relevant to diagnosis, treatment planning, intervention, and outcome evaluation.

Finally, we will attempt to illustrate how the symptom expression and clinical presentation of ethnic minority clients may determine the avenues through which they enter the mental health system, as well as the course of posttreatment reintegration with their communities. Broad cultural influences and specific ethnic differences clearly have an impact on perceptions of symptom severity, precipitating events, and the levels of symptom severity that lead to clinical referral. The clinical evidence strongly suggests that ethnic group norms in large part may determine when referrals are made, community perceptions of symptom severity, and posttreatment acceptance of symptomatic persons into the community.

Symptom Expression across and within Ethnic Groups

Clinical considerations in the expression of psychological symptoms must take into account the methods by which symptoms are elicited and categorized. Methodological issues are also important in the assessment process and in reaching some degree of conceptual validity in formulating diagnoses (also see Chapter 4). Good and Good (1986) have summarized such methodological considerations as follows:

1. *Normative uncertainty* refers to specific cultural assumptions about abnormal behavior and symptoms that are used to inform interpretation of individual symptoms and of their threshold, level, and duration. Good and Good (1986) cite as an example the consistent finding of higher levels of psychological symptoms among Puerto Ricans and the difficulty of determining whether this represents actual differences in psychopathology or culturally patterned variations in the expressions of distress.

2. *Centricultural bias* is by now a well-known problem, in which criteria defined and validated in one culture are used to determine the extent of a psychological disorder in another culture. In addition to cultural differences in the type, frequency, severity, and duration of symptoms, the additional problem exists of failing to recognize the attributed sources and culturally unique expressions of symptoms. Rogler, Malgady, and Rodriguez (1989) have identified the limitations of using preconceived diagnostic categories that may inadvertently omit the more salient mental health problems in Hispanic communities.

3. *Indeterminacy of meaning* occurs in the search for semantic equivalents when symptoms are presumed to have universal referents but are in fact expressed differently, thus producing confusion in the interpretation of symptom similarity across ethnic groups. This is most clearly seen in culturally weighted concepts such as guilt and shame, which take on different symptomatic significance for different cultures (see Weiss & Kleinman, 1988, for a review of relevant literature) and which have been amply demonstrated by Kinzie et al. (1982) in the development and validation of the Vietnamese Depression Scale.

4. *Narrative context* refers to the impact of the location and setting in which client symptoms are discussed. The candor and completeness of symptom disclosure can vary significantly depending on who is asking (e.g., clinician, friend, elder, native healer), where (e.g., clinic, church, community setting), what the person is asking about (e.g., dreams, contact with spirits, taboo objects, family tensions), and how (e.g., directly, or through trance mediums, relatives, or friends; in English or through bilingual interpreters).

5. *Category validity* is seen most clearly in the differential expression of symptoms that are presumed to reflect a common psychological disorder. Perhaps the best example is that provided by Kleinman and Good (1985) in which they pose the question of whether depression expressed primarily in psychological terms associated with strong feelings of remorse and guilt can be equated with depression experienced primarily in somatic terms, as clinical lore suggests is common among Asian Americans.

Ethnic Identity

Strength of identification with a particular ethnic group is an important consideration in recognizing and interpreting psychological symptoms of clinical severity. Most assessment schemata emphasize the importance of using well-developed ethnic identity indices that account for variance attributable to gender and generation differences in comparing the symptomatic expression of different ethnic groups (e.g., Dana, 1993; Marsella & Kameoka, 1989). Unfortunately, such indices are not always available for all ethnic groups nor are they all reliable and valid over time (see Chapter 2).

It is risky to assume that physical characteristics or expressed membership in an ethnic group are equivalent to strength of identification or are strongly reflective of one's affiliation with ethnic traditions. For example, Phinney (1990) points out how the absence of positive attitudes or the presence of negative attitudes toward one's ethnic identity—feelings such as displeasure, dissatisfaction, discontent, and ambivalence—can be seen as a denial of one's ethnic identity and thus as indicators of psychopathology. By contrast, Dana (1993) describes cognitive developmental stage models of ethnicity that are relevant to the assessment of both psychological health and psychopathology. Taking different stages of ethnic identity into account can thus be useful in differentiating emotional expressions of ethnic identity ambivalence from symptoms of more serious psychological disorders.

The following description of symptom expression for different disorders by different ethnic groups should be read with these issues in mind. Although the epidemiological literature provides some indication of the comparability of diagnostic disorders across United States ethnic populations (e.g., Rubio-Stipec, Shrout, Bird, Canino, & Bravo, 1989), little information is available on the similarities and differences in symptom expression within a disorder.

Anxiety Disorders

Past reviews of the cross-cultural literature clearly indicate that anxiety and anxiety disorders are universally present in human societies but that the phenomenology of such disorders varies significantly across cultures (Good & Kleinman, 1985). In their broader review of the literature on culture and anxiety disorders, Good and Kleinman (1985) caution against the category fallacy of reifying a classification such as "anxiety disorders" that may have limited applicability beyond the cultural origins of the concept. Despite such well-founded warnings, there does appear to be ample evidence from epidemiological research that anxiety disorders of clinical severity do occur among United States ethnic minority groups. The more important considerations for this chapter have to do with how anxiety and anxiety disorders are expressed across different ethnic groups, as well as how different expressions may be misperceived by the clinician.

One of the better examples of a culture-specific idiom of expression of anxiety symptoms that has significance for an ethnic minority population is found in the syndrome known as *nervios*. In Costa Rica, Low (1981) found that *nervios* provides a socially acceptable category of expression for symptoms of feeling "out of control" that are generated by disruption and breakdown in family relationships. Symptoms such as headaches, insomnia, lack of appetite, depression, fears, anger or bad character, trembling, disorientation and temporary blindness, fatigue, itching, altered perceptions, and hot sensations were seen by Hispanics as abnormal, undesirable, and uncontrollable physical responses. Although *nervios* has been studied primarily as a Hispanic idiom of distress (e.g., Guarnaccia, DeLaCancela, & Carrillo, 1989), a recent study by Van Schaik (1989) has found "nerves" to be a popular illness category for similar symptom expression in a rural population in Appalachian Kentucky. Koss (1990) provides a detailed discussion of somat- ization among Hispanic populations, which is also relevant for other ethnic minorities to whom somatization tendencies have been attributed, such as Asian Americans.

Depressive Disorders

Depressive disorders of clinical severity have probably received the most cross-cultural attention. Although there appears to be a reasonable degree of consensus that the core symptoms of depression (dysphoria, anhedonia) are manifested in many cultures, there is a considerable problem with clear identification of depressive symptoms across different groups. Marsella, Sartorius, Jablensky, and Fenton (1985) have challenged the cross-cultural validity of depressive disorders on the grounds that there is no word for the disorder in some cultures. However, lack of an explicit word for a disorder in a culture does not preclude its presence. Others have argued for the presence of some form of the disorder in all cultures (Jenkins, Kleinman, & Good, 1991). Part of the problem appears to stem from comparing cultures with clear mind–body distinctions with those that hold more holistic concepts of human behavior. A related problem concerns comparison of the idioms of distress used to convey symptoms that might be considered reflective of clinical depression. Two examples of attempts to understand symptom expression in depressive disorders will be described next.

Using ethnosemantic interviewing techniques to elicit symptoms of distress among the Hopi, Manson, Shore, and Bloom (1985) sought to identify affective, cognitive, and behavioral clusters of symptoms characteristic of depressive experience. Five categories of illness were identified by Hopi informants: (1) *wu wan tu tu ya* (worry sickness), (2) *ka ha la yi* (unhappiness), (3) *uu nung mo kiw ta* (a broken heart), (4) *qo vis ti* (disappointment, pouting), and (5) *ho nak tu tu ya* (drunkenlike craziness, with or without alcohol). Although presented as distinct phenomenological categories, Manson et al. (1985) emphasize that their meaning is situation-specific and requires context for appropriate interpretation. For example, *wu wan tu tu ya* derived its significance from the relationship between symptoms and subsequent help-seeking behavior. In addition, *wu wan tu tu ya* took on added significance if associated with witchcraft, misconduct, spiritual imbalance, or supernatural experiences. Whereas *wu wan tu tu ya* refers to pervasive problems in one's environment, *uu nung mo kiw ta* refers to despair or acute sadness resulting from unrealized expectations or disruptions in interpersonal relationships that were perplexing, shocking, or sudden. Distinctions regarding symptoms, situations, and precipitating sources were also found for the other Hopi depressive experiences.

In light of the number of symptoms elicited that are strongly associated with the concept of depression in psychiatric nomenclature, it is interesting to note that 93 percent of the informants for this study indicated that there was no word or phrase equivalent to the term *depression*. Yet, *uu nung mo kiw ta* was strongly associated with the most salient symptoms of depression and occurred significantly more often among known cases of depressive disorder than among a matched community group. This illustrates quite clearly that the lack of a cross-culturally equivalent verbal designator for a particular emotional phenomenon does not preclude its presence in a given culture.

Southeast Asians are a fast-growing segment of the United States population and present a considerable challenge in the complexity of symptom expressions, as indicated by the cross-cultural convergence and contrasts in the expression of depressive symptoms found by Kinzie et al. (1982). The clinical presentation among Vietnamese Americans thus included the following symptoms:

1. Physical states associated with depression, including poor appetite, pains, exhaustion, and diurnal variation in energy patterns
2. Depressed or sad mood, which could be translated into English only in an awkward way—"sad and bothered," "low-spirited and bored," "down-hearted and low-spirited" (though seemingly redundant in English, these were seen as distinct psychological symptoms by Vietnamese clients)
3. Those unrelated to either lowered mood or the Western concept of depression, including being angry, feeling shameful and dishonored, feeling desperate, and having a feeling of going crazy

The high endorsement of "being angry" as a reported symptom contrasted strikingly with behavior observed in the diagnostic interviews, in which clients did not appear irritated or hostile but, rather, were characterized by psychomotor retardation exceeding the reserved interaction expected of Vietnamese when interacting with people of markedly different status (e.g., physician and patient). In addition, the "shameful and dishonored" symptoms were distinct from Western notions of guilt; they reflected more of a burden in failing to meet current familial obligations, as well as those of the ancestral past. In the absence of psychotic symptoms, "going crazy" as a symptom was interpreted as related to feelings of desperation and loss of control resulting from the extreme discomfort of the affective and physical aspects of the depressive experience.

Mollica, Wyshak, de Marneffe, Khuon, and Lavelle (1987) have found that Cambodian, Laotian, and Vietnamese versions of the Hopkins Symptom Checklist-25 were particularly helpful in assessing victims of trauma in that they were short and nonprovocative and helped in symptom expression by allowing clients to put words around their feelings. More recently, Noh, Avison, and Kaspar (1992) reported a strong cultural tendency among Korean Americans for lowered response to Positive Affect items on the Center for Epidemiological Studies Depression Scale (CES-D). They caution that this is likely to result in overestimates of the degree of psychological distress or psychiatric morbidity.

Depressive symptom expression among African Americans has received less attention in the literature and is consequently more difficult to characterize. An earlier study by Raskin, Crook, and Herman (1975) compared African-American and Anglo patients on presenting symptoms controlling for age, sex, and social class status. Their results indicated that both African-American and Anglo patients were highly similar in presenting the core symptoms of depression, but that African-American patients were more likely to rate themselves higher on negativism and internalization (Buss & Durkee, 1957). African-American males in particular indicated they would respond with verbal or physical attack if they felt their rights were violated, whereas both male and female patients reported a tendency to internalize feelings of rage or anger. In addition, high-risk factors such as suicide threats and attempts and assaultive behavior played a prominent role in the decision to hospitalize African-American patients.

More recent studies confirm the convergence of depressive symptom expression for African Americans and Anglos while clarifying the cultural influences on differential symptom expression (Jones & Gray, 1986). Part of the problem in clearly differentiating depressive symptoms of African Americans stems from earlier studies, which concluded that they rarely suffered from depression or manic-depressive disorders (Kramer, Rosen, & Willis, 1973). Other studies indicate that African-American rates equal or in some cases exceed those of Anglos (Jones, Robinson, Parson, & Gray, 1982; Bell & Mehta, 1981). A particular problem in accurate diagnosis arises in the expression of symptoms that are influenced by cultural factors. For example, the old stereotypic belief that African Americans are generally happy people who seldom suffer from depression could lead to a failure to recognize clinical thresholds for abnormal mood states, as in hypomanic conditions. Conversely, language, mannerisms, and style of relating to Anglo clinicians may be interpreted as depressive symptoms rather than as resistance to the controlling elements in an alien clinical environment.

In a detailed case study of pathological mourning, Cancelmo, Millan, and Vazquez (1990) provide a rich description of the manner in which cultural beliefs influenced symptom expression in a Puerto Rican male patient. This case study is particularly useful in demonstrating the importance of cultural beliefs in making an accurate differential diagnosis, and in the subsequent effectiveness or lack thereof of therapeutic interventions.

Schizophrenic Disorders

Although schizophrenic disorders among ethnic minorities have received considerably less attention than depressive disorders, some important aspects of symptom expression need to be considered. Jones and Gray (1986) indicate that African Americans are more likely to be overdiagnosed as schizophrenic than are Whites because clinicians are unduly impressed by hallucinatory and delusional symptoms. Although studies that use systematic diagnostic criteria have not found differences between African Americans and Whites in the clinical prevalence of schizophrenia (Adebimpe, 1981), the symptom expression of African-American clients is apparently much more likely to result in that diagnosis. This is also true of Hispanic patients. Mukherjee, Shukla, Woodle, Rosen, and Olarte (1983) found that misdiagnosis of schizophrenia was particularly likely if the African-American or Hispanic patient was young and experienced auditory hallucination associated with affective disorders. The combination of affective and psychotic symptoms also presents a complex symptom expression that could result in failure to recognize schizo-affective disorders among African Americans and other ethnic minorities.

One of the more systematic studies of symptom expression in schizophrenia was conducted by Escobar, Randolph, and Hill (1986), who compared Hispanic and Anglo veterans using structured diagnostic interviews. The primary symptoms of schizophrenia, such as hallucinations, delusions, and functional deterioration, were similar for both groups as indicated by outcome data for the Diagnostic Interview Schedule, Brief Psychiatric Rating Scale (BPRS), the Hopkins Symptom Checklist-90 (SCL-90), and the Global Assessment Scale (GAS). However, there was a trend for Hispanic patients to have higher scores in thought disorder items of the BPRS and higher mean severity on the Clinical Global Impressions (CGI), as well as reporting significantly more positive somatic symptoms on the SCL-90, particularly items relating to chest pains, "hot" and/or "cold" spells, and "lump" in the throat.

Interpreting symptom expression in the more severe psychological disorders presents particular difficulties for the clinician who is unfamiliar with ethnic norms in emotional expression, who may misinterpret linguistic styles and behavioral mannerisms, and who generally cannot relate to the life experiences of ethnic clients. As Jones and Gray (1986) indicate, "language not understood is often considered evidence of thought disorder, styles of relating are sometimes misinterpreted as disturbance of affect; and unfamiliar mannerisms are considered bizarre" (p. 63). In addition, cardinal symptoms of schizophrenia such as thought disorder are typically thought to be more common among African-American clients of lower socioeconomic status, a finding that is not supported by the research (Haimo & Holzman, 1979).

Paranoid symptoms can be particularly problematic to diagnose accurately among ethnic minority clients (Loring & Powell, 1988; Mirowsky, 1985; Ndetei, 1986). Newhill (1990) presents several case studies that demonstrate the role of effective differential diagnosis in recognizing paranoid symptoms based on reality and those that represent psychopathology, and argues for the importance of neither minimizing true paranoid symptoms nor mislabeling healthy cultural adaptation.

Our understanding of ethnic variations in symptom expression for schizophrenic disorders has lagged considerably behind that for depressive disorders. More complex issues regarding symptom expression in schizophrenic disorders have been raised by Fabrega (1989), who indicates that a great deal of variation and modification of the disorder will be revealed by attending to "native phenomenologies of psychoses" (p. 277). Other recent reports have expressed similar concerns regarding the interpretation of the symptom complex that is now diagnosed as schizophrenia (Corin, 1990).

Because of the severity and pervasiveness of symptomatic expression in schizophrenic disorders, family and community factors are clearly important. Social values that define thresholds for symptomatic expression and perceptual filters on the types of symptoms considered pathognomonic may lead to divergent conclusions by clinicians and community members. Katz, Sanborn, Lowery, and Ching (1978) found that clinicians and community members differed significantly in describing schizophrenic disorders in the Japanese community of Hawaii. Clinicians focused on symptoms of seclusiveness and shallow and blunted emotional expression. By contrast, community members considered symptoms of uncontrolled emotionality and distrust to be more salient. Cross-cultural studies of the behavioral and expressive qualities of schizophrenia in highly diverse cultures may serve as well to inform clearer understanding of symptom expression among ethnic minorities in the United States (Katz et al., 1988).

The great importance of family factors is seen in Mexican-American families, who prefer the folk category of *nervios* as a way to view schizophrenic illness of relatives (Jenkins, 1988). Although some Mexican Americans involved in Jenkins's study thought that the relationship between *nervios* and mental illness involved a continuum of severity in a developmental sequence, the majority maintained that they are distinct maladies. Jenkins suggests that this cultural preference relates to efforts to reduce stigma and reinforce the strength of family bonds. The indigenous view and labeling process thus acts to identify and mediate the course and outcome of schizophrenic disorder.

Comorbidity of Disorders

A variety of factors involving inconsistent or piecemeal use of treatment facilities increases the probability that ethnic minority clients may display a higher degree of comorbidity (Maser & Cloninger, 1990). Considering the well-documented barriers to mental health service utilization for ethnic minorities, there is an accompanying risk that delay in diagnosis and treatment may result in the development of comorbid conditions that go unrecognized by clinicians (Good, 1993). These and other issues regarding comorbidity among ethnic minorities are addressed in a recent issue of the journal *Culture, Medicine and Psychiatry* (Maser & Dinges, 1993).

Dinges and Duong-Tran (1993) found high comorbid rates of depression, substance abuse, and suicidality among Native American and Alaskan Native adolescents that were significantly related to stressful life events and the accompanying emotional impact of these events. Different types and amounts of stressful life events were related to specific combinations of comorbidity that were interpretable with respect to associated cultural dynamics. For example, a pattern of stressful life events that included the loss of identity-sustaining cultural supports was associated with an increased frequency of suicide attempts with diagnosed depression. O'Nell (1993) provides a related analysis in the form of comorbidity of problem drinking, depression, and suicidality in a Native American tribe as indicating psychopathological distress for one subgroup at high risk for suicide, while reflecting the rupture of social bonds in another subgroup at high risk for suicide.

Stressful life event patterns are obviously relevant to the understanding of symptom expression in comorbid conditions among ethnic minorities. Unfortunately, most stress measures do not include items that can be used to identify specific stressors related to ethnic identity issues or to collective stressors associated with culturally influenced symptom expression. An issue of considerable concern for the future is the identification among United States ethnic minorities of symptom expressions that may be clearly associated with specific acculturative stressors.

The influence of social roles, social role integration, and subcultural membership on comorbid symptom expression is seen in the affliction of "spiritual heart trouble," an idiom of distress found in low-income, disenfranchised African-American Pentecostal church members. The pattern of symptoms is characteristic of that often seen in anxiety and depressive disorders (Camino, 1992). This form of distress is associated with role confusion and conflict over social role priorities, and is experienced as a serious illness that may lead to "spiritual death." The range of symptoms associated with spiritual heart trouble include "heavy heart," "heart beating fast," uncontrollable drowsiness, interrupted sleep, headaches, weakness, dizziness, "saying things I shouldn't," and "loss of spiritual joy or desire" (Camino, 1992). What is striking is that the precipitating events in each case are highly similar and are related to vital Pentecostal beliefs and principles. This relationship is in turn interpreted as a sociosomatic disorder that is mediated by events in the social environment.

Avenues through Which Ethnic Minorities Enter the Mental Health System

The literature contains far more reports of obstacles and barriers to the utilization of mental health services for ethnic minorities than it does analysis of the means by which contact is made and sustained. Appropriate assessment of presenting complaints and symptomatic expression, as well as treatment planning and eventual return to the community, requires a systematic approach to understanding the various pathways by which ethnic minorities may enter the mental health system (Rogler & Cortes, 1993).

Perhaps one of the more clinically relevant conceptual models has been proposed by Lin, Tardiff, Donetz, and Goresky (1978), who attempted to reconstruct and analyze the pathways of help-seeking of severely disabled mental patients from four different ethnic populations in Vancouver: Chinese, Anglo, Middle European, and Native Indians. They developed a help-seeking grid instrument to analyze the major clinical events along the pathways taken to treatment agencies. These events included recognition of the initial manifestations of the problem, the source of recognition of the problem, and a series of attempts to assess and intervene in the problem. A typology of help-seeking patterns was developed that permitted comparisons in terms of the degree of family involvement, medical intervention, and social and legal agency involvement in pathways.

The typology proposed by Lin et al. is summarized as follows:

- Type A was characterized by early and prolonged efforts by the family to intervene. Medical intervention subsequently occurred if the family could not resolve the problem. Intervention by legal or social agencies was rare. The end stage of the path included both inpatient and outpatient treatment.
- Type B was characterized by the families' early referral of the patient to social agencies and outpatient treatment. Multiple social agencies were contacted at an early stage. Inpatient treatment occurred last in the help-seeking path.
- Type C was characterized by early legal and social agency interventions initiated by persons other than family members.
- Type D was reserved for mixed, indefinite patterns of help-seeking and subsequent agency and treatment involvements.

Ethnicity proved to be a major factor in differentiating patterns of help-seeking and the type and severity of problems that were presented. Type A were predominantly Chinese, Type B predominantly Anglo-Saxon and Middle-European, and Type C predominantly Native Indians. The types of problems also differed significantly in that the Type A (Chinese) patients had greater than expected episodes of psychoses and antisocial noncriminal behavior and fewer alcoholic, drug, suicidal, or social problems. Type B (Anglos and Middle Europeans) had a greater number of alcohol or drug problems and psychophysiological disorders, whereas Type C (Native Indians) had more alcohol or drug, social, and suicidal problems.

The Type A pattern has been commonly observed by both ethnic minority and nonminority clinicians alike with respect to Asian-American clients. Thus, remarkably advanced psychotic symptoms are often tolerated as long as the patient is not assaultive or socially disruptive. The family response is to isolate the individual in the home environment in the early stages of the problem. If the symptoms become bizarre or potentially violent, outside intervention may be sought through the family physician. If symptom expression requires external intervention, the family may be considerably less likely to accept the person even after successful treatment. In the Type A pattern, the higher tolerance by the family may be rooted in loyalties and obligations to take care of less fortunate family members. Family elders or teachers are often consulted to assist in correcting the patient's behavior in order to avoid the shame associated with having to seek assistance from mental health providers.

Type B patterns also involved the patient's family, but they played a much less active role. Social services, medical facilities, and mental health agencies were contacted at much earlier stages, presumably reflecting a considerably lower threshold for symptomatic expression and tolerance for deviance by the identified patient. The patients in this type of help-seeking pathway (Anglo and Middle European) bring a different history of utilization and perception of social services and mental health agencies, as well as more familiarity with psychological and sociological theories. This context serves to mitigate the shame or social embarrassment that might otherwise be associated with a family member identified as experiencing a mental disorder. Indeed, failure to make an early referral of a symptomatic family member to a mental health provider may be seen as disloyal, uncaring, and neglectful of one's family responsibilities.

The Type C pattern (Native Indians) demonstrated neither the potentially counterproductive family solidarity of the Type A pathway nor the active use of social and mental health services that characterized the Type B pathway. The all-too-familiar pattern was for these patients to flounder adrift without a supportive social network and to be transferred between social or mental health agencies and the police on the basis of momentary expediency. They did not voluntarily seek treatment, nor did the symptoms that brought them into contact with various agencies engender systematic assessment or treatment planning by the providers with whom they came in contact. The social context and the type of problems presented probably played a much larger role in the Type C pattern than it may have for Type A or Type B. Working with drug and alcohol problems associated with suicidal behavior is one of the most stressful and least rewarding activities of mental health providers, especially when these are viewed as chronic conditions for which minimal social support from the ethnic community is available. These circumstances are seen most graphically for ethnic minorities who may have been forcibly relocated and often wind up attempting to cope with alien urban environments using only their own individual resources.

This model is offered as a pragmatic conceptual framework that can alert the clinician to ethnic, familial, and community norms and values that influence the diversity of pathways by which ethnic minority clients may come to their attention. There is a more theoretically complex literature that also bears on such questions. (e.g., Briones et al., 1990). Kleinman (1977; 1979; 1986; 1988) has written extensively on the social construction of illness, including mental illness, and the theoretical framework he provides is highly relevant to such questions. Of related interest are emerging views of acculturation as an endogenous force in shaping symptom expression, as opposed to more traditional views of acculturation as an exogenous force (Rogler, Cortes, & Malgady, 1991). In the former approach, the mutual acculturative process occurring in the clinical interaction alters both client and clinician definitions of symptoms and their meaning with respect to treatment planning.

Angel and Thoits (1987) have presented a theoretical framework for understanding the impact of culture on the process of symptom recognition, labeling, and help-seeking based on the assumption of learned cognitive structures that filter bodily experience and influence the interpretation of deviations from culturally defined norms. Their model describes the temporal sequence from pre–symptom recognition of physiological and affective changes to the labeling and evaluation of symptoms resulting from contact with experts and treatment providers. Thus, the type of problem presented and the patient's experiences with various treatment agencies may shape subsequent self-recognition of psychological symptoms, as well as the pathways to treatment.

Influences of Symptom Expression and Help-Seeking Pathways on Treatment

As this review indicates, ethnicity may have dramatic influences on the type, mode, and manner of symptom expression and may also lead to different pathways to treatment. The roles of symptom expression and help-seeking patterns on the actual treatment provided to ethnic minorities also need to be considered. Although some aspects of symptom expression may be correlated with ethnic group membership or acculturative status, we emphasize that reducing stereotyping and bias in understanding their impact on the treatment process involves awareness of the client's *individualized* linguistic and sociocultural background. This important point has been made previously by Malgady, Rogler, and Constantino (1987) with respect to ethnocultural and linguistic bias in assessing Hispanics. The same precaution applies as well to other ethnic minorities.

Perhaps the best way to approach this problem is to adopt the *explanatory belief model* proposed by Kleinman (1980) to understand the interaction of symptom expression with help-seeking pathways and eventual treatment. Kleinman describes explanatory models as ideas about an episode of illness (in this case a psychological problem) that are held by all the participants to the eposide. Eliciting explanatory models about a particular illness event serves to reduce problems in clinical communication between the patient and the clinician, as well as to make sense of what is happening and what needs to be done about it. The explanatory models of the identified patient and the clinician may be the most important to understand at the symptom expression stage. The explanatory models of family, friends, and other community members may be more crucial at earlier or later stages of the treatment process, as illustrated by the typology of help-seeking patterns described by Lin et al. (1978) in the previous section.

According to Kleinman (1980), there are five major explanatory model questions that are important to ask of any illness event. These questions are concerned with (1) the cause of the problem; (2) the timing and mode of onset of the symptoms; (3) how the problem works as a pathophysiological process; (4) the course of the illness in terms of severity, acuteness, or chronicity; and (5) the type and length of treatment. Consistent with the goal of *individualized* understanding of symptom expression in relation to treatment goals and processes, explanatory models about a particular illness event or episode may be more important than general ethnic beliefs about illness and health, important as they may be. Kleinman proposes that the clinician first ask general, open-ended questions about the patient's explanatory models, preferably in the home setting. If answers to such questions are unrevealing (as they might be with more serious forms of psychopathology), he then suggests a simpler set of questions that can be used in eliciting explanatory models (Kleinman, 1980, p. 106).

Explanatory models can be used to understand the interaction of symptom expression, help-seeking pathways, and the treatment process, as well as to avoid either overestimating or underestimating the influence of cultural factors. For example, López and Hernandez (1986) examined where and how in the evaluation process culture is considered by therapists. Although clinicians report that culture is assessed in many phases of the evaluation, they actually may take cultural factors into consideration less systematically than they think they do. In addition, there seems to be little firm basis for clinician decisions about whether a symptom or behavior is syntonic with or deviant from the patient's surrounding community.

It is clear that explanatory models can influence the entire process of symptom recognition, labeling, and help-seeking. For example, the traditional distrust often found between White clinicians and Native Americans might be ameliorated by a communication process that elicited the client's explanatory models, as was done in the Manson et al. (1985) study. Recent attempts to use explanatory models in the elicitation, classification, and interpretation of psychological symptoms have been made by the Explanatory Model Interview for Classification (EMIC) project (Weiss & Kleinman, 1988). Preliminary results suggest that lack of understanding of local explanatory models can severely limit the clinician in responding therapeutically to the social tensions associated with ethnic-specific psychological problems that may be rooted in the patient's community.

Explanatory models can also be important in posttreatment reintegration of the client with his or her community. For example, causal beliefs that hold people responsible for their problems or illness events may influence the difficulty or ease of shedding the patient role. Similarly, explanatory models about the course of a disorder may influence family tolerance both for type and severity of symptoms and for the range of deviant behavior permitted by the community. The clinical evidence suggests that the treatment prospects for patients from specific ethnic populations may be seriously influenced by the explanatory models of family and community members. For example, some Southeast Asian populations hold strong beliefs about the heritability and chronicity of serious psychological disorders such as schizophrenia. Not only is the identified patient stigmatized by such beliefs, but the marriage prospects of siblings may be seriously affected. Consequently, extremely bizarre, self-destructive, or assaultive psychological symptoms may have to occur for help-seeking to extend beyond the family, community elders, or trusted local healers.

Summary

This chapter has focused on the varieties of symptom expression for major psychological disorders among ethnic minorities in the United States, as well as the influence of symptom expression on the pathways to treatment. The literature is limited in many respects, and much more clinical research is needed to expand our understanding of the relationship between symptom expression, explanatory belief models, help-seeking pathways, and effective interventions for ethnic minorities. Current and future generations of clinicians will need to attend more carefully to ethnic identity, community dynamics involving gender-based role demands and role dislocations, and the nature of both supportive and dysfunctional social networks, all of which may influence the type, form, combinations, severity, and course of psychological symptoms of clinical severity among ethnic minorities.

References

Adebimpe, V. R. (1981). Overview: White norms and psychiatric diagnosis of Black patients. *American Journal of Psychiatry, 138,* 279–285.

Angel, R., & Thoits, P. (1987). The impact of culture on the cognitive structure of illness. *Culture, Medicine and Psychiatry, 11,* 465–494.

Bell, C. C., & Mehta, H. (1981). Misdiagnosis of Black patients with manic depressive illness: Second in a series. *Journal of the National Medical Association, 73,* 101–107.

Briones, F. D., Heller, P. L., Chalfant, H. P., Roberts, A. E., Aguirre-Hauchbaum, S. F., & Farr, W. F. (1990). Socioeconomic status, ethnicity, psychological distress, and readiness to utilize a mental health facility. *American Journal of Psychiatry, 147,* 1333–1340.

Buss, A. H., & Durkee, A. (1957). An inventory for assessing different kinds of hostility. *Journal of Consulting Psychology, 24,* 343–349.

Camino, L. A. (1992). The cultural epidemiology of spiritual heart trouble. In J. Kirkland, H. F. Mathews, C. W. Sullivan, & K. Baldwin (Eds.), *Herbal and magical medicine: Traditional healing today* (pp. 118–136). Durham, NC: Duke University Press.

Cancelmo, J. A., Millan, F., & Vazquez, C. I. (1990). Culture and symptomatology—The role of personal meaning in diagnosis and treatment: A case study. *The American Journal of Psychoanalysis, 50,* 137–149.

Corin, E. E. (1990). Facts and meaning in psychiatry: An anthropological approach to the lifeworld of schizophrenics. *Culture, Medicine and Psychiatry, 14*, 153–188.

Dana, R. H. (1993). *Multicultural assessment perspectives for professional psychology*. Boston: Allyn and Bacon.

Dinges, N. G., & Duong-Tran, Q. (1993). Stressful life events and comorbidity of depression, suicidality, and substance abuse among American Indian and Alaska Native adolescents. *Culture, Medicine and Psychiatry, 16*, 487–502.

Escobar, J. I., Randolph, E. T., & Hill, M. (1986). Symptoms of schizophrenia in Hispanic and Anglo veterans. *Culture, Medicine and Psychiatry, 10*, 259–276.

Fabrega, H. (1989). The self and schizophrenia: A cultural perspective. *Schizophrenia Bulletin, 15*, 277–290.

Good, B. (1993). Culture, diagnosis, and comorbidity. *Culture, Medicine and Psychiatry, 16*, 427–446.

Good, B., & Good M. D. (1986). The cultural context of diagnosis and therapy: A view from medical anthropology. In M. Miranda & H. Kitano (Eds.), *Mental health research and practice in minority communities: Development of culturally sensitive training programs* (DHHS Publication No. ADM 86-1466) (pp. 1–28). Rockville, MD: National Institute of Mental Health.

Good, B., & Kleinman, A. (1985). Culture and anxiety: Cross-cultural evidence for the patterning of anxiety disorders. In A. H. Tuma & J. Maser (Eds.), *Anxiety and the anxiety disorders* (pp. 297–324). Hillsdale, NJ: Lawrence Erlbaum.

Guarnaccia, P. J., DeLaCancela, V., & Carrillo, E. (1989). The multiple meanings of *ataques de nervios* in the Latino community. *Medical Anthropology, 11*, 47–62.

Haimo, S. F., & Holzman, P. S. (1979). Thought disorder in schizophrenics and normal controls: Social class and race differences. *Journal of Consulting and Clinical Psychology, 47*, 963–967.

Jenkins, J. H. (1988). Ethnopsychiatric interpretations of schizophrenic illness: The problem of *nervios* within Mexican-American families. *Culture, Medicine and Psychiatry, 12*, 301–329.

Jenkins, J., Kleinman, A., & Good, B. J. (1991). Cross-cultural studies of depression. In J. Becker & A. Kleinman (Eds.), *Psychosocial aspects of depression* (pp. 67–99). Hillsdale, NJ: Lawrence Erlbaum.

Jones, B. E., & Gray, B. A. (1986). Problems in diagnosing schizophrenia and affective disorders among Blacks. *Hospital and Community Psychiatry, 37*, 61–65.

Jones, B. E., Robinson, W. M., Parson, E. B., & Gray, B. A. (1982). The clinical picture of mania in manic-depressive Black patients. *Journal of the National Medical Association, 74*, 553–557.

Katz, M. M., Marsella, A., Dube, K. C., Olatawura, M., Takahashi, R., Nakane, Y., Wynne, L. C., Gift, T., Brennan, J., Sartorius, N., & Jablensky, A. (1988). On the expression of psychosis in different cultures: Schizophrenia in an Indian and in a Nigerian community. *Culture, Medicine and Psychiatry, 12*, 331–355.

Katz, M. M., Sanborn, K. O., Lowery, H. A., & Ching, J. (1978). Ethnic studies in Hawaii: On psychopathology and social deviance. In L. Wynne, R. Cromwell, & S. Methysse (Eds.), *The nature of schizophrenia: New approaches to research and treatment* (pp. 572–585). New York: Wiley.

Kinzie, J. D., Manson, S. M., Vinh, D. T., Nguyen, T. T., Anh, B., & Pho, T. N. (1982). Development and validation of a Vietnamese-language depression rating scale. *American Journal of Psychiatry, 139*, 1276–1281.

Kleinman, A. (1977). Depression, somatization, and the new cross-cultural psychiatry. *Social Science and Medicine, 11*, 3–10.

Kleinman, A. (1979). Sickness as cultural semantics: Issues for an anthropological medicine and psychiatry. In P. Ahmed & G. Coehlo (Eds.), *Toward a new definition of health: Psychosocial dimensions* (pp. 53–65). New York: Plenum Press.

Kleinman, A. (1980). *Patients and healers in the context of culture*. Berkeley: University of California Press.

Kleinman, A. (1986). *Social origins of distress and disease: Depression, neurasthenia, and pain in modern China*. New Haven, CT: Yale University Press.

Kleinman, A. (1988). *Rethinking psychiatry: From cultural category to personal experience*. New York: Free Press.

Kleinman, A., & Good, B. (1985). Introduction: Culture and depression. In A. Kleinman & B. Good

(Eds.), *Culture and depression* (pp. 1–33). Berkeley: University of California Press.

Koss, J. D. (1990). Somatization and somatic complaint syndromes among Hispanics: Overview and ethnopsychological perspectives. *Transcultural Psychiatric Research Review, 27,* 5–29.

Kramer, M., Rosen, B., & Willis, E. (1973). Definitions of mental health disorders in a racist society. In C. V. Willie, B. M. Kramer, & B. S. Brown (Eds.), *Racism and mental health* (pp. 353–459). Pittsburgh: University of Pittsburgh Press.

Lin, T. Y., Tardiff, K., Donetz, G., & Goresky, W. (1978). Ethnicity and patterns of help-seeking. *Culture, Medicine and Psychiatry, 2,* 3–13.

López, S., & Hernandez, P. (1986). How culture is considered in evaluations of psychopathology. *Journal of Nervous and Mental Disease, 176,* 598–606.

Loring, M., & Powell, B. (1988). Gender, race, and DSM-III: A study of the objectivity of psychiatric diagnostic behavior. *Journal of Health and Social Behavior, 29,* 1–22.

Low, S. M. (1981). The meaning of *nervios*: A sociocultural analysis of symptom presentation in San José, Costa Rica. *Culture, Medicine and Psychiatry, 5,* 25–48.

Malgady, R. G., Rogler, L. H., & Costantino, G. (1987). Ethnocultural and linguistic bias in mental health evaluation of Hispanics. *American Psychologist, 42,* 228–234.

Manson, S. M., Shore, J. H., & Bloom, J. D. (1985). The depressive experience in American Indian communities: A challenge for psychiatric theory and diagnosis. In B. Good & A. Kleinman (Eds.), *Culture and depression* (pp. 331–368). Berkeley: University of California Press.

Marsella, A. J., & Kameoka, V. A. (1989). Ethnocultural issues in the assessment of psychopathology. In S. Wetzler (Ed.), *Measuring mental illness: Psychometric assessment for clinicians* (pp. 231–256). Washington, DC: American Psychiatric Press.

Marsella, A. J., Sartorius, N., Jablensky, A., & Fenton, F. R. (1985). Cross-cultural studies of depressive disorders: An overview. In A. Kleinman & B. Good (Eds.), *Culture and depression* (pp. 299–324). Berkeley: University of California Press.

Maser, J. D., & Cloninger, C. R. (1990). Comorbidity of anxiety and mood disorders: Introduction and overview. In J. D. Maser & C. R. Cloninger (Eds.), *Comorbidity of mood and anxiety disorders* (pp. 3–12). Washington, DC: American Psychiatric Press.

Maser, J. D., & Dinges, N. G. (1993). Comorbidity: Meaning and uses in cross-cultural clinical research. *Culture, Medicine and Psychiatry, 16,* 409–426.

Mirowsky, J. (1985). Disorder and its context: Paranoid beliefs as thematic elements of thought problems, hallucinations, and delusions under threatening social conditions. *Research in Community and Mental Health, 5,* 185–204.

Mollica, R. F., Wyshak, G., de Marneffe, D., Khuon, F., & Lavelle, J. (1987). Indochinese versions of the Hopkins Symptom Checklist-25: A screening instrument for the psychiatric care of refugees. *American Journal of Psychiatry, 144,* 497–500.

Mukherjee, S., Shukla, S. S., Woodle, J., Rosen, A. M., & Olarte, S. (1983). Misdiagnosis of schizophrenia in bipolar patients: A multiethnic comparison. *American Journal of Psychiatry, 140,* 1571–1574.

Ndetei, D. M. (1986). Paranoid disorder—Environmental, cultural or constitutional phenomenon? *Acta Psychiatrica Scandinavica, 74,* 50–54.

Newhill, C. E. (1990). The role of culture in the development of paranoid symptomatology. *American Journal of Orthopsychiatry, 60,* 176–185.

Noh, S., Avison, W. R., & Kaspar, V. (1992). Depressive symptoms among Korean immigrants: Assessment of a translation of the Center for Epidemiologic Studies—Depression Scale. *Psychological Assessment, 4,* 84–91.

O'Nell, T. D. (1993). "Feeling worthless": An ethnographic investigation of depression and problem drinking at the Flathead reservation. *Culture, Medicine and Psychiatry, 16,* 447–470.

Phinney, J. (1990). Ethnic identity in adolescents and adults: Reviews of research. *Psychological Bulletin, 108,* 499–514.

Raskin, A., Crook, T. H., & Herman, K. D. (1975). Psychiatric history and symptom differences in Black and White depressed inpatients. *Journal of Consulting and Clinical Psychiatry, 43,* 73–80.

Rogler, L., & Cortes, D. (1993). Help-seeking pathways: A unifying concept in mental health care. *American Journal of Psychiatry, 150,* 554–561.

Rogler, L., Cortes, D., & Malgady, R. (1991). Acculturation and mental health status among Hispanics. *American Psychologist, 46,* 585–597.

Rogler, L., Malgady, R., & Rodriguez, G. (1989). *Hispanics and mental health: A framework for research.* Malabar, FL: Krieger.

Rubio-Stipec, M., Shrout, P. E., Bird, H., Canino, G., & Bravo, M. (1989). Symptom scales of the Diagnostic Interview Schedule: Factor results in Hispanic and Anglo samples. *Psychological Assessment: A Journal of Consulting and Clinical Psychology, 1,* 30–34.

Van Schaik, E. (1989). Paradigms underlying the study of nerves as a popular illness term in Eastern Kentucky. *Medical Anthropology, 11,* 15–28.

Weiss, M. G., & Kleinman, A. (1988). Depression in cross-cultural perspective: Developing a culturally informed model. In P. R. Dasen, J. W. Berry, & N. Sartorius (Eds.), *Health and cross-cultural psychology* (pp. 179–206). Newbury Park, CA: Sage.

Chapter 4

Impact of the Use of Standard Psychological Assessment on the Diagnosis and Treatment of Ethnic Minorities

RICHARD H. DANA

This chapter has several purposes: (1) to list and provide a rationale for the seven tests currently used in standard psychological assessment in the United States; (2) to describe a technology using moderator variables to distinguish among assimilated, traditional, bicultural, and marginal cultural orientations as a necessary precursor to standard psychological assessment; (3) to describe some deficits in standard psychological assessment in construction, administration, and interpretation (including distortion, pathologization, caricature, and dehumanization) for those individuals within each ethnic minority group who do not have an assimilated cultural orientation; (4) to examine the usefulness of the standard psychological tests for psychodiagnosis, personality, and intelligence with ethnic minority populations; and (5) to present a format for culturally competent psychological assessment services.

Standard Psychological Assessment

Standard psychological assessment refers to the small number of tests used since 1960 for clinical diagnosis, personality description, and measurement of intelligence. Piotrowski and Keller (1989) found that only seven tests were used in 80 percent of their surveyed outpatient mental health facilities. These tests were the Wechsler Adult Intelligence Test (WAIS), the Wechsler Intelligence Tests for Children and Infants (WISC-R/WPPSI), Figure Drawings, Sentence Completions, the Rorschach, the Bender-Gestalt and the Minnesota Multiphasic Personality Inventory (MMPI). When recommendations from APA-approved doctoral programs are included (Craig & Horowitz, 1990; O'Donohue, Plaud, Mowatt, & Fearon, 1989), the Thematic Apperception Test (TAT) is added to this list. Neither scientist-practitioner nor practitioner-scholar models of training have differed in their assessment curricula (Dana, 1992).

Students in the majority of doctoral programs are still not trained to administer these tests using culturally acceptable styles of service delivery, or a social etiquette for interpersonal transactions that is acceptable to ethnic minority clients. In addition, students are only infrequently provided with experiences in examining culture-specific perspectives that would be relevant for interpretation of test protocols (as in López et al., 1989). As a result, training in standard psychological assessment is deficient for practice with ethnic minority populations. The failure to incorporate culture-specific tests into the assessment curriculum has further reduced the likelihood of providing acceptable services for these populations. In the absence of cultural competence, the practice of standard psychological assessment has unforeseen consequences. These may include not only faulty diagnosis, but also caricature and distortion in personality description by minimizing differences and stereotyping client behaviors.

Within each ethnic minority group, standard psychological assessment will be suitable for some members but inappropriate for others because of their varying degrees of assimilation. Moreover, the percentages of persons who are assimilated differ greatly among ethnic minority groups. As a result, it is always mandatory to distinguish those individuals within each minority population who are assimilated and for whom standard psychological assessment is appropriate. This may be done by assessment of cultural orientation using moderator variables (Dana, 1992).

Cultural Orientation and Moderator Variables

Four possible cultural orientations are usually distinguished. A *traditional orientation* is defined as retention of an original culture, whereas *nontraditional* refers to assimilation into the majority Anglo-American culture. *Bicultural* individuals have retained many aspects of their original culture while simultaneously functioning in a manner acceptable to and understood within the majority culture. *Marginality* implies rejection of substantial segments of both the original and the dominant society cultures. A fifth cultural orientation, *transitional*, has been used to describe Native Americans who are bilingual but who question their traditional religion and values (LaFromboise, Trimble, & Mohatt, 1990).

Although complete information on the number of persons fitting each cultural orientation category is not known at this time, a few studies provide some relevant information. Native Americans probably have the lowest percentage of nontraditional or assimilated individuals, as few as 9 percent in a college population, with an approximately equal division among the remaining three orientations (Johnson & Lashley, 1989). Another source reported a 20 percent traditional orientation, 65 percent marginality, and 15 percent assimilated and/or bicultural (French, 1989). These discrepancies reflect not only college versus noncollege samples but also the ambiguity of definitions that are not derived from moderator variables. For African Americans, it was estimated using moderator variables that as many as 77 percent of male students in one Southern urban college were assimilated in their cultural orientation (Whatley & Dana, 1989). Comparable data for Asian Americans and Hispanic Americans has not been located.

Moderator variables are now available to measure cultural orientation for some of the major ethnic minority populations in the United States. Mandatory use of these variables has only been suggested in a few recent sources (e.g., Dana, 1993; Ibrahim & Arredondo, 1986; Velásquez & Callahan, 1992). Nonetheless, cultural competence in assessment practice requires information on client cultural orientation that is obtained prior to the onset of assessment services. This information will suggest not only the specific tests to use but also the likelihood of bias using standard psychological assessment.

There is insufficient space in this chapter for discussion of comparisons among available moderators for each ethnic minority population. A listing of selected measures is provided in Table 4-1. (For details, see Chapter 2 of this book and Chapter 7 in Dana, 1993.) Most of these measures are bilevel; they provide information not only on traditional culture but also on the acquisition of dominant society values. The listed measures differ in psychometric adequacy, but all of them meet minimum standards. A measure or measures of cultural orientation should be routinely employed because the current categorization of cultural orientations is

TABLE 4-1   Selected Moderator Variables for Assessment of Cultural Orientation

Measure	Source
Developmental Inventory of Black Consciousness	Milliones (1980)
Racial Identity Attitude Scale	Helms (1990)
African Self-Consciousness Scale	Baldwin & Bell (1985)
Suin-Lew Asian Self-Identity Acculturation Scale	Suinn, Rickard-Figueroa, Lew, & Vigil (1987)
Acculturation Scale for Mexican Americans	Cuellar, Harris, & Jasso (1980)
Hispanic Acculturation Scale	Marín, Sabogal, VanOss Marín, Otero-Sabogal, & Perez-Sable (1987b)
Native Generations Diagnosis	Brown (1982, May)
Rosebud Personal Opinion Survey	Hoffman, Dana, & Bolton (1985)
Individualism–Collectivism Scale	Hui (1988)
Scale to Assess World Views	Ibrahim & Kahn (1987)

only a gross classification, and there are empirically demonstrated pathologization consequences of not using culture as a moderator variable (e.g., Dana & Whatley, 1991; Hoffman, Dana, & Bolton, 1985; Montgomery & Orozco, 1985).

Measures for African Americans describe Nigrescence, a process of identity awareness, and Africentrism, or Afrocentrism, a behavioral redintegration of African heritage. For Asian Americans, there are a variety of group-specific measures, none of which is ready for clinical application at the present time. However, the Suinn-Lew measure, an adaptation of the Acculturation Scale for Mexican Americans for persons of Chinese, Japanese, and Korean ethnic origin, is acceptable for cautious assessment applications. For Southeast Asian refugees and other Asian immigrants, it is often preferable to infer cultural orientation from information collected in an interview. This information should include willingness to acculturate, current phase of acculturation process, current group sociocultural data, and individual psychological characteristics. This information is available in checklist format (Dana, 1993, p. 114). For Hispanic Americans, a variety of psychometrically sound instruments are available for subgroups of Cuban Americans and Mexican Americans, with separate measures for children, in addition to the Hispanic Acculturation Scale (Marín, Sabogal, VanOss Marín, Otero-Sabogal, & Perez-Sable, 1987a).

Assessment of Native American cultural orientation in reservation settings should use tribe-specific measures whenever feasible. For urban residents, however, the Brown interview technique is recommended regardless of tribal origin. This technique provides a descriptive chart for acculturation in terms of family relationships, social-recreational activities, spiritual-religious practices, and training-education preferences (Brown, 1982, May). Finally, whenever an application of group-specific measures is unavailable or unfeasible, more general measures of world view, or world view components, may be used. These measures, however, usually will not be as appropriate for Native Americans as moderators that are tribe-specific tests or the Brown Pan-Indian interview technique.

Deficiencies in Standard Psychological Assessment for Cross-Cultural Practice

Test Construction

The standard psychological assessment instruments were constructed on the basis of unquestioning acceptance and use of a psychometric paradigm that has been applied in the United States and Western Europe primarily by White male psychologists. As a result, these tests are culture-specific and usable only in a European-American cultural context with English-speaking persons who have a Eurocentric world view, as a result of either early childhood socialization or assimilation as an adult. *World view* embraces shared group and individual identity components, consensual values and beliefs, and common language.

Contemporary psychometric practices have developed in a context of Western science. To be sure, the underlying model of science is now in the throes of change in the direction of a social constructionism (Dana, 1987). Assessment practice is being informed indirectly by this paradigm shift toward an emphasis on persons in social contexts with specific and interactive causes of behavior, and using modified methods to achieve these purposes. This new assessment perspective expands the concept of individual differences by adding dimensions based on culture and gender.

The details of culture-specific assessment technology and service delivery style have not yet been forthcoming for all ethnic minority groups. Research agendas primarily for Hispanic populations (Marín & Marín, 1991; Ponterotto & Casas, 1991; Rogler, Malgady, & Rodriguez, 1989) were precursors to an edited book for assessment of Hispanics (Geisinger, 1992). Snowden and Todman (1982) have provided a major resource for assessment of African Americans. Competent reviews of assessment issues with Asian Americans (Sue & Sue, 1987) and refugees (Williams, 1986) are available. For Native Americans, there has been an emphasis on reviews of more limited assessment domains (e.g., Dana, 1986; Manson, Walker, & Kivlahan, 1987).

Matarazzo (1992) has predicted that assessment during the next century will emphasize individual differences, using new types of tests to measure mental abilities and personality in the form of "specific psychological styles and predispositions" (p. 1014) within the general nonpathological population. Moreover, assessment of specific forms of psychopathology using narrow band measures will supplement the use of restandardized versions of the contemporary MMPI. These glances into the future are consistent with an increasing practice of culturally competent assessment.

Test Administration

The assessment process in Anglo-American society is a professional relationship with established rules for acceptable client behaviors that were derived from the medical model of service delivery for physical health problems. This model emphasizes patient compliance in the face of provider expertise and credibility based on formal credentials provided by educational experience and professional licensing—what Naisbitt (1982) calls "high technology and low touch." As a consequence, the interaction between health service providers and consumers in this society has been somewhat impersonal, structured, and formal, with minimal give-and-take questioning and relevant discussion.

This model is no longer comfortable or acceptable even for many Anglo-American consumers of health and/or mental health services who may accept a medical model conception of their psychological distress (Dana, 1985). Nonetheless, to the extent that this service delivery model has been institutionalized and has system characteristics, change has not occurred rapidly. Although Anglo-American clients may be restive and somewhat put off or dissatisfied with this relatively impersonal service delivery style, they do have lifelong familiarity with this style and have learned a variety of coping behaviors in an effort to receive the best services possible.

Clients with traditional orientations representing non-Anglo-American cultures may not accept services proferred in an impersonal manner, especially when their conceptions of mental illness and legitimate remediations differ from the standard nomenclature and interventions.

Distinct culture-specific styles of assessment service delivery can increase rapport and willingness to participate in an assessment process. African Americans are often reluctant to engage immediately in the expected task orientation that is necessary for any assessment process. This process has been described in stages of guarded appraisal, investigative challenges to determine culturally relevant experience, partial identification by personal relationship overtures, personal regard, and finally task engagement (Gibbs, 1985). This process of sizing up and checking out cannot always be accomplished in a single session.

Asian Americans conform to role relationships on the basis of gender, age, and expertise and have expectations for immediate benefit—a "gift" that strengthens the relationship sufficiently for subsequent services to occur (Sue & Zane, 1987). Credibility in these relationships occurs if the assessor is male; older than the client; and confident in communicating educational, experiential, and personal credentials (Lee, 1982).

Hispanic Americans respond to a cultural script for social interaction called *simpatía* (Triandis, Marín, Lisansky, & Betancourt, 1984). This etiquette includes leisurely chatting, or *platicando;* attention that is informal and personal, or *personalismo;* an atmosphere of warmth called *ambiente;* and role relationships invoking respect, or *respeto* (e.g., younger to older persons, women to men, to persons in authority). The intent of *simpatía* is to evoke *confianza en confianza,* or mutual trust. Moreover, for Hispanics, use of a client's first language is mandatory because affect communication and self-disclosure may be impaired and speech distortions may occur in the second language.

An acceptable service delivery style for Native Americans mirrors the sequence of talk and begins with informal chitchat on topics of mutual interest. Of course, this implies a basis for the conversation arising from shared activities occurring in other settings and from a relationship that has existed prior to the assessment service. Not only is tribe-specific cultural knowledge required, but there should be a personal basis for the relationship that already permits acceptance and trust. Whenever this context of relationship is not feasible, the test materials may be meager and incomplete. Subsequent interpretations of these data will often be faulty because the text protocols will appear to be adequate and self-revealing when, in fact, they represent only an attempt at task compliance without the investment of self that can occur only for a friend or relative.

Test Interpretation

Test interpretation is informed by a variety of unverbalized expectations and preconceptions for client responsivity to the standard assessment process and tests. Four of these conditions that can lead to implicit assessor bias will be examined: (1) distortion as a result of minimizing differences among persons, (2) pathologization by use of inappropriate diagnostic nomenclature, (3) caricature as a result of stereotypy, and (4) dehumanization as a consequence of inapplicable personality theories.

Distortion

Unwitting distortion of information contained in test protocols may occur on the basis of an often unacknowledged assessor belief that all persons should be assimilated as Americans so that historic differences in ethnicity are blurred in the "melting pot" of the United States. Nonetheless, ethnorelativism is a necessary hallmark of a multicultural society, and training for ethnorelativistic thinking is vital for human services that are responsive to individual differences. Bennett (1986) has described a six-stage ethnocentrism–ethnorelativism continuum that includes Denial, Defense, Minimization, Acceptance, Adaptation, and Integration. Many Anglo-American service providers trivialize differences in culture in order to preserve the intactness of their own world view. Training for ethnorelativistic thinking is a necessary component of professional training for culturally competent assessment.

Pathologization

Pathologization refers to interpretation that renders assessees more disturbed than in fact they are. The *Diagnostic and Statistical Manual of Mental Disorders*, third edition, revised (DSM-III-R) (American Psychiatric Association [APA], 1987) recognized only that religious and cultural beliefs should not be used for diagnosis because they may be confounded with schizophrenic delusions or hallucinations. Because there is worldwide distribution of only a small number of conditions (Kleinman, 1991, July), the DSM-III-R categories should be used with caution for individuals in the United States who do not have the dominant society's Anglo-American cultural orientation.

With the development and publishing of the DSM-IV, cultural content has been incorporated into the new classification system (American Psychiatric Association, 1994; NIMH-Sponsored Group on Culture and Diagnosis, January, 1993). The inclusion of Appendix I in the DSM-IV provides some assistance in incorporating cultural issues and conditions into the diagnostic process. Although a DSM cultural axis may be desirable in the future, in the current system there is a possibility of stereotypy in the absence of accepted diagnostic procedures for establishing cultural orientation.

The DSM is the criterion for checklist and rating scale measures of psychology. Since the DSM historically has made mind–body, disease process, and disease course assumptions that are inapplicable to a majority of the world population, it not surprising that López and Núñez (1987) found only a perfunctory DSM acknowledgment of cultural influences in measures used for structured diagnostic interviews. The resistance to any DSM modifications for culture appears to stem from minimization of cultural differences and a psychometric foundation for our current assessment paradigm that has been accepted as cross-culturally valid.

Caricature

Caricature is used here to refer to a distortion of assessees' personality and/or psychopathology that occurs as a result of stereotypy. For example, African-American group differences are often labeled as deficits by Anglo-American service providers (Wyatt, Powell, & Bass, 1982). Codependence, as a second example, may be considered as evidence of disturbance by Anglo-Americans. For many persons, however, particularly Asian Americans, codependence may not be unwillingness or inability to assume personal responsibility but simply an allocation of this responsibility to others. Finally, clients may be judged by their Anglo-American assessors on the basis of their ethnicity to have characteristics that would indicate psychopathology in Anglo-Americans. Attributions of anxiety, confusion, and reserve are made of Chinese clients (Li-Repac, 1980) while African-American clients' sexuality may be perceived as inappropriate (Wyatt et al., 1982).

Dehumanization

Dehumanization is a strong word, but the application of personality theory developed in one culture to persons in another culture can have exactly this effect. Psychoanalysis provides a convenient example because this personality theory of European-American origin was espoused by many anthropologists and psychologists of an earlier generation and was used as a basis for cross-cultural personality research, often with projective techniques. Psychoanalysis as a personality theory or a method of psychotherapy can be applied to persons who are not of European origins. Whenever this occurs, however, this theory should be used with caution because it may not constitute a universal framework for understanding human beings.

To my knowledge, the most egregious example of dehumanization by application of psychoanalytic theory to an assessee occurred using the Rorschach with a Mescalero Apache shaman. This shaman was diagnosed as a "character disorder with oral and phallic fixations . . . with occasional hysterical dissociations" (Klopfer & Boyer, 1961, p. 178). Such a diagnosis on the basis of the Rorschach alone needs to be placed in a frame of reference that includes the reservation community and peer judgment, since there is culturally relevant personality theory that may be invoked to account for the Rorschach protocol (Dana, 1993, p. 156). My intent in using this example is not to stigmatize psychoanalysis per se, but to argue that culture-specific personality theories are a necessary component of cultural competence in assessment. Unfortunately, there are few such theories at the present time (e.g., for African Americans: Jenkins, 1982; Steele, 1990). In their absence, one should use existing theories with caution and with appreciation of their limited generality.

The Current Status of Cross-Cultural Validity in Standard Tests

This description will include the seven tests used in standard psychological assessment and some other tests that have had cross-cultural usage. The Minnesota

Multiphasic Personality Inventory will be examined separately because it is now the most widely used test for psychopathology and personality. Two projective techniques for personality assessment—the Rorschach and the TAT—will be discussed in a context of other inkblot and picture-story techniques. The Sentence Completions, Bender Gestalt, and Figure Drawings will be considered together under the heading "Other Projective Techniques." In addition, the standard intelligence tests for adults and children will be considered. Other intelligence tests with cross-cultural applications will also be dscribed. Several additional tests that tap limited assessment domains not included in the standard list based on frequency of usage will also be described. Finally, there will be consideration of the kinds of measures that have been largely omitted in psychological assessment, particularly culture-specific or *emic* methods.

Minnesota Multiphasic Personality Inventory (MMPI, MMPI-2)

The MMPI has been translated into 150 languages for use in diagnosis and personality description in more than 50 countries. Translations of standard tests are required for those persons in the United States whose first or primary language is not English. Nonetheless, there has been relatively little interest in the development and use of translations for cultural minority groups in the United States, with the exception of Hispanics. For Spanish-speaking persons, several translations of varying quality do exist, but except for a Puerto Rican version (Diaz, Nogueras, & Draguns, 1984) these translations do not appear to be directly comparable to the English version. Many bicultural, bilingual Hispanic Americans should have a choice of English or Spanish test versions.

Many of the MMPI translations used in other parts of the world have not controlled for accuracy or linguistic equivalence (Williams, 1986) and are of questionable cross-cultural validity. Cross-culturally valid translations should be carried out according to acceptable criteria for linguistic and construct equivalence. In addition to the translations, the formats for item presentation, the item contents (including contexts), and cultural restrictions for self-disclosure are relevant for cross-cultural validity. Because the MMPI scales were constructed without the use of factor analysis, a major cross-cultural validation technique, replicatory factor analysis, cannot be employed. For details on ways to increase MMPI cross-cultural validity, readers should examine Ben-Porath (1990).

There are notable differences between the MMPI-1 profiles of ethnic minority groups and Anglo-American normative groups. For example, African Americans may have high scores on scales F, 6, 8, and 9 as a result of Nigrescence, a process of becoming Afrocentric, while Hispanic Americans exhibit elevated scores on these scales on the basis of being traditional in cultural orientation (see Chapter 7 in Dana, 1993). However, Native American psychiatric patients, regardless of diagnosis, cultural orientation, or tribal affiliation, show similar profiles with elevations on F, 4, and 8 (Pollack & Shore, 1980). These issues are further compounded by a large group comparison literature containing inappropriate statistics, inadequate socio-economic criteria, and inconsistent definitions of ethnicity (Greene, 1987).

Some caveats for MMPI usage with ethnic minority populations in this country have been abbreviated from a more complete description of these issues for presentation here (Dana, 1993). The MMPI-1 should be used only when the assessee has been demonstrated to be comparable to the standardization population on demographic variables, including world view as measured by moderator variables, and speaks English as a first language. Even the MMPI-2 has only small and unrepresentative samples from several ethnic minority groups, and the cultural orientations of these individuals are unknown. The use of the MMPI with Native Americans/Alaskan Natives is more problematic than for other ethnic minority populations (Hoffmann et al., 1985). Even with use of moderator variables, tribe-specific norms are necessary for reservation residents.

Projective Techniques for Personality Assessment

Inkblot Measures: Rorschach, Exner Comprehensive Rorschach, and
Holtzman Inkblot Test

The original Rorschach was used for anthropological studies of many cultures, usually with a psychoanalytic interpretative stance or attention to model personality, although the cross-cultural validity has been questioned (Lindzey, 1961). The Exner Comprehensive Rorschach system relies on diagnostic indices and normative data for interpretation. However, there are no special norms for ethnic minority groups in this country. The Holtzman Inkblot Test (HIT) was constructed to provide an inkblot test that had psychometric properties acceptable to most psychologists. The HIT has been used in many different cultural settings, with factor analysis used to establish cross-cultural validity. Although the same factors do appear in different cultures, these factors have different loadings and there have been no conpensatory item weighting revisions (Eysenck & Eysenck, 1983).

Lindzey's questioning of the Rorschach's potential cross-cultural validity can be countered only in terms of the theory underlying the Rorschach inkblots. Hermann Rorschach certainly believed that *Erlebnistypus,* or the Experience-Balance, extraversion–introversion system, was universal. This system was consistently apparent in factor-analytic studies of the HIT (Swartz, Reinehr, & Holtzman, 1983) and received independent confirmation when all published Rorschach factor-analytic studies were reanalyzed using a principal-components analysis (Dana, Hinman, & Bolton, 1977). The HIT, despite the fact that it is not among the tests included in the frequency definition of standard psychological tests, is the only inkblot test that can be recommended for cross-cultural assessment at this time.

Picture-Story Techniques

The picture-story techniques described here include the TAT, the TEMAS (an acronym for "tell me a story"), and a variety of other culture-specific sets of pictures. The culture-specific picture-story techniques used by anthropologists also have been criticized for their use of psychoanalytic theory and reliance on findings that were not verified by direct observation (Mensh & Henry, 1953). In addition, there is neither a consensual TAT scoring system that accounts for all protocol data nor an underlying personality theory that claims universality.

Picture-story TAT variants developed for African Americans include the Thompson Modification (T-TAT) with redrawn Murray pictures (Thompson, 1949) and the Themes Concerning Blacks Test (TCB) (Williams, 1972). The TCB test may be used provisionally in preference to the T-TAT because of the culture-specific nature of the TCB cards, although more research on the scoring categories is needed. It should also be noted that an Anglo-American assessor who is a stranger to the assessee may encounter what Snowden and Todman (1982) have called "reticence," a characteristic caution, vagueness, and inhibition of storytelling.

For Hispanic Americans, TEMAS, a culture-specific set of picture-story cards, is available (Costantino, Malgady, & Rogler, 1988). The TEMAS was developed for bilingual administration to children from 5 to 18 years of age. Everyday interpersonal relationships involving conflict are presented in culturally relevant and gender-balanced chromatic pictures of moderate ambiguity. A variety of personality and cognitive functions are scored. There are limited norms for Anglo-Americans, African Americans, Puerto Ricans, and other Hispanic Americans. Parallel versions for Anglo-American children and Asian-American children are being developed. Validation studies suggest that personality constructs are being measured and that TEMAS can be used for diagnostic screening and prediction of therapy outcome.

For Native Americans, many sets of tribe-specific pictures have been developed on the basis of criteria for designing pictures (Sherwood, 1957). Tribe-specific pictures are available for Blood, Eskimo, Hopi, Menomini, Northern Cheyenne, Navajo, and Sioux. For reservation residents, tribe-specific pictures are preferred, and it is recommended that pictures be drawn on the basis of Sherwood (1957) design criteria.

However, there are no scoring systems that can be recommended for interpretation of the picture-story protocols of Native Americans. Instead, assessors should be familiar with the history, customs, ethnography, fiction, and published life histories of individuals for any tribe whose members are assessed using picture story techniques. Inservice training for assessors is available in language, healing practices, spirituality, and tribal law in many tribal colleges. In addition, there is a set of guidelines for interpretation of stories provided by acculturated and traditional Native Americans to the Murray TAT cards (Dana, 1993, pp. 152–155; Monopoli, 1984).

Other Projective Techniques: Sentence Completions and Figure Drawings
These techniques all provide a stimulus situation that offers considerable promise for their use in multicultural assessment settings. An early review (Holtzman, 1980) indicated problems in translation of item stems for use in completion techniques. These techniques also have to demonstrate psychological equivalence of meanings across cultures (Manaster & Havighurst, 1972). Completion techniques developed in the language of a particular culture have merit as *emic* measures.

Human figure drawings have a long history of cross-cultural use as measures of intelligence and personality, especially for values and cognitions (Barnouw, 1963, pp. 347–348). Any cross-cultural application of existing scoring systems for intelligence for personality is probably unwise in the absence of cultural validity for the constructs used in the scoring systems.

Intelligence Tests

Standard intelligence tests are used routinely with all ethnic minority populations in this country. These tests have minimized cultural bias by careful matching on some demographic variables, although factor invariance has not been demonstrated for Native Americans and Hispanic Americans. English versions of these tests usually have been administered. A Spanish translation of the WAIS-R, the Escala de Inteligencia Wechsler para Adultos (EIWA), is available; but this translation is not comparable, especially in conversions of raw scores to scaled scores, and should be limited in use to clients who are rural, language-impaired, and have limited education (López & Romero, 1988). Moreover, users of test data are seldom informed of the normative data used for comparison of the performances of ethnic minority individuals. Assessors who examine the intelligence of ethnic minority individuals should inform themselves of the cross-cultural validity literature for that group. For example, Verbal Scale scores for Native Americans may suggest academic expectations in Anglo-American classrooms; Performance Scale measures will provide more reliable estimates of intellectual functioning in other settings. Moreover, the numbers of factors and factorial structure are also culturally distinct for Native Americans (e.g., Dana, 1984).

Consideration should be given to the use of alternative tests of intelligence for ethnic minority populations. The System of Multicultural Pluralistic Assessment (Mercer & Lewis, 1978), the Kaufman Assessment Battery for Children, and the McCarthy Scales of Children's Abilities are all preferable to Wechsler tests for children. Although each of these tests also presents some problems for assessors of non-Anglo-American children, the Kaufman battery is the preferred alternative (Dana, 1993, pp. 188–190).

Limited Domain Measures

Although the purpose of this chapter is to provide information on the usefulness of standard psychological assessment with ethnic minority populations in the United States, it would be unfair not to indicate that there are a variety of tests with more limited measurement purposes that do have acceptable cross-cultural validity. Three selected measures of anxiety and depression will be noted here (see Chapter 9 for more measures; Dana, 1993).

The State-Trait Anxiety Inventory (STAI) provides brief, self-report measures of state, or general nervousness, and trait, or chronic anxiety (Spielberger, 1976). This inventory and a companion measure for children were factorially derived and have been translated into more than 40 languages using acceptable procedures to maximize idiomatic equivalency. Research on a Spanish-language version including confirmatory factor analysis has suggested cross-cultural validity and the desirability of use in this country with Spanish-speaking individuals.

The Inventory to Diagnose Depression (IDS) was developed to include criteria for major depressive disorders and an ongoing summary of symptom severity not included in other measures. The IDS has been used with Native American adolescents (Zimmerman, Coryell, & Wilson, 1986). The Vietnamese Depression Scale (VDS) represents careful and systematic translation procedures that included opportunity to provide a culturally consistent array of symptoms including somatization, depressed mood, and symptoms unrelated to lowered mood or Western depression (Kinsie et al., 1982).

Culture-Specific Measures

These measures include behavior observations/ethnographies, life history/case studies, the accounts method, and methods for studying life events (Dana, 1993, pp. 142–146). They become culture-specific on the basis of the development of narratives or categories within a cultural setting, with major assistance from local residents, a collection of local normative data, and an intent to include the context and meaning of behaviors. The accounts method is useful to identify problems, specify adaptive/maladaptive coping styles, and recommend culturally appropriate interventions with community input at each stage of the process (Jones & Thorne, 1987).

Methods for studying life events provide a life span approach to the delineation of culture-specific problems-in-living. The Social Readjustment Rating Scale (Holmes & Rahe, 1967) has been adapted for ethnic minority groups by the addition of stressors related to cultural practices and discrimination. Checklists of stressors are available for urban minority youth (Mosley & Lex, 1990), Hispanic immigrants and Hispanic Americans (Cervantes, Padilla, & deSnyder, 1991), and Native Americans (Dana, Hornby, & Hoffman, 1984).

A Format for Description of Culturally Competent Psychological Assessment Services

Cultural competence includes not only cultural sensitivity but also the skills required to establish and maintain comfortable relationships with assessment clients. In addition, a knowledge of the limitations of standard psychological assessment with persons from cultural minority groups is necessary. Awareness of acceptable translations of standard psychological tests and competence in the client's first language are highly desirable. Selection and/or modification of appropriate existing tests and other assessment materials with cultural validity is also required. In addition, in some settings for some cultural groups, the creation of new culture-specific or *emic* tests will be desirable.

A suggested format for culturally relevant assessment procedures would include these cultural competence ingredients as well as culture-specific feedback procedures to maximize the likelihood of client interest in subsequent interventions. Individuals from minority cultures who are traditional in orientation often may experience standard psychological assessment as neither appropriate nor fair. Alternative assessment procedures are then required. These alternatives may consist of modifications or adaptations of standard psychological assessment instruments, including translations, or the creation of new culture-specific measures. Bicultural and transitional individuals should be encouraged to make an informed choice between standard psychological assessment and culture-specific measures, whenever such measures are available. Marginal persons may often be uninterested, unmotivated, and/or unwilling participants in any assessment process. These persons require a time-limited and problem-specific mix of standard and culture-specific technologies, often with a behavioral emphasis.

Assessment findings may need to be communicated to the client and/or to family members or other advocates. In this communication process, attention should be given to the expectations for intervention procedures and service providers that have resulted from specific beliefs about health and illness. These beliefs need to be examined in a context of available intervention resources and with the person(s) who are responsible for implementing and intervention.

At present, the practice of culturally competent assessment is rare indeed. Despite awareness and formal pressure from program accreditation guidelines and site visitors, there is a paucity of relevant training available to students. In addition, the assessment establishment remains skeptical regarding the necessity of translations, local or group norms, moderator variables, culture-specific service delivery styles, or any need for new *emic* tests for ethnic minority groups in the United States. The solution to these dilemmas lies in greater understanding of the cultural specificity of the Anglo-American world view as expressed in our assessment technology. Such understanding requires an ethnorelativism that honors and is responsive to a much wider range of individual differences than occurs at the present time. Implementation of cultural competence in assessment training will require not only a greater ethnic minority faculty presence in training but also political persuasion that will occur only when a larger proportion of the United States population represents various ethnic minorities.

References

American Psychiatric Association. (1987). *Diagnostic and statistical manual of mental disorders* (DSM-III-R) (3rd ed., revised). Washington, DC: Author.

American Psychiatric Association. (1994). *Diagnostic and statistical manual of mental disorders* (DSM-IV) (4th ed.). Washington, DC: Author.

Baldwin, J. A., & Bell, Y. R. (1985). The African Self-Consciousness Scale: An Africentric personality questionnaire. *Western Journal of Black Studies, 13*(2), 27–41.

Barnouw, V. (1963). *Culture and personality.* Homewood, IL: Dorsey.

Bennett, M. J. (1986). A developmental approach to training for interpersonal sensitivity. *Journal of Intercultural Relations, 10,* 179–196.

Ben-Porath, Y. S. (1990). Cross-cultural assessment of personality: The case for replicatory factor analysis. In J. N. Butcher & C. D. Spielberger (Eds.), *Advances in personality assessment* (Vol. 4, pp. 27–48). Hillsdale, NJ: Lawrence Erlbaum.

Brown, S. (1982, May). *Native generations diagnosis and placement on the conflicts/resolutions chart.* Paper presented at the annual meeting of the School of Addiction Studies, Center for Alcohol and Addiction Studies, University of Alaska, Anchorage.

Cervantes, R. C., Padilla, A. M., & deSnyder, N. S. (1991). The Hispanic Stress Inventory: A culturally relevant approach to psychosocial assessment. *Psychological Assessment: A Journal of Consulting and Clinical Psychology, 3,* 438–447.

Costantino, G., Malgady, R. G., & Rogler, L. H. (1988). *TEMAS (Tell-Me-a-Story) manual.* Los Angeles: Western Psychological Services.

Craig, R. J., & Horowitz, M. (1990). Current utilization of psychological tests at diagnostic practicum sites. *Clinical Psychologist, 43,* 29–36.

Cuellar, I., Harris, I. C., & Jasso, R. (1980). An acculturation scale for Mexican American normal and clinical populations. *Hispanic Journal of Behavioral Science, 2,* 199–217.

Dana, R. H. (1984). Intelligence testing of American Indian children: Sidesteps in quest of ethical practice. *White Cloud Journal, 3*(3), 35–43.

Dana, R. H. (1985). A service-delivery paradigm for personality assessment. *Journal of Personality Assessment, 49,* 598–604.

Dana, R. H. (1986). Personality assessment of Native Americans. *Journal of Personality Assessment, 50,* 480–500.

Dana, R. H. (1987). Training for professional psychology: Science, practice, and identity. *Professional Psychology: Research and Practice, 18,* 9–16.

Dana, R. H. (1992). A commentary on assessment training in Boulder and Vail Model programs: In praise of differences! *Journal of Training and Practice in Professional Psychology, 6*(2), 19–26.

Dana, R. H. (1993). *Multicultural assessment perspectives for professional psychology.* Boston: Allyn and Bacon.

Dana, R. H., Hinman, S., & Bolton, B. (1977). Dimensions of examinees' responses to the Rorschach: An empirical synthesis. *Psychological Reports, 40,* 1147–1153.

Dana, R. H., Hornby, R., & Hoffmann, T. (1984). Local norms of personality assessment for Rosebud Sioux. *White Cloud Journal, 3*(2), 17–25.

Dana, R. H., & Whatley, P. R. (1991). When does a difference make a difference? MMPI scores and African Americans. *Journal of Clinical Psychology, 47,* 417–440.

Diaz, J. O. P., Nogueras, J. A., & Draguns, J. (1984). MMPI (Spanish translation) in Puerto Rican adolescents: Preliminary data on reliability and validity. Hispanic *Journal of Behavioral Science, 6*(2), 179–189.

Eysenck, H. J., & Eysenck, S. B. G. (1983). Recent advances in the cross-cultural study of personality. In J. N. Butcher & C. D. Spielberger (Eds.), *Advances in personality assessment* (Vol. 2, pp. 41–69). Hillsdale, NJ: Lawrence Erlbaum.

French, L. (1989). Native American alcoholism: A transcultural counseling perspective. *Counseling Psychology Quarterly, 2*(2), 153–166.

Geisinger, K. (Ed.). (1992). *Psychological testing for Hispanics.* Washington, DC: American Psychological Association.

Gibbs, J. T. (1985). Treatment relationships with Black clients: Interpersonal vs. instrumental strategies. *Advances in clinical social work.* Silver Spring, MD: National Association of Social Workers.

Greene, R. L. (1987). Ethnicity and MMPI performance: A review. *Journal of Consulting and Clinical Psychology, 55,* 497–512.

Helms, J. E. (Ed.). (1990). *Black and White racial identity: Theory, research, and practice.* New York: Greenwood.

Hoffmann, T., Dana, R. H., & Bolton, B. (1985). Measured acculturation and the MMPI-168. *Journal of Cross-Cultural Psychology, 16,* 243–256.

Holmes, T. H., & Rahe, R. H. (1967). The Social Readjustment Rating Scale. *Journal of Psychosomatic Research, 11,* 213–218.

Holtzman, W. H. (1980). Projective techniques. In H. C. Triandis & J. W. Berry (Eds.), *Handbook of cross-cultural psychology: Vol 2. Methodology* (pp. 245–278). Boston: Allyn and Bacon.

Hui, C. H. (1988). Measurement of individualism–collectivism. *Journal of Research in Personality, 22,* 17–36.

Ibrahim, F. A., & Arredondo, P. M. (1986). Ethical standards for cross-cultural counseling, counselor preparation, practice, assessment, and research. *Journal of Counseling & Development, 64,* 349–352.

Ibrahim, F. A., & Kahn, H. (1987). Assessment of world views. *Psychological Reports, 60,* 163–176.

Jenkins, A. H. (1982). *The psychology of the Afro-American: A humanistic approach.* New York: Pergamon Press.

Johnson, M. E., & Lashley, K. H. (1989). Influence of Native Americans' cultural commitment on preferences for counselor ethnicity and expectations about counseling. *Journal of Multicultural Counseling and Development, 17,* 115–122.

Jones, E. E., & Thorne, A. (1987). Rediscovery of the subject: Intercultural approaches to clinical assessment. *Journal of Consulting and Clinical Psychology, 55,* 488–495.

Kinsie, J. D., Manson, S. M., Vinh, D. T., Tolan, N. T., Anh, B., & Pho, T. N. (1982). Development and validation of a Vietnamese-language depression rating scale. *American Journal of Psychiatry, 139,* 1276–1281.

Kleinman, A. (1991, July). The psychiatry of culture and the culture of psychiatry. *Harvard Mental Health Letter, 8*(1), 4–6.

Klopfer, B., & Boyer, L. B. (1961). Notes on the personality structure of a North American Indian shaman: Rorschach interpretation. *Journal of Personality Assessment, 25,* 170–178.

LaFromboise, T. D., Trimble, J. E., & Mohatt, G. V. (1990). Counseling intervention and American Indian traditions: An integrative approach. *The Counseling Psychologist, 18,* 628–654.

Lee, E. (1982). A social systems approach to assessment and treatment for Chinese American families. In M. McGoldrick, J. K. Pierce, & J. Giordano (Eds.), *Ethnicity and family therapy* (pp. 527–551). New York: Guilford Press.

Li-Repac, D. (1980). Cultural influences on perception: A comparison between Caucasian and Chinese-American therapists. *Journal of Cross-Cultural Psychology, 11,* 327–342.

Lindzey, G. (1961). *Projective techniques and cross-cultural research.* New York: Appleton-Century-Crofts.

López, S. R., Grover, K. P., Holland, D., Johnson, M. J., Kain, C. D., Kanel, K., & Mellins, S. A. (1989). Development of culturally sensitive psychotherapists. *Professional Psychology: Research and Practice, 20,* 369–376.

López, S. R., & Núñez, J. A. (1987). Cultural factors

considered in selected diagnostic criteria and interview schedules. *Journal of Abnormal Psychology, 96,* 270–272.

López, S. R., & Romero, A. (1988). Assessing the intellectual functioning of Spanish-speaking adults: Comparison of the EIWA and the WAIS. *Professional Psychology: Research and Practice, 19,* 263–270.

Manaster, G. J., & Havighurst, R. J. (1972). *Cross-national research: Socio-psychological methods and problems.* Boston: Houghton-Mifflin.

Manson, S. M., Walker, R. D., & Kivlahan, D. R. (1987). Psychiatric assessment and treatment of American Indians and Alaska Natives. *Hospital and Community Psychiatry, 38*(2), 165–173.

Marín, G., & Marín, B. V. (1991). *Research with Hispanic populations.* Newbury Park, CA: Sage.

Marín, G., Sabogal, F., VanOss Marín, B., Otero-Sabogal, R., & Perez-Sable, E. J. (1987). Development of a short acculturation scale for Hispanics. *Hispanic Journal of Behavioral Science, 9,* 183–205.

Matarazzo, J. D. (1992). Psychological testing and assessment in the 21st century. *American Psychologist, 47,* 1007–1118.

Mensh, I. N., & Henry, J. (1953). Direct observation and psychological tests in anthropological studies. *American Anthropologist, 55,* 461–480.

Mercer, J., & Lewis, J. (1978). *System of Multicultural Pluralistic Assessment.* New York: Psychological Corporation.

Milliones, J. (1980). Construction of a Black consciousness measure: Psychotherapeutic implications. *Psychotherapy: Theory, Research and Practice, 17,* 175–182.

Monopoli, J. (1984). *A culture-specific interpretation of thematic test protocols for American Indians.* Unpublished master's thesis, University of Arkansas, Fayetteville, AR.

Montgomery, G. T., & Orozco, S. (1985). Mexican Americans' performance on the MMPI as a function of level of acculturation. *Journal of Clinical Psychology, 41,* 203–212.

Mosley, J. C., & Lex, A. (1990). Identification of potentially stressful life events experienced by a population of urban minority youth. *Journal of Multicultural Counseling and Development, 18,* 118–125.

Naisbitt, J. (1982). *Megatrends.* New York: Warner.

NIMH-Sponsored Group on Culture and Diagnosis, Steering Committee. (1993, January). *Cultural Proposals and Supporting Papers for DSM-IV (3rd Rev.).* Pittsburgh: University of Pittsburgh Medical School.

O'Donohue, W., Plaud, J. J., Mowatt, A. M., & Fearon, J. R. (1989). Current status of curricula of doctoral training programs in clinical psychology. *Professional Psychology: Research and Practice, 20,* 196–197.

Piotrowski, C., & Keller, J. W. (1989). Psychological testing in outpatient mental health facilities: A national study. *Professional Psychology: Research and Practice, 20,* 423–425.

Pollack, D., & Shore, J. H. (1980). Validity of the MMPI with Native Americans. *American Journal of Psychiatry, 137,* 946–950.

Ponterotto, J. G., & Casas, J. M. (1991). *Handbook of racial/ethnic minority counseling research.* Springfield, IL: Thomas.

Rogler, L. H., Malgady, R. G., & Rodriguez, O. (1989). *Hispanics and mental health: A framework for research.* Malabar, FL: Krieger.

Sherwood, E. T. (1957). On the designing of TAT pictures, with special reference to a set for an African people assimilating Western culture. *Journal of Social Psychology, 45,* 161–190.

Snowden, L., & Todman, P. (1982). The psychological assessment of Blacks: new and needed developments. In E. E. Jones, & S. J. Korchin (Eds.), *Minority mental health* (pp. 193–226). New York: Praeger.

Spielberger, C. D. (1976). The nature and measurement of anxiety. In C. D. Spielberger & R. Diaz-Guerrero (Eds.), *The nature and measurement of anxiety* (Vol. 1, pp. 1–11). Washington, DC: Hemisphere.

Steele, S. (1990). *The content of our character: A new vision of race in America.* New York: Harper Perennial.

Sue, D., & Sue, S. (1987). Cultural factors in the clinical assessment of Asian Americans. *Journal of Consulting and Clinical Psychology, 55,* 479–487.

Sue, S., & Zane, N. (1987). The role of culture and cultural techniques in psychotherapy: A critique and reformulation. *American Psychologist, 42,* 37–45.

Suinn, R. M., Rickard-Figueroa, K., Lew, S., & Vigil, S. (1987). The Suinn-Lew Asian Self-Identity Acculturation Scale: An initial report. *Educational and Psychological Measurement, 47,* 401–407.

Swartz, J. D., Reinehr, R. C., & Holtzman, W. H. (1983). *Holtzman Inkblot Technique, 1956–1962: An annotated bibliography.* Austin: Hogg Foundation for Mental Health, University of Texas.

Thompson, C. E. (1949). The Thompson modification of the Thematic Apperception Text. *Rorschach Research Exchange and Journal of Projective Techniques, 13,* 469–478.

Triandis, H. C., Marín, G., Lisansky, J., & Betancourt, H. (1984). Simpatía as a cultural script of Hispanics. *Journal of Personality and Social Psychology, 47,* 1363–1375.

Velásquez, R. J., & Callahan, W. J. (1992). Psychological testing of Hispanic Americans in clinical settings: Overview and issues. In K. F. Geisinger (Ed.), *Psychological testing of Hispanics* (pp. 253–265). Washington, DC: American Psychological Association.

Whatley, P. R., & Dana, R. H. (1989). *Racial identity and MMPI group differences.* Fayetteville: University of Arkansas.

Williams, C. L. (1986). Mental health assessment of refugees. In C. L. Williams & J. Wstermeyer (Eds.), *Refugee mental health in resettlement countries* (pp. 175–188). New York: Hemisphere.

Williams, R. L. (1972). *Themes concerning Blacks.* St. Louis, MO: Williams & Associates.

Wyatt, G. E., Powell, G. J., & Bass, B. A. (1982). The Survey of Afro-American Behavior: Its development and use in research. In B. A. Bass, G. E. Wyatt, & G. T. Powell (Eds.), *The Afro-American family: Assessment, treatment, and research issues* (pp. 13–33). New York: Grune & Stratton.

Zimmerman, M., Coryell, C., & Wilson, S. (1986). A self-report scale to diagnose major depressive disorder. *Archives of General Psychiatry, 43,* 1076–1081.

Chapter 5

Traditional Individual Psychotherapy and Ethnic Minorities

JULIAN WOHL

The primary audience envisioned for this chapter is composed of White, mainstream counselors and psychotherapists whose clients[1] will include members from among the four ethnic groups with which this book is concerned. Despite efforts to develop an ethnically diverse pool of service providers, these providers represent only a small portion of those who deliver such services. The normative situation in providing service to ethnic minority group members remains one in which a White, mainstream clinician renders the service (Mays & Albee, 1992).

This chapter concentrates on the applicability of some basic psychotherapeutic concepts and practices to a population of clients who are ethnically and culturally different from White, middle- and upper-class European-Americans ("mainstream"), the source and usual target of traditional individual psychotherapy. In contrast to the majority of the chapters in this book, the focus is less on individual ethnic groups and the treatment problems specific to them, and more on the application of general principles of psychotherapy to ethnic groups which differ culturally from those to which psychotherapy has traditionally been applied.

Very early in the history of modern psychotherapy, Freud (1919/1953) said that it would be necessary to modify his psychoanalytic method in order to treat people who might be in need but might not be suitable candidates for psychoanalysis. He suggested, for example, that psychoanalysis could be supplemented with direct suggestion. The approach taken in this chapter is consistent with that idea of adapting established approaches to make them functional with a different kind of

74

patient. The intent is to help a practitioner trained in basic psychotherapeutic theory and practice to make use of that knowledge in work with nontraditional clients. These clients might not fit the conventional criteria for traditional individual psychotherapy but nevertheless might benefit from it.

Cultural Embeddedness and Adaptation

Any system of psychotherapy is embedded within a particular cultural-historical context, which shaped and conditioned the thought processes and values of both its practitioners and the clientele for which it was designed. Psychoanalysis with its variants and derivatives, behaviorism and its cognitive modifications, and the humanistic-experiential approaches make up the three major categories of contemporary psychotherapy. In addition to these major categories are movements aimed at integrating various theories and methods (Arkowitz, 1992; Norcross & Goldfried, 1992).

Despite the differences among and within these categories, they comprise methods created largely by White, middle-class practitioners, intended to be applied to people presumed to share with the European and North American creators of these methods cultural content such as value orientations, cause–effect relationships, and cognitive modes ("world views"). This broad framework of psychotherapy developed gradually through the latter half of the nineteenth century and the first half of the twentieth. In the last half of this century, however, and accelerating dramatically in the last third, the claim that this framework was universally valid and suitable for all comers has been forcefully challenged as the ethnic and cultural character of the target population changed (see Chapter 1).

These changes shattered the comfortable assumption that everyone was more or less alike and more or less equally susceptible to the application of basic methods of psychotherapy. It became clear that for many of this new class of patients, the structure, framework, "contract," or "ground rules" of psychotherapy were not automatically comprehended, and the procedures therapists wished to employ were not immediately acceptable. Two conclusions emerged from these perceptions. The first of these is the positive, healthy rediscovery of the principle that cultural variation among patients and cultural differences between patients and therapists always exist to varying degrees in psychotherapy and require the attention of therapists. No pairing of patient and psychotherapist will be without its cultural variety in some way, however minute, and the wise therapist should make no assumption about cultural commonality with patients that is not left open to question. Appreciating the ubiquity of cultural variation and the importance of cultural issues in psychotherapy can do much to heighten the consciousness of therapists and foster a sharpening of skill and an enhancement of their therapeutic efforts.

Such appreciation, however, does not automatically require that a whole new brand of psychotherapy be manufactured for each cultural, subcultural, or ethnic variant of client. Yet a second conclusion sometimes drawn with regard to acknowledging the multicultural nature of United States society and therefore the ethnic diversity of clinical clientele, is the therapeutically nihilistic one that so-called traditional therapies cannot be used effectively with cultural minorities and should be replaced by some new "culturally specific" techniques. Culturally specific approaches are psychotherapeutic methods designed to be congruent with the cultural characteristics of a particular ethnic clientele, or for problems believed to be especially prominent in a particular ethnic group or to ethnic groups in general (for an example of one such approach, see Ramirez, 1991; for an overall review see Sue, 1990).

Although such experimentation to develop more efficacious means of treating ethnic minorities using culturally specific techniques is desirable, these efforts should not be taken to rule out the use of traditional psychotherapies. Weiner (1975) notes that race and socioeconomic class differences between patient and therapist do not automatically make basic psychotherapy an inappropriate choice. "What is needed," he says, "is for the therapist to know *how to conduct psychotherapy* with groups of people who differ from him, and *not* to conclude that it is inapplicable" (p. 21), emphasis in original.

To decide simply on the basis of ethnicity, race, religion, socioeconomic class, age, or sex that a particular client will be unsuitable for a "talking therapy" or a therapy involving some degree of self-scrutiny constitutes by itself an insult and, if the issue is ethnicity, an ethnic slur (Wohl, 1989b). Such a conclusion is an example of cultural imperialism, violative of ethical and clinical rules of practice. Psychotherapists and psychological counselors are not supposed to prejudge and make treatment decisions about clients prior to having the opportunity to assess them. Any reasonable review of the literature shows no justification for the sweeping conclusion that would dismiss traditional psychotherapies out of hand (Atkinson, 1985; Parloff, Waskow, & Wolfe, 1978; Ponteretto, 1984; Sue, 1988; Sue, Chun, & Gee, this volume). To the contrary, evidence exists to support the opposite notion, that basic psychotherapeutic approaches can work effectively with United States subcultures and minority groups (Jones, 1987; Jones & Matsumoto, 1982; Lerner, 1972; Meadow, 1982; Wilkinson & Spurlock, 1986).

Traditional psychotherapies can be used, but they must be adapted and flexibly applied by taking into account social, economic, cultural, ethnic, and political determinants of the patient's situation. This approach is consistent with what Jackson (1990) in her discussion of various models of "ethnocultural psychotherapy" characterizes as a model that combines a traditional treatment approach with an appreciation of cultural factors. There is no escape in psychotherapy from the requirement that the therapist become conscious of any factors that might affect or condition the patient's reactions within the therapeutic situation and bear upon the patient's life outside that situation.

When faced with ethnic minority (or other) clients who seem not to fit their conventional criteria for psychotherapy, therapists may well be tempted to discard or forego what they have learned are useful approaches to engaging people in psychotherapy. In working with these clients, therapists must walk one of the several fine lines that are found in psychotherapy. A balance must be struck between the impulse on the one hand to discard as inappropriate or useless basic psychotherapeutic methods, and, on the other, to insist that a particular construction of psychotherapy be maintained when it obviously presents profound difficulties for patients or provokes their rejection. Avoidance of the pitfall requires a careful attention to the path. To change metaphors, while the bathwater drains, one wants to preserve the baby.

Beginning Psychotherapy

The most crucial point in psychotherapy with people for whom psychotherapy clearly presents a culturally different adaptational experience, and perhaps even for any potential patient, is the very beginning (Brammer, Abrego, & Shostrum, 1993: Griffith & Jones, 1978). Here is where the effort to engage the client must pass its most serious test, and here is where the failure of many therapists to draw the client into treatment is rooted. At the point of entry, when patient and therapist first meet, before the structure and procedure are understood by the patient, the two participants stand poised, facing each other across a canyon. To construct the bridge across that space is the first responsibility of the psychotherapist. Failure to do so can signal the onset of a spiral of miscommunication ending in an early termination of unsuccessful psychotherapy. To begin to close the gap is to initiate what just about all theories of psychotherapy insist is vital and basic: the special therapeutic relationship (Frank & Frank, 1973; Frank, 1982; Lambert & Bergin, 1992; Langs, 1973: Strupp, 1973, 1982).

Culturally different clients may require more introduction to the process than a sentence or two about how talking is useful and that the therapist wants the patient to express thoughts, feelings, and problems and that the patient should feel free to do so. Ethnic minority patients, on the basis of past experience, may have no reason to accept and trust what the nonminority, mainstream White therapist says, the more so when the whole idea just presented as a procedure may be inconsistent with prevailing norms about getting help in a particular minority group or subgroup (Kaplan & Johnson, 1964; Pedersen, 1982).

Emerging from psychoanalysis, but applicable to all psychotherapy, is the concept of resistance. One of the oldest concepts in psychotherapy, it has proved very helpful in understanding client conduct in treatment, but it is all too easy to misuse it with ethnically or culturally different patients. In brief, resistance refers to reactions of patients inspired by threat perceived in the psychotherapeutic situation. Ultimately, that threat for the client is that protective illusions may have to be confronted and that significant, valued aspects of the self may have to be changed.

Resistance is an internal process and occurs in all patients. It will, therefore, be a part of the ethnic minority patient's repertoire also. But it would be a serious mistake to lay all confusion, reluctance, hesitation, skepticism, or suspicion displayed initially by the patient at the door of an internally rooted resistance and nothing else. Enmeshed in the emotional component may well be a purely cognitive puzzlement that an appropriate introduction to psychotherapy by the therapist can dispel, thus reducing some of what appears to be classical resistance (Wohl, 1989b). Also resembling internally rooted resistance is the protective garb of reluctance, caution, and wariness worn by members of minority groups as a result of prior discrimination and frustration in their relations with private and governmental bureaucracies.

Although we focus now on barriers to treatment that might be mistaken for internally based resistance but are a product of external experiences, rarely if ever will such a distinction between an inner barrier and an outer one be complete. The psychotherapist needs always to realize that even the most realistic, culturally based reasons for a patient's reluctance or difficulty in initiating psychotherapy will have also its inner correlate, which may well have to be handled. At this point, we need to emphasize that before one moves in that direction, the external, reality-based aspects should be confronted. Upon encountering a culturally different client, it is helpful to bear in mind (and perhaps especially comforting to the beginner) that not everyone who enters the office is suitable for psychotherapy or for a particular therapist's way of conducting it. The nature or severity of the disorder on the one side, and the skills, theoretical orientation, or experience of the therapist on the other may argue against a particular patient–therapist combination. This observation, of course, applies across the board and not just to the culturally different patient.

In intercultural psychotherapy situations, many candidates for help can be found whose differences from the therapist and from the therapist's concepts of disorders and remediation are so great that the gap cannot be closed. The most extreme examples of this can be found in reports of the application of Western psychotherapy to patients in non-Western societies. The record of success is not encouraging, and even where it seems successful, substantial modifications in procedure are evident (Wohl, 1989a). But large gaps, too great for individual psychotherapy to close, can be found much closer to home.

In this book (Chapter 9), Koss-Chioino discusses the difficult problem of treating minimally acculturated Native Americans with Western psychotherapies. On the other hand, Devereaux (1951; 1953) reported satisfactory psychoanalytic psychotherapy results with well-acculturated Plains Indians. Trained in anthropology as well as in psychoanalysis, Devereaux emphasized that despite their degree of acculturation, therapy required him to understand the patient's cultural traditions in order to deal appropriately with the therapeutic relationship, dreams, and the goals of therapy. A person's degree of acculturation can greatly affect the feasibility of employing individual psychotherapy with that person. It seems that one measure of the usefulness of individual psychotherapy across cultural-ethnic divides is the degree of acculturation to the majority culture, in combination with the strength of the person's ethnic identity (Kitano, 1989).

In responding to cultural (including ethnic, linguistic, religious, and class) diversity in patients that differentiates them from the therapist, a basic psychotherapy framework can be used. In initiating work with members of ethnic and cultural minorities, psychotherapists should maintain the psychotherapeutic stance, mode of understanding, and empathic quality consistent with their psychotherapy theories. At the same time, they must take into account issues presented by the client's cultural context. This approach derives from and reaffirms the basic principle that although therapists work within a theoretical framework, they stand ready to appreciate and respond flexibly to the idiosyncrasies of individual patients.

By way of illustration, the mainstream, highly intelligent, verbally facile patient may or may not be sophisticated about psychotherapy. Such patients tempt therapists to assume that they are knowledgeable. Wiser therapeutic practice recommends that therapists await confirmation from the patient. But regardless of the patients' actual understanding of psychotherapy, therapists will tailor their language and form of presentation to the intellectual level of the patient so that the cognitive element in the therapist's message is delivered while the self-esteem of the patient is protected. At the other extreme, in working with patients with limited formal education and no particular enlightenment regarding psychotherapy, again therapists will utilize language and conduct designed to inform the patient and to avoid damaging the patient's self-esteem.

Making a Relationship

In these simple illustrative contexts, the therapist responds to identified sociocultural and intellectual or cognitive differences. Therapists recognize that they must establish working conditions with their patients and that they need to communicate certain information about the procedure in order to do so. Normally, we would do this more or less automatically without thinking that we are doing something "cross-culturally." Effective therapeutic communication tailored to the patient's situation and status is advocated and nicely demonstrated by Schafer (1974) in his appropriately titled paper, "Talking to Patients in Psychotherapy." No departure from sound psychotherapeutic principles is required. The difference is that in interethnic, intercultural situations, one must pay much more attention to the work of establishing the basis for a communicative relationship than in those where this factor is not evident.

The therapist's appreciation of the patient's social, educational, and intellectual position, and the use of tactful interventions derived from that knowledge, are basic and general psychotherapeutic characteristics in any treatment context and in any and all theories of psychotherapy. We modify or adapt our "method," "procedure," or "technique" to fit the concrete facts of the clinical situation. We finely tune the mode of communication, including vocabulary, language level, and style of relating, so that we effectively communicate what we think we need to get across in order to create a good collaborative working arrangement.

Furthermore, the manner in which we proceed in these initial steps demonstrates for the patient civility, quiet rationality, careful listening, respectful attention, and genuine interest—a syndrome of attitudes, values, and conduct that the therapist takes for granted as part of the professional culture (if not invariably of one's personal life). But this complex of social interaction is not necessarily as familiar to the patient as to the therapist and thus may itself constitute a significant "cultural difference," which requires adaptation on the patient's part and recognition of the patient's struggle with it on the therapist's. As therapists, we consider our characteristics and conduct as normal, humane, desirable, and appropriate ways of interacting, but they may not necessarily appear so to clients, in whose lives such modes of conduct may be neither commonplace nor even infrequently evident.

A second reason that a therapist's psychotherapeutically correct conduct might surprise a patient lies in quite another direction. Many people who in their everyday lives would hope, enjoy, and expect to be treated in the aforementioned manner by their fellows do not expect such egalitarian conduct from their authorities, among whom are included their "doctors." This group includes people from many countries around the world, some of whom now reside in this country, as well as the descendants of such immigrants who perpetuate at least some of the traditional ways of their predecessors. The literature, for example, tells us that Asians tend to expect a more direct, forceful, authoritative manner and a less personal demeanor in their experts, whereas Hispanics are said to want authoritativeness blended with a greater degree of personal intimacy than the principles prescribe for the patient more familiar to the clinician (Leong, 1986; Maduro, 1982; Owan, 1985;). Roll, Millen and Martinez (1980) present an exceptionally thoughtful discussion of relationship issues along with common errors and suggestions for avoiding them in the treatment of Latinos. Similarly, Tsui and Schultz (1985) describe mistakes and explicate relationship issues in the interethnic treatment of Asians.

Confronting Noticeable Differences

Thus far this discussion has concentrated on the idea of modifications and adaptations of basic psychotherapy to individual patient requirements that are so minimal that they are not conventionally referred to as "culturally" rooted. The general principle in dealing with larger cultural differences—that is, more obviously different differences—remains the same. When we note unusual characteristics of the kind conventionally labeled as cultural—dialect, accent, skin color, name, religion, or other indicators of ethnic identity—we know that more than normal attention needs to be devoted to clarifying with the patient an array of matters about the psychotherapeutic process and procedure.

To begin to do so, ideally we might want to know the patient's conceptions of the nature and source of the problems being experienced, the patient's expectations about what will happen, and the patient's construction of the ways in which the therapist will help. From the patient, and perhaps from other sources of information about the patient's general cultural background, we might expect, and actually discover, deviations from our normative expectations or conceptions of the cause of the troubles, unusual metaphoric representation of difficulties, and ideas about the role of third parties in treatment that contradict ours.

Kleinman (1980) has provided a comprehensive approach to the question of bridging the gap between patients' views of their troubles and those of the therapists. He uses the concept of "explanatory model" to refer to conceptions that both clients and therapists maintain of etiology, course, appropriate sick role behavior, and treatment. Kleinman also suggests an array of specific questions aimed at eliciting the patient's explanatory model. (This approach is discussed in greater detail in Chapter 3 in connection with pathways to treatment.) If the explanatory models of the clinician and the patient are far apart and the distance between them is not negotiated, treatment will flounder. If the therapist sees the patient's abdominal discomfort as a reaction to inner conflict or as a learned way of reacting to stress, and the patient sees it as the revenge of an offended ancestor, little basis for a common approach to the problem exists.

In such extreme situations, psychotherapy is well nigh impossible because the two parties apply contradictory explanatory principles and conceptual frameworks to the same events. They maintain contrary constructions of their experience and cognitive systems, their ways of comprehending reality. Such gross disparities exemplify one aspect of the "world view" problem (Frank & Frank, 1991; Torrey, 1986; see also Chapter 2 for a description of the "world view" concept.) Another aspect of the world view issue shows itself when language differences exist between the two participants in a psychotherapy situation. Language and thought are intimately related (Sapir, 1949; Whorf, 1941). Both reflect an individual's "assumptive world" (Frank & Frank, 1991) or "world view" (Torrey, 1986). When two people in a psychotherapy interaction are linguistically different from each other, their cognitive worlds also differ.

A language difference between therapist and patient can provide a truly formidable barrier to their effective collaboration in individual psychotherapy. When one party speaks French and the other Japanese, unless a third common language is available, psychotherapy cannot occur. Interpreters can be used in the assessment and problem definition stage of an inquiry, though not without error (Marcos, 1979), but the therapy itself requires a substantially shared language and the interaction of the participants alone together. The interpreter's presence creates a triangular situation with many potential complications.

In a less extreme and more common situation than a complete absence of a common language, one participant might speak English as a second language or be a native speaker of nonstandard English while the other uses standard English (see Chapter 2 for a discussion of language, or Russell, 1988, and Sue, 1981, who discusses language as a barrier to psychotherapy). Another frequently found situation would include some degree of bilingualism and the need to find a convenient common tongue. Where both parties are relatively fluent in two languages (Spanish and English are the most obvious examples), shifting back and forth might occur.

The issues associated with bilingual communication in psychotherapy have been explored in detailed in a series of papers by Marcos and his associates (Marcos, 1976a, 1976b; Marcos & Alpert, 1976; Marcos & Urcuyo, 1979; Pitta, Marcos, & Alpert, 1978) and by Marrero, (1983). Despite the complexity introduced by a bilingual situation, such therapy can be effective. In one experimental study, a well-qualified bilingual psychiatrist, speaking English with one group of six bilingual patients and Spanish with the other group of six bilingual patients, used brief, psychodynamic psychotherapy and achieved equally positive results with both groups (Gomez, Ruiz, & Laval, 1982).

In a more recent paper, Marcos (1988) argues that a cognitive framework the psychotherapist might apply appropriately to an "Anglo-American patient cannot be equally appropriate for the . . . Hispanic patients" who must "communicate across the cultural as well as the language barriers" (p. 37). The fact that clients are bilingual does not mean that when speaking English they share the Anglo world view. It is likely that differences in world views and explanatory models between patients and psychotherapists would be greater in situations where the patient is less assimilated by the mainstream culture. But with bilingual Hispanic clients, at least, acculturation is not directly measured by English-language proficiency (Marcos, 1988). In addition to oral language differences and the problems they create, the silent component of communication also reflects cultural characteristics and another dimension of communicative stress (Sue, 1990).

Working from our appreciation of the patient's point of departure, we negotiate the distance between that conceptual framework and the one we want to construct. We need to communicate what we are doing, what we expect the patient to be doing, and how we expect to interact. In instances of obvious, blatant cultural differences, we become hypersensitive to these matters, but the point is that in psychotherapy we need always to pay attention to the same issues even when the person is ostensibly a member of the majority culture and presumably understands the ways of helping and being helped with personal difficulties in our culture. Short of the patient's being a member of our encapsulated professional subculture, we really ought not to take anything for granted about what a client's conceptions of treatment and its rationale might be.

The literature in psychotherapy and counseling abounds with information, warnings, and advice to therapists on working with cultural minorities and culturally different people in general. It insists repeatedly that therapists embarking on such activities need to acquire knowledge about the culture of the people they will be treating (Abel, Metraux, & Roll, 1987; Marsella & Pedersen, 1981; Pedersen, 1987; Pedersen, Draguns, Lonner, & Trimble, 1989; Sue, 1981). Advice runs the gamut from reading suitable sociological and anthropological works to immersing oneself in the everyday life of the group in question. Psychotherapists who are to devote all or most of their professional time to a particular cultural, subcultural, or ethnic group would be wise to learn as much as possible about the folkways, communication styles, traditions, belief systems, mores, and values of the group.

Reading can be very helpful in this educational process. Living closely and informally within the group, participating in its social activities, and developing friendships can obviously enhance and deepen immeasurably any such externally developed knowledge. It can provide a very useful sense of the context of a patient's life. The realities and practicalities of professional life, however, do not allow most practitioners the luxury of such intensive, virtually anthropological, fieldwork immersion. Depending on the nature of the practice, contacts with members of different cultural groups will not absorb a major part of the practice, and therapists will have to content themeves with a less thoroughgoing investment in learning about the culture in question. But although such knowledge can be helpful, it also raises the peril of stereotyping.

Students of ethnic relations and conflicts, as well as many writers in the clinical literature on interracial and interethnic psychotherapy, have warned of the danger of stereotyping (Smith, 1981; Sue, 1981). Usually, concern centers on situations where the therapist, ignorant of both the cultural background and the individual situation of the patient, might impose on the patient and the patient's life situation prejudices and preconceptions based on a stereotypic image within the therapist. From this comes the frequently expressed injunction to learn as much about the culture as possible before initiating therapy with members of the particular group, as well as coming to appreciate one's own prejudices and values. Knowledge about the group in question combined with a substantial degree of self-awareness can do a great deal to overcome that kind of threat.

But with that knowledge comes another peril. Here we encounter a perhaps more insidious threat of stereotyping, in the form of the old adage that a little knowledge is a dangerous thing. The danger here is that, armed with a superficial knowledge of the culture, the therapist will cast the patient into the mold of the generalized member of that particular culture and lose sight of the individual. We need to remember that knowledge gained from studying about a group is generalized and expressive of many truths about members of the group, but that no individual member of the group will be a living representation of all the generalizations. Neither is any group so homogeneous that all generalizations about the group apply to all members of the group.

With any American ethnic or subcultural minority, the therapist must consider the patient's degree of assimilation by the majority group. United States society is pluralistic, but most members of subcultures participate to varying degrees in the larger culture, and the psychotherapist will want to ascertain the degree of acculturation to that larger culture (see Chapter 2). This issue of multiple cultural identities can itself be a major component of the psychological difficulties besetting the patient. In sum, stereotyping can derive from the therapist's personal prejudices and biases, but it can also emerge from the therapist's honest effort to deny those prejudices their power by learning about the culture in question. In either case, the result is the treatment of the individual patient as a member of a class or a category rather than as a real human person who is also a member of a specific social, cultural, racial, or ethnic group.

An alternative to the "anthropological" approach is exemplified nicely in a statement by Dr. Peter Ng, a pediatrician at Asian Health Services, a clinic in Oakland, California's Chinatown, "There are 20 zillion cultures out there and there's no way you can know every quirk. What we can do as providers is be curious. We have to ask, and then ask again. . . . It's about caring, and out of caring searching out what we need to know" (Gross, 1992, p. 10). Understanding and caring are crucial and universal values in psychotherapy as well as in medicine. Caring is reflected in the clinician's effort to understand the client's meanings, and care is demonstrated in the compassionate and thoughtful fashion in which that understanding is sought. Psychotherapists from outside the patient's ethnic group cannot be expected to know the ins and outs of the client's group, and pretending to do so is quickly detectable by the patient as fraudulent. Such pretense also violates the values of honesty and openness in relationships that are supposed to characterize our psychotherapy systems. The correct position for therapists must be an open, receptive readiness to learn from the client so that the client's world view can be understood.

From both conscious and unconscious revelations, we learn patients' ideas about the nature and origins of their troubles, the personal meaning of "treatment" or "therapy" or "counseling" or whatever terms they use to refer to whatever they expect will take place between the participants. When the "cultural" differences between the participants are greater than the average expectable cultural difference (a phrase adapted from Hartmann, 1958), therapists need to be more conscious of the possibility that they might misread the patient's communications, and they need to be more than usually careful to investigate ambiguities or uncertainties in their understanding of references and terminology. But here once again we see a quantitative difference, not a qualitative one. Any psychotherapist seeks understanding of the patient through the patient's communications; clarification of meaning is a part of that process.

Historically Oppressed Minorities as Clients

Because of our special American agony in race relationships, the term *intercultural* is too pallid and puny to characterize interracial and interethnic clinical relationships adequately. Every clinical interaction between a White clinician and a Black patient occurs in the historical context of relationships between Black and White people in this country and the psychocultural effects of those relations on both patient and therapist. The heritage of slavery, oppression, brutality, dehumanization, segregation, and discrimination gives a special quality to this particular clinical situation. Given the tradition of racism in the United States, this applies as well to clinical relationships between White therapists and Native Americans, Latinos, and Asian Americans (Jones, 1990; Toupin, 1980). (A summary of this "tradition" for each of the minority groups referred to in this book appears in Chapter 2.)

The White therapist–Black patient interaction perhaps most dramatically demonstrates the problem and is where that much used, even abused term *sensitivity* forces itself into play. Certainly our services need to be "culturally sensitive" (Rogler, Malgady, Costantino, & Blumenthal, 1987), but they must also be highly responsive to the ethnic sensitivities of individual clients. Overwhelmingly, those who address the issue in the literature agree that White psychotherapists need to appreciate the importance of race and the pervasiveness of racial sensitivity in Black patients (Block, 1984; Brantley, 1983: Butts, 1980; Ridley, 1989; Wohl, 1983). This is most crucial in the earliest stage of therapy when trying to establish a collaborative working relationship, and it remains important all through the work. Race is omnipresent for the patient, consciously and unconsciously, as well as for the therapist (in whom we hope *conscious* appreciation of it dominates).

Much of the literature notes that therapists' race problems pose as great a difficulty as do those of patients, and argues that therapists must first treat their own racism before that can well serve their patients in interracial psychotherapy. Block (1981), Lorion and Parron (1987), and Griffith (1977) join others who have observed that therapists carry into clinical relationships with poor and minority patients preconceptions, assumptions, and stereotypes about them that can blind them to the real potential of these patients to respond favorably to treatment.

The history and prevalence of racial and ethnic prejudice in the United States and the existence of unconscious stereotypes means that therapists will be peculiarly vulnerable to experiencing inappropriate and distorted reactions to ethnically different clients. Such countertransference reactions that spring more from their own personal backgrounds than from the material communicated by the client impair and interfere with their effective functioning. As Jones (1987) observes, countertransference is "perhaps the most extensively addressed topic in discussions of the Black patient" (p. 178). It may also be the most fundamental and crucial issue in interethnic psychotherapy.

The possibilities for countertransference distortion are virtually unlimited. Commonly noted manifestations of such effects in interethnic psychotherapy are those stemming from "White guilt." These can include avoidance of dealing with issues that might be seen as distressing to the client, and overidentification with the client's suffering, or that part of it viewed as due to ethnic/racial discrimination. Other typical reactions might be fear of the client's latent "Black rage" (Grier & Cobb, 1969) and therefore a tendency to avoid saying things that might be thought to provoke it; difficulty with sexual material because of stereotypic images about the "primitive" sexuality of ethnic group members; avoidance of the topic of ethnicity/race and denial of racial awareness; inappropriate injection of race or insistence on exploring racial feelings when the client is concerned with other matters. Interethnic treatment can evoke personal reactions in therapists that are more or less unique to the interethnic situation (Gorkin, 1987; Jones & Seagull, 1977).

In the last analysis, all the warnings and cautions in the literature telling psychotherapists and counselors to beware of stereotyping, forego prejudice, be "sensitive," hear the client accurately, be empathic, know their own biases, and be tuned in to their own cognitive and emotional processes are dealing with the same issue. The point is that effective psychotherapeutic performance, with any patient, requires that the therapist manage the countertransference. In this context, that management means preventing one's own cognitive and emotional reactions from intruding and interfering with the therapist's proper functioning.

Unconscious racist derogation can be as insidious as it is destructive. An early paper on the topic of White therapist–Black patient therapy (Adams, 1950) gives advice that may seem gratuitous to today's sophisticated practitioner. The author warns against referring to Blacks as "you people" or "your people," which, he notes, "makes the Negro patient suspicious, wary and fearful of being patronized" (p. 305). (For a review of the early literature, see Griffith, 1977; for a more recent assessment of White therapist–Black patient issues, see Jones, 1990.) Although this particular example may, we hope, no longer be relevant, the general point about sensitivity to derogation still holds. One very common example of derogating patients is calling them by their first names without authorizing patients to return the favor. This practice is of course not limited to interethnic work. We all too often observe young male service providers address older female patients this way, and poorly trained receptionists in professional offices frequently assume a first-name relationship with all comers, regardless of race, color, creed, age, sex, or national origin.

Sometimes we do not know what it takes to offend, but we may sense the result, perhaps in a chilling of the atmosphere, a subtle withdrawal, a sullen smoldering anger, or an open outburst. An American trying to work with a Thai patient might say or do something inappropriate in a Thai context while trying to be useful. The Thai might think the American foolish or ignorant of Thai ways but generally will tolerate the lapse because the poor fool is a foreigner and the Thai does not expect foreigners to understand Thai ways. The Thai will not be so ready to personalize the error as derogation because there has not been such a bitter tradition of pain-laden relations between Thais and Americans. By contrast, interethnic therapy in the United States with a Native American, Latino, or African-American client, an offense, equally innocent and unknown to the therapist, might have much more destructive consequences.

Working with traditionally oppressed minorities threatens the therapist's ability to walk a fine line in several ways. One of these follows from acknowledging that race is a real factor in interracial psychotherapy. Having granted that, then what to do about it becomes the question. The general alternatives are available. One would have therapists introduce the topic of race and its possible impact on the therapeutic relationship openly at the outset of psychotherapy. Presumably this would lead to an exploration of the patient's attitudes about and difficulties with ethnic conflict and ethnic identity. It would also serve the purpose of communicating the therapist's courageous readiness to deal with this touchy topic, thereby contributing to building the patient's trust and forging the therapeutic alliance, that more or less tacit agreement between the participants to cooperate in an effort to bring the therapy to a successful conclusion.

The other position holds that therapists should be willing to discuss racial issues but provides no specific technical guidance about how they are to be introduced and by which participant. Psychoanalytic psychotherapy theory would instruct the therapist to wait until the patient, either manifestly or in disguised derivative form, introduces the subject of race before commenting on it (Langs, 1973). The fine line in this instance, then, is to balance out readiness to deal with a problem that is believed to be a part of the therapeutic interaction against the sense that generally it is better to wait until one has evidence that the issue exerts sufficient pressure within the patient that would make dealing with it fruitful. Above all, it is important to avoid the comfort of an intellectualized discussion of race and the evils of racism.

Psychotherapy and Reality

Prior to about 1970, at least in the psychodynamically informed literature, White psychotherapists found themselves instructed in "color blindness" in their work with Black patients (Griffith, 1977). As Adams (1950) passionately expressed it, the patient must be helped "to face the core of his inner problems which are the same kind that haunt, enslave, torture and degrade men of all races" (p. 310). The ideal seemed to be for therapists to work with Black patients as they would with anyone else. This presumptively egalitarian view held sway in the period when psychoanalytic theory, with its concentration on internal dynamics and with minimal attention given to "reality" factors such as social, economic, cultural, political, and ethnic influences, dominated psychotherapy. In this framework, therapists would tend to regard patients' references to racial issues such as discrimination or segregation as reflections of an inner resistance to the treatment that exploited plausible external realities. Therapists were warned to beware of confusing inner resistance with external reality, to stick to clinical problems, and to avoid getting caught up in attempts to solve the social problems of the patient that were realities of an unjust society (Heine, 1950).

By the late 1960s, with the civil rights movement in high gear, with psychoanalytic theories competing with and losing popularity to a variety of approaches that emphasized the importance of external forces rather than internal influences and of immediate rather than past experience, with many therapists politicized and committing themselves in their work to social activism, the emphasis shifted. Now many psychotherapists came to view minority patients' difficulties as rational and appropriate responses to intolerable abuse and privation. The tendency to attribute problems to societal oppression and discrimination while minimizing or denying entirely their neurotic, self-maintaining aspects increased (see, for example, Majors & Nikelly, 1983). Here again another fine line is introduced for the psychotherapist. At one extreme, one can be color-blind, deny the significance of race, and see racial references only as serving resistance. At the other, one can ignore the internal conflictual struggles of the patients, avoid the unpleasantness of helping them to confront their inner truths, and concentrate on the struggle against the social environment as the culprit.

Reality—the reality of the social environment in which many African Americans, Asian Americans, Hispanics, and Native Americans grow up—is cruel and unfair. The neurotic conflicts that beset people, whatever their ethnicity, are to a significant degree the results of developmental experience in their social environments. To the extent that interpersonal struggles and conflicts have been internalized and lie within, the problems do not get solved or changed by attacking the external sources. Nor is psychotherapy a tool for changing the external forces that sustain the patient's suffering. It can only hope to improve and strengthen the patient's ability to feel more comfortable and to operate more effectively upon the environment.

Throughout this book are discussions of a variety of problems and approaches to them that do not depend on traditional individual psychotherapy. Many of these confront directly the familial, social, economic, and political forces that contribute to the miseries of clients. Such external approaches will often have more power and practicality than psychotherapy can claim. There are many ways to attack human difficulties. Individual psychotherapy is only one of them and, measured against the scale of human suffering, not a very powerful one. Freud (1905/1953) noted that psychotherapy can be practiced in many ways but that the important criterion is whether the patient is helped. We may extend this and say that there are many ways to help clients and any that work are satisfactory.

Traditional psychotherapy is peculiarly designed to cope with those aspects of the client's difficulties that are internally based. This is the underlying justification for the admonition not to confuse resistance with reality. That warning holds true for any therapist working with any patient. The fact that an event or circumstance is true and real in the patient's life makes it more functional as a vehicle of resistance. All of us do, after all, want to appear reasonable as we struggle to avoid anxiety and evade the pain of the therapeutic process. In these protective efforts we use whatever lies handy. Something factual is always available; fiction is not required. The psychotherapeutic task is to use professional knowledge and human understanding to help patients to know their own truths, to come to grips with themselves, and to promote their psychological freedom, thereby enabling them to function more effectively.

Note

1. Recipients or consumers of individual psychotherapy services are usually referred to either as *clients* or *patients*. The term used depends on various factors, such as whether the treatment context is a medical or nonmedical one, and on the provider's personal and theoretically based preferences. In keeping with the eclectic direction of this chapter, both terms are used throughout as equivalents.

References

Abel, T., Metraux, R., & Roll, S. (1987). *Psychotherapy and culture*. Albuquerque: University of New Mexico Press.

Adams, W. A. (1950). The Negro patient in psychiatric treatment. *American Journal of Orthopsychiatry, 20*, 305–310.

Arkowitz, H. (1992). Integrative theories of therapy. In D. K. Freedman (Ed.), *History of psychotherapy: A century of change* (pp. 261–303).

Washington, DC: American Psychological Association.

Atkinson, D. R. (1985). Research on cross-cultural counseling and psychotherapy: Overview and update of reviews. In P. B. Pedersen (Ed.), *The handbook of cross-cultural counseling and psychotherapy* (pp. 191–197). New York: Praeger.

Block, C. B. (1981). Black Americans and the cross-cultural counseling experience. In A. J.

Marsella & P. B. Pedersen (Eds.), *Cross-cultural counseling and psychotherapy* (pp. 177–194). New York: Pergamon Press.

Block, C. B. (1984). Diagnostic and treatment issues for Black patients. *The Clinical Psychologist, 37,* 51–54.

Brammer, L. M., Abrego, P. J., & Shostrom, E. L. (1993). *Therapeutic counseling and psychotherapy* (6th ed.). Englewood Cliffs, NJ: Prentice-Hall.

Brantley, T. (1983). Racism and its impact on psychotherapy. *American Journal of Psychiatry, 140,* 1605–1608.

Butts, H. F. (1980). Racial issues in psychotherapy. In T. B. Karasu & L. Bellak (Eds.), *Specialized techniques in individual psychotherapy* (pp. 352–381). New York: Bruner/Mazel.

Devereaux, G. (1951). Three technical problems in the psychotherapy of a Plains Indian woman. *American Journal of Psychotherapy, 5,* 411–423.

Devereaux, G. (1953). Cultural factors in psychoanalytic therapy. *Journal of the American Psychoanalytic Association, 1,* 629–635.

Frank, J. D. (1982). Therapeutic components shared by all psychotherapies. In J. H. Harvey & M. M. Parks (Eds.), *Psychotherapy research and behavior change* (pp. 5–37). Washington, DC: American Psychological Association.

Frank, J. D., & Frank, J. B. (1991). *Persuasion and healing* (3rd ed.). Baltimore: Johns Hopkins University Press.

Freud, S. (1905/1953). On psychotherapy. *Standard edition of the complete psychological works, Vol. 7* (pp. 255–269). London: Hogarth.

Freud, S. (1919/1953). Lines of advance in psychoanalytic therapy. *Standard edition of the complete psychological works, Vol. 17* (pp. 157–168). London: Hogarth.

Gomez, E., Ruiz, P., & Laval, R. (1982). Psychotherapy and bilingulaism: Is acculturation important? *Journal of Operational Psychiatry, 13,* 13–16.

Gorkin, M. (1987). *The uses of countertransference.* New York: Jason Aronson.

Grier, W., & Cobb, P. M. (1969). *Black rage.* New York: Bantam.

Griffith, M. (1977). The influence of race on the psychotherapeutic relationship. *Psychiatry, 40,* 27–40.

Griffith, M., & Jones, E. E. (1978). Race and psychotherapy: Changing perspectives. In J. H. Masserman (Ed.), *Current psychiatric therapies, Vol. 18.* New York: Grune & Stratton.

Gross, J. (1992, June 28). Clinics help Asian immigrants feel at home. *New York Times,* Section 1, p. 10.

Hartmann, H. (1958). *Ego psychology and the problem of adaptation.* New York: International Universities Press.

Heine, R. (1950). The Negro patient in psychotherapy. *Journal of Clinical Psychology, 6,* 373–376.

Jackson, A. M. (1990). Evolution of ethnocultural psychotherapy. *Psychotherapy, 27,* 28–35.

Jones, A., & Seagull, A. (1977). Dimensions of the relationship between the Black client and the White therapist. *American Psychologist, 32,* 850–855.

Jones, E. E. (1987). Psychotherapy and counseling with Black clients. In P. B. Pedersen (Ed.), *Handbook of cross-cultural counseling and psychotherapy* (pp. 173–179). Westport, CT: Praeger.

Jones, E. E., & Matsumoto, D. R. (1982). Psychotherapy with the underserved: Recent developments. In L. R. Snowden (Ed.), *Reaching the underserved: Mental health needs of neglected populations* (pp. 207–228). Beverly Hills, CA: Sage.

Jones, N. (1990). Black/White issues in psychotherapy. *Journal of Social Behavior and Personality, 5,* 305–322.

Kaplan, B., & Johnson, D. (1964). The social meaning of Navajo psychopathology and psychotherapy. In A. Kiev (Ed.), *Magic, faith, and healing* (pp. 203–229). New York: Free Press.

Kitano, H. H. L. (1989). A model for counseling Asian Americans. In P. Pedersen, J. Draguns, W. Lonner, & J. Trimble (Eds.), *Counseling across cultures* (pp. 139–151). Honolulu: University of Hawaii Press.

Kleinman, A. (1980). *Patients and healers in the context of culture.* Berkeley: University of California Press.

Lambert, M. J., & Bergin, A. E. (1992). Achievements and limitations of psychotherapy research. In D. K. Freedham (Ed.), *History of psychotherapy: A century of change* (pp. 360–390). Washington, DC: American Psychological Association.

Langs, R. (1973). *The technique of psychoanalytic psychotherapy, Vol. 1.* New York: Jason Aronson.

Leong, F. T. L. (1986). Counseling and psychotherapy with Asian-Americans. *Journal of Counseling Psychology, 33,* 196–206.

Lerner, B. (1972). *Therapy in the ghetto: Political impotence and personal disintegration*. Baltimore: Johns Hopkins University Press.

Lorion, R. P., & Parron, D. L. (1987). Countering the countertransference: A strategy for treating the untreatable. In P. B. Pedersen (Ed.), *Handbook of cross-cultural counseling and psychotherapy* (pp. 79–86). Westport, CT: Praeger.

Maduro, R. J. (1982). Working with Latinos and the use of dream analysis. *Journal of the American Academy of Psychoanalysis, 10,* 609–628.

Majors, R., & Nikelly, A. (1983). Serving the Black minority: A new direction for psychotherapy. *Journal of Non-White Concerns, 11,* 142–151.

Marcos, L. R. (1976a). Bilinguals in psychotherapy: Language as an emotional barrier. *American Journal of Psychotherapy, 30,* 552–560.

Marcos, L. R. (1976b). Linguistic dimensions in the bilingual patient. *American Journal of Psychoanalysis, 36,* 347–354.

Marcos, L. R. (1979). Effects of interpreters on the evaluation of psychopathology in non-English-speaking patients. *American Journal of Psychiatry, 136,* 171–174.

Marcos, L. R. (1988). Understanding ethnicity in psychotherapy with Hispanic patients. *American Journal of Psychoanalysis, 48,* 35–42.

Marcos, L. R., & Alpert, M. (1976). Strategies and risks in psychotherapy with bilingual patients: The phenomenon of language independence. *American Journal of Psychiatry, 133,* 1275–1278.

Marcos, L. R., & Urcuyo, L. (1979). Dynamic psychotherapy with the bilingual patient. *American Journal of Psychotherapy, 33,* 331–338.

Marrero, R., (1983). Bilingualism and biculturalism: Issues in psychotherapy with Hispanics. *Psychotherapy in Private Practice, 1,* 57–64.

Marsella, A. J., & Pedersen, P. B. (Eds.). (1981). *Cross-cultural counseling and psychotherapy.* New York: Pergamon Press.

Mays, V., & Albee, G. (1992). Psychotherapy and ethnic minorities. In D. K. Freedheim (Ed.), *History of psychotherapy: A century of change* (pp. 552–570). Washington, DC: American Psychological Association.

Meadow, A. (1982). Psychopathology, psychotherapy and the Mexican-American patient. In E. E. Jones & S. J. Korchin (Eds.), *Minority mental health* (pp. 331–361). New York: Praeger.

Norcross, J. C., & Goldfried, M. R. (Eds.). (1992). *Handbook of psychotherapy integration.* New York: Basic Books.

Owan, T. C. (Ed.). (1985). *Southeast Asian mental health: treatment, prevention, services, training, and research.* Rockville, MD: National Institute of Mental Health.

Parloff, M. B., Waskow, I. E., & Wolfe, B. S. (1978). Research on therapist variables in relation to process and outcome. In S. L. Garfield & S. A. Bergin (Eds.), *Handbook of psychotherapy and behavior change* (2nd ed.). (pp. 233–282). New York: Wiley.

Pedersen, P. (1982). The intercultural context of counseling and pyschotherapy. In A. J. Marsella & G. M. White (Eds.), *Cultural conceptions of mental health and therapy* (pp. 333–358). Dordrecht, Holland: Reidel.

Pedersen, P. (Ed.). (1987). *Handbook of cross-cultural counseling and psychotherapy.* Westport, CT: Praeger.

Pedersen, P., Draguns, J., Lonner, W., & Trimble, J. (Eds.). (1989). *Counseling across cultures* (3rd ed.). Honolulu: University of Hawaii Press.

Pitta, P., Marcos, L. R., & Alpert, M. (1978). Language switching as a treatment strategy with bilingual patients. *American Journal of Psychoanalysis, 38,* 255–258.

Ponteretto, J. G. (1984). Racial/ethnic minority research in *The Journal of Counseling Psychology:* A content analysis and methodological critique. *Journal of Counseling Psychology, 35,* 410–418.

Ramirez, M. (1991). *Psychotherapy and counseling with minorities.* New York: Pergamon Press.

Ridley, C. R. (1989). Racism in counseling as an aversive behavioral process. In P. Pedersen, J. Draguns, W. Lonner, & J. Trimble (Eds.), *Counseling across cultures* (3rd ed.) (pp. 55–77). Honolulu: University of Hawaii Press.

Rogler, L. H., Malgady, R. G., Costantino, G., & Blumenthal, R. (1987). What do culturally sensitive services mean? The case of Hispanics. *American Psychologist, 42,* 565–570.

Roll, S., Millen, L., & Martinez, R. (1980). Common errors in psychotherapy with Chicanos. *Psychotherapy: Theory, Research and Practice. 17,* 158–168.

Russell, D. M. (1988). Language and psychotherapy: The influence of nonstandard English in clinical practice. In L. Comas-Díaz & E. E. H.

Griffith (Eds.), *Clinical guidelines in cross cultural mental health* (pp. 33–68). New York: Wiley.

Sapir, E. (1949). *Selected writings of Edward Sapir.* Berkeley and Los Angeles: University of California Press.

Schafer, R. (1974). Talking to patients in psychotherapy, *Bulletin of the Menninger Clinic, 38,* 503–515.

Smith, E. (1981). Cultural and historical perspectives in counseling Blacks. In D. W. Sue (Ed.), *Counseling the culturally different* (pp. 141–185). New York: Wiley.

Sue, D. W. (1981). *Counseling the culturally different.* New York: Wiley.

Sue, D. W. (1990). Culture-specific strategies in counseling: A conceptual framework. *Professional Psychology: Research and Practice, 21,* 424–433.

Sue, S. (1988). Psychotherapeutic services for ethnic minorities: Two decades of research findings. *American Psychologist, 43,* 301–308.

Strupp, H. H. (1973). Toward a reformulation of the psychotherapeutic influence. *International Journal of Psychiatry, 11,* 263–365.

Strupp, H. H. (1982). The outcome problem in psychotherapy: Contemporary perspectives. In J. H. Harvey & M. Parks (Eds.), *Psychotherapy research and behavior change* (pp. 39–71). Washington, DC: American Psychological Association.

Torrey, E. F. (1986). *The mind game.* New York: Harper & Row.

Toupin, E. S. W. A. (1980). Counseling Asians: Psychotherapy in the context of racism and Asian-American history. *American Journal of Orthopsychiatry, 50,* 76–86.

Tsui, P., & Schultz, G. L. (1985). Failure of rapport: Why psychotherapeutic engagement fails in the treatment of Asian clients. *American Journal of Orthopsychiatry, 55,* 561–569.

Weiner, I. B. (1975). *Principles of psychotherapy.* New York: Wiley.

Whorf, B. L. (1941). The relation of habitual thought and behavior to language. In B. L. Whorf (Ed.), *Four articles on metalinguistics* (pp. 20–38). Washington, DC: Foreign Service Institute, U.S. Department of State.

Wilkinson, C. B., & Spurlock, J. (1986). Mental health of Black Americans. In C. B. Wilkinson (Ed.), *Ethnic psychiatry* (pp. 13–60). New York: Plenum Press.

Wohl, J. (1983, October). *White therapists and Black patients: Advice from the experts.* Paper presented at the meetings of the Arkansas Psychological Association.

Wohl, J. (1989a). Cross-cultural psychotherapy. In P. B. Pedersen, J. G. Draguns, W. J. Lonner, & J. E. Trimble (Eds.), *Counseling across cultures* (3rd ed.) (pp. 79–113). Honolulu: University of Hawaii Press.

Wohl, J. (1989b). Integration of cultural awareness into psychotherapy. *American Journal of Psychotherapy, 43,* 343–355.

Chapter **6**

Cultural Relativistic Approach toward Ethnic Minorities in Family Therapy

MELVIN N. WILSON
DI-ANN G. PHILLIP
LAURA P. KOHN
JUDITH A. CURRY-EL

It is important to understand the role of ethnicity in the psychological intervention and treatment of ethnic minority families in this country (Wilkinson, 1987). Problems in living are not only the products of aberrant intrapsychic development and familial dysfunctions, but also a consequence of the specific political, social, economic, and legal histories that ethnic minorities have had in the United States. Past conditions of slavery, legal discrimination and segregation, immigration exclusion and restrictions, internment, and forced removal to reservations have influenced the attitudes, perceptions, and behavioral patterns of ethnic minorities. In effect, the larger society has played a major role in the developmental etiology of certain mental health disturbances and in the way mental health professionals have responded to these groups.

The mental health delivery system has long struggled with understanding the context of one's experiences in the etiology of mental illnesses (Cheung & Snowden, 1990). The system has sought to develop services that reflect acceptance and accommodation of the differences among Americans, rather than reflecting the assimilation of those differences to the cultural majority. Unfortunately, the recognition of contextual influences has not always translated into appropriate services to diverse populations. Because of the small number of ethnic minority professionals, indigenous paraprofessionals have often been employed in the delivery of mental health services to ethnic minority communities. However, paraprofessionals often do not possess the professional sophistication needed to understand the role of ethnicity in the etiology and treatment of mental disturbances.

The definitions and treatment of abnormal behavior endorsed by ethnic minority groups are often very different from those of the majority population (see Chapter 9 of this book). Indeed, it is often important to appreciate indigenous definitions of abnormal behavior and curative procedures in order to gain entry and deliver mental health services effectively to the ethnic minority communities. Service providers need to acquire a clear understanding and appreciation of these cultural differences. Cultural empathy on the part of the service provider instructs minority clients about the mental health professional's understanding of the culture-specific proprieties of their problems and symptoms.

Most important for this chapter is the increase in the number of minority families and children in the general population (Ashburg & DeVita, 1992; O'Hare, 1992). Differences among ethnic groups' traumatic historical relationships with non-minority Americans and experiences with discrimination have led to differences in adaptation experiences. These experiences are related to economic success and the preservation of familial stability. Furthermore, this chapter argues that mental health practitioners must consider differences in adaptation experiences in their intervention and treatment plans with ethnic minority families.

Some cautions are warranted as well. Although we provide information regarding the variation within each of the ethnic groups, we sometimes fall victim to discussing each ethnic group and their families as a homogeneous entity. This is especially troublesome if one is trying to acquire improved clinical interviewing and diagnostic strategies that are culturally sensitive to ethnic minorities. Diversity and variation commonly occur within each ethnic minority group (Hirabayashi & Saram, 1980; O'Hare, 1992). Variation exists in living conditions, in languages, and thus in cultural values and practices. A review of ethnic groups may describe characteristics that are applicable to most of the members but not to all of them. Accordingly, this chapter will not attempt an exhaustive exploration of specific subgroup characteristics. Instead, it will focus primarily on characteristics that are generally applicable to most groups.

Family Life among Ethnic Minority Americans

Until fairly recently, the "normal" family was synonymous with nuclear structure based on immediate family membership (Saba, Karrer, & Hardy, 1990). As a result, all else was labeled aberrant (Moynihan, 1965). However, changing demographic patterns (delayed marriages, higher divorce rates, unemployment, and urban migratory trends) have all influenced and broadened the traditional definition of the "family" (London & Devore, 1988; McGoldrick, Pearce, & Giordano, 1982; Wilson, 1986). While all groups have been affected by these trends to some degree, the greatest impact has been on minority and immigrant groups. Unfortunately, services to the groups most affected by demographic and economic fluctuations are the least adequate in the mental health system.

For cultural and social reasons, family and family life took on special meaning for ethnic minority groups. The extended family is the most important common element shared by ethnic minorities. By *extended family*, we refer to family composition, structure, and interaction that goes beyond the nuclear family unit to include consanguine, in-law, conjugal, and fictive relationships (Foster, 1983). The extended family directly influences the primary values, beliefs, and behaviors of its members. A consistent finding across ethnic groups is the supportive role and mutual-aid function of the extended family. The extended-family network is an alternative structure of support that supplements the nuclear family. In this respect, the extended family is both a tangible family unit of kin and non-kin and an intangible cohesive force in ethnic minority communities. Extended families are the centers of economical activity, decision making, and care for children and other dependents (Wilson, 1989). Moreover, extended families transmit values, including emotional closeness, economic cooperation, child care, and social regulation.

African-American Families

Historically, Africans had elaborate support networks and extended family relationships (Franklin, 1988; Nobles, 1988; Sudarkasa, 1988). Before enslavement, Africans were members of a diverse population, with different languages and cultural practices (Karst, 1986). This cultural diversity, combined with the practice of slave masters separating family members, forced African-American slaves into situations that disrupted familial ties and/or social support. Nevertheless, the African-American family developed and maintained strong ties (Nobles, 1988; Sudarkasa, 1988). African-American slaves formed support networks made up of biologically related and nonbiologically related members (Sudarkasa, 1988). The persistence of African familial networks throughout slavery suggests that they are an example of an enduring cultural phenomenon (Franklin, 1988; Wilson, 1986; Wilson & Tolson, 1990).

Currently, African-American families are characterized by the high prevalence of mother-only households, due primarily to high fertility rates among single African-American women and the high rate of unemployment among African-American men, rather than to rising divorce rates (Glick, 1988; U.S. Bureau of Census, 1990). In addition, African Americans consistently delay marriage as opposed to other American groups, and there is a rising proportion of African Americans in their twenties and thirties who have never been married. Until recently, most African-American families consisted of married couples. Since 1970, however, there has been a decline in the number of married couples with young children, and an increase in the proportion of children being raised in single-parent homes (McAdoo, 1991).

In sum, the current social difficulties facing African-American families include high birth rates among single women, the predominance of mother-only households, and large numbers of marital dissolutions (see Chapter 1). African-American families also experience poverty more often than do majority families (O'Hare, Pollard, Mann, & Kent, 1991). In addition, African-American families are often exposed to violent crime, particularly assaults and homicides directed at males. Such experiences make them vulnerable to economic and social stress, which can have a detrimental impact on their psychological well-being.

American Indian Families

Native Americans often maintain strong tribal identification and high degrees of respect for their heritage (Brown & Shaughnessay, 1981; Lewis, 1970). Native American communities can also be characterized as having an important regard for the land, highly democratic governmental societies, and great respect for their elders (Brown & Shaughnessay, 1981; London & Devore, 1988). Similarly, Native Americans portray a strong sense of communalism, generosity, and harmony. These concepts stem from the prevalence of the extended family, the sense of biological relationship within the clan and/or the tribe, and the belief that Native Americans discover themselves through interpersonal relationships (Anderson, 1989; Brown & Shaughnessay, 1981; Ho, 1987).

Native American cultural tradition is noteworthy for the positive value it places on children (Brown & Shaughnessay, 1981; Garbarino, 1985). Among the Crows of the Plains, children of conquered tribes were adopted into families of the victors. Among the Tlingit of the Northwest coast, children were rarely punished but were socialized instead through shaming and praise (Bergman, 1977; Byler, 1977; Garbarino, 1985). Utmost care was taken to ensure the child's happiness among the Camas because it was believed that if the infant child was not happy, he or she could choose to return to heaven (Bird & Melendy, 1977; Lewis, 1970). While traditional family structure, attitude, and practices toward children provide a healthy form of child rearing, other experiences, such as those with federal boarding schools, have had a detrimental impact on Native American children (Tafoya, 1989).

Native Americans experience a variety of problems, including social and mental health problems, alcoholism, child abuse and neglect, adolescent delinquency, and violent deaths (LaFromboise, 1988). Although the demand for mental health services by Native Americans has recently increased, contact between Native American families and mental health agencies has often been negatively colored by previous experiences with mainstream social agencies (Ho, 1987). In addition, many Native Americans have been inappropriately and ineffectively served by mental health agencies (LaFromboise, 1988; Westermeyer, 1977a, 1977b).

Latino Families

Although it appears that the nuclear family structure is the most common form of family life in the Latino community, others have observed a great deal of diversity in Latino family organization (Klor de Alva, 1988). The Latino nuclear family tends to be embedded in an extended family network that includes other relatives (Acosta-

Belen, 1988; Anderson, 1989; Davis, Haub, & Willette, 1988; Ho, 1987; Vega, 1990). According to Klor de Alva (1988), extended family members tend to live near but not with each other, except during periods of transition. As families become acculturated, they tend not to live in the same household but may still reside in the same neighborhood.

Although a great deal of diversity exists within Latino groups (Valdivieso & Davis, 1988), there is an increasing trend toward mother-only households. The proportion of mother-only households has increased by approximately 10 percent while the proportion of dual-parent households has decreased by almost 6 percent over the last decade (U.S. Bureau of Census, 1992). This trend has been augmented by high birth and poverty rates among Latino groups (Ashburg & DeVita, 1992). These changes increase the stress on Latino families and can contribute to psychological dysfunction.

Asian-American Families

Generally, marriage rates are higher and divorce rates are lower among Asian Americans than among other ethnic minority Americans. In addition, the traditional Southeast Asian family tends to be extended (Anderson, 1989; Ruetrakul, 1987). The father assumes a family leadership role, and sons are sometimes valued more highly than daughters (Ho, 1987). From an early age, children are taught to respect parents, elders, and ancestors, and obedience toward parents is expected. Interpersonal harmony is highly regarded; therefore, Asian Americans may choose to conceal their true feelings when harmony is at stake (Anderson, 1989).

Family Therapy Approaches with Ethnic Minority Families

Our discussion of family therapy approaches includes an examination of the current models of family therapy described in the literature, including the culturalist, ecological, ecostructural, and family systems models, and the degree to which they are being utilized. The rationale for the use of family therapy with specific ethnic minority groups is also presented. Finally, we discuss the issues and problems that may be faced in working with ethnic minority families, as well as guidelines for engaging in culturally relevant family therapy.

Family therapy successfully coalesced as a treatment method during the late 1960s. Since then, family interventions have taken many forms, the techniques have been expanded and refined, and family therapy continues to be an effective and widely used model of treatment. This approach began with the recognition of the connection between child disturbances and parental problems. A wide range of methods of family assessment are in use, reflecting the numerous conceptual models about how families function. Regardless of the general method or theory preferred, in order to ensure that ethnic minority families have opportunities for appropriate help, it is vital that the therapist be culturally sensitive and competent (Hill & Strozier, 1992).

Not only must we be aware of the culture of the clients, we must also gain perspective on our own culture and how our constructs and paradigms are interpreted in another culture. Similarly, Wilkinson (1987) indicated that professionals should recognize the need for understanding ethnic minorities, particularly how disparate life-styles, attitudes, and behaviors of minority ethnic persons are perceived and/or misperceived by others. It would be incorrect to assume that mental disturbance in the individual results solely from intrapsychic development and is not influenced by the political, social, economic, and legal histories that ethnic minorities have experienced in the United States.

Theoretical Models of Family Therapy

According to Minuchin (1974), family therapy involves the process of feedback between situations and the individual. Altering the position of a person in relation to the situation changes the experience of that person. Different experiences that are produced in therapy reinforce the new method of relating to the circumstances and are therefore likely to generalize to other situations outside of treatment (Minuchin, 1974). A critical activity of therapy involves the therapist joining with the family to begin to facilitate interventions directed at change. Change occurs at the basic structural level of the family and is organized around changing familial organization and interactions by using alternative modalities of transaction (Minuchin, 1974).

Of the many family therapy models, a few have been consistently cited in the literature. Some of these models include family systems, culturalist, ecological, structural, ecostructural, and Bowenian models. The family systems model posits that family structure and process is primary; therefore, examination of the hierarchies and boundaries through observation of family interaction is the core of family therapy (Inclan, 1990). The culturalist perspective further contends that culture is the primary source of behavior patterns that are both prevalent and condoned by members of the culture (Inclan, 1990).

The culturalist model has been criticized because it tends to view culture as fixed and ahistorical and may result in justifying culturally sanctioned behaviors that are maladaptive (Inclan, 1990; Rogler, Malgady, Costantino, & Blumenthal, 1987). Conversely, a strict family systems approach examines family process while completely ignoring the social reality that creates the context in which these processes are manifested (Inclan, 1990). Ecological therapy seeks to integrate the culturalist and family systems approaches by viewing families and their social context as one integrated process (Aponte, 1991; Boyd-Franklin, 1987; Inclan, 1990). Therefore, it has been asserted that ecological therapy is particularly useful for ethnic minority families who are often undergoing both cultural and intrafamilial transitions.

The structural approach expands the definition of the traditional family in order to accommodate three-generational familial structures and parent–child issues (Boyd-Franklin, 1989a, 1989b). This form of therapy provides a method for assessing family structure (Boyd-Franklin, 1987). In so doing, it allows for the identification of areas of difficulty and facilitates restructuring of the family system in order to produce change (Minuchin, 1974). Strengths of the model include a problem-solving approach that is focused, concrete, and offers direct resolutions (Boyd-Franklin, 1987, 1989a).

Ecostructural therapy is similar to ecological therapy in that it is an elaborated treatment model that emphasizes engagement and problem-solving techniques. Furthermore, ecostructural therapy seeks to include other institutions that impinge on some families in therapy (Aponte, 1991). Thus, the ecostructural model presumes that therapists must always consider a family's environment and community as relevant to the diagnostic process and planning of treatment (Inclan, 1990). In some instances, therapists may find it necessary to restructure or to help the family renegotiate its relationship with a particular agency.

The Bowenian model has been mentioned in the literature as an appropriate approach with ethnic minority clients (Boyd-Franklin, 1989a, 1989b). This approach has two major strengths in that it provides strategies for exploring extended family dynamics and also creates a theoretical framework useful in generating hypotheses regarding familial patterns (Boyd-Franklin, 1987). Genograms are diagrams of family relationships across generations that include significant family members and institutions outside the family. Genograms have been advocated as a primary agent for gathering extended ethnic family information (Moore-Hines & Boyd-Franklin, 1982; Boyd-Franklin, 1989a, 1989b).

Extended Family Structure and Family Therapy

It is important that family therapy approaches accommodate the characteristics of the extended family structure. Within these structures there exist reciprocal obligations, considerable influence on decision-making and membership roles, and reinforcement of traditional values and patterns (Boyd-Franklin, 1989a, 1989b; McGoldrick et al., 1982). Interdependent extended family structures that promote survival within the family are essential to obtaining and maintaining familial health. In other words, because the family relies on extended membership and intergenerational relations, it is logical that this same network would be crucial to ensuring optimal mental health. Incorporating the extended family members into therapy allows many minority groups to work in an environment that most closely mirrors their real-life experience. Creating such an environment facilitates both the therapeutic process and improved familial functioning.

The presence of grandparents as primary caregivers as well as other extended family members in ethnic minority families speaks to the necessary inclusion of these members in therapy (Attneave, 1982; Boyd-Franklin, 1989a, 1989b; Everett, Proctor, & Cartmell, 1983; Harrison, Wilson, Pine, Chan, & Buriel, 1990; Moore-Hines & Boyd-Franklin, 1982; LaFromboise, Trimble, & Mohatt, 1990) and reflects the familial structure. Omission of these members would mean the loss of valuable information regarding familial structure and processes. For example, Wilson (1984) has shown that grandmothers in the home perform a significant amount of the child-rearing tasks, particularly in single-parent households.

Some authors have noted that within the Asian family structure the individual is often considered a part of the whole and is therefore subordinated to the extended family (Chin, 1983; Shon & Ja, 1982). Specific hierarchical family roles are emphasized, with formalized rules of behavior for each member within the group. It has been suggested that family therapy is particularly suitable for these Asian families because the process brings the kin into the treatment naturally, thereby more accurately reflecting the familial environment. Family therapy allows an interactive and contextual perspective of the roles of Asian-American family members (Ho, 1987).

Given the primary influence of intergenerational family members, often the focus of conflict is between generations within the family, each struggling with differing sets of cultural expectations and norms depending on the level of acculturation (Lee, 1989; Shon & Ja, 1982; Vazquez-Nuttal, Avila-Vivas, & Morales-Barreto, 1984). Family therapy can address these intergenerational conflicts and resolve them within the extended familial context that includes all relevant members present. A multigenerational approach to therapy is an efficient and effective method for handling the problems that occur across the generations within one family.

Cultural Characteristics and Family Therapy

Other cultural features of ethnic minority families support the use of family therapy as a particularly effective form of treatment. For example, the therapists' use of self is an important indicator of an intervention's success (Aponte, 1991). Among Latino populations, the term *personalismo* refers to the establishment of relationships through personal and effective bonds (Inclan, 1990). *Personalismo* can enhance the development of trust between therapists and their Latino clients. Given that most models of family therapy require extensive use of the therapist's personality and increased activity level to help direct and guide successful joining with the family, there is a greater chance that *personalismo* will develop at a faster rate than in traditional forms of therapy (Inclan, 1990).

Similar to modern day multisystems approaches, traditional Native American healing ceremonies have been conducted within an extended family setting. These traditional ceremonies included public disclosure, confession, and storytelling (Everett et al., 1983; LaFromboise et al., 1990; Tafoya, 1989). According to Tafoya (1989), usage of such techniques provided a nonthreatening and indirect way of structuring the problem and served as a "therapeutic metaphor." Stories or case histories of other family members, particularly elders, can be used within family therapy to triangulate the problem, thereby providing a comfortable distance between family members. Furthermore, resolution of these stories provides valuable insight into the way in which the family conceptualizes their current difficulties.

Tharp (1991) has suggested that family therapy rather than individual therapy, may be particularly appropriate with ethnic minority groups since the family is a central mechanism for the development of ethnic identity. Furthermore, with family therapy the potential for stereotypes and racial attitudes held by White therapists to hurt treatment is diminished because the therapist must operate within the context of the family's ethnicity. Since immediate problem solving is the primary focus of structural family therapy, therapist biases may be avoided because psychological interpretations are minimal and interventions tend to be specific and direct.

Immediate problem solving, as a feature of structural family therapy, is a particularly attractive feature for ethnic minority families who often face numerous economic and social hardships. Using a multisystems model, the therapist is able to conceptualize interventions with any family at many different levels, and the model builds on problem-solving techniques. Targeting particular problems allows the therapist to keep the family problem focused and empowers them to intervene at the appropriate system levels. In particular, Boyd-Franklin (1987) noted that African-American families can benefit from concrete, goal-oriented, short-term therapy. Such an approach reduces the presence of threatening outsiders, incorporates the inherent strengths of the family, and addresses the daily stresses often experienced by these families (Moore-Hines & Boyd-Franklin, 1982).

Issues and Problems in Family Therapy

Despite the characteristics that lend themselves to the appropriateness of family interventions with ethnic minority families, several issues may arise around suspiciousness among groups, myths of sameness, treatment expectations, process of acculturation, and language barriers. Traditionally, members of ethnic minority groups have relied on informal support networks such as extended family and the church (Attneave, 1982; Boyd-Franklin, 1987; London & Devore, 1988). Investigators have speculated that reliance on natural support systems results in fewer feelings of guilt, defeat, humiliation, and powerlessness when compared with reliance on outside institutions (McGoldrick et al., 1982). Although more ethnic minorities are starting to utilize family therapy, these issues and problems must be addressed before full integration and trust can be developed.

Suspicion has often led to unusually high attrition rates, with many clients not returning after the first few sessions and in some cases not after the initial session (Everett et al., 1983; London & Devore, 1988). Boyd-Franklin (1987), notes that among African Americans a defensive, guarded reception to intervention might be seen as appropriate, given the historical experience of this group in the United States. Relying on outsiders to solve intimate family problems is often perceived as a violation of family confidentiality. As such, until the therapist can be trusted, the client will maintain his or her distance.

Myths of Sameness

Although ethnicity has begun to be addressed in the family therapy literature, the view of ethnic minority families as being similar to nonminority families continues to dominate the field. Hardy (1989) has referred to this universal approach as a "theoretical myth of sameness," whereby the epistemological assumption for most family therapy training is that all ethnic families are the same. Hardy asserts it would be more appropriate to focus on the ways in which minority and nonminority families are different as well as similar. For instance, the diverse familial structures found in African-American, Native American, Latino, and Asian-American cultures have yet to be addressed in mainstream family therapy literature.

The universal approach is compounded by insufficient multicultural training, which leads to misunderstanding and misinterpretation of social and cultural mores displayed by members of ethnic groups. For instance, among some Native Americans a firm handshake is perceived as competitive, and therefore a very light grasp is used (Everett et al., 1983). Such an initial greeting or handshake can be misinterpreted as distant, which may disrupt the working relationship between the client and therapist. Such misunderstandings could ultimately result in premature termination by the Native American client. Clinical training programs need to include an emphasis on understanding the sociopsychological and family reality of ethnic minorities from a system sociopsychological perspective.

Treatment Expectations

Another problem that contributes to early attrition of clients is differing expectations of treatment, depending on the families' values and perception of mental health intervention. A study of Puerto Rican patients found that they expected their doctor to be active and concrete, either giving advice or prescribing medication. Confronted with a traditional psychological approach, in which the therapist role is supposed to be passive, while the client is expected to discuss and reflect on the problems, the Puerto Rican client may choose to terminate treatment permaturely (Abad, Ramos, & Boyce, 1974).

Dauphinais, LaFromboise, and Rowe (1980) conducted a similar study to determine the expectations of Native American clients. The researchers concluded that knowledge and appreciation of the client's cultural values and the willingness to participate in community activities were qualities Native Americans sought from an effective counselor. Furthermore, the tendency of some Native American clients neither to ask direct questions nor to challenge treatment may be misperceived as a lack of involvement in the therapy process and thus may maintain distance between the therapist and the client (Everett et al., 1983).

Introspective and insight-oriented therapies utilizing techniques such as reflective listening may also have little or no relevance to many Native American clients or to members of other minority groups (Atkinson, Morton, & Sue, 1989). In contrast, some self-disclosure by the therapist may greatly aid the therapeutic process by enhancing trust and rapport (Everett et al., 1983; Ho, 1987). Many Native American clients become impatient and will terminate therapy that is primarily client-centered or reflective; therefore, strategic and directive interventions may be preferred (LaFromboise et al., 1990; Unger, 1977).

Process of Acculturation

A salient issue for recent immigrants concerns the level of acculturation of each family member and the resulting conflict when generations in the family are acculturating to the host country at differing rates. Baptiste's work with Latino immigrant families showed that several characteristics of the recent migration experiences caused conflict and were consistent across families despite their differing national heritage (Baptiste, 1987). For example, family members were often unaware of the difficulties resulting from migration and acculturation experiences. Thus, parents tended to attribute the cause of conflict to their children having been negatively influenced by American culture (Baptiste, 1987). The task of therapy was often focused on recognizing the stress associated with migration, grieving the loss of the "old country," and reconciling unrealized expectations for their new life. In addition, therapy can help the family adapt old family functioning rules to new ones that are more adaptive in the new country (Baptiste, 1987).

Chin's work with Chinese-American families indicates that families' differing rates of acculturation depends on several variables, such as number of years in the United States, age at the time of migration, amount of exposure to Western culture, and amount of contact with American peers (Chin, 1983). Similarly, Southeastern Asian refugee families have many difficulties that stem from intergenerational tension and differing values as a result of acculturation differences among the family members (Lee, 1989). Such differences and their ensuing consequences need to be acknowledged and addressed in the therapeutic process.

Native Americans have been found to vary regarding their degree of commitment to preserving their cultural and tribal legacy (LaFromboise et al., 1990; Unger, 1977). At least five levels of acculturation have been identified by LaFromboise and her colleagues among Native Americans: traditional, transitional, marginal, assimilated, and bicultural. Prior to any intervention, a thorough assessment must be made in order to determine where the family is along the acculturation continuum and the degree to which they identify with their culture (see Chapter 2). By being cognizant of these diverse levels of acculturation, therapists will be better able to help Native American clients cope with their concerns.

Language Barriers

Language is one of the most salient barriers to treatment, particularly among first- and second-generation migrant families (see Chapter 2). Working with Spanish-speaking families can be a complex process because members often vary in their command of English and Spanish (Fillmore, 1991; Sciarra & Ponterotto, 1991). A classification of bilingual status has been developed and may be helpful in determining how the process of bilingual family therapy proceeds (Marcos, 1976). For example, the degree of proficiency in either language has implications for langauge preference in therapy, ability to convey affective experiences, and the amount of language switching that takes place within a session (Sciarra & Ponterotto, 1991).

Despite the limited information addressing bilingualism in therapy, several recommendations are offered. The therapist should be aware of the dynamics of bilingualism and the communication patterns among family members, and should have some knowledge of the level of language proficiency of the family members (Sciarra & Ponterotto, 1991). In addition, evidence suggests that the presence of bilingual staff and trained translators from the community increases treatment utilization (see Chapter 8; Rogler et al., 1987). When translators are used, care needs to be taken to ensure understanding of mental health terms and accuracy of the translations.

Recommendations and Guidelines for Treatment

Guidelines for treatment of ethnic minority families include assessment prior to treatment with particular emphasis on ecostructural or contextual factors. Also, avoidance of universal models of family functioning is important. Many of the issues such as level of acculturation, linguistic proficiency, expectations of treatment, definition of family, and familial roles must be explored when assessing ethnic minority families. Other areas should be examined, such as the ecological context, socioeconomic level, employment history, and involvement and experiences with outside institutions and agencies.

For families that are relatively recent migrants, it would be necessary to assess premigratory family life and experiences, the actual migration experience, and the impact of migration on the individual family members (see Chapter 1). In some instances, information regarding physical health, medication history, and reliance on indigenous healers may be salient. Indigenous healers are frequently used by Native Americans and various Latinos and Asian subgroups and may need to be incorporated into the treatment process (see Chapter 9).

Although it is also important to determine the nature and the degree of support provided by the extended family and the community to which the person belongs, overreliance on cultural conceptualizations and interpretations can lead to misguided expectations that the therapeutic process should precisely reflect cultural principles and standards. However, obtaining optimal functioning may require adjusting these cultural characteristics (Padilla, Ruiz, & Alvarez, 1975; Rogler et al., 1987). The difficulty arises in deciding what constitutes "optimal functioning," and ways in which the therapeutic goals and cultural characteristics interact and are processed with family members in treatment.

With ethnic minority families as with nonminority families, it is important to communicate acceptance of the family and approach the problem in a manner similar to the way the family chooses to frame it (Baptiste, 1987; Ho, 1987; Sciarra & Ponterotto, 1991). It is imperative that therapists be aware of their own attitudes toward the ethnic group and the culture with which they are working. In addition, therapists must educate themselves about differences within groups, to avoid subscribing to the convenient and prevailing "cookbook" approach, which divides minority groups into four broad categories (i.e., Americans of Asian, Latino, African, or Native descent). Self-exploration of feelings helps therapists resist ethnocentric bias and avoid pseudoinsight. Attempting to learn about the family's culture from the family rather than operating under prior assumptions will prevent stereotyping and misunderstanding.

Although the ethnic identity of family members will often be addressed in therapy, it is particularly important not to limit therapy to the issues that revolve exclusively around this topic (see Chapter 2; Sciarra & Ponterotto, 1991). Therapy generally works best when it is direct, active, and highly focused on a limited number of issues that are salient to the client (Sciarra & Ponterotto, 1991). Many times intervention must be altered to incorporate education and information about the process of therapy itself (McGoldrick et al., 1982). The process of therapy may need to be further modified to extend beyond the family to include nontraditional members and organizations that affect the family.

Therapy with families who have recently migrated must address the issues of loss of community and support networks (Sciarra & Ponterotto, 1991). Often it is necessary to give the family permission to mourn the loss of country of origin, while they deal with the issues of discrepant expectations and the actual reality of the new country (Baptiste, 1987). Also, differential rates of assimilation may occur across generations in the family resulting in stress and conflict (Szapocznik et al., 1986). Older family members may be less inclined to be assimilated into the majority culture or may have more difficulty than younger ones in doing so.

It is useful to form social and cultural alliances with families that include an initial focus on highly structured informative sessions. Early sessions should provide information about the therapeutic process, including the expectations and limitations of therapy. Additionally, alliances with influential family members serve to acknowledge the therapist's appreciation of the culture. With many Asian families, it is important to show respect for traditional roles—for example, by initially reinforcing the fathers' role as head of family. It is also important to avoid interpreting the mother–child relationship as overdependent and to recognize the family's expectations of each sibling.

Other specific recommendations can be made for providing family therapy to particular ethnic minority families. It has been suggested that structural family therapy is the preferred approach in providing treatment for Asian Americans because of the indirect communication style, patterns of expression, and process of disagreement that exist in some Asian-American families (Kim, 1985; Lee, 1989). Structural family therapy emphasizes the active restructuring of family interactions to create change without relying heavily on direct and open expression in families (Shon & Ja, 1982). Furthermore, the use of family therapy with Chinese-American immigrant families should focus on a holistic view that includes a psychoeducational approach while reinforcing culturally sanctioned coping mechanisms and cultural strengths (Shon & Ja, 1982).

When addressing the needs of African-American families, a multisystems approach has been consistently advocated as the optimal means of intervention (Boyd-Franklin, 1987; 1989b; Moore-Hines & Boyd-Franklin, 1982; Willis, 1988). This model directly empowers the family by directly incorporating strengths such as the extended family, role flexibility, and religion into treatment (Boyd-Franklin, 1989b). Moreover, with regard to African-American clients, it has been suggested that they should be approached in an egalitarian manner that reduces status differences. Since family therapy focuses on the broader community and social context, rather than on the individual, these goals are best facilitated by the family and multisystems models (Moore-Hines & Boyd-Franklin, 1982).

In many African-American families, role flexibility is a commonly utilized coping strategy, particularly in single-parent homes. Role flexibility often results in children assuming adult roles and responsibilities at an earlier age than would be expected. Such patterns must be interpreted in the context of the specific familial situation. A complete and thorough assessment of these roles must be made before the arrangement is deemed dysfunctional, leading to the prescription of inappropriate interventions that may in fact lead to family disequilibrium. It may in fact be appropriate and therapeutic for the therapist to be supportive of role flexibility in the African-American family.

Network therapy has been consistently cited as the treatment of choice when working with Native Americans (LaFromboise et al., 1990). This form of intervention has been noted to be most compatible with traditional Native American healing approaches, and, although it has been primarily utilized with individual clients, it has many broad and valuable implications for use with families (Attneave, 1977, 1982). The network approach utilizes the extended family and community system as an integral part of the treatment plan and as a "social force" or network that can provide social support. Broadening treatment beyond the immediate family provides greater likelihood that support and improvements made during therapy will continue after termination.

Concluding Remarks

It is apparent that the basic premise of family therapy is potentially consistent with the life beliefs and styles of many ethnic minority Americans. To use this approach with ethnic minority families, practitioners will need to possess sensible and sensitive appreciations of cultural differences. Although the appreciation of cultural differences as a therapeutic objective is easier than its implementation in practice, it is reasonable to assume that clinical training programs could address many of the issues raised in this chapter. Our point is that familial problems of ethnic minority Americans are influenced by social, ecological, and cultural contexts. Put another way, when things go wrong, it is important that we understand the family's problem within a unique cultural and ethnic framework. In doing less, we are ineptly applying universal solutions that could do more harm than good.

Finally, the objective of the various phases of family therapy is to obtain two fundamental kinds of information. First, the nature of the problem must be determined. Second, the problem's context must be understood. Both types of information require the ability to comprehend the cultural and ethnic background of the families being helped. Appreciating the contribution of culture and ethnicity will improve service to this significantly underserved portion of the United States. A better understanding and recognition of cultural differences will make training relevant to ethnic minority families. Clients who are culturally different understand the nature of their differences. It is time that professional training and services do the same.

References

Abad, V., Ramos, J., & Boyce, E. (1974). A model for delivery of mental health services to Spanish-speaking minorities. *American Journal of Orthopsychiatry, 44,* 584–595.

Acosta-Belen, E. (1988). From settlers to newcomers: The Hispanic legacy in the United States. In E. Acosta-Belen & B. R. Sjostrom (Eds.), *The Hispanic experience in the United States: Contemporary issues and perspectives* (pp. 1–33). New York: Praeger.

Anderson, P. P. (1989). Issues in serving culturally diverse families of young children with disabilities. *Early Child Development and Care, 50,* 167–188.

Aponte, H. J. (1991). Training on the person of the therapist for work with the poor and minorities. *Journal of Independent Social Work, 5,* 23–39.

Ashburg, D. A., & DeVita, C. J. (1992). New realities of the American family. *Population Bulletin, 47*(2), 1–44.

Atkinson, D. R., Morton, G., & Sue, D. W. (1989). *Counseling American minorities* (3rd ed.). Dubuque, IA: Brown.

Attneave, C. (1977). The wasted strengths of Indian families. In S. Unger (Ed.), *The destruction of American Indian families* (pp. 29–33). New York: Association on American Indian Affairs.

Attneave, C. (1982). American Indians and Alaska Native families: Emigrants in their own homeland. In M. McGoldrick, J. K. Pearce, & J. Giordano (Eds.), *Ethnicity and family therapy* (pp. 55–83). New York: Gardner.

Baptiste, D. A. (1987). Family therapy with Spanish-heritage immigrant families in cultural transition. *Contemporary Family Therapy, 9,* 229–250.

Bergman, R. (1977). The human cost of removing Indian children from their families. In S. Unger

(Ed.), *The destruction of American Indian families* (pp. 34–36). New York: Association on American Indian Affairs.

Bird, A. R., & Melendy, P. (1977). Indian child welfare in Oregon. In S. Unger (Ed.), *The destruction of American Indian families* (pp. 43–46). New York: Association on American Indian Affairs.

Boyd-Franklin, N. (1987). The contribution of family therapy models to the treatment of Black families. *Psychotherapy, 24,* 621–629.

Boyd-Franklin, N. (1989a). *Black families in therapy.* New York: Guilford Press.

Boyd-Franklin, N. (1989b). Five key factors in the treatment of Black families. *Journal of Psychotherapy and the Family, 6,* 53–69.

Brown, E. F., & Shaughnessay, T. F. (1981). *Education for social work practice with American Indian families: Introductory text. Child Welfare Training* (DHHS Report No. OHDS 81-30298). Washington, DC: Children's Bureau.

Byler, W. (1977). The destruction of American Indian families. In S. Unger (Ed.), *The destruction of American Indian families* (pp. 1–11). New York: Association on American Indian Affairs.

Cheung, F. K., & Snowden, L. R. (1990). Community mental health and ethnic populations. *Community Mental Health Journal, 26,* 277–291.

Chin, J. L. (1983). Diagnostic considerations in working with Asian-Americans. *American Journal of Orthopsychiatry, 53,* 100–109.

Dauphinais, P., LaFromboise, T., & Rowe, W. (1980). Perceived problems and sources of help for American Indian students. *Counselor Education and Supervision, 21,* 37–46.

Davis, C., Haub, C., & Willette, L. (1988). U.S. Hispanics: Changing the face of America. In E. Acosta-Belen & B. Sjostrom (Eds.), *The Hispanic experience in the United States: Contemporary issues and perspectives* (pp. 3–56). New York: Praeger.

Everett, F., Proctor, N., & Cartmell, B. (1983). Providing psychological services to American Indian children and families. *Professional Psychology: Research and Practice, 14,* 588–601.

Fillmore, L. W. (1991). When learning a second language means losing the first. *Early Childhood Research Quarterly, 6,* 323–346.

Foster, H. J. (1983). African patterns in Afro-American family. *Journal of Black Studies, 14,* 201–232.

Franklin, J. H. (1988). A historical note on Black families. In H. P. McAdoo (Ed.), *Black families* (2nd ed.) (pp. 23–26). Newbury Park, CA: Sage.

Garbarino, M. (1985). *Native American heritage* (2nd ed.). Prospect Heights, IL: Waveland.

Glick, P. C. (1988). Demographic pictures of Black families. In H. P. McAdoo (Ed.), *Black families* (2nd ed.) (pp. 111–132). Newbury Park, CA: Sage.

Hardy, K. V. (1989). The theoretical myth of sameness: A critical issue in family therapy training and treatment. *Journal of Psychotherapy and the Family, 6,* 17–33.

Harrison, A. O., Wilson, M. N., Pine, C. J., Chan, S. Q., & Buriel, R. (1990). Family ecologies of ethnic minority children. *Child Development, 61,* 347–362.

Hill, H. I., & Strozier, A. L. (1992). Multicultural training in APA-approved counseling psychological program: A survey. *Professional Psychology, 23,* 43–51.

Hirabayashi, G., & Saram, P. A. (1980). Some issues regarding ethnic relations research. In K. V. Ujimoto & G. Hirabayshi (Eds.), *Visible minorities and multiculturalism: Asians in Canada* (pp. 379–388). Toronto: Butterworths.

Ho, M. K. (1987). *Family therapy with ethnic minorities.* Newbury Park, CA: Sage.

Inclan, J. (1990). Understanding Hispanic families: A curriculum outline. *Journal of Strategic and Systemic Therapies, 9,* 64–82.

Karst, K. L. (1986). Paths to belonging: The Constitution and cultural identity. *North Carolina Law Review, 64,* 303–377.

Kim, S. C. (1985). Family therapy for Asian-Americans: A strategic structural framework. *Psychotherapy, 22,* 343–348.

Klor de Alva, J. J. (1988). Telling Hispanics apart: Latino sociocultural diversity. In E. Acosta-Belen & B. R. Sjostrom (Eds.), *The Hispanic experience in the United States* (pp. 107–136). New York: Praeger.

LaFromboise, T. D. (1988). American Indian mental health policy. *American Psychologist, 43,* 388–397.

LaFromboise, T. D., Trimble, J. E., & Mohatt, G. V. (1990). Counseling intervention and American Indian tradition: An integrative approach. *The Counseling Psychologist, 18,* 628–654.

Lee, E. (1989). Assessment and treatment of Chinese-American immigrant families. *Journal of Psychotherapy and the Family, 6,* 99–122.

Lewis, C. (1970). *Indian families of the Northwest coast: The impact of change.* Chicago: University of Chicago Press.

London, H., & Devore, W. (1988). Layers of understanding: Counseling ethnic minority families. *Family Relations, 37,* 310–314.

Marcos, L. R. (1976). Linguistic dimensions in the bilingual patient. *American Journal of Psychoanalysis, 36,* 347–354.

McAdoo, H. P. (1991). Family values and outcomes for children. *Journal of Negro Education, 60,* 361–365.

McGoldrick, M., Pearce, J., & Giordano, J. (Eds.). (1982). *Ethnicity and family therapy.* New York: Gardner.

Minuchin, S. (1974). *Families and family therapy.* Cambridge, MA: Harvard University Press.

Moore-Hines, P., & Boyd-Franklin, N. (1982). Black families. In M. McGoldrick, J. K. Pearce, & J. Giordano (Eds.), *Ethnicity and family therapy* (pp. 84–107). New York: Gardner.

Moynihan, D. P. (1965). *The Negro family, the case for national action: Moynihan report.* Washington, DC: U.S. Government Printing Office.

Nobles, W. W. (1988). African-American family life: An instrument of culture. In H. P. McAdoo (Ed.), *Black families* (2nd ed.) (pp. 44–53). Newbury Park, CA: Sage.

O'Hare, W. P. (1992). America's minorities—The demographics of diversity. *Population Bulletin, 47*(4), 1–47.

O'Hare, W. P., Pollard, K. M., Mann, T. L., & Kent, K. M. (1991). African Americans in the 1990s. *Population Bulletin, 46,* 1–40.

Padilla, A. M., Ruiz, R. A., & Alvarez, R. (1975).

Community mental health services for the Spanish-speaking/surnamed population. *American Psychologist, 30,* 892–905.

Rogler, L. H., Malgady, R. G., Costantino, G., & Blumenthal, R. (1987). What do culturally sensitive mental health services mean? *American Psychologist, 42,* 565–570.

Ruetrakul, P. (1987). *A study of problems and stress of Southeast Asian students with accompanying families at the University of Pittsburgh.* Paper presented at the annual meeting of the Comparative and International Education Society, Washington, DC.

Saba, G. W., Karrer, B. M., & Hardy, K. Y. (Eds.). (1990). *Minorities and family therapy.* New York: Haworth.

Sciarra, D. T., & Ponterotto, J. G. (1991). Counseling the Hispanic bilingual family: Challenges to the therapeutic process. *Psychotherapy, 28,* 473–479.

Shon, S. P., & Ja, D. Y. (1982). Asian families. In M. McGoldrick, J. K. Pearce, & J. Giordano (Eds.), *Ethnicity and family therapy* (pp. 208–228). New York: Gardner.

Sudarkasa, N. (1988). Interpreting the African heritage in Afro-American family organization. In H. P. McAdoo (Ed.), *Black families* (2nd ed.) (pp. 27–43). Newbury Park, CA: Sage.

Szapocznik, J., Rio, A., Perez-Vidal, A., Kurtines, W., Hervis, O., & Santiste-Ban, D. (1986). Bicultural Effectiveness Training (BET): An experimental test of an intervention modality for families experiencing intergenerational/intercultural conflict. *Hispanic Journal of Behavioral Sciences, 8,* 303–330.

Tafoya, T. (1989). Circles and cedar: Native Americans and family therapy. *Journal of Psychotherapy and the Family, 6,* 71–98.

Tharp, R. G. (1991). Cultural diversity and treatment of children. *Journal of Consulting and Clinical Psychology, 59,* 799–812.

Unger, S. (Ed.). (1977). *The destruction of American Indian families.* New York: Association on American Indian Affairs.

U.S. Bureau of the Census (1990). *Fertility of American women: June 1990, Current Population Reports, Series P-20, No. 454.* Washington, DC: U.S. Government Printing Office.

U.S. Bureau of the Census (1992). *Statistical abstract of the United States: 1992.* Washington, DC: U.S. Government Printing Office.

Vazquez-Nuttal, E., Avila-Vivas, Z., & Morales-Barreto, G. (1984). Working with Latin American families. *Family Therapy Collections, 9,* 75–90.

Valdivieso, R., & Davis, C. (1988). *U.S. Hispanics: Challenging issues for the 1990s.* Washington, DC: Population Reference Bureau.

Vega, W. A. (1990). Hispanic families in the 1980's: A decade of research. *Journal of Marriage and the Family, 52,* 1015–1024.

Westermeyer, J. (1977a). The drunken Indian: Myths and realities. In S. Unger (Ed.), *The destruction of American Indian families* (pp. 22–28). New York: Association on American Indian Affairs.

Westermeyer, J. (1977b). The ravage of Indian families in crisis. In S. Unger (Ed.), *The destruction of American Indian families* (pp. 47–56). New York: Association on American Indian Affairs.

Wilkinson, C. B. (1987). Introduction. In C. B. Wilkinson (Ed.), *Ethnic psychiatry* (pp. 1–11). New York: Plenum Press.

Willis, J. T. (1988). An effective counseling model for treating the Black family. *Family Therapy, 15,* 185–194.

Wilson, M. N. (1984). Mother's and grandmothers' perceptions of parental behavior in three generational Black families. *Child Development, 55,* 1333–1339.

Wilson, M. N. (1986). The Black extended family: An analytical review. *Developmental Psychology, 22,* 246–258.

Wilson, M. N. (1989). Child development in the context of the Black extended family. *American Psychologist, 44,* 380–385.

Wilson, M. N., & Tolson, T. F. J. (1990). Familial support in the Black community. *Journal of Clinical Child Psychology, 19,* 347–355.

Chapter 7

Group Interventions and Treatment with Ethnic Minorities

MELBA J. T. VASQUEZ
AY LING HAN

Group interventions have long been considered the treatment of choice for various kinds of problems and difficulties (Kaplan & Sadock, 1993; Kaul & Bednar, 1986). Group therapy may be the treatment of choice for ethnic minorities, who often struggle with issues such as confidence, self-esteem, empowerment, and identity (Boyd-Franklin, 1991; Ho, 1984; Mays, 1986; Nayman, 1983). The approach is seen as relevant for populations whose primary concerns often focus on feelings of loneliness and social isolation and the need for support, as well as stresses in interpersonal relationships (Boyd-Franklin, 1987; Ettin, 1988; Talley & Rockwell, 1985; Yalom, 1985).

As with other forms of psychological intervention, the unique cultural needs and variations of ethnic group members must be taken into account in preparing and providing group treatment (Boyd-Franklin, 1991; Comas-Díaz, 1984; Nayman, 1983). Therapists, regardless of ethnicity, must be aware that ethnicity in group therapy is a salient personal and interpersonal factor and, thus, always has significance for both group members and leaders (Davis, 1984). In addition to understanding group dynamics and processes, it is vital to understand the role of culture and ethnicity, as described in other sections of this book (see Chapter 2). Group leaders should also subscribe to the *Guidelines of Psychological Services to Ethnic, Linguistic, and Culturally Diverse Populations* (American Psychological Association, 1993).

Philosophy of Group Treatment with Ethnic Minority Clients

Group interventions and treatments can vary from traditional group psychotherapy to intensive small-group experiences such as basic skills training, laboratory training, and encounter groups (Kaplan & Sadock, 1993; Lubin, 1983). Group therapy approaches can differ according to theoretical orientation (e.g., psychoanalytic, Adlerian, psychodrama, person-centered, Gestalt, behavioral), composition (e.g., heterogeneous, homogeneous), structure (e.g., open-ended, closed-ended), and setting (e.g., outpatient, inpatient, partial hospitalization) (Kaplan & Sadock, 1993; Corey, 1990). All groups typically progress through identifable stages or phases in which issues emerge that need to be addressed by the group leaders (Corey, 1990). Group therapy can be viewed as a microcosm of the members' lives outside the group and should also be considered as a microcosm of the members' society at large (Yalom, 1985).

Multicultural and feminist approaches, particularly the relational approach to psychological development (Miller, 1986) and the application of that approach to group therapy (Fedele & Harrington, 1990), have largely influenced the authors' treatment philosophy for working with ethnic minorities. In addition, Yalom's (1985) process-oriented approach and the "curative factors" that characterize that approach have strongly influenced our group practice.

Yet, given that group psychological approaches have Eurocentric assumptions about the primacy of the individual in treatment and intervention for personal and interpersonal concerns, certain assumptions about what is effective may be problematic for some ethnic minority clients. For example, Yalom's (1985) "curative factors," which pertain to socializing techniques and skills, imitative behaviors, and interpersonal learning, assume that assertiveness and expression of negative feelings are curative for various interpersonal difficulties. Although they may be curative for many members of the dominant society in the United States, for the client whose ethnic heritage considers family or group belongingness primary and the individual secondary, such direct expressiveness could be considered impolite, presumptuous, and unacceptable, and could even precipitate intrapsychic and familial bicultural or multicultural conflicts.

Important components of group treatment philosophy with ethnic minorities are "valuing diversity" and "bicultural/multicultural competence," of which the development of bicultural identity is a part. "Valuing diversity" refers to a philosophical and treatment outlook that (1) acknowledges the ways that ethnic minorities have unique or different sets of experiences, and (2) recognizes and embraces the goal of appreciating both minority and majority cultural contexts, and to develop an ease in "switching" back and forth (Padilla, 1993), depending on the minority person's choices in the particular context. The minority person's task is to internalize a more positive sense of racial or ethnic identity (Tatum, 1993), and to develop a clear and integrated sense of self (Comas-Díaz, 1988). This process embraces a bicultural identification with one's multiple heritages rather than over-defining one cultural/racial dimension at the cost of the other (Padilla, 1993).

Culture-sensitive approaches in group interventions should include an acknowledgment of American/Eurocentric assumptions regarding the primacy of individuality, exploration of implications of such learning in the member's own bicultural/multicultural contexts, and an incorporation of bicultural/multicultural appreciation and learning.

Fedele and Harrington (1990) describe four healing factors operative in group treatment with women, which, we believe, in addition to other healing processes, are particularly relevant for all ethnic minorities in facilitating bicultural/multicultural appreciation and competence. These healing factors are based on a relational approach (Miller, 1986), which suggests that groups that foster particular types of interactions and connections between people promote psychological growth and the healing of emotional wounds. The four salient healing factors include validation of one's experience, empowerment to act in relationships, development of self-empathy, and mutuality. A description of each of these factors follows, as well as their relevance to ethnic minority persons.

Validation as a Healing Factor

Unfortunately, persons of color encounter numerous messages and experiences in society that diminish their feelings of worth (Atkinson, Morten, & Sue, 1989; Comas-Díaz & Griffith, 1988); thus, the messages that become internalized include that one's needs, experiences, and perceptions are not important or valid. In groups, ethnic minorities can understand and validate each other's experiences, needs, realities, and value. The feeling of being understood validates one's sense of reality and self-worth. Sharing one's pain in a group can promote healing. Healing occurs when a person returns to the pain of the past and finds that he or she is not alone this time (Jordan, 1989), an experience that can be particularly compelling for ethnic minorities.

Validation as a healing factor for group interventions with ethnic minorities includes acknowledgment and affirmation of the following experiences: historically unrecognized, invalidated, or devalued relationships; devaluations or idealizations of successes; and pathologization or undue criticism and/or punishments of otherwise normal difficulties or mistakes. The composition of an ethnically or racially mixed group parallels the dynamics and processes of the larger society and, without careful facilitation, runs the risk of reenacting the dynamics and processes of oppression, silence, and invalidation.

Empowerment as a Healing Factor

One of the goals of effective group treatment is to empower group members. Ethnic minority group members, many of whom have experienced various degrees of disempowerment in society, can benefit from a group approach that emphasizes empowerment. An empowering consequence of group validation of ethnic minorities' previously unacknowledged or silenced experiences may include not only letting go of any internalized negative and positive stereotypes, but also internalizing more reality-based and affirming images about oneself and others so that they may experience the legitimacy of their complex identity and experience. Thus, it is important that groups provide a context in which these members not only validate their struggles as ethnic minorities but also encourage each other's ability to be effective. This process can help heal injuries from past abuses and messages that have resulted in the diminished ethnic minority group members' capacities to feel powerful, and their willingness to exercise power (Fedele & Harrington, 1990).

Self-Empathy as a Healing Factor

Self-empathy includes the ability to have compassion for oneself and to accept that which is human in ourselves (Fedele & Harrington, 1990; Jordan, 1989). Ethnic minority group members who have experienced harsh or judgmental relationships (with parents, teachers, peers, and other significant persons in their lives), as well as negative societal messages, may have developed a harsh or judging approach to themselves. Ethnic minority individuals may tend to define themselves as "failures" when an error is made, instead of realizing that errors and mistakes are natural parts of living and learning. The relative lack of ethnic minority role models in key power positions in society contributes significantly to that negative self-perception.

Primary reference groups (the gender, ethnic, socioeconomic, religious, and other groups with which one most identifies) influence one's view of oneself and others. If one views one's primary reference group as unentitled or a relative failure in society, then the tendency is to either see oneself as a failure or to disengage from that primary reference group. Coupled with pervasive, insidious, and explicit negative messages from significant others and society, the potential for self-harshness increases. Jordan and her colleagues write that "in order to empathize one must have a well-differentiated sense of self in addition to an appreciation of and sensitivity to the differentness as well as the sameness of another person" (Jordan, Surrey, & Kaplan, 1991, p. 29). The process of healing occurs when group members learn to hear about each other's deepest fears, insecurities, shame, and mistakes, in the context of nonjudgmental, caring relationships, which in turn helps group members develop self-empathy and compassion for their own vulnerabilities, imperfections, and past mistakes. The need to develop compassion for oneself, as well as positive perception of one's primary reference group, is crucial, and group therapy provides a unique forum for the promotion for such empathy and compassion.

In a heterogeneous group, mutual empathy among members must involve the facilitation of trust and safety for minority members to share experiences they do not usually discuss in mixed groups and for White members to hear these experiences without undue defensiveness. When issues of racial or ethnic oppression come up, White members may struggle with feelings of fear, shame, guilt, remorse, sadness, or anger. Thus, self-empathy must also be a clear goal for White members in the group. Self-empathy is facilitated when co-leaders are able to model empathy for White members of the group—communicating understanding without condoning oppression—so that they themselves are able to reach a paradoxical stance toward themselves, one that depersonalizes yet also assumes responsibility for the oppressor in them, where they are able to see that they are recipients of a racist cultural heritage and that they have a choice over their attitudes and behaviors in relation to diversity.

Mutuality as a Healing Factor

Mutuality is the ability to tune into the subjective, inner experience of another person at a cognitive and affective level (Fedele & Harrington, 1990; Jordan, 1989). It involves the ability to understand fully, appreciate, and convey respect for the other person's experience and uniqueness and a willingness to allow others to have an impact on oneself and to understand and appreciate one's impact on others. Mutuality means respecting the other person's pain and valuing his or her growth without being threatened. Mutual relationships result in more energy, more ability to act, more awareness and understanding of others, a greater sense of worth, and a heightened experience of closeness and connection with others (Miller, 1986).

People of color have often experienced imbalances in mutuality. That is, societal roles often leave ethnic minorities in positions where interactions are less than mutual. Tatum (1993), in her paper on the experiences of Black women growing up in predominantly White communities, described failures of empathy and the challenges of mutuality for Black and White women. Minor imbalances in relationships are challenging and painful, but pervasive and traumatic disconnections and imbalances in mutuality can lead to psychological wounds, some of which can include an inhibition of the ability to act, especially when one's experience in that relationship leads to emotional difficulties and turmoil. Miller (1988) described other consequences of loss of mutuality in relationships, including loss of self-understanding, a diminished sense of self-worth, a decrease in energy, and a confusing sense of isolation. She also described long-term effects, such as a seriously distorted view of the self and others, the inability to express feelings, overreliance on maladaptive coping mechanisms, and isolation and/or unfulfilling attachments.

Basic Group Processes

Developmental Nature of the Group

Group treatment tends to be developmental in nature, and a number of writers have described the phases through which groups progress (Bennis & Shepard, 1974; Corey, 1990). Although these phases may tend to be consistent aspects of group development, they do not necessarily occur in a predictable order, and long-term groups may recycle through various aspects of these phases several times. Among the phases through which groups can progress are the following: trust and cohesion, conflict and struggle, cohesion, mature working group, and termination (Bennis & Shepard, 1974). Different issues emerge for ethnic persons in each of these phases.

Trust and Cohesion

The initial phase in groups is establishing trust and cohesion. Ethnic minority group members who are open to intimacy will tend to be involved in this phase; those who have difficulty with trust and intimacy will tend not to participate. These difficulties may be due to negative experiences with trust that were personal, familial, and/or cultural in origin. Initially, the group may focus on a discussion of interpersonal problems external to the group as members search for commonalities. In addition, members have a tendency to search for a role, which often parallels the role they take in other group situations as well as within their families. Unfortunately, the sociopolitical history of many ethnic minority groups is one riddled with betrayal. Therefore, an all-ethnic or mixed-ethnic group may initially be characterized by distrust of the sponsoring agency, other group members, and/or the leader. Knowing the history of group members, through a pregroup interview, discussion with other therapists, and/or a history form, is important and helpful. Interventions must be designed carefully to promote an atmosphere of trust and safety; otherwise, potential consequences of distrust or lack of a sense of safety may include attrition, lack of in-depth disclosure, and low member participation (Davis, 1984).

Conflict and Struggle

The next phase of group development typically involves issues of conflict and struggle, with power and interpersonal dominance taking the form of anger, disagreement, or disappointment. For some ethnic minority members, especially women of color, such feelings may be difficult to acknowledge and express. It is often easier to express anger about the external world and injustices. The danger for these ethnic minorities is that they will be scapegoated or punished. Those who are fearful of conflict may flee. They may flee by not going deeper into their feelings, by participating more superficially, and/or by decreasing or terminating their attendance. It is important to validate those feelings and the unjust realities of social construction of ethnicity and gender in our society. It is also important to facilitate the focus on anger within the group where it may be relevant. For example, an activist Latino group member, who may be generally angry at conservative Hispanics who disengage from ethnic identity, may also be resentful of a group member who is biracial (part Hispanic and part White) and non-Spanish-speaking.

In this phase, group members may also experience disappointment in group leaders for what is or is not happening. It is important that this process be acknowledged and validated as important and constructive; leaders should be able to draw anger to themselves and to separate personal attacks from attacks on the role of leader. This phase presents an opportunity for group members to learn effective ways of experiencing hurts, disappointments, and admission of wrongdoing. It is also important that group leaders model nondestructive ways of expressing anger. Boundaries about the expression of anger (that members talk constructively about their anger, not talk or act from it in destructive ways) can be effective in making this phase safer.

Cohesion

After a period of conflict, the group gradually develops into a cohesive unit, with increased morale, mutual trust, and self-disclosure (Corey, 1990; Lakin, 1985). More in-depth communication, including "painful secrets" or "real" reasons for coming to the group, are shared, and intimacy and closeness are chief concerns. Although emotional support and validation from leaders and members are important, the usual therapeutic proscription against providing more concrete help or advice does not necessarily apply in cases of group therapy with ethnic minorities. Group therapists in this context must often provide advocacy and psychoeducational interventions. For example, the therapist may provide an immigrant mother whose undocumented worker family member is being harassed or abused by an unscrupulous employer with information or referral to resources about immigrant worker rights.

Mature Working Group

During this phase, group members take on many leadership roles and tasks (Corey, 1990). There is a clear sense of purpose and direction to the group, and the atmosphere is relatively comfortable, genuine, and focused. The group also has resources to resolve internal conflicts and mobilize its resources. Group members are more comfortable with differences and tolerate a wide range of diversity. For example, a cynical professional group member may be open to hearing about herbs to help depression and lack of energy; an angry separatist is considerate of interpreting for the minimally Spanish-speaking member when the need arises. Issues affecting group members not only within the group but also outside the group are addressed openly and effectively.

Termination

If the group is a time-limited one, there is a tendency to want to continue. If the group is an ongoing one where individual members end their participation on the basis of their own needs and timing, group members will clearly feel the loss of the departing member. During this phase, leaders must help the group not deny endings and should facilitate goodbyes, expression of diappointment or regret, consolidations of learning, and exploration of future needs. It can be damaging to the trust in the group if group members simply drop out without acknowledgment, and it is valuable both to communicate concern about premature departures and to celebrate the accomplishment of a group member who feels ready to terminate. Endings can stir up feelings of abandonment, especially for those who have a history of problematic abandonments in their life. For a time-limited group, when the entire group terminates at once, it is important to reserve at least two full group sessions of one and one-half hours each for this process.

Process Orientation of the Group

A process-oriented approach to group work (Yalom, 1985) facilitates members' involvement with and responsiveness to each other. Leaders make observations and comments about the process, themes, and dynamics underlying the content of the group and teach group members to do the same. The leader becomes more involved in the group, is less distant, and is more immediate and genuine by focusing on the here-and-now group process. This approach to leadership facilitates the empowerment of ethnic minority members who have not necessarily experienced the validation of their perceptions and the value of their contributions in group settings.

Central Process Issues in Groups

Power
Power is a central issue in any relationship, particularly for groups with ethnic minority members. As members of oppressed groups, ethnic minorities and women are often uncomfortable with the notion of power as domination, control or mastery, competition, or winning over others. Psychological empowerment, on the other hand, is defined by Surrey (1987) as "the motivation, freedom, and capacity to act purposefully, with mobilization of the energy, resources, strengths, or power of each person through a mutual relational process" (p. 3). This approach to empowerment facilitates working with clients such as Asian, Hispanic, African-American, Native American, and other minority group members whose values promote dignity and respect and who favor collaboration and interdependence over confrontation and competition.

Self-Esteem, Identity, and Intimacy
For many ethnic minorities, issues of self-esteem, identity, and intimacy are central and are interwoven with being minority members of United States society, where stereotypic and prejudicial messages are pervasive. The internalization of these messages can influence self-esteem, identity, and intimacy. Minority self-identity issues may range from confusion ("Who am I?"), to conflicts about one's sense of identity and belongingness ("Am I Chinese? American? Chinese-American?"), often complicated by perceptions that differ from those of others (e.g., a Chinese person being called "Jap" by White Americans or, similarly, a Japanese American being called "traitor" by relatively more traditional Japanese counterparts), to making an arbitrary choice of one cultural heritage to the exclusion of the other (e.g., "I am American, not Hispanic").

Various writers have elaborated on ways of thinking about minority identity in general (e.g., Atkinson et al., 1989), African-American racial identity (Cross, 1991), and White racial identity (Helms, 1990). Some investigators found that exploration of identity issues was significantly higher among minority group subjects than among a comparison White group, and that self-esteem was related to the extent that minority subjects had thought about and resolved issues of ethnicity (Phinney & Alipuria, 1990). In addition, subjects who reported a strong ethnic identification (rather than a bicultural identification) were significantly more "separatist," engaged in less cross-ethnic contact out of school and reported more cross-ethnic conflict (Rotheram-Borus, 1990). Moreover, higher ratings of "moratorium" identity status were associated with significantly more behavioral problems, less social competence, and lower self-esteem (Rotheram-Borus, 1989).

Thus, group interventions with minorities should address issues of self-esteem and identity. Comas-Díaz and Jacobsen (1987) suggest three major therapeutic functions for helping a client deal with issues of identity: (1) reflection of the client's identity and societal/environmental sources of his or her identity that contribute to the client's issues with identity, (2) psychoeducation and examination of the client's inconsistencies in self-identity, and (3) mediation between the client's ethnocultural identity and personal identity to achieve a more integrated and consolidated sense of self. A risk for an ethnic minority person in an ethnically or racially mixed group where he or she is a minority member is that he or she may only share experiences and parts of identity that are "Americanized" or similar to those of the majority of the group members.

Group Leadership

Group leadership style will vary according to the goals and focus of the group and the theoretical orientation of the leaders (Corey, 1990; Lakin, 1985). Group leaders may be called upon to engage in a variety of roles and tasks, such as seeking and giving information, responding to feelings, summarizing, confronting, and modeling for the group (Bertcher, 1979). This section will deal with the ethnicity of the group leader and the specific tasks of group leaders for working with ethnic groups that emerge from the models and treatment philosophies of Fedele and Harrington (1990), Miller (1986), and Yalom (1985).

Ethnicity of the Group Leader

There are mixed and controversial findings with regard to ethnic minorities' preferences for the ethnicity of their psychotherapist (Atkinson & Wampold, 1993; López, López, & Fong, 1991; López & López, 1993). Typically, Mexican Americans, for example, prefer counselors of the same ethnicity, but some research implies that this may be a weak preference in relation to other counselor characteristics, such as counselor effectiveness. Sue, Fujino, Hu, Takeuchi, and Zane (1991), in a naturalistic five-year study, examined the relationship of treatment process and outcome to ethnic match between mental health professional and client. The researchers found that ethnic match was significantly related to fewer dropouts after one session, a greater number of treatment sessions, and significantly improved outcomes as measured on a global evaluation measure.

Davis (1984) described how White leaders of ethnic minority group members may be subject to challenges of their leadership for philosophical, political, or personal reasons, as well as their knowledge of ethnic minority culture. On the other hand, challenges to minority group leaders may also come from both White and ethnic minority group members. Because a position of leadership is inconsistent with "ascribed lower status" of minorities in society, and because both White and ethnic minority group members may have internalized that oppressive perception, ethnic minority group leaders may experience more aggression or lack of credibility from participants. In both sets of challenges, the leaders' processing and discussion of the significance of their ethnicity relative to each other and to others in the group can be a healthy and productive process. Moreover, ethnic minority leaders are also more likely to be targets for members' projections of their own personal sense of inadequacies.

Tasks for Group Leaders

Provide Psychoeducation and Promote Trust and Safety
A primary task in providing group therapy to ethnic minorities is to promote interactions that provide a bicultural/multicultural perspective and build trust and safety. While most clients entering group treatment have anxieties about confidentiality and about being understood, accepted, and respected, these concerns are particularly intensified for ethnic minorities. Several factors account for ethnic minorities' hesitancy to utilize mental health services: lack of familiarity with counseling as a helping resource, cultural imperatives against talking about personal problems to strangers, language barriers and cultural differences in encoding and decoding verbal and nonverbal communication, lack of ethnic minority mental health professionals, and lack of culturally relevant and sensitive services (Sue, 1981). Given these barriers, promotion of trust and safety is a particularly important goal. A potential ethnic minority member should be instructed about group treatment in order to alleviate any anxieties about being "mainstreamed" without respect for diversity.

During a screening interview and throughout group treatment, co-leaders should assess an ethnic minority person's extent of identification with and acculturation to both the minority background and the dominant culture (see Chapter 2). Leaders can do much to promote safety and trust by using this information when establishing ground rules around issues such as confidentiality and expectations of the members' and leaders' involvement, as well as cancellation policy and fees. Generally, the greater a potential member's identification with his or her ethnic background, the greater the effort that should be made by the leaders to explore the member's reactions to such psychoeducation and to frame expectations in bicultural terms. A group leader can promote trust and safety by modeling openness, respect and caring, genuineness, and honesty. Active involvement of group members responding to one another, rather than the group leader, can also promote trust and safety.

Focus on Group Members' Strengths
An important task for the leaders of ethnic minority groups is to emphasize strengths rather than pathology. Psychotherapy in general tends to focus on problems and to emphasize behaviors and attitudes for which clients are responsible that contribute to their difficulties in living. While such exploration and challenge is

helpful to clients, it is also important to facilitate exploration of the minority client's strengths, abilities, and resiliency. Moving in that direction, the therapist and the group validate and mirror aspects of the ethnic minority client's personality and functioning that are undervalued in society, thereby enhancing rather than undermining the self-esteem of the client.

Promote Empowerment of Group Members

Empowering group members means that the therapist implements interventions to help members begin to trust their own observations and feelings. To do so, we as group leaders must be able to ask ourselves "if we are prepared to hear, see, and understand [our ethnic or racial minorities'] authentically told experiences. Unless the answer is 'yes,' we will not be able to help facilitate the empowerment of [ethnic minority clients]" (Tatum, 1993, p. 6). The group leader can support and challenge group members to develop awareness of themselves and their needs, and to learn ways of responding on the basis of their personal meaning rather than relying exclusively on meanings as defined by others. Ethnic minority group participants, particularly women of color, have often been denied validation of their perceptions, experiences, and sense of the world. Group leaders can help clients learn to listen, respect, and feel entitled to their experiences, perceptions, and needs, and to express these observations and feelings in the open interactions that characterize groups.

Promote Skills of Communication and Assertiveness

Group leaders may help group members develop skills of communication and assertiveness (Bertcher, 1979). When group members realize that they can assert their needs and influence the group or individual members directly and powerfully, they will begin to develop trust and confidence in themselves. An important function of the leader is to promote the use of communication in ways that build connection and enhance everyone's personal power. An empowering interactive process results in increased zest, knowledge, self-worth, salience, and desire for more connection. Group members are then able to apply those skills outside the group setting. With an ethnic or racial minority member, group leaders can frame such learning in terms of expanding or enhancing the minority person's repertoire of bicultural competence, increasing his or her ability to negotiate different social interactions and cultural contexts.

Facilitate Expression of Negative Feelings

Most ethnic minority group members value connectedness, cooperation, interpersonal relationships, and family (Atkinson et al., 1989; Comas-Díaz & Griffith, 1988). Because of this, it is sometimes difficult for ethnic minority participants, particularly women, to address feelings and behaviors related to anger, conflict, and competition. Thus, the group leader can create norms that facilitate the exploration of these and the issues associated with them. It is important, for example, to teach that expressing anger is vital to recognizing and challenging the restrictiveness of role expectations, and deepening authenticity in relationships. It is also important to model the ability to hear, receive, and validate others' anger and yet still remain "connected." With a minority member, it is important to acknowledge that direct expressions of negative feelings may be counterproductive in certain cultural contexts. In these cases, leaders may encourage a minority person to explore more culturally acceptable yet personally productive ways of dealing with negative feelings in their lives.

Promote "Here-and-Now" Focus

Because people tend to recapitulate their interpersonal problems in the therapy group, progress can occur when members express "here-and-now" emotional experiences and examine them in order to understand their defensiveness or resistance to dealing with interpersonal difficulties (Yalom, 1985). The group therapist explores unconscious patterns and events that may have been useful in the past but are no longer functional in the individual's current life and relationships. Healing and change come partly from helping clients understand the connection between experiences of the past and current behavior and, for ethnic minorities, from helping them integrate historically unvoiced or devalued multicultural concerns with here-and-now and/or relatively more personal issues.

Focus on Sociocultural Issues

The group leader can support and challenge change not only at the individual but also at the group and societal levels. One of the basic tenets of both multicultural and feminist therapy is that environmental, social, and political forces influence the development of the individual, and that a primary goal is helping clients understand the impact of these influences. Regardless of history in this country, ethnic minority groups face many social, economic, and political pressures. Despite advances in the past few decades, minority Americans find themselves far behind the larger society in education, occupational status, income, housing, political representation, and professional roles (see Chapter 1). These life stresses and forces cannot be ignored in the context of group psychotherapy.

Group Composition

Groups may consist of both ethnic minority and White members or of ethnic minority members only. Integrated groups that have ethnic and nonethnic members often reflect attitudes and behaviors of the external world and may provide more information and mutual understandings, as well as skills in interacting with each other. On the other hand, homogeneous groups of ethnic minorities provide the opportunity for more immediate trust and cultural understanding, which can enhance and foster group cohesion. One study (Shen, Sanchez, & Huang, 1984) examined the verbal participation of Anglos, Mexican Americans, and Native Americans with comparable educational backgrounds in group therapy sessions for alcoholic patients. The researchers found that Anglo patients had significantly higher verbal participation than either of the two other ethnic groups and suggested the need to consider the advantages and disadvantages of homogeneous and heterogeneous ethnic groupings in group therapy for alcoholic patients.

Other research suggests that decision making about ethnically homogeneous and heterogeneous groupings should consider the importance of factors that will facilitate members' verbal participation. Chu and Sue (1984) suggested that Asians may be initially disadvantaged in racially heterogeneous groups. Because of a strong adherence to the cultural value of politeness, Asians may tend toward lower verbal participation for fear of interrupting others. Hispanics may be more comfortable in a homogeneous Spanish-speaking group if they are able to move in and out of Spanish and English without fear of offending non–Spanish speakers. The important consideration is that higher verbal participation yields greater positive change in the clients' views of themselves (Corey, 1990; Yalom, 1985). If a heterogeneous grouping is chosen, then the degree of verbal participation by all members should be attended to and addressed.

Homogeneous groups of ethnic minority members provide the opportunity for more immediate trust and cultural understanding, which can enhance and foster group cohesion and promote more in-depth self-disclosure (Davis, 1984). Homogeneous groups typically have as their goal the enhancement of the ethnic identity of the group members. Given differences in experiences with acculturation and oppression, the opportunity exists to acknowledge differences in ethnic identity among the group members and to explore the significance of the differences in their own view of themselves, their view of their own and other ethnic groups, and their view of the majority group (see Chapter 2).

Integrated groups that have ethnic and nonethnic members may present a number of challenges as well as opportunities. It is important to note that being "one of a kind" in a group, for example the only ethnic minority, lesbian, or woman, can be isolating and may make it difficult for that member to relate to others in the group. Davis (1984) notes that the ethnicity of the group members and leader is always of importance, even when ethnicity as such is unrelated to the goals of the members. The risks of being the most "different" in any group, for both leader and member, include the following: being the recipient of underidentification from other members, being scapegoated as the "identified patient" so that other members may project their own issues onto the ethnic minority person and do not take responsibility for their own actions and reactions; and being over- or underprotected by the leaders.

In either homogeneous or heterogeneous ethnic groups, leaders also may wish to consider whether the group should be limited to one sex or should include both men and women. Proponents of same-sex groups describe the advantages of such a composition. Bernardez (1983) considers women's groups the treatment of choice for most women. She believes that single-sex groups allow women to focus on their unique experiences as women, to practice assertiveness, and to redefine goals and notions of womanly behavior. Likewise, there are advantages to organizing an all-men's group. While recruiting men for such a group may be a challenge, men in single-sex groups seem to feel greater freedom to express feelings without being bound by the traditional role restrictions they may experience with women present, to focus on their unique issues and experiences as men, and to explore new ways of expressing needs and feelings with one another (Kaufman & Timmers, 1986; McLeod & Pemberton, 1984; Van Wormer, 1989).

Alonso (1987) advocates mixed-sex groups in the belief that such groups offer more options for working through sex-role issues. In their study on differences in verbal behavior between an all-female, an all-male, and a mixed-sex group, Verdi and Wheelan (1992) found that same-sex groups generated more flight, pairing, counterpairing, dependency, and work compared with mixed-sex groups; in the latter, flight increased across time, and work decreased. Fedele and Harrington (1990) suggest that both same- and mixed-sex group perspectives have merit. At certain developmental times, an individual may need to be in a same-sex group to focus on gender identity issues. At other times, a mixed group can provide the possibility of integrating women's and men's experiences into a "coherent and dynamic understanding of the human experience" (Fedele & Harrington, 1990, p. 3), as well as offering skills in relating with one another—for example, resolving long-standing differences and misunderstandings between men and women (Tannen, 1990).

Group Applications to Ethnic Minorities

The focus of group intervention may be largely psychotherapeutic, developmental, or preventive (Drum & Lawler, 1988). A *psychotherapeutic* group is designed primarily to help members repair or reconstruct the self, overcome recurring crises, and resolve lifelong traumas. A *developmental* group is typically designed "to facilitate normal development by assisting people in adding new skills or dimensions to their lives, or by providing strategies to help in the resolution of critical issues" (Drum & Lawler, 1988, p. 17). Drum and Lawler (1988) describe a *preventive* group as one designed to "prevent or forestall the onset of a problem or need through anticipation of the consequences of non-action" (p. 17). Each of these types of group intervention may be helpful in designing groups to work with ethnic minority populations.

The literature indicates that group interventions can be effective for ethnic and culturally diverse populations. Levine and Padilla (1980) reported positive results in their review of a number of studies which examined group therapy interventions with Hispanic children, adolescents, and young adults. Comas-Díaz (1981) found that low-income Puerto Rican women who participated in either cognitive or behavioral group therapy showed significant reductions in depression compared to control group patients who received no immediate treatment. Kinzie et al. (1988) found that South Asian refugees' acceptance of group therapy was enhanced when the group maintained a bicultural focus, provided practical information, met concrete needs, and was flexible. Boulette (1976), who compared assertiveness training with nondirective psychotherapy, found that Mexican-American women showed greater gains in self-esteem and in assertiveness through participation in an assertiveness-training group.

Psychotherapeutic Groups

The primary purpose of ongoing, moderate- to long-term psychotherapy (i.e., months to years) is to repair or reconstruct entrenched, dysfunctional life patterns as well as to provide support with major recurring crises (Drum & Lawler, 1988). Psychotherapy for ethnic minorities offers the opportunity to deal with a number of unique issues. For example, one of the strengths for the Hispanic individual is the family, which promotes connection in human relationships. A number of writers have pointed out the importance of the Hispanic extended family (Atkinson et al., 1989; Levine & Padilla, 1980; Martinez, 1993; Romos-McKay, Comas-Díaz, & Rivera, 1988; Sabogal, Marin, Otero-Sabogal, Martin, & Perez-Stable, 1987). A child who grows up within the culture of a Hispanic family network learns the existence of many sources of love and support. When the normal family structure and function are disrupted, however, as with abuse and specifically with incest, psychological development is damaged and significant psychological trauma exists.

Wyatt (1990) reviewed the literature on sexual abuse of ethnic minority children. Although she did not find differences in prevalence of child sexual abuse among ethnic minority groups, she did hypothesize that other forms of victimization (the trauma of negative sexual stereotypes, racism and discrimination, stigmatization of being "less than good," powerlessness, etc.) may complicate professionals' understanding of the sequaelae associated with child sexual abuse and their interpretation of those events. She cited one study (Stein, Golding, Siegel, Burnam, & Sorenson, 1988) that indicated that more depressive disorders, alcohol and drug abuse, phobias, and panic disorders were noted in Hispanic male and female child abuse victim when compared with a non-Hispanic cohort. Wyatt suggested that although initial reactions to sexual abuse may not reveal ethnic differences, especially when Black–White comparisons are made, the other aspects of victimization inherent in ethnic minority children's lives affect long-term adjustment to sexual abuse trauma.

Women's groups in particular typically have group members who have experienced abuse of some kind. The rate of sexual and physical abuse of women before the age of 21 ranges from 37 percent to 50 percent (McGrath, Keita, Strickland, & Russo, 1990). Posttraumatic stress disorder is one of the most common effects of sexual abuse, and the symptoms may include chronic depression, periodic nightmares, insomnia, anxiety, inability to feel safe, inability to trust in relationships, volatility, acting-out behavior, and an inability to persist in accomplishing goals. Long-term group psychotherapy is the treatment of choice, in addition to some individual psychotherapy to work through the detrimental effects of such abuse.

Developmental Group Interventions

Developmental group interventions are similar to preventive group interventions in that both are highly preplanned, are focused on a single issue, and attempt to raise consciousness and educate, but they empower through promoting the acquisition or enhancement of crucial life skills after the need for help arises. Moving into adulthood brings with it many developmental tasks. One of those tasks involves redefining one's relationship with one's parents. For instance, an ongoing developmental task of adulthood involves changing and refining the ways one relates to one's parents, from being a dependent child to an independent adult. Ethnic minorities have the same developmental task as other young adults; however, some ethnic minority group members may experience complications in that process, especially if their cultural values place the family over the individual (Sung, 1985; Szapocznik et al., 1986). A person from a Hispanic or Asian family may experience confusion and perhaps even conflict in the process of changing his or her relationships with parents, especially if White peers are used as models for that process. A goal of a developmental group intervention for Hispanics or Asians would thus be to support and strengthen the relationship of ethnic minority group members with their mothers and fathers in a context which recognizes, values, and integrates their bicultural or multicultural realities.

Preventive Group Interventions

Preventive group interventions are designed to help anticipate and prevent problems; they are intended to occur before the need for help arises (Drum & Lawler, 1988). Often, learning theories form the foundation of preventive and developmental group interventions, but both behavioral and experiential, in-depth psychodynamic exploration can be effective in all group interventions at times. A time limited structured group is generally the format of a preventive group intervention. Preventive groups, as previously mentioned, also tend to focus on a single issue and typically have a consciousness-raising and educational component.

Summary

In this chapter, we presented our treatment philosophy for providing group interventions and treatment with ethnic minorities. We used multicultural, feminist, and process-oriented perspectives to discuss factors that contribute to effective group work, group leadership, group composition, and group approaches with ethnic minorities. We hold the assumption that the group is a microcosm for the ethnic minority person's life outside the group and in society at large. We proposed a treatment philosophy that includes the principles of "valuing diversity" and "bicultural/multicultural competence," principles that incorporate the minority's unique minority and majority cultural heritages and experiences with majority–minority dynamics in this society.

Curative factors as discussed by Fedele and Harrington (1990) were elaborated in terms of their application to work with ethnic minorities. Due to ethnic minorities' common experiences as members of an oppressed group, validation, empowerment, self-empathy, and mutuality are considered particularly salient healing factors in group interventions and treatment. Issues of power, self-esteem, identity, and intimacy are also central issues in groups with ethnic minorities. Ethnic or racial composition of group members and leaders was considered, as homogeneous and heterogeneous compositions significantly influence the particular dynamics and processes that arise in a given group. We explored the advantages, challenges, and risks for group members and leaders in homogeneous and heterogeneous ethnic and gender group compositions. Finally, we discussed the use of psychotherapeutic, developmental, and preventive group interventions.

References

Alonso, A. (1987). Discussion of women's groups led by women. *International Journal of Group Psychotherapy, 37*, 155–162.

American Psychological Association. (1993). Guidelines for providers of psychological services to ethnic, linguistic and culturally diverse populations. *American Psychologist, 48*, 45–48.

Atkinson, D., Morten, G., & Sue, D. W. (1989). *Counseling American minorities*. Dubuque, IA: Brown.

Atkinson, D. R., & Wampold, B. E. (1993). Mexican Americans' initial preference counselors: Simple choice can be misleading—Comment on López, López, and Fong (1991). *Journal of Counseling Psychology, 40*, 245–248.

Bennis, W. G., & Shepard, H. A. (1974). A theory of group development. In G. S. Gibbard, J. H. Hartman, & R. Mann (Eds.), *Analysis of groups: Contributions to theory, research and practice* (pp. 127–153). San Francisco: Jossey-Bass.

Bernardez, T. (1983). Women's groups. In M. Rosenbaum (Ed.), *Handbook of short term therapy groups* (pp. 119–138). New York: McGraw-Hill.

Bertcher, J. J. (1979). *Group participation: Techniques for leaders and members*. Beverly Hills, CA: Sage.

Boulette, R. T. (1976). Assertive training with low-income Mexican American women. In M. R. Miranda (Ed.), *Psychotherapy with the Spanish-speaking: Issues in research and service delivery. Monograph 3* (pp. 73–84). Los Angeles: Spanish Speaking Mental Health Research Center, University of California.

Boyd-Franklin, N. (1987). Group therapy for Black women: A therapeutic support model. *American Journal of Orthopsychiatry, 57*, 394–401.

Boyd-Franklin, N. (1991). Recurrent themes in the treatment of African-American women in group psychotherapy. *Women & Therapy, 11*, 25–40.

Chu, J., & Sue, S. (1984). Asian/Pacific Americans and group practice. *Social Work with Groups, 7*, 23–36.

Comas-Díaz, L. (1984). *Ethnicity in group work practice*. New York: Haworth.

Comas-Díaz, L. (1988). Cross-cultural mental health treatment. In L. Comas-Díaz & E. E. H. Griffith (Eds.), *Clinical guidelines in cross-cultural mental health* (pp. 337–361). New York: Wiley.

Comas-Díaz, L. (1981). Effects of cognitive and behavioral group treatment on the depressive symptomatology of Puerto Rican women. *Journal of Consulting and Clinical Psychology, 49*, 627–632.

Comas-Díaz, L., & Griffith, E. E. H. (Eds.). (1988). *Clinical guidelines in cross-cultural mental health*. New York: Wiley.

Comas-Díaz, L., & Jacobsen, F. M. (1987). Ethnocultural identification in psychotherapy. *Psychiatry, 50*, 232–241.

Corey, G. (1990). *Theory and practice of group counseling* (3rd ed.). Pacific Grove, CA: Brooks/Cole.

Cross, W. E., Jr. (1991). *Shades of Black: Diversity in African-American identity*. Philadelphia: Temple University Press.

Davis, L. E. (1984). Essential components of group work with Black Americans. *Ethnicity in Group Work Practice, 7*, 97–109.

Drum, D. J., & Lawler, A. C. (1988). *Developmental interventions: Theories, principles and practice*. Columbus, OH: Merrill.

Ettin, M. (1988). The advent of group psychotherapy. *International Journal of Group Psychology, 38,* 139–167.

Fedele, N. M., & Harrington, E. A. (1990). Women's groups: How connections heal. *Work in progress, No. 47.* Wellesley, MA: Stone Center Working Paper Series.

Helms, J. E. (Ed.). (1990). *Black and White racial identity: Theory, research and practice.* Westport, CT: Greenwood.

Ho, M. K. (1984). Social group work with Asian/Pacific-Americans. In L. E. Davis (Ed.), *Ethnicity in social work practice* (pp. 49–61). New York: Haworth.

Jordan, J. (1989). Relational development: Therapeutic implications of empathy and shame. *Work in progress, No. 23.* Wellesley, MA: Stone Center Working Paper Series.

Jordan, J. V., Surrey, J. L., & Kaplan, A. G. (1991). Women and empathy: Implications for psychological development and psychotherapy. In J. V. Jordan, A. G. Kaplan, J. B. Miller, I. Stiver, & J. Surrey (Eds.), *Women's growth in connection: Writings from the Stone Center* (pp. 27–50). New York: Guilford Press.

Kaplan, H. I., & Sadock, B. J. (Eds.). (1993). *Comprehensive group psychotherapy* (3rd ed.). Baltimore: Williams & Wilkins.

Kaufman, J., & Timmers, R. L. (1986). Searching for the hairy man. *Women & Therapy, 4,* 45–57.

Kaul, J. J., & Bednar, R. L. (1986). Experiential group research: Results, questions, and suggestions. In S. L. Garfield & A. E. Bergin (Eds.), *Handbook of psychotherapy and behavior change* (3rd ed.) (pp. 671–714). New York: Wiley.

Kinzie, J. D., Leung, P., Bui, A., Ben, R., Keopraseuth, K. G., Riley, C., Fleck, J., & Ades, M. (1988). Group therapy with Southeast Asian refugees. *Community Mental Health Journal, 24,* 157–166.

Lakin, M. (1985). *The helping group: Therapeutic principles and issues.* Reading, MA: Addison-Wesley.

Levine, E. S., & Padilla, A. M. (1980). *Crossing cultures in therapy: Pluralistic counseling for the Hispanic.* Monterey, CA: Brooks/Cole.

López, S. R., & López, A. A. (1993). Mexican Americans' initial preferences for counselors: Research methodologies or researchers' values? *Journal of Counseling Psychology, 40,* 249–251.

López, S. R., López, A. A., & Fong, K. T. (1991). Mexican Americans' initial preferences for counselors: The role of ethnic factors. *Journal of Counseling Psychology, 38,* 487–496.

Lubin, B. (1983). Group therapy. In I. B. Weiner (Ed.), *Clinical methods in psychology* (2nd ed.) (pp. 389–446). New York: Wiley.

Martinez, C., Jr. (1993). Psychiatric care of Mexican Americans. In A. C. Gaw (Ed.), *Culture, ethnicity, and mental illness* (pp. 431–466). Washington, DC: American Psychiatric Press.

Mays, V. M. (1986). Black women and stress: Utilization of self-help groups for stress reduction, *Women & Therapy, 4,* 67–79.

McGrath, E., Keita, G. P., Strickland, B. R., & Russo, N. F. (1990). *Women and depression: Risk factors and treatment issues.* Washington, DC: American Psychological Association.

McLeod, L. W., & Pemberton, B. K. (1984). Men together in group therapy. *Voices: Art and Science of Psychotherapy, 20,* 63–69.

Miller, J. B. (1986). *Toward a new psychology of women* (2nd ed.). Boston: Beacon.

Miller, J. B. (1988). Connections, disconnections and violations. *Work in progress, No. 33.* Wellesley, MA.: Stone Center Working Paper Series.

Nayman, R. L. (1983). Group work with Black women: Some issues and guidelines. *Journal for Specialists in Group Work, 8,* 31–38.

Padilla, A. M. (1993, February). *Growing up in two cultures.* Keynote speech presented at the Tenth Annual Teachers College Winter Roundtable on Cross-Cultural Counseling and Psychotherapy, New York City.

Phinney, J. S., & Alipuria, L. L. (1990). Ethnic identity in college students from four ethnic groups. *Journal of Adolescence, 13,* 171–183.

Romos-McKay, J. M., Comas-Díaz, L., & Rivera, L. A. (1988). Puerto Ricans. In L. Comas-Díaz & E. E. H. Griffith (Eds.), *Clinical guidelines in cross-cultural mental health* (pp. 204–232). New York: Wiley.

Rotheram-Borus, M. J. (1989). Ethnic differences in adolescents' identity status and associated behavioral problems. Special issue: Adolescent identity: An appraisal of health and intervention. *Journal of Adolescence, 12,* 361–374.

Rotheram-Borus, M. J. (1990). Adolescents' reference-group choices, self-esteem, and adjustment. *Journal of Personality and Social Psychology, 59,* 1075–1081.

Sabogal, F., Marin, G., Otero-Sabogal, R., Martin, B. V., & Perez-Stable, E. J. (1987). Hispanic familism and acculturation: What changes and what doesn't? *Hispanic Journal of Behavioral Sciences, 9,* 397–412.

Shen, W. W., Sanchez, A. M., & Huang, T. (1984). Verbal participation in group therapy: A comparative study on New Mexico ethnic groups. *Hispanic Journal of Behavior Sciences, 6,* 277–284.

Stein, J. A., Golding, J. M., Siegel, J. M., Burnam, A., & Sorenson, S. (1988). Long-term psychological sequelae of child sexual abuse: The Los Angeles Epidemiologic Catchment Area Study. In G. E. Wyatt & G. J. Powell (Eds.), *The lasting effects of child sexual abuse* (pp. 135–154). Newbury Park, CA: Sage.

Sue, D. W. (1981). *Counseling the culturally different: Theory and practice.* New York: Wiley.

Sue, S., Fujino, D. C., Hu, L., Takeuchi, D. T., & Zane, N. W. S. (1991). Community mental health services for ethnic minority groups: A test of the cultural responsiveness hypothesis. *Journal of Consulting and Clinical Psychology, 59,* 533–540.

Sung, B. L. (1985). Bicultural conflicts in Chinese immigrant children. Special issue: Family, kinship, and ethnic identity among the overseas Chinese. *Journal of Comparative Family Studies, 16,* 255–269.

Surrey, J. L. (1987). Relationship and empower-ment. *Work in progress, No. 30.* Wellesley, MA: Stone Center Working Paper Series.

Szapocznik, J., Rio, A., Perez-Vidal, A., Kurtines, W., Hervis, O., & Santiste-Ban, D. (1986). Bicultural Effectiveness Training (BET): An experimental test of an intervention modality for families experiencing intergenerational/intercultural conflict. *Hispanic Journal of Behavioral Sciences, 8,* 303–330.

Talley, J. E., & Rockwell, W. J. (1985). *Counseling and psychotherapy services for university students.* Springfield, IL: Thomas.

Tannen, D. (1990). *You just don't understand: Men and women in conversation.* New York: Ballantine.

Tatum, B. D. (1993). Racial identity development and relational theory: The case of Black women in White communities. *Work in progress, No. 63.* Wellesley, MA: Stone Center Working Paper Series.

Van Wormer, K. (1989). The male-specific group in alcoholism treatment. *Small Group Behavior, 20,* 228–242.

Verdi, A. F., & Wheelan, S. A. (1992). Developmental patterns in same-sex and mixed-sex groups. *Small Group Research, 23,* 356–378.

Wyatt, G. E. (1990). Sexual abuse of ethnic minority children: Identifying dimensions of victimization. *Professional Psychology: Research and Practice, 21,* 338–343.

Yalom, I. (1985). *The theory and practice of group psychotherapy* (3rd ed.). New York: Basic Books.

Chapter *8*

Community Approaches with Ethnic Groups

JOSEPH F. APONTE
CATHERINE A. MORROW

Goodstein and Sandler (1978) identified several approaches by which the field of psychology can be used to enhance human welfare. These approaches included clinical psychology, community mental health, community psychology, and public policy psychology. This chapter will focus on the *community mental health* and *community psychology* models and the strategies inherent in them. Both of these approaches extend their interventions beyond "troubled individuals" to the community as reflected in the community mental health model, and to social systems that are important in socializing, supporting, and controlling people (e.g., school system, churches, prisons, judicial system) as exemplified in the community psychology model.

These approaches focus on the environmental, social, community, and institutional forces that lead to the development of problems or prevent people from developing as effective human beings. Such a framework is particularly important for ethnic persons, who are often blamed for their plight while oftentimes being the victims of oppression, racism, prejudice, and discrimination (Shapiro, 1975). An approach that focuses on the community will begin to address these experiences and their consequences.

This chapter will focus on community-based approaches. A discussion of *community mental health* approaches and their effectiveness with ethnic clientele is followed by a description of *community psychology* and alternative service delivery models and their common elements. Particular emphasis is placed on prevention and consultation efforts, elements that cut across these models. Several illustrative programs created for ethnic populations that exemplify these common elements are discussed. Finally, guidelines for providing community-based services and intervention strategies are presented.

Community Mental Health Approaches

The community mental health revolution had its roots in the early work of such pioneers as Dorothea Dix, Samuel Tuke, Clifford Beers, Adolph Meyer, Eric Lindemann, and Maxwell Jones (Bloom, 1984; Cutler, 1992), eventually culminating in the formation of the Joint Commission on Mental Illness and Mental Health and the subsequent publication of the commission's 1961 report, *Action for Mental Health* (Appel & Bartemeier, 1961). This report was the basis for President John F. Kennedy's historical proposal for a new national mental health program and the appropriation of funds for planning grants for the program (Kennedy, 1963).

After the death of President Kennedy, Public Law 88-164 (the Community Mental Health Centers Act of 1963) was passed by the U.S. Congress. This and subsequent legislation provided funding for the construction and staffing of a network of community mental health centers (CMHCs) to be located in 1500 designated catchment areas in the United States. The act required that the centers provide five essential services: inpatient, outpatient, emergency, partial hospitalization, and consultation and education. These basic services were viewed as the vehicles for addressing the mental health needs of the country.

Bloom (1984) has noted a number of characteristics of the community mental health movement that were embedded in CMHCs, several of which have direct relevance to ethnic groups. These include the emphasis on (1) the delivery of services or practice in the community, (2) the comprehensiveness and continuity of services, (3) disease prevention and health promotion services, (4) innovative clinical strategies designed to meet the needs of community residents, (5) tapping new sources of personnel including paraprofessionals and indigenous mental health workers, (6) community control, and (7) identifying and eliminating sources of stress within the community.

The early years of the community mental health movement were characterized by great enthusiasm, high expectations, optimism, and rapid development of CMHCs (Cutler, 1992). Many amendments to the original CMHC legislation provided additional funding for the centers, either for categorical services (e.g., substance abuse), or for specific populations (e.g., children, chronically mentally ill, elderly). Ethnic minorities were also recognized as an underserved population in the 1960s and 1970s (Vega & Murphy, 1990). However, efforts to increase funding for these and other high-risk groups, were scuttled by the Omnibus Budget Reconciliation Act of President Reagan, which deeply cut finding for all mental health programs (Foley & Sharfstein, 1983).

Despite the Reagan administration's budget cuts, the majority of the CMHCs remained open (Hadley & Culhane, 1993). During the 1990s, however, in an effort to contain health care costs, a variety of "managed care systems" were developed, including Utilization Review Organizations (UROs), Health Maintenance Organizations (HMOs), and Preferred Provider Organizations (PPOs). These systems are basically designed to reduce either the rates at which services are used or the average cost per unit of service (Herzlinger & Calkins, 1986). Some CMHCs are already operating as managed care systems, perhaps because of the opportunity this approach affords to generate revenues for programs, particularly in light of escalating health care costs and dwindling financial resources (Broskowski & Marks, 1992).

Although ethnic groups were clearly an underserved targeted population in the community mental health movement, the efforts of planners, service providers, and practitioners have met with mixed results. Some studies have found that African Americans and Native Americans overutilized services in comparison to their proportion of the general population, whereas Hispanics and Asian Americans underutilized services (Sue, 1977). More recent investigations reported similar utilization rates in comparison to their respective populations (O'Sullivan, Peterson, Cox, & Kirkeby, 1989), while others have found trends similar to the older data (Bui & Takeuchi, 1992; Snowden & Cheung, 1990; Sue, Fujino, Hu, Takeuchi, & Zane, 1991).

Early research consistently found that ethnic clients had more premature terminations and stayed in treatment for fewer sessions than Whites (Sue, 1977). More recent research showed that these differences have diminished (O'Sullivan et al., 1989); it has been noted, however, that large differences among ethnic groups still remain (Sue et al., 1991; Hu, Snowden, Jerrell, & Nguyen, 1991). Sue and his colleagues (1991) found that African Americans had a significantly higher proportion of treatment dropouts than all other groups, whereas Asian Americans had a lower proportion of dropouts than Whites. Asian Americans tended to stay in treatment longer and African Americans tended to stay in treatment for shorter periods than Whites (Bui & Takeuchi, 1992; Sue et al., 1991).

Little research has been published on treatment outcomes for mental health services received by ethnic clients (see Chapter 16 for an extensive discussion of this topic). The data available indicate that ethnic clients, in general, do not experience outcomes as successful as those of White clients. Closer scrutiny of studies reveals differential outcomes among ethnic groups: African Americans do not have treatment outcomes as successful as Whites, Hispanics, or Asian American clients, even when socioeconomic status is controlled (Sue et al., 1991). These findings, coupled with disproportionately high dropout rates and shorter lengths of stay in treatment, put African Americans at high risk in the mental health system.

Many of the studies available have not controlled for differences in socioeconomic status (SES) and diagnosis (Cheung & Snowden, 1990; Snowden, Storey, & Clancy, 1989). When such variables are controlled statistically, differences in utilization rates, premature termination, treatment duration, and treatment outcomes tend to diminish. Despite these attenuation effects, however, many barriers to service utilization by ethnic populations still exist, including lack of familiarity with mental health services (Keefe & Casas, 1980; Loo, Tong, & True, 1989; Takeuchi, Leaf, & Kuo, 1980), lack of availability of services (LaFromboise, 1988; Solomon,

1988), cost of services (Taube & Rupp, 1986), organizational barriers (Cheung & Snowden, 1990; Zane, Sue, Castro, & George, 1982), and culturally unresponsive services.

Community Psychology Approaches

The previous discussion of traditional community mental health services offered to ethnic clients through the local CMHC described the underutilization of existing services, high dropout rates, premature termination, and general dissatisfaction with these services. The overall effectiveness of the model and its implementation with all groups has also been challenged (Bloom, 1984; Chue, 1974). Many psychologists argued that rather than correcting those shortcomings of the community mental health movement, it was necessary to turn to another approach with a different theoretical, practice, and research base. Such an approach was that of community psychology, which developed in part because of dissatisfaction with more traditional approaches to helping people (Anderson et al., 1966).

Psychologists adhering to a community psychology approach focus on identifying and helping to eliminate deleterious environmental, social, and institutional conditions that affect all members of a population (Iscoe, Bloom, & Spielberger, 1977; Rappaport, 1977). Community psychologists do not restrict the scope of their concern to those with established disorders (Heller et al., 1984). Instead, they focus on situational or contextual contributors to an individual's problems and argue that, whereas individual change can promote a better person–environment fit, efforts to change the environment and social context are often more appropriate targets for intervention.

A community psychology approach to mental health service delivery is decidedly different in its assumptions, goals, research, and practices from the traditional clinical and community mental health approaches (Iscoe et al., 1977). Community psychology has an organizational–community, nondeficit, competence-building, and primary prevention focus (Bloom, 1984; McClure et al., 1980). Differentiation from community mental health, however, according to McClure et al., (1980) has been realized only in its theoretical underpinnings, not in its practice. One key ingredient to a community psychology approach is the construct of *empowerment* (Florin & Wandersman, 1990; Heller et al., 1984; Zimmerman, 1990).

Rappaport (1984) suggests that empowerment can best be understood in the context of what it is not—by seeing it as the absence of alienation, powerlessness, and helplessness. These feelings are often experienced and endured by ethnic group members who are subjected to oppression, racism, and discrimination. Parsons (1989) speaks of empowerment as a process that enables people to master their environment and achieve self-determination. Galan (1988) defines empowerment as self-accountability, a developmental process by which individuals first come to believe in their own competencies for self-mastery, and second, become willing to act in their own best interests. Gutiérrez and Ortega (1991) describe three levels of empowerment: personal, interpersonal, and political. The last level emphasizes the goals of social action and social change.

Common Elements of Alternative Community Service Delivery Models

Alternative community service delivery models seek to incorporate approaches that can have, or have had, demonstrated effectiveness with ethnic populations and clientele. Such approaches, subsumed under the heading of alternative community service delivery models, have been used in both urban and rural settings and with different ethnic groups. Borrowing from the community mental health model, there is a focus on the "catchment area" or community being served, coupled with a strong emphasis on active community board leadership. From the community psychology model, alternative programs also focus on efforts to remediate negative environmental, social, and institutional forces.

Alternative community service delivery models emphasize a number of common elements: (1) ecological validity, (2) a multiproblem approach, (3) a commitment to interagency collaboration and coordination, (4) employment of bilingual and bicultural staff, (5) use of paraprofessionals, (6) development of cultural competency with helping networks, (7) strengthening social support networks, and (8) use of prevention and consultation strategies. Each of these elements is particularly relevant to ethnic persons and will be discussed in the following sections.

Emphasis on Ecological Validity

To achieve ecological validity, the delivery of mental health services must be designed to be consonant with, and not disruptive of, the ongoing relationships, strengths, and resources within the "ecosystem" or community. Rather than relying on the traditional office-based model, nearly all alternative models advocate and deliver treatment in the community. Many programs offer services through local churches, housing projects, beauty and barber shops, malls, and other community facilities frequented by ethnic persons. Such increased availability of services enhance their utilization by low-income groups who may have had difficulty accessing traditional office-based services because of transportation problems.

Going to where clients are, especially ethnic clients whose cultural environment may be quite different from that of the mental health professional, lessens client defenses and encourages the development of empathy, understanding, and rapport on the part of the mental health professional by providing him or her with a realistic and practical understanding of that client's daily demands and stressors. Furthermore, community-based service produces a more accurate needs assessment picture, consequent goal setting, and outcome evaluation. Because of a more accurate assessment, the duration, type, and intensity of services can be tailored to meet the specific needs of the individual client. Given the heterogeneity of ethnic groups, such individualization of service delivery is by far more appropriate than the often traditional reliance on "prepackaged" services (Vega & Murphy, 1990).

Emphasis on a Multiproblem Approach

Most traditional human service delivery systems are organized and financed around targeted categories of problems—for example, income needs, housing, delinquency, substance abuse, and mental health. The ever-increasing caseloads for human service workers may also contribute to a narrowing of focus in that workers rarely consult with each other and may even develop treatment goals that run counter to each other. For ethnic people in need of many services, such decentralization requires clients to establish several effective working relationships with White middle-class staff, successfully negotiate each agency's procedures, organize their appointments, and work toward diverse goals.

Alternative community service delivery models assume a systemic perspective in which adaptive individual and family functioning has, most likely, been impaired by many different and interacting problems. Service providers in these models are deliberately charged with the responsibility to recognize and respond to a range of presenting needs, a tenet that requires that the services offered be holistic and comprehensive (Vega & Murphy, 1990). Effective service delivery to those with multiple problems requires the mental health worker to slip in and out of many roles: teacher, therapist, advocate, organizer, and case manager, to name a few. A broader, more comprehensive focus must be maintained if ethnic clients are to be empowered to act more effectively on their own behalf.

Commitment to Interagency Collaboration and Coordination

Because of the array and complexity of problems with which ethnic clients tend to present to service agencies (Acosta, Yamamoto, & Evans, 1982), particularly if they come from low-SES or immigrant backgrounds, it is imperative that community agencies collaborate with each other. Such efforts would avoid duplication of services and maintain continuity of care, while also ensuring that community needs are being met. To achieve this latter goal, the value of maintaining an open dialogue with community representatives cannot be overemphasized.

Gordon (1991) illustrates how conflicting attitudes and inaccurate beliefs regarding agency practices on the part of other community agencies, as well as indigenous leaders, can result in a drop in referral rates and negative expectations regarding the likelihood of receiving effective treatment. In instances where formal and informal linkages were achieved with community groups (e.g., churches), ethnic persons were more aware of services and were also more likely to use them in times of need (Starrett, Todd, Decker, & Walters, 1989). Eng and Hatch (1991) describe an effective lay health advisory model for networking between Black churches and agencies.

Marburg (1983) suggested several mechanisms by which better relations among community organizations could be formed. These included monthly, reciprocal inservice training presentations to provide detailed descriptions of available ser-vices, community forums to discuss gaps in service delivery with suggestions for remediation, and attempts to open avenues of communication for the purposes of reducing atmospheres conducive to "turf wars." Such efforts would be beneficial to all service recipients but would be particularly helpful for providers, who frequently lack cultural knowledge and practical experience in working with ethnic clientele.

Employment of Bilingual and Bicultural Staff

High visibility of bilingual, and preferably bicultural, staff not only encourages ethnic group members to seek out services initially, but also aids in establishing rapport and helps to build trust among the client, the service provider, and the agency in general (Reeves, 1986). The mental health provider who can converse in the particular language or dialect spoken in the community is in a much better position to understand the symbolism, idiosyncrasies, and life experiences of his or her clients and, therefore, to provide appropriate services (see Chapter 2). An additional benefit of employing ethnically similar personnel is the opportunity for these professionals to serve as role models for the ethnic client (Curtis, 1990).

Use of Paraprofessionals

Well-organized alternative programs realize that one of the best ways to establish effective working relationships with ethnic communities is to utilize indigenous resources and paraprofessionals (Lefley & Bestman, 1991; Snowden, 1987). Gordon (1991) reported that the most important resource for identification and intervention with Hispanic alcohol abusers is not the treatment professional but, rather, the Hispanic female paraprofessional from the neighborhood with whom the client may already be acquainted. Hispanic women, especially, tended to disclose information regarding alcohol-abusing spouses to Hispanic workers but not to the physician or counselor. Consequently, Gordon suggests that ethnic paraprofessionals should receive special training in problem identification and in motivating clients to commit to treatment.

Development of Cultural Competency with Helping Networks

Unlike White majority persons, ethnic persons must continuously grapple with issues of ethnic identity (see Chapter 2). Through this process, many members of ethnic groups adaptively struggle to develop cultural competencies with both their culture and the majority culture, thereby filtering advantages from both as best they can. Whereas some are remarkably successful in their endeavors, others experience rejection and ridicule, and lack a sense of truly belonging to either group. Given the fact that they often come into mental health treatment via other community agen-cies, such as the court, social services, or school, some ethnic clients may lack sophistication regarding the different responsibilities of the many agencies to which they are referred. Such experiences, coupled with the insensitivity sometimes exhibited by White middle-class professionals, can lead to problems for the ethnic person in the mental health system.

Many alternative models recognize the need to teach ethnic clients how to network with formal supports available in the community (e.g., job training, public school personnel, medical care professionals, mental health professionals, civic organizations). Workers from programs may accompany ethnic clients on appointments with other service workers to provide support and to model appropriate ways of gathering information, enlisting services, and clearly detailing contractual responsibilities so that the service provider and the client walk away with mutual understanding. In the same way that service providers need to be culturally competent with ethnic cultures, clients need the requisite skills to represent their needs, abilities, and expectations effectively to the majority culture.

Strengthening Social Support Networks

Social support networks are used extensively by African Americans, Hispanics, Asian Americans, and Native Americans (see Chapter 2). African Americans who receive informal support from family, friends, and other respected individuals in their community tend to utilize formal service networks to a greater degree than do those with less social support (Eng & Hatch, 1991; Mindel & Wright, 1982; Spence & Atherton, 1991). Building social support networks into treatment interventions through the involvement of family members can lead to enhanced levels of mutual support among family members, more effective dealings with community agencies, and the development of advocacy groups to deal with common social issues (Aponte, Zarski, Bixenstine, & Cibik, 1991; Keefe & Casas, 1980).

Instead of traditional strategies, which focus on the community agency as the sole deliverer of services, alternative models suggest that ethnic minorities who may be hesitant to seek formal services may best be helped by utilizing agency resources to organize and strengthen natural helping networks within the community (Mays, 1986). Such self-help groups serve many purposes. They provide mutual support (Gottlieb, 1982), reduce isolation and alienation (Mays, 1986; Parsons, 1989), afford a sense of community and in-group membership (Katz, 1981), encourage the development of personal empowerment to better manage one's own life, and provide opportunities for people to form social action groups for political empowerment (Gutierrez & Ortega, 1991).

Prevention and Consultation Strategies

Prevention and consultation strategies are often used with alternative community service delivery models. Prevention has traditionally been divided into three categories: primary, secondary, and tertiary prevention. Heller et al. (1984) suggest the following definitions: *Primary prevention* refers to efforts aimed at keeping mental disorders from occurring at all; *secondary prevention* refers to reducing the duration and severity of disorders which do occur; and *tertiary prevention* attempts to minimize the extent of disability of impairment that may result from disorders. Forgays (1991) argues that secondary and tertiary prevention are not really prevention, and it is in the focus on primary prevention that community-based programs can have a significant impact on its population.

Heller et al. (1984) define *consultation* as "an approach to social change through improvement of existing community organizations and institutions" (p. 231). Consultation efforts are often included in primary prevention programs (Bell, 1987; Mann, 1987) but are more commonly included within secondary prevention programs (DeBruyn, Hymbaugh, & Valdez, 1988; Tolan, Perry, & Jones, 1987; Tyler, Cohen, & Clark, 1982). Consultation efforts target existing networks of primary caregivers and agents of social control, such as teachers, police, ministers, physicians, and welfare workers. Implicit in the operating principles of consultation is that the community has the strengths and expertise to solve its own problems; consultants merely act as catalysts and assistants to motivate and mobilize indigenous community leaders to take action.

Examples of Community-Based Programs

To illustrate the aforementioned elements of alternative community approaches, several programs will be described in this section: (1) the Black on Black Violence Program developed by Bell (1987); (2) the Hispanic Program designed by Delgado and Scott (1979); (3) the South Cove Community Health Center, which targeted Chinese elderly (Lee & Yee, 1988); and (4) the Mental Health Program at Keams Canyon Indian Hospital and Clinics (Marburg, 1983). Though targeting specific groups, each of these programs has relevance to all ethnic populations.

Black on Black Violence

Bell (1987) reports that Black males have a 1 in 21 chance of being murdered, whereas White males have a 1 in 121 chance. Similarly, Black females have a 1 in 194 chance, White females a 1 in 369 chance. Homicide is the leading cause of death among young Black males; they are 7.6 times more likely to be killed by homicide than their White counterparts (O'Hare, Pollard, Mann, & Kent, 1991). Furthermore, two-thirds to three-quarters of Black homicide victims will know their murderer as family member, friend, or acquaintance. Thus, a majority of Black-on-Black murders occur in the context of familiar interpersonal relationships.

To address the devastating effects of such violence on the African-American community, Bell's initial efforts were aimed at consciousness raising and support building from both community agencies and the community at large. Toward that end, the following strategies were employed: A series of question-and-answer sessions staffed by experts in interpersonal violence were broadcast on call-in radio programs; an advisory board to the local CMHC was formed; and a citywide, multimedia blitz billed as "No Crime Day" was held. Such efforts had the impact of making the community more aware of the seriousness and nature of the problem.

Surveys of several CMHCs' catchment area schools resulted in alarming statistics: 31 percent of second, fourth, sixth, and eighth graders had seen someone shot; 34 percent had seen a person stabbed; and 84 percent had witnessed someone being beaten. Armed with these data, the local CMHC sponsored a retreat for concerned families in order to develop strategies to reduce family volence. Out of this retreat grew a women's support group for battered and abused women and an Elderly Respite Care Service. Other primary prevention strategies included vocational programs to help clients start their own businesses and programs, which provided recreational activities to community youth as an alternative to gang membership.

Secondary prevention efforts included the development of a screening instrument used at the CMHC to identify victims of violence. Once identified, clients were referred to the CMHC's Victim Assistance Service for information regarding legal aid. CMHC staff also developed liaison relationships with a community women's shelter in order to safely harbor women and children, and with community ministers to raise their sensitivity to issues of family violence. Thus, both primary and secondary prevention components of the program were comprehensive and involved continuity of services through an array of networks.

The Hispanic Program

To meet the unmet mental health needs in the Puerto Rican subcommunity of their city, Delgado and Scott (1979) developed a series of innovative programs that they described as a "strategic intervention." Given that the Puerto Rican population of their catchment area had expanded rapidly but that utilization rates were even lower than those of other ethnic groups, their overriding goal was to encourage culturally-relevant service provision through various avenues, including (1) community/institutional consultation and education programs, (2) advocacy efforts, and (3) the "barrio service center" model.

To help other social agencies and institutions improve their services to Puerto Ricans, program staff trained their non-Hispanic staff to understand Puerto Rican culture. They also targeted public school teachers to provide a conceptual framework for appreciating assimilation issues and the role that environmental factors play in intrapsychic conflicts (see Chapter 2). Additionally, the program applied for and received a grant to identify and train a host of indigenous community leaders for potential membership on social agency boards. To help them learn the bureaucratic language and processes, training covered issues of organizational bylaws, parliamentary procedures, budgets, fund raising, and general priniciples of community organization.

Needs assessment efforts identified that many community agencies seemed to hire only one Hispanic staff member to serve nearly all their Hispanic clientele, which suggested that turnover and burnout from excessive clinical responsibilities were likely to occur. Consequently, the program advocated hiring additional Hispanic professionals and paraprofessionals, and also collaborated with agencies by agreeing to provide ongoing training, consultation, and program development to new recruits brought in by agencies. Finally, additional needs assessments were carried out in order to identify the most pressing needs of the Hispanic community. Armed with those data, program consultants were able to bring increased pressure on service delivery systems to address specifically the areas of documented need.

Direct services to Hispanic residents were provided via the "barrio service center" model. Program offices were located in the sections of town with the highest concentration of Puerto Ricans, staff were bilingual and bicultural, and family members were included in the treatment process whenever possible. Importantly, program clinicians often visited the homes of their Puerto Rican clients to observe family interactions directly and to model appropriate coping and problem-solving skills in vivo.

The South Cove Community Health Center (SCCHC)

Lee and Yee (1988) suggest that the tendency for Asian immigrant populations to live in and depend on close-knit ethnic enclaves (e.g., Chinatowns) may serve to maintain barriers when interacting in Western society. Of particular concern to these authors is the process by which traditional Chinese beliefs about health and illness, language, and the lack of continuity of care act as cultural barriers to adequate health care services for Asian elderly. For example, traditional Chinese thought considers blood a vital entity that cannot be replaced. As a result, many elderly persons actively avoid Western health practitioners who order blood tests for diagnostic purposes.

To improve the accessibility and quality of health care for Chinese elderly in their community, these authors initiated a three-pronged intervention. First, they developed home health care services for debilitated elderly. Staffed by bilingual nurse practitioners, this program provided primary care services in the patient's home. Second, they centralized health care services by establishing satellite medical clinics, also staffed by bilingual personnel, in several elderly housing complexes in and around Chinatown. Third, a health eduation program, presented to regular meetings of elderly people, provided instruction on various health-related topics as well as a forum in which elderly persons could discuss cultural barriers, learn about the Western system, and learn how better to obtain services for themselves.

Despite these efforts, however, inadequate interagency communication created a lack of effectively coordinated services. To address this lack of coordination, the SCCHC initiated a new project to introduce the role and concept of case management to the Chinese elderly community, to help elderly patients and their families coordinate posthospital care, and to respond to the loneliness and isolation experienced by many homebound elderly. To address this latter issue, a volunteer program of primarily bilingual high school and college students was developed to visit homebound elderly persons regularly for companionship.

Mental Health Program at Keam's Canyon Indian Hospital and Clinics

Operating on a culturally consistent model that stresses the integration of physical and mental health, Marburg (1983) describes a rural, hospital-based community mental health program that utilizes an array of remedial, developmental, and preventive strategies to respond to the unique needs of Native Americans. Located on the Hopi Indian Reservation, the program includes as components inpatient services, outpatient services, outreach efforts, aftercare services, and the development of consulting networks in the community.

An integral part of coordinated inpatient service delivery is a mental health consultation team, led by a senior psychologist who has full clinical and voting privileges as a member of the medical staff. Congruent with the goals of implementing the biopsychosocial approach to holistic health care, mental health consultation staff collaborate with physicians and attend medical rounds daily. Outpatient services include the full spectrum of therapy options, such as individual psychotherapy, marital and family therapy, and substance abuse counseling. Among the Hopi and Navajo served, these therapies are frequently expanded to include multigenerational intervention strategies and more often than not require the services of an expert translator.

Outreach and aftercare services were founded on the premise that continuity of care following hospitalization is crucial. One aspect of continuity is helping the client develop or strengthen his or her personal social networks within the community. Helping the client to open communication channels with family members and other significant members in his or her community, such as traditional healers, clan leaders, or village chiefs, greatly facilitates meaningful psychosocial reintegration into the community. Additionally, the program sought to develop and strengthen a system of formal and informal consultation networks by which to respond to pressing clinical issues raised by community groups such as school psychologists, non-Western traditional healers, Tribal Alcoholism Centers, Tribal Court, and Tribal Police.

Each of these community-based programs has elements of the alternative community service delivery models. The programs were particularly consistent with the values, beliefs, and practices within the community; all involved a miltiproblem approach, included interagency collaboration and coordination, focused on the ethnic individual developing personal competency in dealing with helping networks, and encouraged the development of social support networks. Some of the programs utilized bilingual staff and paraprofessionals to deliver their services. It was evident from the published reports that all the programs were sensitive and responsive to those community residents they served.

Guidelines for Using Community-Based Approaches with Ethnic Groups

Effective delivery of alternative community services and programs requires effective planning. Such planning needs to be based on detailed information about the community and its residents (Humm-Delgado & Delgado, 1986; Vega & Murphy, 1990). Ethnic community leaders and residents should be invited and warmly welcomed to participate in needs assessment planning in order to ensure that program goals are consistent with community-held values and to customize services, thereby enhancing a sense of community ownership of the program (Bell, 1987; Heller, 1992; Tyler, Cohen, & Clark, 1982). The needs assessment can take the form of using key informant, community survey, and social area analysis strategies (Aponte, 1983; Aponte & Young, 1981).

Those services and programs directed at ethnic populations need to be conceptualized, developed, and implemented at multiple levels within society and the community. The impact of environmental and social forces such as poverty, racism, and oppression on individuals from ethnic groups cannot be overlooked. Community psychology and its subareas, such as social ecology, need to move beyond merely classifying social environments and forces to developing and implementing interventions that clearly achieve environmental changes for the improved psychological well-being of people (Insel, 1980).

Developers of alternative community service models directed at ethnic populations may find it helpful to use unorthodox methods of marketing, such as advertisement on ethnic radio stations, television commercials, billboards, fliers in ethnic grocery stores, and restaurants to provide outreach efforts in disseminating service and program information (Spence & Atherton, 1991). Other useful techniques are to make bilingual staff highly visible in the ethnic community via speaking engagements at church and civic organizations. Such efforts should clarify how the service model operates and how it may be different from the traditional services they may have received in the past.

Service delivery must be flexible to meet the needs of individual communities (Applewhite, Wong, & Daley, 1991). After a careful needs assessment for the targeted population, services should be organized and designed to achieve an appropriate balance between direct and indirect service provision. Those services that are provided through CMHCs should be culturally sensitive, compatible, and relevant (Campinha-Bacote, 1991; Flaskerud, 1986; Rogler, Malgady, & Costantino, 1987) and may require the use of different service delivery models (Campinha-Bacote, 1991; Padilla, Ruiz, & Alvarez, 1975; Uba, 1982) that allow services to be delivered more directly and effectively to various ethnic groups in the community.

Services should be organized in such a way that ethnic clients are asked to disclose personal information to as few program representatives as possible. For example, many traditional CMHCs operate in hierarchical fashion, so that a client may be interviewed by one person for the intake, another for assessment, then finally the therapist. Because many ethnic clients present with an understandably suspicious demeanor, such organizational hierarchies may simply add to feelings of frustration and pessimism about the likelihood of benefit. By contrast, interacting with few, preferably bilingual, staff members seems much more "user-friendly" and is likely to facilitate trust and positive expectations from clients.

Outside community agencies must accurately understand the goals of the alternative program, its intended target population, and what it is *not* intended to do. If other community agencies do not have accurate perceptions of new programs, inappropriate referrals may occur. All links in the community chain must work together to provide integrated services. Those agencies that should be targeted in any community include but are not limited to the following: vocational rehabilitation services, hospital emergency rooms and walk-in medical clinics, state psychiatric facilities, local CMCHs, local substance abuse centers, public school personnel, housing authority, rape crisis centers, homeless shelters, and social service agencies.

Thus far, several guidelines by which alternative models can be implemented have been discussed. Careful needs assessment, multilevel intervention, creative marketing, flexibility of direct and indirect service provision, a streamlined "intake" process, and ongoing efforts to maintain interagency collaboration are all necessary but not sufficient elements of community change. No matter how well organized the program or how skilled the staff, the ethnic community itself remains the most powerful resource for improving the quality of life for its ethnic citizens. The sense of community involvement and ability to effect change is essential to combating helplessness, lack of power, and pessimism in ethnic persons.

Community-based approaches may begin by sending empowering messages to the community via ongoing community education, outreach advertisement, and recruitment of volunteer help in order to create an awareness of the community's needs, resources, and strengths. Efforts need to be directed toward strengthening informal social networks of community members and encouraging strong indigenous leadership. Education programs designed to emphasize shared cultural history, values, and accomplishments can be used to develop cohesion and team building. Encouraging pride and the development of positive aspects of ethnic identity reduces feelings of powerlessness, helplessness, and lack of involvement. In the final analysis, empowerment remains the key for initiating and maintaining effective communitywide change.

References

Acosta, F. X., Yamamoto, J., & Evans, L. A. (1982). *Effective psychotherapy for low-income and minority patients.* New York: Plenum Press.

Anderson, L. S., Cooper, S., Hassol, L., Klein, D. C., Rosenblum, G., & Bennett, C. C. (1966). *Community psychology: A report of the Boston Conference on the Education of Psychologists for Community Mental Health.* Boston: Boston University.

Aponte, J. F. (1983). Need assessment: The state of the art and future directions. In R. A. Bell, M. Sundel, J. F. Aponte, S. A. Murrell, & E. Lin (Eds.), *Assessing human service needs: Concepts, methods, and applications* (pp. 285–302). New York: Human Sciences Press.

Aponte, J. F., & Young, R. (1981). *Need assessments with minority groups: Conceptual, methodological, and utilization issues.* Paper presented at the Third National Conference on Needs Assessment in Health and Human Service Systems, Louisville, KY.

Aponte, H. J., Zarski, J. J., Bixenstine, C., & Cibik, P. (1991). Home/community-based services: A two-tier approach. *American Journal of Orthopsychiatry, 61,* 403-408

Appel, K. E., & Bartemeier, L. H. (1961). *Action for mental health: Final report of the Joint Commission on Mental Illness and Health.* New York: Basic Books.

Applewhite, S. R., Wong, P., & Daley, J. M. (1991).

Service approaches and issues in Hispanic agencies. *Administration and Policy in Mental Health, 19*, 27–37

Bell, C. C. (1987). Preventive strategies for dealing with violence among Blacks. *Community Mental Health Journal, 23*, 217–228.

Bloom, B. L. (1984). *Community mental health: A general introduction* (2nd ed.). Monterey, CA: Brooks/Cole.

Broskowski, A., & Marks, E. (1992). Managed mental health care. In S. Cooper & T. H. Lentner (Eds.), *Innovations in community mental health* (pp. 23–49). Sarasota, FL: Professional Resource Press.

Bui, K. T., & Takeuchi, D. T. (1992). Ethnic minority adolescents and the use of community mental health care services. *American Journal of Community Psychology, 20*, 403–417.

Campinha-Bacote, J. (1991). Community mental health services for the underserved: A culturally specific model. *Archives of Psychiatry Nursing, 5*, 229–235.

Cheung, F. K., & Snowden, L. R. (1990). Community mental health and ethnic minority populations. *Community Mental Health Journal, 26*, 277–291.

Chu, F. D. (1974). The Nader report: One author's perspective. *American Journal of Psychiatry, 131*, 775–779.

Curtis, P. A. (1990). The consequences of acculturation to service delivery and research with Hispanic families. *Child and Adolescent Social Work, 7*, 147–160.

Cutler, D. L. (1992). A historical overview of community mental health centers in the United States. In S. Cooper & T. H. Lentner (Eds.), *Innovations in community mental health* (pp. 1–22). Sarasota, FL: Professional Resource Press.

De Bruyn, L. M., Hymbaugh, K., & Valdez, N. (1988). Helping communities address suicide and violence: The Special Initiatives Team of the Indian Health Service. *American Indian and Alaska Native Mental Health Research, 1*, 56–65.

Delgado, M., & Scott, J. F. (1979). Strategic intervention: A mental health program for the Hispanic community. *Journal of Community Psychology, 7*, 187–197.

Eng, E., & Hatch, J. W. (1991). Networking between agencies and Black churches: The lay adviser model. *Prevention in Human Services, 10*, 123–146.

Flaskerud, J. H. (1986). The effects of culture-compatible intervention on the utilization of mental health services by minority clients. *Community Mental Health Journal, 22*, 127–141.

Florin, P., & Wandersman, A. (1990). An introduction to citizen participation, voluntary organizations, and community development: Insights for empowerment through research. *American Journal of Community Psychology, 18*, 41–54.

Foley, H. A., & Sharfstein, S. S. (1983). *Madness in government: Who cares for the mentally ill?* Washington, DC: American Psychiatric Press.

Forgays, D. G. (1991). Primary prevention of psychopathology. In M. Hersen, A. E. Kazdin, & A. S. Bellack (Eds.), *The clinical psychology handbook* (2nd ed.) (pp. 743–761). New York: Pergamon Press.

Galan, F. J. (1988). Alcoholism prevention and Hispanic youth. *Journal of Drug Issues, 18*, 49–58.

Goodstein, L. D., & Sandler, I. (1978). Using psychology to promote human welfare: A conceptual analysis of the role of community psychology. *American Psychologist, 33*, 882–892.

Gordon, A. J. (1991). Alcoholism treatment services to Hispanics: An ethnographic examination of a community's services. *Family and Community Health, 13*, 12–24.

Gottlieb, B. H. (1982). Mutual help groups: Members' views of their benefits and of roles for professionals. *Prevention in Human Services, 1*, 55–67.

Gutiérrez, L. M., & Ortega, R. (1991). Developing methods to empower Latinos: The importance of groups. *Social Work with Groups, 14*, 23–43.

Hadley, T. R., & Culhane, D. P. (1993). The status of community mental health centers ten years into block grant financing. *Community Mental Health Journal, 29*, 95–102.

Heller, K. (1992). Ingredients for effective community change: Some field observations. *American Journal of Community Psychology, 20*, 143–160.

Heller, K., Price, R. H., Reinharz, S., Riger, S., Wandersman, A., & D'Aunno, T. A. (1984). *Psychology and community change: Challenges of the future* (2nd ed.). Pacific Grove, CA: Brooks/Cole.

Herzlinger, R., & Calkins, D. (1986). How companies tackle health care costs: Part III. *Harvard Business Review, 64,* 70–80.

Hu, T., Snowden, L. R., Jerrell, J. M., & Nguyen, T. D. (1991). Ethnic populations in public mental health: Services choice and level of use. *American Journal of Public Health, 81,* 1429–1434.

Humm-Delgado, D., & Delgado, M. (1986). Gaining community entrée to assess service needs of Hispanics. *Social Casework, 67,* 80–89.

Insel, P. M. (1980). Task force report: The social climate of mental health. *Community Mental Health Journal, 16,* 62–78.

Iscoe, I., Bloom, B. L., & Spielberger, C. D. (Eds.). (1977). *Community psychology in transition: Proceedings of the National Conference on Training in Community Psychology.* New York: Hemisphere.

Katz, A. H. (1981). Self-help and mutual aid: An emerging social movement. *Annual Review of Sociology, 7,* 129–155.

Keefe, S. E., & Casas, J. M. (1980). Mexican Americans and mental health: A selected review and recommendations for mental health service delivery. *American Journal of Community Psychology, 8,* 303–326.

Kennedy, J. F. (1963). *Message from the President of the United States Relative to Mental Illness and Mental Retardation* (88th Congress, 1st Session, Document 58). Washington, DC: U.S. Governmant Printing Office.

LaFromboise, T. D. (1988). American Indian mental health policy. *American Psychologist, 43,* 388–397.

Lee, S. S., & Yee, A. K. (1988). The development of community-based health services for minority elderly in Boston's Chinatown. *Pride Institute Journal of Long-Term Home Health Care, 7,* 3–9.

Lefley, H. P., & Bestman, E. W. (1991). Public-academic linkages for culturally sensitive community mental health. *Community Mental Health Journal, 27,* 473–488.

Loo, C., Tong, B., & True, R. (1989). A bitter bean: Mental health status and attitudes in Chinatown. *Journal of Community Psychology, 17,* 283–296.

Mann, P. A. (1987). Prevention of child abuse: Two contrasting social support services. *Prevention in Human Services, 4,* 73–111.

Marburg, G. S. (1983). Mental health and native Americans: Responding to the challenge of the biopsychosocial model. *White Cloud Journal, 3,* 43–51.

Mays, V. (1986). Black women and stress utilization of self-help groups for stress reduction. *Women & Therapy, 4,* 67–79.

McClure, L., Cannon, D., Belton, E., D'Ascoli, C., Sullivan, B., Allen, S., Connor, P., Stone, P., & McClure, G. (1980). Community psychology concepts and research base: Promise and product. *American Psychologist, 35,* 1000–1011.

Mindel, C. H., & Wright, R., Jr. (1982). The use of social services by Black and White elderly: The role of social support systems. *Journal of Gerontological Social Work, 4,* 107–120.

O'Hare, W. P., Pollard, K. M., Mann, T. L., & Kent, K. M. (1991). African Americans in the 1990s. *Population Bulletin, 46,* 1–40.

O'Sullivan, M. J., Peterson, P. D., Cox, G. B., & Kirkeby, J. (1989). Ethnic populations: Community mental health services ten years later. *American Journal of Community Psychology, 17,* 17–30.

Padilla, A. M., Ruiz, R. A., & Alvarez, R. (1975). Community mental health services for the Spanish-speaking/surnamed population. *American Psychologist, 20,* 892–905.

Parsons, R. J. (1989). Empowerment for role alternatives for low income minority girls: A group work approach. *Social Work with Groups, 11,* 27–45.

Rappaport, J. (1977). *Community psychology: Values, research, and action.* New York: Holt, Rinehart & Winston.

Rappaport, J. (1984). Studies in empowerment: Introduction to the issue. *Prevention in Human Services, 3,* 1–7.

Reeves, K. (1986). Hispanic utilization of an ethnic mental health clinic. *Journal of Psychosocial Nursing and Mental Health Services, 24,* 23–26.

Rogler, L. H., Malgady, R. G., & Costantino, G. (1987). What do culturally sensitive mental health services mean? The case of Hispanics. *American Psychologist, 42,* 565–570.

Shapiro, R. (1975). Discrimination and community mental health. *Civil Rights Digest, 8,* 19–23.

Snowden, L. R. (1987). The peculiar successes of community psychology: Service delivery to ethnic minorities and the poor. *American Journal of Community Psychology, 15,* 575–586.

Snowden, L. R., & Cheung, F. K. (1990). Use of inpatient mental health services by members of ethnic minority groups. *American Psychologist, 45,* 347–355.

Snowden, L. R., Storey, C., & Clancy, T. (1989). Ethnicity and continuation in treatment at a Black community mental health center. *Journal of Community Psychology, 17,* 111–118.

Solomon, P. (1988). Racial factors in mental health service utilization. *Psychosocial Rehabilitation Journal, 11,* 3–12.

Spence, S. A., & Atherton, C. R. (1991). The Black elderly and the social service delivery system: A study of factors influencing the use of community-based services. *Journal of Gerontological Social Work, 16,* 19–35.

Starrett, R. A., Todd, A. M., Decker, J. T., & Walters, G. (1989). The use of formal helping networks to meet the psychological needs of the Hispanic elderly. *Hispanic Journal of Behavioral Sciences, 11,* 259–273.

Sue, S. (1977). Community mental health services to minority groups: Some optimism, some pessimism. *American Psychologist, 32,* 616–624.

Sue, S., Fujino, D. C., Hu, L. T., Takeuchi, D. T., & Zane, N. W. S. (1991). Community mental health services for ethnic minority groups: A test of the cultural responsiveness hypothesis. *Journal of Consulting and Clinical Psychology, 59,* 533–540.

Takeuchi, D. T., Leaf, P. J., & Kuo, H. S. (1980). Ethnic differences in the perception of barriers to help seeking. *Social Psychiatry and Psychiatric Epidemiology, 23,* 273–280.

Taube, C., & Rupp, A. (1986). The effect of Medicaid on access to ambulatory mental health care for the poor and near-poor under 65. *Medical Care, 24,* 677–686.

Tolan, P. H., Perry, M. S., & Jones, T. (1987). Delinquency prevention: An example of consultation in rural community mental health. *Journal of Community Psychology, 15,* 43–50.

Tyler, J. D., Cohen, K. N., & Clark, J. S. (1982). Providing community consultation in a reservation setting. *Journal of Rural Community Psychology, 3,* 49–58.

Uba, L. (1982). Meeting the mental health needs of Asian Americans: Mainstream or segregated services. *Professional Psychology, 13,* 215–221.

Vega, W. A., & Murphy, J. W. (1990). *Culture and the restructuring of community mental health.* New York: Greenwood.

Zane, N., Sue, S., Castro, E. G., & George, W. (1982). Service system models for ethnic minorities. In L. R. Snowden (Ed.), *Reaching the underserved: Mental health needs of neglected populations* (pp. 229–258). Beverly Hills, CA: Sage.

Zimmerman, M. A. (1990). Taking aim on empowerment research: On the distinction between individual and psychological conceptions. *American Journal of Community Psychology, 18,* 169–177.

Chapter 9

Traditional and Folk Approaches among Ethnic Minorities

JOAN D. KOSS-CHIOINO

While anthropologists have had a long-standing interest in traditional and folk healing (referred to in this chapter as "ethnomedical systems"), psychologists and other behavioral scientists have only recently begun to consider the importance of these practices to ethnic minority peoples. All ethnic groups have transferred to the United States many or all of their main beliefs and practices connected to healing. There is evidence that these practices have undergone significant changes and in some cases have even intensified as a result of the difficult adaptations ethnic minority persons face in a societal environment that can be economically and psychologically stressful, even hostile, for newcomers. These difficult conditions become even more salient for ethnomedical practice when we consider that healing beliefs and practices are multivocal in terms of what they symbolize for both practitioners and clients.

Symbols inherent in ethnomedical practices connote and represent concerns about ethnic identity, selfhood, world view, expressions of family and community values, and reaffirmations of cultural cohesiveness and tradition. Additionally, traditional and folk healing systems are commonly interrelated with or encompassed by religious and political goals. Unlike what is often described for biomedicine, that it serves only to prevent or cure disease, or for psychotherapy, that it is aimed mainly at treating emotional disorders (although these perspectives are more ideal than actual, since both marginally serve many other goals), alternative healing systems in ethnic minority communities are formally multidimensional, in part because they are often embedded in the processes by which ethnic individuals and their communities adapt to their adopted environments. It must also be noted that alternative healing practices can also be found in White-majority, middle-class suburban communities (McGuire, 1988) implying fulfillment of needs that go beyond those served by either biomedicine or psychotherapy.

Scope of the Chapter

This chapter first presents an overview of ethnomedical systems in the larger ethnic minority populations in the United States (Hispanic-American, African-American, Asian-American, Native American), beginning with a relatively detailed description of Hispanic ethnomedical systems as models of traditional perspectives on etiology, diagnosis, healing process, healer initiation and training, beliefs, ritual practices, and patterns of utilization. Finally, the nature of the interface between psychotherapeutic treatment and ethnomedicine in ethnic minority groups is explored, as are the possibilities of integrating ethnomedical approaches into standard treatment modalities. Since there are many ethnic groups as well as variations within both the groups and their healing systems, only highlights of these phenomena can be described here. The intent is to illustrate variability in types and modes of traditional healing found in the United States. Each ethnic category includes very different cultural traditions, such as Puerto Rican, Cuban, and Mexican in the Hispanic cultural tradition, and these will be examined separately.

Individual cultural differences are reflected in indigenous traditional healing practices; however, extensive borrowing and some cross-utilization also takes place. Despite variations associated with different Hispanic cultures, the reader will appreciate that there are also a number of broad similarities, such as these:

1. There is a widespread belief that the cause of illness and misfortune has a locus external to the individual and is mostly spiritual (or spiritual combined with physical aspects).
2. Frequent group participation in healing ritual is often preferred to individual sessions.
3. The individual as sufferer is most often treated as if within a family or community.
4. Morality, as both cause of illness and condition for recovery, is integral to healing.
5. The healing process depends largely on nonverbal and symbolic interactions (Koss, 1986; Koss-Chioino, 1992).

In these and other ways, traditional healing in Hispanic populations (as well as in other ethnic groups) is very different from the psychology-based concepts and practices found in standard psychotherapeutic treatments. However, interpretations can be made (many are found in the literature) that describe parallel psychological processes and effects (such as catharsis). Some of these parallels will be included in the descriptions that follow.

Before we proceed, a number of background assumptions must be explained. Basic to understanding traditional healing systems is that they are conceptually constructed and organized on their own terms. They often ignore (simply do not consider) the mind–body distinction and are not based on the logicodeductive scientific paradigm of biomedicine that focuses on the body as most relevant to diagnosis and treatment, and secondarily focuses on "mind" or psyche, both of which are assumed to have a physical structure and locus (Koss-Chioino, 1992). Salient differences in paradigms between healing systems will be discussed. The main contrasting paradigms are what have been labeled in the literature as *etic* (scientific, universal) versus *emic* (the insider, relativistic view), and may be associated with biomedical and ethnomedical (traditional, folk) systems, respectively. It can be argued, however that all medical/healing systems are shaped by the values, world, and self-views of the cultures in which they develop and are utilized; therefore, all healing systems are "ethnomedical." The far-reaching implication is that not every healing system or practice can be assessed by the same (standard, universal) measures. Each is constructed of its own set of meanings and views of self and world. Each has its own set of rules and a particular logic within a paradigm and structure made up of interrelated (however loosely) parts.

These perspectives will be illustrated in the following descriptions of the healing systems in each of the ethnic subcultures to be discussed. It is also important to note that the terms *traditional* and *folk* do not represent hard and fast categories that are easily differentiated. Generally, these terms allude to the history of the healing system. Chinese medicine, for example, is widespread throughout Asia and has a long written tradition permitting a high degree of codification. In contrast, shamanic healing systems in particular tribes of Native North Americans are local in their provenance and in their clientele. They are generally not codified in written form nor are they formally regulated by societal bodies, but are passed on as oral traditions and informally regulated through custom and patronage. Both categories could be dubbed "popular" medicine in the sense that they are most often informally regulated by healers and clients, as opposed to professional biomedicine regulated by government-based licensing boards. However, these distinctions are not definitive in that the rules and principles guiding ethnomedical as opposed to biomedical systems are usually of a different genre altogether. It is therefore very difficult to compare types of medical systems systematically.

Hispanic Healing Systems

Three widespread ethnomedical systems are found in the United States among Hispanics—*Espiritismo* (Spiritism), *Santería,* and *Curanderismo*—associated with the three major ethnic communities of Puerto Ricans, Cubans, and Mexican Americans (see Garrison, 1977; Gonzalez-Wippler, 1973; Harwood, 1977; Kay, 1977; Koss-

Chioino, 1992; Sandoval, 1977, for more detailed descriptions). Each is a synthesis of beliefs and practices derived from separate neocolonial histories: Spiritism from the conjunction of European (French) and Afro-Caribbean traditions; *Santería* from a conjunction of folk Catholicism and West African traditions; and *Curanderismo* from a synthesis of folk Catholicism and Mexican Indian traditions. Spiritualism (a variation of Spiritism with a similar European and folk Catholicism background) is also found in Mexico and on the United States–Mexico border (Finkler, 1985; Trotter & Chavira, 1981).

Illness Etiologies

The major causal paradigm for all these systems is that malicious or unaware other-than-human beings or forces are the final causes of physical suffering, emotional distress, or personal problems. Spirits in Spiritism or saints/gods in *Santería* are the direct cause of suffering in those systems. In *Curanderismo*, the will of God is invoked as causal in many cases, but there are also a number of provoking agents in Mexican-American belief: spoiled food; environmental factors (*aires*); contact with persons wishing harm, consciously or inadvertently (*mal de ojo, el ojo*—the evil eye); immoral excesses of sex or money acquisition; deviant behavior; congenital or hereditary characteristics; and witchcraft (Kay, 1977; Koss-Chioino & Cañive, 1993; Trotter & Chavira, 1981). Age and general weakness, as well as a "weak character," add to the effect of the agents listed here. Vestiges of these etiological beliefs are also found in Spiritism and *Santería*; probably the most important is bewitchment (Koss-Chioino, 1992).

The unifying theme for all of these systems is that of harmony and balance. To heal (*sanar* or *curar*) also means "to restore to health," the latter interpreted as harmony within individuals, between them, and within the cosmos. What are referred to in orthodox Western thought as the physical, social, and existential dimensions of health are inexorably bound up together in Hispanic healing. In Spiritism, the spiritual (the Holy Spirit and His realm) encompasses all of these dimensions; in *Santería*, the rule of the gods or saints is very similar to concepts of the spirit world in Spiritist belief and practice. One phrasing of "harmony/balance," much described in the literature among less acculturated Mexican Americans and Mexicans, is the theory of balance between hot and cold. For example, foods that are too "hot" cause "hot" illnesses, and "cold" herbal remedies are prescribed by *curanderas* (healers). Although extremes in change of climate or contact with heat or cold are believed to cause illness, temperature per se is not what is at risk; rather, hot–cold is a metaphoric symbology that expresses excesses and an ever-present awareness of the danger of imbalance. However, this symbolic paradigm appears to be dropping out of the belief systems of Mexican Americans and Puerto Ricans in the United States (Kay, 1977; Koss, 1987). In all Hispanic healing systems, imbalance is a moral issue; thus, in Spiritism, illness-causing (*causa*) spirits are attracted to persons who behave immorally. In *Curanderismo* or *Espiritismo*, those who "break the rules" (including "uncleanliness" in the moral sense) often become ill because they threaten the integrity of social fabric. Transgressions are sinful both because they unbalance the "good" within an individual and because they generate conflict among persons.

Diagnosis: Identifying the Illness

Hispanic healers make few significant distinctions between physical illness, emotional disorder, and social problems such as being criminally charged or failing in business. There is an informal practice of referring complaints assessed as *"material"* (somatic) to medical doctors while simultaneously apportioning spiritual aspects of the distress to traditional treatments. All complaints are interpreted as having similar etiologies, and diagnosis proceeds in much the same way regardless of the type of complaint. As we shall see later, remedies may differ according to type of complaint (but not systematically); the cause of the distress, such as "bewitchment" or "nervousness," often becomes the label for the distressing condition. Distinctions between somatic and other types of complaints (i.e., psychological or spiritual) are also unsystematic; for example, some of the Spiritist healers in Puerto Rico asserted that "nerves are almost always physical" but also maintained that a particular *causa* spirit (sent by a woman who desired the client's husband) could cause her "pain and nerve sickness" or that nerves run in the family (see Koss-Chioino, 1992). However, the common ground in a condition labeled "nerves" is that of conflict in interpersonal, usually intimate, relationships, which generates extreme emotions, particularly anger.

The process of diagnosis in traditional healing is quite different from the method of either biomedicine or psychotherapy. Clients rarely describe their complaints as the main step in the intake process; rather, the healer is expected to "know" what the client's complaints are without verbal input from the client. In *Santería* the diagnostic process is divinatory and is called a *registro*. The *santero* (healer) who specializes in reading the shells (*los caracoles,* modeled after West African cowrie shells) is known as an *italero* (Gonzalez-Wippler, 1973). The eighteen shells, called the "mouthpieces of the gods," are for sale in any *botanica* (shops that sell remedies, prayers, herbs, candles, and other prescriptions and ritual objects). Sixteen or twelve (if the diviner is not yet a priest) are thrown four times onto a straw mat, and the patterns are interpreted according to the position of the shells. Each letter or pattern "speaks" for one or more *orishas* and is interpreted according to a legend or proverb associated with it; this is standardized in the "Table of *Ifá*." The diviner then particularizes the interpretation for a specific client and his or her problem. Not only do priests *(santeros, babalawos)* deal with problems and disordered emotions, but they also prescribe herbal remedies and amulets *(resguardos)* to protect against future injury or to bring about a desired event. It is these latter services, actual manipulations of the future, that appear most sought after.

A different type of "diagnostic" divination is found among Spiritists. First, their personal spirit guides help them "see" into the spirit world to identify the spirit causing a client's problems. Then a process of probing takes place in which the healer describes the client's complaints (somatic distress, feelings, persistent interpersonal or social problems) and the client confirms (most frequently) or denies them. The *causa* spirit is then called down to possess the body of one of the healers and enjoined to explain its actions. Spirit and client carry on a largely one-sided dialogue in which the social context (usually interpersonal relations) of the client's problems or complaints, including circumstances and relationships in past lives, is revealed. Much of the remedy (intervention or solution) is symbolically or meta- phorically contained within this spirit–client interchange. Medium-healers at the healing table, who are not possessed, dialogue, cajole, and exhort the *causa* spirit to leave the suffering client. The spirit usually expresses the recognition of his or her wrongdoing in molesting the client and agrees to leave once the client forgives it for causing the distress. Other remedies to be carried out at home (prayers, candle lighting, herbs, aromatic baths, ritual cleansing of various kinds) may also be prescribed by healers, who "receive" this knowledge from their spirit guides.

Healing Process

Both one-on-one consultations and group ritual sessions are contexts for healing; individuals as clients are most frequent, but couples, small groups of relatives, or even places (i.e., one's home or shop) may be "treated," the last with a purification process employing incense or other aromatic materials. Again, it might be noted that balance and harmony are central to healing, whether the etiological belief is in spirits, gods, the devil versus God, natural forces, energies, or vibrations. This focus on other-than-natural forces beyond visible reality and daily life events results in a number of significant differences in the ways healing is carried out and experienced.

In Spiritism, among Puerto Ricans and other Latinos in the United States, the medium-healer is not the agent of intervention but only a vehicle, an instrument to bring about change in the sufferer's condition. Briefly described, the group healing ritual consists of the mediums (mostly adepts but also some novices) sitting behind a table. The session is opened by the recitation of prayers to the Holy Spirit, Jesus (often the "Our Father" and other items of Catholic liturgy). Then the mediums exhort the audience of potential clients to relax by directing them to meditate and to become part of the spirit world by seeking visual experience of it. The mediums commonly follow suit and become possessed for a brief moment by their main protector-guide spirit, who then stands behind each medium-healer and presides over the session. The group of mediums then concentrate on the spirit world and on certain *videncias* (visions) that indicate the relationship of a certain spirit to someone in the audience. That client is then singled out, according to a visual description given by the spirit to the medium, and is summoned to the table (on which sits only a vessel of blessed water in which the spirit fluids are encapsulated). The "diagnostic" process described above then takes place.

The central feature of Spiritist healing is the use of image and metaphor in these spirit-produced explanations. Much of what takes place can only be described as the manipulation of symbolic material that somehow gets "inside" the sufferer. How this happens can be explained in part by belief in and experience of *plas- mación*—that is, that the healer feels the client's complaint within his or her own body. The feelings of clients are literally "shaped" or "formed" inside the healer through the action of the particular spirit causing the distressing feelings in the suffering client. Symbols, in spirit communication, are not representational but, instead, refer to feelings and emotions. Spiritist healer-mediums model these feelings and emotions; through messages (visions) or direct bodily transfer of feelings from spirits, they mirror them for clients. A cycle of resonating feelings is set up, including not only the medium-healers and often other mediums working at a table (at a group session), but also the audience of participants. The Spiritist ritual healing session in its group form has been compared with psychodrama and likened to an imaginal theatrical performance (Seda Bonilla, 1964; Koss, 1979).

The implication of this kind of healing process is the power it conveys to the suffering client in terms of concern and caring, as well as shared experience and intimacy among persons who know about suffering (see also McClain, 1989). The facts of the healers' former suffering, as central to the initiation into the healer role (to be described), are not usually known to clients, but the feelings are readily available upon contact with a healer, especially during the ritual process. The altered states phenomena (ritual trance and possession-trance) illustrate the healer's contact with suffering as well as her or his ability to control distressing feelings and emotions.

This same interpretation can also be applied to Spiritualist and *Santería* healing practices among Mexican Americans and Cubans, both of whom utilize altered states of consciousness in their ritual healing. In the latter, *santeros* and *babalawos* undergo elaborate initiations and are usually self-selected during bouts of problems or illness. In *Curanderismo*, healers receive their healing avocations both as a gift from God *(el don)*, and through apprenticeship to an elderly relative. Often, however, they are selected for the healer role because they are recognized to possess high sensitivity and interest in the suffering of other persons, for whose benefit they renew connection with God and the saints. In this way, their relationships with clients appear to have similar features to those of spiritists and *Santeros*; they are open to sharing their clients' pain as a route to facilitating their healing, and to the incorporation of other-than-human forces in the healing process.

Patterns of Utilization

Very little epidemiological data is available for utilization of ethnomedical treatments by Hispanics in the United States. In California, *Curanderismo* is variously reported to be used by 5 to 8 percent of Mexican-American parents for their children in Santa Barbara (Gilbert, 1980); Keefe (1981) found 7 percent of her sample in Los Angeles had been to a *curandero*; and Chavez (1984) reported that 23 percent of Mexican immigrants to San Diego said they would use a *curandero*, but only 1 percent actually reported using such services. In urban barrios in Colorado and South Texas, reported uitilization was found to be much higher, 32 percent in the former and 54 percent in the latter (Rivera, 1988; Trotter & Chavira, 1981; see especially Mayers, 1989). There is little objective evidence for the extent of utilization of Spiritism (and its variations) or *Santería*, but older studies of the New York City area (Garrison, 1977; Harwood, 1977) describe the widespread use of Spiritism in the 1970s, and subsequent studies in small eastern cities such as Hartford, Connecticut (Singer & Borrero, 1984), show this to be the case wherever there is a large concentration of Puerto Ricans. Similarly, various studies (Brandon, 1991; Sandoval, 1977) indicate that *Santería* is a flourishing health and mental health alternative in Miami, Florida, as well as in other areas of concentrated Cuban population. Some studies separate the belief in traditional healing practices from records of actual use. This suggests both use as a potential resource and the common use of home remedies and rituals, which has not been well documented but is frequently observed (Harwood, 1977; Mayers, 1989; Trotter, 1981).

Healers in each of the Hispanic ethnomedical systems described here commonly describe themselves as generalists. But in *Curanderismo*, for example, various investigators (Kay, 1977; Rivera & Wanderer, 1986) point out that these healers are most widely used by women, frequently for their children's illnesses but also for their own health problems. The mental health aspects of *Curanderismo* among Mexican Americans in the United States have not been well studied (but see Koss-Chioino & Cañive, 1993 and Newton, 1978). Conditions generally perceived as physical illnesses—*susto, empacho, bilis, caida de la mollera,* and *mal de ojo*—have emotional concommitants, and bewitchment and *nervios* have direct relationship to emotional distress, as well as to somatic distress. Because these popular illnesses are culturally constructed as syntheses of somatic and psychological causal factors, and this paradigm differs from that of biomedicine, where soma and psyche are separately considered as primary in diagnostic schemata, they are presented to folk healers who understand them in these *emic* ways. The treatments for them are usually also synthetic in terms of the soma/psyche axis.

African-American Ethnomedicine

Snow (1977) characterizes the underlying belief system of African-American ethnomedicine as "a composite of the classical medicine of an earlier day, European folklore regarding the natural world, rare African traits, and selected beliefs derived from modern scientific medicine" (p. 83). All this is blended with fundamentalist Christianity and with elements from West Indian voodoo (including basically similar "magical" practices of rootwork, hoodoo, "crossing up," hexing, and witchcraft). There is so much diversity in the description of beliefs, practices, and types of healers that one gets the impression of several overlapping healing systems, in part distributed according to locale, with differences in the northern and southern states as well as in places of special tradition such as the Sea Islands of South Carolina and Louisiana (Baer, 1985; Blake, 1984; Hall & Bourne, 1973; Watson, 1984b). As pointed out by Baer (1985), however, there is little systematic or representative data to clarify the types of healers, the systems, or their distribution.

Baer (1985) suggests a typology based on two main types of African-American healers: "independent" and "cultic." (The same division could be made for Hispanic healers, since *Curanderos* generally work independently and *Santeros* within cult groups; spiritists are almost always members of healing cults but also may hold private consultations.) Within this division, however, he classifies healers according to whether they are generalists or specialists. This then neatly accounts for an amazing variety: Independent generalists (conjurers, spiritualists) deal with illnesses and problems of "unnatural cause" (Snow, 1978); specialized independents (midwives, herbalists, "magic" vendors, neighborhood "prophets") are local healers, supplying herbs or occult articles (perfumed oils, candles), or counseling, prayer, and prophecy for common problems. In this category also are found healers in the rural South (bone-setters, blood-stoppers) who still, though in lesser number, treat physical ailments. Cultic generalists work within groups and are identified as Spiritualists, some fewer as voodoo (or "hoodoo") priests or priestesses, and a few as Black Muslim or Black Hebrew healers (these last are sectarian organizations with religiopolitical tenets and goals). Finally, cultic specialists function within religious organizations as "divine" or "faith" healers in evangelistic congregations such as the Holiness, Pentecostal, or Baptist churches. These healers are well known, but their ways of healing have not been well studied.

Etiology and Diagnosis of Illness

Snow (1978, 1993) points to the prevalent belief that good health is an instance of good fortune that includes a good job, a faithful spouse, and loving children. "The cure for one, therefore, might cure them all" (Snow, 1978, p. 70). Here again there is no real separation between illness and other types of distress, nor is there a significant difference between psyche and soma in folk theory. Moreover, diagnosis focuses not on symptoms but on causes. The most prevalent of causes is that conceived as failure to avoid dangerous situations that bring on illness or misfortune. Appropriate and timely action can neutralize danger from attack by other humans, natural events, or nonhuman beings such as ghosts, ancestors, or evil spirits. While symptoms are fluid and may change easily or be shifted to another causal category (i.e., natural to unnatural), knowing the cause of the illness is essential to finding the right healer and treatment even when shifts may be made between types of healers.

Etiological notions divide into natural and unnatural categories. The former have to do with beliefs in proper action according to God's plan for people aimed at maintaining both harmony and well-being. Unhealthy life-styles and excesses will lead to illness, or God may take punitive action for failure in one's duty to serve him. Although physicians or herbalists can cure the former, the latter demands a contract with God or the intercession of a religious healer.

With regard to unnatural illness (i.e., listed by Snow, 1978, as caused by excessive, nonproductive worry, evil influence, or sorcery/magic), this type of distress is probably closest to the problems treated by psychotherapists. It is often caused by "fixes" or "hexes" (also referred to as *voodoo, hoodoo, root work, crossing-up*) carried out by human agents, usually intimate others who are envious or angry with the victim and therefore require the help of a specialist with unusual powers. This healer should have a special bond with God for a successful intervention that counteracts the beyond-human quality of the causal factors, such as Satan or magical attack. Folk diagnosis of magical illness includes poisoning to account for gastrointestinal symptoms or weight loss, a hex worked on clothes or items worn near to the body to explain behavior that feels out of personal control, and any unusual symptoms such as the feelings that an animal (spider, lizard, snake) has intruded itself into one's body.

Patterns of Utilization

Decisions of African Americans regarding utilization of professional health care services are reported as unrelated to income; however, a national survey showed that the problems experienced by those with lower income were more serious (Neighbors, 1984). A general pattern of underutilization was revealed in which somewhat more than half of those who reported a serious problem (phrased as a "nervous breakdown") did not seek professional assistance. The conclusion of the investigator, that African Americans widely utilize a "lay network" as a source of assistance, confirms the descriptive studies cited here. A systematic survey in Detroit, Michigan, found that even for hypertension, defined as a "natural" illness in the folk system, 24 percent women and about 10 percent men reported using folk or "personal" care treatments; 41 percent women said they were likely to use an ethnocare therapy as compared to Anglo-American women (14 percent) (Bailey, 1991). Although various authors (Blake, 1984; Watson, 1984a) describe the widespread use of home remedies and ethnomedical healing in isolated rural populations because of the lack of professional medical services or conservation of tradition, it seems clear that these are not the most important factors in the decision to utilize ethnomedicine.

Ethnomedicine among Asian-Americans

As in the Hispanic-American community, there is a great degree of variation between ethnomedical systems among Chinese, Japanese, Vietnamese, and tribal peoples such as the Hmong or Lao. The basic tenets of Chinese medicine were set out in written documents dating to the thirteenth and fourteenth centuries B.C.; in them health and disease were recognized as subject to the principles of the natural world (Xiu, 1988). Shamanic healing probably diminished in importance by the third century B.C. and with the publication of *The Canon of Internal Medicine*, the first Chinese medical textbook. However, shamanic healers are still working in Taiwan, although they have not been reported for the United States (Kleinman, 1980). A complex system of herbal remedies is of great antiquity as part of both ethnomedical systems (Xiu, 1988) but the religious ideas and ritual practices associated with the beginnings of Chinese medicine have largely dropped out, and physical/bodily manipulation or exercises are central, such as acupuncture, moxibustion, massage, and breathing exercises (i.e., *Tai Chi, Oigong*).

Although current diagnosis and treatment appear focused on the somatic, a psychological approach is an integral aspect; in particular, there is a stipulated relationship between a person's mind and his or her state of health (Wu, 1984). A balanced and disciplined life maintains health; this includes regulations of emotions and desires, a balanced diet, and adjustment when physical changes occur. The central tenet of the Chinese conception of health is balance, both inner and outer (with nature and the world), particularly between *yin* (dark, heavy, inner, female) and *yang* (bright, light, outer, male). Good health depends on the equilibrium of the basic emotions and organs. Body physiology is made up of five *yin* viscera and five *yang* organs, each responsible for a bodily function and associated to an external part of the body. The heart presides over all the organ systems and governs all mental activities. If the heart malfunctions (i.e., symbolic imbalance), palpitations, memory loss, insomnia, or mental disorders can occur. Illness etiology differentiates between inner and outer causes: External causes include the six evils: wind, cold, heat, wetness, dryness, and fire; internal causes are the seven emotions, excesses of which can cause imbalance, blockage of *ch'i* (life force, energy), and malfunction of the organs. Irregularity of food and drink and fatigue can also lead to illness. Imbalances can also occur because transitions over time are inevitable and cause instabilities. External, cosmic imbalances should be avoided; astrological almanacs are consulted for mating as well as for important times of transition such as weddings and funerals.

Currently, Chinese medicine has given up treating external imbalances that have moral dimensions; these are handled by Buddhist or Taoist priests or by spirit healers. Chinese medicine takes as its focus internal imbalances within the human being, whereas ritual experts deal with the external. The Taoist system metaphorically relates immoral actions to five demons conjured up by antisocial human behavior. Buddhist concepts of rebirth account for imbalances such as antipathies between a parent and child because of a relationship in a past life, or label a child's irritability as "fright" due to an imbalance among animating forces, including the Buddhist soul (Topley, 1976). Traditionally, these healing systems were used in an alternative or complementary way dependent on the course of events (particularly the illness), recommendations by family elders or diagnoses of the problem.

With regard to mental health, traditional Chinese medicine took the position that the human mind was unable to remain normal if distracted by extreme emotions such as worry, fear, anger or fixed desires (Li, 1984). Various investigators, such as Kleinman and Kleinman (1985), analyze the ways in which emotions are "somatized" and expressed as physical illness when mood disorders are present. Because the biomedical categories of illnesses of the mind and of the body are not found in Chinese ethnomedical nosology, which instead has categories best characterized as "psychosomatic" (for want of a better term to connote their synthesis), some dispute the validity of "somatization" as an explanatory psychological process that accounts for the ample expression of somatic symptoms and few affective ones (Kawanishi, 1992). It has been further suggested that this leads to high levels of errors in diagnosing mood or anxiety disorders on the basis of somatic symptomatology among Asians; instead, somatic symptom expression may be related to obstacles to legitimate entry into the sick role, or to ways of relating to non-Asian therapists.

Given limitations of space, all that can be said here about ethnomedicine among Japanese-Americans is that it is based in part on Chinese traditional medicine and similar types of religious healing within the Buddhist and Shinto traditions (Otsuka, 1976). However, there are a number of innovative healing cults such as the Salvation Cult (Gedatsukai), and new "standard" therapies, such as Morita and Naikan, specifically responsive to Japanese cultural values (Lebra, 1984; Murase, 1984; Reynolds & Kiefer, 1977). Murase (1984) shows how both of these innovative therapies are based on the Japanese concept of *sunao*, which refers to a pristine state of mind, like that of a baby, an unconditional state of trust in others. *Sunao* is closely linked with Shintoism; other aspects of these therapies are linked to Buddhist and Confucian traditions.

Among Southeast Asians, the hill tribes (Hmong and Mien) in the United States see shamans when available and generally continue their traditional beliefs and practices regarding herbal remedies (Muecke, 1983; see also Westermeyer, 1988 for descriptions of Hmong and Lao ethnomedicine). Central concepts of their traditional medical systems include the notion that continued health depends on the continued residence of many souls; absence of one or more causes illness or death. In addition, spirits *(phii)* are omnipresent throughout nature and associated with places; they can either cause or heal illness and must be respected. Magic and sorcery can be employed to cause illness, but illness can also result from inherited defects in "blood" or "wind" (akin to the elements in Chinese medicine). As with the Chinese, too much thinking or worrying can cause illness and disturb balance. Among the Lao as compared to the hill tribes (Hmong), Buddhist concepts have been more influential and prayer and bodily cleanliness are more important. We have almost no studies of the extent to which these beliefs and practices survive in the United States setting, but several investigators have documented their presence in the United States (D. Kinzie, E. Foulks, personal communication).

Traditional Healing among Native Americans

Extensive diversity in ethnomedical practices is found in this population, since traditional healing systems vary along tribal lines (there are 500 federally recognized tribes) and are largely, though not entirely, shamanic (that is, made up of independent practitioners and culture-specific beliefs and practices). An ample literature can be consulted for descriptions of traditional healing in each tribe or area (see, especially, the Smithsonian Institution's *Handbook of North American Indians*, 1978; also Vogel, 1977, who presents a descriptive overview of therapeutic techniques and healing plants among Native Americans; and individual studies such as Bahr, Gregorio, Lopez, & Alvarez, 1974 [Pima]; Jilek, 1982 [Pacific Northwest]; Kunitz, 1983; and Levy, Neutra, & Parker, 1987 [Navaho], among many others).

Two popular religious healing traditions transcend tribal boundaries: the Native American Church and Pentecostalism, found in all ethnic minority populations. I will briefly discuss the former from the perspective of how these types of organization and healing ideologies radically differ from psychotherapy, making attempts at inclusion or cooperation extremely difficult. This discussion is a preface to the final section of this chapter, which will deal with perspectives on interfacing or integrating traditional healing systems and psychotherapy.

The Native American Church is a pan-Indian religion based on a ritual that facilitates direct contact with the Great Spirit (also God) through peyote, pipe and cigarette smoking, drumming, and songs and prayer (Bergman, 1974). Imported from Mexico in the last decades of the nineteenth century, it incorporates many elements of traditional Native American cultures, especially those of the Plains peoples integrated with elements of Christianity (Aberle, 1966; Anderson, 1980). Predominantly revivalistic and oriented toward Native American ethnicity (rather than tribal identity), it meets the needs of some, especially younger persons who undergo intensive conversion experiences. Therapeutic effects are engendered in two ways: first, through a curing ceremony in which members of the church are treated for specific problems, often physical but also psychosocial (e.g., alcoholism) or emotional in nature. One traditional technique used is that of sucking out the evil spirit in the patient while other members sing and pray. Confession of sins at the ceremony is also employed. Second, the ceremony itself includes a number of therapeutic aspects: Conversion occurs by taking peyote and having a revelation, then being purged of sins through the physical purging brought on by the drug. Strong emotions in all participants are facilitated by the ceremony, accompanied by clear moral injunctions regarding abstinence from alcohol, marital fidelity, restraint from vengeance and fighting, and so on. As in many types of small-group religious ceremonies, a high degree of communality is fostered when food, cigarettes or pipe, emotions, and problems are all shared without distinction. One investigator comments that he felt accepted, even as a White man, despite the official emphasis on pan-Indian nationalism.

The Native American Church is one of many examples of widespread, new, cultic religions, based on goals of cultural nationalism, that have specific as well as general healing aspects (some were identified as "revitalization movements" by Wallace, 1961). These are formed through individual need arising out of far-reaching cultural change, and are typified by emphases on a traditional ethos synthesized with newer symbols. They return people to a community to replace one that has become fragmented and chaotic, providing the opportunity for a new type of personal commitment to social goals (Jones & Korchin, 1982).

These are most always group experiences intending resocialization and validating personal change within a reconstructed social arena. As Topper (1987) points out, the traditional Navaho healing ceremony, led by the medicine man as a community leader, is a group phenomenon, attended by family and close neighbors. Moreover, it symbolically recreates the cosmos for the sufferer with the intent of restoring harmony. These basic attributes are extremely difficult to reproduce within behavioral or psychodynamic psychotherapies (even group and family modalities) given their predominant individualistic orientation (Jones & Korchin, 1982; Topper, 1987).

Interface or Integration?

The question of how to interface with traditional healing among ethnic minority patients can be discussed at four levels: (1) therapist–client interaction, (2) consultation with or referrals to traditional healers on behalf of clients, (3) institutional attempts to work with traditional healers, and (4) innovation of synthesized therapies combining standard and ethnomedical approaches. All of these approaches are complex and full of difficulties, theoretical, practical, and ethical. Each level will be discussed briefly with examples from the literature and the author's experience.

Therapist–Client Interaction

Some authors suggest that attributes of the healer–client relationship, and the conceptual bases of their ethnomedicine, are so different as to make some psychotherapies invalid or inappropriate for certain clients. Topper (1987) makes a strong case that therapies that promote self-exploration or restructuring of the personality (and thus bring up emotional conflicts) are negative and divisive within the context of traditional Navaho culture. This would directly counter the Navaho healing goal of restoration of harmony in all life (and nonhuman) spheres. However, because ethnic minority persons do utilize mental health services, inevitably, considerations of content as well as prior expectations about healer–client relationships or revealing certain types of personal information will be introduced into the therapeutic situation.

At the simplest level in the therapy process, the therapist needs to inform himself or herself with regard to the relationship of these aspects to the client's experiences with traditional healing. Secondary sources may have potential for suggestion, but an attitude of ethnographic inquiry, in which the client becomes the teacher of his or her experience, is probably most productive in eliciting the content and importance of his or her ethnomedical beliefs and practices. The therapist as "clinical" ethnographer must be open, accepting, and humble at this juncture in the relationship. The most important aspect is the willingness of the client to bring this content into therapy. As illustrated in a recent book (Vargas & Koss-Chioino, 1992) therapists of similar ethnic background seem to find that clients bring this material into therapy if an opening is made. Although this is not well documented, indications exist that the therapist's attitude toward this material and his or her interest and prior experience may be the salient factors (Maduro, 1975).

Snow (1978) discusses cases where physicians or psychotherapists claimed success in treating symptoms and illnesses defined ethnomedically by patients. Biomedical remedies were justified as ethnomedical preparations, or folk remedies were used as placebos. Not only the ethical issues but also the possibility of disruption of the therapeutic relationship make such approaches highly undesirable for use with ethnic minority clients (Koss-Chioino & Cañive, 1993).

Cooperation with Healers

In my experiences in Puerto Rico and New Mexico, consultations with healers about general matters were easy to obtain; dealing with a specific patient led directly into ethical issues as well as questions involving the entire structure and organization of the healing professions (both ethnomedical and biomedical); see Dinges et al., (1981), for a discussion of these issues for American Indians and Alaskan natives. With regard to ethical issues, a client must request such services as either consultation or treatment. Issues of credibility of the traditional healer must be defined and defended; fees for service must be negotiated (particularly difficult when traditional healers do not charge or accept gifts); the form and content of reporting must be agreed on (including confidentiality requirements) and some way of synthesizing the two very different approaches to the disorder must be negotiated to the satisfaction of all concerned. As illustrated for Puerto Rico (Koss-Chioino, 1992), even where there is a pattern of frequent dual use of alternative treatments for the same episode of illness, it may be difficult to establish areas of complementarity. An example of this type of difficulty is when a healer insists that antipsychotic medication interferes with her or his spiritual treatment of a diagnosed schizophrenic patient with a prescribed regimen of halperidol or stelazine.

Institutional Arrangements for Interface

A number of experimental projects have been attempted, such as the School for Medicine Men (Bergman, 1973), the Therapist-Spiritist Training Project in Puerto Rico (Koss, 1980; Koss-Chioino, 1992) and the employment of Spiritists at Lincoln Hospital in New York (Ruiz & Langrod, 1976). A number of informal efforts to bring traditional healers into a clinic setting are anecdotally reported, especially for the southwestern United States. Most of these projects publicize these efforts as educational, a way to make clinicians aware of ethnomedical beliefs and practices. This tactic, though a step toward understanding and tolerance, creates the problem of recognizing the true value of the healers to their ethnic clients. They are perceived as either foreign or marginal to the clinic and its mandates, and are often considered both socially inferior to biomedical or psychological healers and outside of professional boundaries.

In its efforts to incorporate ethnomedicine into its services, the Indian Health Service has installed hogan-like rooms in some of its newer hospitals in New Mexico and Arizona to encourage Navaho medicine men to come into the clinics to work with patients. Navaho staff reported that these internal hogans were not really used as intended, even though medicine men regularly visited their clients in the hospitals. The issue is one of possible cooptation, in which healers working within biomedical institutional settings would change their techniques or be compromised by monetary reimbursements otherwise unavailable to them. On this point, I observed the reactions of over fifty Spiritist healers in Puerto Rico, steadfastly maintained that they could not accept payment or carry out much of their usual healing work in a clinical setting. However, they did act as willing consultants and also worked directly with patients in hospitals or clinics who requested them. My experience in that project led to the conclusion that referral to the places where alternative healing rites take place is the best policy if the aforementioned issues can be worked out.

New Therapeutic Syntheses

There are a number of examples of innovative therapies that incorporate ethnomedical beliefs or practices in combination with standard psychotherapeutic techniques of Western, biomedical origin. The Japanese therapies, Naikan and Morita, have been mentioned; they are considered quite successful with persons suffering particular syndromes, such as anxiety disorders. At one extreme, there is the incorporation of specific techniques, particularly where parallels have been drawn, such as between mainstream psychotherapy and Spiritism (Comas-Díaz, 1981). At the other extreme, there has been wholesale adoption of a segment of ritual healing practice where it has been deemed effective for a particular disorder or problem. Wilson (1993) analyzes in detail how the Sweat Lodge ritual works among Native Americans, including its psychological and psychobiological dimensions, and then suggests that it could function as an efficacious form of treatment for anxiety, depression, and stress-related disorders. It is not clear if he feels this adoption would be efficacious for other than Native American sufferers, nor does it appear that he has attempted to measure its effects or outcomes.

Another type of synthesis is described by Gonzalez (1990) who describes her program of Treatment with Dignity "as based in methods and theories found in the fields of anthropology, communication, psychology and sociology" (p. 6). Her program is geared toward perpetrators and adult victims of child abuse and is an individual modality built upon a series of stage-wise exercises. This approach uses Native American tenets and practices (stories, metaphors, ceremonies) as a culturally open-ended format for other than Indian persons. Again, this program has not been evaluated systematically, but its approach has probably been carried out informally by many therapists.

It is clearly extremely difficult to evaluate the efficacy of ethnomedical healing since the types of measures utilized in studies of psychotherapy would make very little sense when concepts, beliefs, and practices differ so widely (Pillsbury, 1982). Some guidelines for both the development of new, culturally responsive therapies and their evaluation are presented in Vargas and Koss-Chioino (1992). The main thrust is to synthesize form and process with culture, defined as both context and content. The content of the therapy could be drawn from ethnomedical beliefs or a set of practices incorporated into process or structure. This and other similar formulations need to be operationalized and the manualized therapies carefully assessed using experimental methodologies. This task could occupy a complete generation of researchers. It appears that ethnicity and ethnomedicine in the United

States will not disappear but will continue to provide opportunities and challenges for practice and research.

References

Aberle, D. (1966). *The peyote religion among the Navaho.* Chicago: Aldine.

Anderson, E. F. (1980). *Peyote: The divine cactus.* Tucson: University of Arizona Press.

Baer, H. A. (1985). Toward a systematic typology of Black folk healers. *Phylon, 43,* 327–343.

Bahr, D. M., Gregorio, J., Lopex, D. I., & Alvarez, A. (1974). *Piman shamanism and staying sickness.* Tucson: University of Arizona Press.

Bailey, E. J. (1991). Hypertension: An analysis of Detroit African-American health care treatment patterns. *Human Organization, 50,* 287–296.

Bergman, R. L. (1973). A school for medicine men. *American Journal of Psychiatry, 130,* 663–666.

Bergman, R. L. (1974). The peyote religion and healing. In R. H. Cox (Ed.), *Religion and psychotherapy* (pp. 296–306). Springfield, IL: Thomas.

Blake, J. H. (1984). "Doctor can't do me no good": Social concomitants of health care attitudes and practices among elderly Blacks in isolated rural populations. In W. H. Watson (Ed.), *Black folk medicine* (pp. 33–40). New Brunswick, NJ: Transaction.

Brandon, G. (1991). The uses of plants in healing in an Afro-Cuban religion, Santería. Special issue: African aesthetics in Nigeria and the diaspora. *Journal of Black Studies, 22,* 55–76.

Chavez, L. R. (1984). Doctors, *curanderos,* and *brujas*: Health care delivery and Mexican immigrants in San Diego. *Medical Anthropology Quarterly, 15,* 31–37.

Comas-Díaz, L. (1981). Puerto Rican *espiritismo* and psychotherapy. *American Journal of Orthopsychiatry, 51,* 636–645.

Dinges, N. G., Trimble, J. E., Manson, S. M., & Pasquale, F. L. (1981). The social ecology of counseling and psychotherapy with American Indians and Alaskan natives. In A. J. Marsella & P. Pedersen (Eds.), *Cross-cultural counseling and psychotherapy: Foundations, evaluation, cultural considerations* (pp. 243–276). Elmsford, NY: Pergamon Press.

Finkler, K. (1985). *Spiritualist healing in Mexico: Successes and failures of alternative therapies.* Hadley, MA: Bergin & Garvey.

Garrison, V. (1977). The Puerto Rican syndrome in *espiritismo.* In V. Crapanzano & V. Garrison (Eds.), *Case studies in spirit possession* (pp. 383–450). New York: Wiley.

Gilbert, M. J. (1980). *Mexican-Americans parents' perceptions of folk childhood disease: Little evidence of a strong folk tradition.* Paper presented at the annual meeting of the American Anthropological Association, Los Angeles.

Gonzalez, M. C. (1990). *Treatment with dignity: A method for working with perpetrators and adult victims of child abuse.* Paper presented at the eighth annual National American Indian Conference on Child Abuse and Neglect, Falls Church, VA.

Gonzalez-Wippler, M. (1973). *Santería: African magic in Latin America.* New York: Julian Press.

Hall, A. L., & Bourne, P. G. (1973). Indigenous therapists in a southern Black urban community. *Archives of General Psychiatry 28,* 137–142.

Harwood, A. (1977). *Rx: Spiritist as needed.* New York: Wiley.

Jilek, W. G. (1982). *Indian healing: Shamanic ceremonialism in the Pacific Northwest today.* Blaine, WA: Hancock House.

Jones, E. E., & Korchin, S. J. (1982). Minority mental health perspectives. In E. E. Jones & S. J. Korchin (Eds.), *Minority mental health* (pp. 3–36). New York: Praeger.

Kay, M. (1977). Health and illness in a Mexican-American barrio. In E. H. Spicer (Ed.), *Ethnic medicine in the Southwest* (pp. 99–166). Tucson: University of Arizona Press.

Kawanishi, Y. (1992). Somatization of Asians: An artifact of Western medicalization? *Transcultural Psychiatric Research, 29,* 5–36.

Keefe, S. M. (1981). Folk medicine among urban Mexican-Americans: Cultural persistence, change and displacement. *Hispanic Journal of Behavioral Sciences, 3,* 41–58.

Kleinman, A. (1980). *Patients and healers in the context of culture.* Berkeley: University of California Press.

Kleinman, A., & Kleinman, J. (1985). Somatization: The interconnectedness in Chinese society among culture, depressive experience, and the meaning of pain. In A. Kleinman & B. Good (Eds.), *Culture and depression* (pp. 429–490). Berkeley: University of California Press.

Koss, J. (1979). On the normal and abnormal from a contemporary viewpoint: Commentary. *Journal of Operational Psychiatry, 10,* 113–118.

Koss, J. D. (1980). The Therapist-Spiritist Training Project in Puerto Rico: An experiment to relate the traditional healing system to the public health system. *Social Science and Medicine, 14,* 373–410.

Koss, J. D. (1986). Symbolic transformations in traditional healing rituals: A perspective from analytical psychology. *Journal of Analytical Psychology, 31,* 341–355.

Koss, J. D. (1987). Expectations and outcomes for patients given mental health care or spiritist healing in Puerto Rico. *American Journal of Psychiatry, 144,* 56–61.

Koss-Chioino, J. D. (1992). *Women as healers, women as patients: Mental health care and traditional healing in Puerto Rico.* San Francisco: Westview.

Koss-Chioino, J., & Cañive, J. (1993). The interaction of cultural and clinical diagnostic labeling: The case of *embrujado. Medical Anthropology, 15,* 171–188.

Kunitz, S. J. (1983). *Disease change and the role of medicine: The Navajo experience.* Berkeley: University of California Press.

Lebra, T. S. (1984). Self-reconstruction in Japanese religious psychotherapy. In A. J. Marsella & G. M. White (Eds.), *Cultural conceptions of mental health and therapy* (pp. 269–283). Boston: Reidel.

Levy, J. E., Neutra, R., & Parker, D. (1987). *Hand trembling, frenzy witchcraft and moth madness: A study of Navaho seizure disorder.* Tucson: University of Arizona Press.

Li, Z. Z. (1984). Traditional Chinese concepts of mental health. *Journal of the American Medical Association, 252,* 3169–3171.

Maduro, R. (1975). Hoodoo possession in San Francisco. *Ethos, 3,* 424–447.

Mayers, R. S. (1989). Use of folk medicine by elderly Mexican-American women. *Journal of Drug Issues, 19,* 283–295.

McClain, C. S. (1989). Reinterpreting women in healing roles. In C. S. McClain (Ed.), *Women as healers: Cross-cultural perspectives* (pp. 1–19). New Brunswick, NJ: Rutgers University Press.

McGuire, M. B. (1988). Ritual healing in suburban America. *Culture, Medicine and Psychiatry, 14,* 133–138.

Muecke, M. A. (1983). In search of healers: Southeast Asian refugees in the American health care system. *Western Journal of Medicine, 139,* 835–840.

Murase, T. (1984). Sunao: A central value in Japanese psychotherapy. In A. J. Marsella & G. M. White (Eds.), *Cultural conceptions of mental health and therapy* (pp. 317–329). Boston: Reidel.

Neighbors, H. W. (1984). Professional help use among Black Americans: Implications for unmet need. *American Journal of Community Psychology, 12,* 551–566.

Newton, F. (1978). The Mexican-American *emic* system of mental illness: An exploratory study. In J. M. Casas & S. E. Keefe (Eds.), *Family and mental health in the Mexican-American community* (pp. 69–89). Los Angeles: Spanish Speaking Mental Health Research Center.

Otsuka, Y. (1976). Chinese traditional medicine in Japan. In C. Leslie (Ed.), *Asian medical systems* (pp. 322–340). Berkeley: University of California Press.

Pillsbury, B. L. K. (1982). Policy and evaluation perspectives on traditional health practitioners in national health care systems. *Social Science and Medicine, 16,* 1825–1834.

Reynolds, D. K., & Kiefer, C. W. (1977). Cultural adaptability as an attribute of therapies: The case of Morita psychotherapy. *Culture, Medicine and Psychiatry, 1,* 395–412.

Rivera, G., Jr. (1988). Hispanic folk medicine utilization in urban Colorado. *Social Science Review, 72,* 237–241.

Rivera, G., Jr., & Wanderer, J. J. (1986). *Curanderismo* and childhood illnesses. *Social Science Journal, 23,* 361–372.

Ruiz, P., & Langrod, J. (1976). Psychiatry and folk healing: A dichotomy? *American Journal of Psychiatry, 133,* 95–97.

Sandoval, M. C. (1977). Afro-Cuban concepts of

disease and its treatment in Miami. *Journal of Operational Psychiatry, 8,* 52–63.

Seda Bonilla, E. (1964). *Interacción social y personalidad en una comunidad en Puerto Rico.* Puerto Rico: Ediciones Edil.

Singer, M., & Borrero, M. (1984). Indigenous treatment for alcoholism: The case of Puerto Rican spiritism. *Medical Anthropology, 8,* 246–273.

Smithsonian Institution (1978–). *Handbook of North American Indians.* W. C. Sturtevant (General Ed.). Washington, DC: Smithsonian Institution Press.

Snow, L. (1977). Popular medicine in a Black neighborhood. In E. H. Spicer (Ed.), *Ethnic medicine in the Southwest* (pp. 19–95). Tucson: University of Arizona Press.

Snow, L. (1978). Sorcerers, saints and charlatans: Black folk healers in urban America. *Culture, Medicine and Psychiatry, 2,* 69–106.

Snow, L. (1993). *Walkin' on medicine.* Boulder, CO: Westview.

Topley, M. (1976). Chinese traditional etiology and methods of cure in Hong Kong. In C. Leslie (Ed.), *Asian medical systems* (pp. 243–265). Berkeley: University of California Press.

Topper, M. D. (1987). The traditional Navajo medicine man: Therapist, counselor, and community leader. *Journal of Psychoanalytic Anthropology, 10,* 217–249.

Trotter, R. T. (1981). Folk remedies as indicators of common illnesses: Examples from the United States–Mexico border. *Journal of Ethnopharmacology, 4,* 207–221.

Trotter, R., & Chavira, J. (1981). *Curanderismo: Mexican folk healing.* Athens, GA: University of Georgia Press.

Vargas, L.A., & Koss-Chioino, J. D. (1992). *Working with culture: Psychotherapeutic interventions with ethnic minority children and adolescents.* San Francisco: Jossey-Bass.

Vogel, V. J. (1977, 4th printing). *American Indian medicine.* Norman: University of Oklahoma Press.

Wallace, A. (1961). *Religion: An anthropological view.* New York: Random House.

Watson, W. H. (1984a). Central tendencies in the practice of folk medicine. In W. H. Watson (Ed.), *Black folk medicine* (pp. 87–97). New Brunswick, NJ: Transaction.

Watson, W. H. (1984b). Folk medicine and older Blacks in southern United States. In W. H. Watson (Ed.), *Black folk medicine* (pp. 53–66). New Brunswick, NJ: Transaction.

Westermyer, J. (1988). Folk medicine in Laos: A comparison between two ethnic groups. *Social Science & Medicine, 27,* 769–778.

Wilson, J. P. (1993). Culture and trauma: The sacred pipe revisited. In J. P. Wilson (Ed.), *Trauma, transformation, and healing: An integrative approach to theory, research, and post-traumatic therapy* (pp. 38–71). New York: Brunner/Mazel.

Wu, D. Y. H. (1984). Psychotherapy and emotion in traditional Chinese medicine. In A. J. Marsella & G. M. White (Eds.), *Cultural conceptions of mental health and therapy* (pp. 285–301). Boston: Reidel.

Xiu, R. J. (1988). Microcirculation and traditional Chinese medicine. *Journal of the American Medical Association, 260,* 1755–1757.

Chapter *10*

Understanding and Treating Ethnic Minority Youth

ROBIN YOUNG RIVERS
CATHERINE A. MORROW

Ethnic minority children and adolescents are the largest growing segment of the United States population. By the year 2000, ethnic minority youth will make up approximately 30 percent of the population. This change will be due primarily to increased birth rates among Hispanics and rising immigration rates among Asians (Gibbs & Huang, 1989; see Chapter 1 of this book). Although the rate of growth of Black youth has been stable over the last decade, they still constitute 34 percent of the African-American population (U.S. Bureau of Census, 1992). The Native American population has the largest percentage of children and adolescents (Berlin, 1987), with 37.4 percent under 18 years of age (U.S. Bureau of Census, 1992).

Ethnic minority youth present unique mental health issues because of their developmental status and membership in their ethnic culture. Some of the issues are related to sociocultural conditions (e.g., poverty, prejudice, racism), whereas others are developmental issues faced by all youth. Developmental tasks, however, are also influenced by cultural factors (Berlin, 1982). All children grow up within the context of a family, whose members bear primary responsibility for the socialization of the children. When working therapeutically with ethnic minority youth, it is important to understand the culture's concept of family so that effective interventions can be developed and implemented.

This chapter will explore issues related to the treatment of ethnic minority children and adolescents. The focus of the chapter will be on African-American, Native American, Asian-American, and Latin American (Hispanic) youth. Although comparisons will be made across these groups, variations within groups also need to be recognized. Sociocultural conditions and mental health problems experienced by ethnic minority children and adolescents, the types of interventions directed toward these children and adolescents, and some of the issues involved in treating them will be discussed.

Sociocultural Factors

Sociocultural factors often interfere with the ethnic minority youth's mastery of developmental tasks. Poverty, language barriers, and negative stereotypes restrict perceived as well as real access to environmental resources. As a result, the effective clinician must assess the youth's environment. Such practical issues may include helping caretakers develop transportation options to sessions, arranging tutorial services for youth and educational resources for parents, and openly discussing with youth the impact of daily exposure to discrimination, conflicting values, and racial stereotypes. Clinicians who directly observe the ethnic minority youth in their classrooms and home environment gain more accurate knowledge of their peer relationship skills, attitudes toward authority, study habits, and degree to which primary needs such as safety, shelter, hygiene, and nutrition are being met. In summary, the effective clinician must address practical sociocultural issues in addition to intrapsychic concerns.

Poverty and Low Socioeconomic Status (SES)

The high rates of poverty in Black, Hispanic, Asian-American, and Native American families has been well established in the census data and in the literature (U.S. Bureau of Census, 1990; see Chapter 1). However, variations in poverty rates within each of these groups need to be recognized (Liu, Yu, Chang, & Fernandez, 1990; Ramirez, 1989). Perhaps the most direct effect of poverty is restricted access to environmental resources with which to combat substandard housing, lack of comprehensive health care, and inadequate nutrition. Several studies lend strong support to the relationship of low SES, its concomitant stressors, and high rates of psychological maladjustment among ethnic minority youth (Gibbs, 1984; Myers, 1989; Tolmach, 1985; Wissow, Gittelsohn, Szklo, Starfield, & Mussman, 1988).

Language Issues

Children generally learn second languages more easily and more quickly than adults. As a result, the language skills of bilingual children may threaten the traditionally strict hierarchical role of monolingual parents and children, particularly for first-generation Asian and Hispanic families (Curtis, 1990; Ho, 1992; Huang, 1994). Language issues may also interfere with academic achievement for ethnic minority youth. Traditional learning styles for Native American children, for example, rely heavily on nonverbal communication, observation, and enactment, as well as linguistic structures that are entirely different from those of English. As a result, the English skills of Native American children are among the poorest of any group in the United States, which partially explains their historical academic underachievement (Ho, 1992).

Although African-American children may experience the least difficulty in learning standard English, many develop two forms, a "Black English" and the more standard English (Russell, 1988). In fact, many African-American youth may intentionally oscillate between them ("code switching") in an attempt to regulate distance and emotional intimacy (see Chapter 2). Such language facility on the African-American youth's part requires an astute clinician to understand the function of code switching and to ask for feedback to ensure accurate understanding and communication between the clinician and the client.

Stereotypes

Stereotypes are transmitted through overtly negative images and attitudes as well as in covert omissions of the positive aspects of minority cultures. These pervasive messages can become internalized if not countered by evidence to the contrary. When they are internalized, identity exploration may be restricted and a dichotomous mode of thinking can result (e.g., White is "good," ethnic minority is "bad"). One must choose between identifying with dominant White values in order to "achieve" or to "hang ethnic," thereby fulfilling the prophecy and acting out the negative stereotype. Such dichotomies are represented in the derogatory slurs that ethnic minority adolescents sometimes use to refer to one who has "sold out" to the dominant culture: "Oreo" refers to an African American who is considered "Black on the outside but White on the inside." Similarly, the terms "banana," "coconut," and "apple" are used for Asian Americans, Latin Americans, and Native Americans, respectively.

Academic Underachievement and School Dropout

The frequency of school dropout for the general population ranges from 5 to 30 percent. Comparable rates for dropout among Puerto Rican youth in New York City range from 42 to 80 percent (Fitzpatrick, 1987); for Native American students on reservations and in boarding schools, 50 percent drop out (Coladarci, 1983); for Black inner-city youth, 40 to 60 percent drop out (Gibbs, 1990). Fewer than half of all Hispanics complete high school (Malone, 1985). In contrast, Liu et al. (1990) report lower dropout rates for Asian-American adolescents than for Whites.

Major Psychological and Social Issues

Identity Conflicts

Ethnic identity is conceptually separate from one's personal identity and from one's ethnicity, or sense of group membership. Ethnic identity is thought to be achieved through a process of crisis (exploration of alternatives) followed by commitment (decisions that reflect personal investment) (Phinney & Alipuria, 1990). Marcia (1966) provides a stage model of ethnic identity. *Identity achievement* is characterized by exploration of relevant issues and commitment to an identity; *moratorium* status exists when one is engaged in ongoing exploration without commitment; a *foreclosed* identity refers to commitment after little or no exploration; and identity *diffusion* refers to the absence of both exploration and commitment.

Research with Marcia's model has fairly consistently reported that minority adolescents tend to score higher in *foreclosure* than do White adolescents (Abraham, 1986; Hauser, 1972; Streitmatter, 1988). As Spencer and Markstrom-Adams (1990) point out, a viable explanation for these results may lie in the life-style preferences, migration patterns, and acculturation rates of the ethnic group that serve to encourage premature *foreclosure*. For example, Native American youth living on reservations may, adaptively, foreclose identity explorations under pressure from parents and community leaders to adhere to traditional cultural norms. However, consistent failure to explore ethnic issues critically can leave minority youth at risk for long-term psychological maladjustment (Parham & Helms, 1985; Phinney, 1989).

Although most of the research regarding ethnic identity has focused on ethnic minority adolescents, this developmental process undoubtedly has its roots in childhood, particularly with the precursor constructs of self-concept and self-esteem. Ethnic minority children are exposed at an early age to negative messages about ethnic groups. As they develop more cognitive maturity (e.g., inference making, self–other comparisons), they begin to take an increasingly sophisticated approach to the self-concept. As a result of societal experiences, however, ethnic minority children may begin to feel they have more limited options than majority children, which can lead to a sense of inferiority, resentment, and frustration.

Everett, Proctor, and Cartmell (1983) refer to an old Iroquois saying that one cannot for long have one's feet in two canoes. This has relevance for ethnic minority youth who are confronted with daily conflicts between the values of the larger dominant culture and those of their own reference group. Adherence to the rules of one group is usually regarded as rejection of the other group. For example, respectful love of one's parents *(oya-koko)* requires Japanese youth to show unquestionable loyalty to lineage and parents; they are expected to comply with familial authority even to the point of sacrificing their personal desires and ambitions (Ho, 1992). Such clashes may foster or contribute to identity diffusion or an inability to develop bicultural competencies (i.e., successful adaptations to both cultures).

Phinney, Lochner, and Murphy (1990) discuss four coping strategies frequently used by ethnic youth as they struggle with identity conflicts: (1) *alienation/marginalization*—accepting a negative self-image, which leads to alienation from one's own culture and an inability to adapt to the majority culture; (2) *assimilation*—attempting to become part of the dominant culture without maintaining ties to the ethnic culture; (3) *withdrawal or separation*—seeking insulation within one's own culture and avoiding contact with the dominant group; and (4) *integration/biculturalism*—retaining ethnic culture and learning the necessary skills to maneuver or adapt to the dominant culture. Biculturally competent adolescents are able to assert their own ethnic values without rejecting those of the majority and can demonstrate ethnic pride without disparaging other ethnic groups.

Substance Abuse

Although substance experimentation is relatively common among the general population of adolescents, unique characteristics emerge among ethnic minority adolescents (see Chapter 13). Many researchers using school populations report that alcohol and other drug use is lower among Black and Hispanic teenagers than among White youth (Barnes & Welte, 1986; Harford, 1985; Harper, 1988). Because of the positive association between school dropout and substance abuse (Schinke, Moncher, Palleja, Zayas, & Schilling, 1988), however, such results may be confounded with the sampling methodology. If those students who drop out are considered, substance abuse rates among ethnic adolescents would appear to be much higher.

Researchers have documented the early, habitual, and widespread use of alcohol among Hispanic males, who frequently begin drinking regularly before the teen years (Caetano, 1986; Comas-Díaz, 1986; Malone, 1986a). Research has also found that Native American adolescents use drugs and alcohol earlier, more heavily, and with more dire consequences than any other ethnic/racial population in the United States (Beauvais & LaBoueff, 1985; Okwumabua & Duryea, 1987; Welte & Barnes, 1987). Native Americans lead the nation in rates of alcohol-related cirrhoses, diabetes, fetal abnormalities, accident fatalities, and homicide (Moncher, Holden, & Trimble, 1990).

Teenage Pregnancy

Whereas teenage mothers account for 12 percent of all births among White Americans, comparable proportions among Hispanics, Blacks, and Native Americans are 18 percent, 25 percent, and 22 percent, respectively (Malone, 1986b). Approximately 4 out of 10 Whites and 6 out of 10 Blacks become pregnant at least once by age 20 (McGowan & Kohn, 1990). In addition, the Black infant mortality rate is almost twice the rate for White infants (U.S. Department of Health and Human Services, 1984). As Schinke, Schilling, Palleja, and Zayas (1987) report, teenage pregnancy and parenthood are associated with educational setbacks, unemployment, family and marital problems, welfare dependency, and increased infant morbidity and mortality.

Given the relatively high rate of teenage pregnancy among ethnic minorities, Scott, Shifman, Orr, Owen, and Fawcett (1988) measured the popular beliefs and level of knowledge regarding sexuality and contraception among Black and Hispanic inner-city adolescents. The results indicated that males of both groups outscored females in accurate knowledge; Hispanic males were by far the most knowledgeable and Hispanic females the least knowledgeable. The authors suggest that these differences in sexual knowledge between Hispanic men and women can be understood within the context of two core values: *machismo* (values relating to virility) and *marianismo* (values related to virginity). Traditional Hispanic sex roles dictate that the male is assertive and deals with the outside world, whereas the female is submissive, sexually naive, and concerned only with home life.

Other reasons have been proposed for the lack of effective contraceptive use to prevent adolescent pregnancy. In the Black community, Allen-Meares (1989) suggests that one barrier is the suspicion that birth control methods and programs are a form of Black genocide imposed by the dominant White society. Other researchers suggest that many adolescents have accurate information about preventing pregnancy but may choose to have a baby as a way of assuming the adult female role (Falk, Gispert, & Baucom, 1981; Ladner, 1972). Given the lack of role models, skills, and self-confidence necessary to pursue alternative life paths, many ethnic minority girls, especially those from low-SES families, may actively seek the traditional role of mother as the only rite of passage by which to enter into adult womanhood.

Suicide and Homicide

Native Americans have the highest rate of completed suicide of any ethnic group. Suicide is the second leading cause of death for Native American adolescents, with 23.6 deaths per 100,000 in the 15–19-year cohort (U.S. Congress, 1986). Rates vary, however, from tribe to tribe (Berlin, 1985). Among those factors found to be related to Native American adolescent suicide attempts are boarding school attendance prior to ninth grade, family disruption, and marked residential mobility even when families stayed together (Dizmang, Watson, May, & Bopp, 1974; May & Dizmang, 1974; Teicher, 1979). Young (1988) suggests that alcohol abuse is a critical risk factor for suicidal behavior on the basis of the finding that 80 percent of Native American adolescent suicide attempters also abuse alcohol.

Liu et al. (1990) report minimal change in the suicide rate for Asian-American youth from 1970 to 1980 after adjusting for population increases. Proportional mortality rates for suicide during this time, however, showed that suicide accounts for a much larger proportion of deaths among Asian-American youth than among White American cohorts. For both Japanese- and Chinese-American adolescents, the suicide death rate has been reported to be consistently higher for foreign-born than for American-born adolescents. Such differences can be attributed either to cultural beliefs and practices and/or to the stress associated with acculturation to United States society.

Although suicidal behavior for Black adolescents is increasing, suicide rates for this group are much lower than for White adolescents (Gibbs, 1990). Gibbs (1990) warns, however, that the incidence of suicide for Black youth may be underestimated given that actual suicidal behavior may be masked by acting out and high-risk behaviors, thereby making suicidal intent more difficult to assess. Little consistent data is available regarding recent suicide rates for Hispanic adolescents (Heacock, 1990; Wyche & Rotheram-Borus, 1990). The general consensus is that the Mexican-American rate is approximately half that of Whites (Hope & Martin, 1986).

In 1986, the leading cause of death for Black males aged 15–19 was homicide, perhaps because of the rapid rise of drug-related activity and violent crime. Black-on-Black homicide is the leading cause of death among young Black males (Bell, 1987). Hispanic homicide, often substance related, has a rate of 88 per 100,000 as compared to 19 per 100,000 for non-Hispanic young males (Centers for Disease Control, 1988; Loya et al., 1986). In New York City, for example, Hispanics disproportionately account for 42 percent of all drug-related deaths, a figure far in excess of their representation in the city's population (Schinke et al., 1988).

Delinquency

Research has found that male and female ethnic minority adolescents have higher incarceration rates than White adolescents (Krisberg et al., 1987). Several studies also report that Black juvenile delinquents have higher rates of depression and of other psychological and neurological symptoms than their White counterparts and that these disorders are frequently undetected, undiagnosed, and untreated (Dembo, 1988; Gibbs, 1982). These authors point out that whereas White youth with similar behaviors are more likely to be referred to the mental health system, Black offenders are channeled into the juvenile justice system.

Chavez, Oetting, and Swaim (1994) investigated delinquent behavior among a large sample of Mexican-American and White adolescents and found a consistent relationship between academic status and every type of delinquent behavior studied for both groups. These results suggest that Mexican-American dropouts are no more delinquent than White dropouts. Proportionally, however, there are more of them. Given the strong relationship between delinquency and achievement, the remediation of social and learning conditions that prevent Mexican-American children from succeeding academically should be targeted in prevention programs. Such efforts would not only reduce dropout but also contribute to reducing delinquency.

Impact of Psychological and Social Issues

In summary, it is important to understand how the sociocultural and ethnic group contexts influence the development of mental health problems in ethnic minority youth. Some researchers (Phinney et al., 1990) postulate that the common element among ethnic youth at risk for future psychological maladjustment is the maintenance of a foreclosed or diffuse identity status. In addition, cultural marginality and the stress associated with acculturation results in heightened anxiety, lowered self-esteem, and aggressive acting-out or withdrawal behavior, which can contribute to such problems as substance abuse, academic underachievement or dropout, teenage pregnancy, delinquency, and suicide and homicide among ethnic minority youth.

Treatment Issues

Trust is a major issue in the therapeutic relationship, for it enhances rapport and contributes to change in the client. With ethnic minority clients and White therapists, however, there is often a lack of trust based on the client's personal and historical experiences with Whites and helping professionals (Everett et al., 1983; Gibbs & Huang, 1989). Even with ethnically similar therapists and clients, there may be a lack of trust arising from the perception that the therapist has sold out and supports the values of the White middle class. Trust is usually a major issue with ethnic minority adolescents, who are typically coming to therapy involuntarily (Gibbs & Huang, 1989; Sykes, 1987). Like most adolescents, they often do not perceive they have a problem, nor do they trust that talking about issues with an adult will help.

One way to enhance trust with ethnic minority youth is for the therapist to be self-disclosing and to share limited personal information. This accomplishes three things:

1. It provides a model for self-disclosure to the adolescent who may feel uncomfortable discussing intimate feelings.
2. It enhances rapport with the adolescent.
3. It facilitates open communication (Gibbs & Huang, 1989).

Other important behaviors that can aid in the development of trust are educating the client about the therapist's role, the client's role, and the process of therapy; reinforcing the parents as the authority; emphasizing confidentiality; discussing racial differences; and displaying ethnic material in the office.

A second important issue is transference. Some ethnic minority cultures (e.g., Asian Americans) tend to view professionals as experts and authority figures. Therefore, there may be a tendency for the ethnic minority child or adolescent to view the therapist as an authority or parental figure (Sykes, 1987). Consequently, the child or adolescent may not feel free to express his or her feelings without some fear of "parental" reprisal or sanction. Anger is also frequently part of the transference, particularly from ethnic minority adolescent males. It is important for the therapist to be aware of and understand the sociocultural, historical, and immediate source of the anger rather than ascribing it to the narrow transference context.

Countertransference can also hinder the effectiveness of therapy with ethnic minority children and adolescents (Hobbs, 1985). Countertransferential reactions or feelings can be a problem with ethnically dissimilar as well as similar therapists. There may be misunderstandings between ethnically similar therapists and clients when the therapist fails to explore unique client issues because of assumptions of shared meaning based on a common cultural background. Maki (1990) has identified several obstacles to therapy related to the countertransference between ethnically similar clients and therapists: (1) an assumption of cultural themes, (2) a denial of identification or overidentification, (3) manifestations of aggression, and (4) avoidance of envy.

White therapists may experience countertransferential feelings of fear, intimidation, hatred, aggression, patronization, or denial, which can inhibit exploration of significant issues and themes with the client (Spurlock, 1985). For example, the White therapist may attempt to deny racial differences with the ethnic minority child or adolescent by trying to appear "color-blind." Such a position invalidates the client's ethnic and/or racial identity and denies his or her daily experiences. In addition, the therapist may fail to set and/or enforce limits, particularly with African-American male adolescents, who often express anger at the external controls placed on their behavior by the larger society as well as by the therapist (Hobbs, 1985). In working with ethnic minority youth, it is important for the therapist to be aware of and understand his or her own feelings of ethnicity, racism, stereotypes, and oppression (Hull, 1982; Spurlock, 1985; Sykes, 1987).

Treatment Approaches

Therapeutic intervention with ethnic minority children and adolescents requires a culturally sensitive, well-organized, and theoretically sound framework (Ho, 1992; Malgady, Rogler, & Costantino, 1990). As with ethnic minority adults, many contextual factors must be considered, such as the client's culture, level of acculturation and bicultural competency skills, English verbal ability, developmental levels, family traditions and structure, and attitudes toward help-seeking behaviors. In the following sections, three modes of intervention will be discussed: (1) individual therapy for the ethnic minority child or adolescent, (2) family therapy, and (3) group therapy. Within each approach, specific examples will be offered to illustrate ways in which these can be modified to demonstrate cultural sensitivity to ethnic minority youth.

Individual Therapy

Perhaps the first task of the therapist who hopes to engage an ethnic minority child or adolescent in individual therapy is to enlist parental cooperation and collaboration for the child's treatment. Failure to do so is perhaps the primary cause of premature termination among ethnic minority children and adolescents (Ho, 1992). An integral part of this invitation process is the therapist's ability to demonstrate awareness of and sensitivity toward cultural norms and social mores. For example, more traditional Native American children and adults consider direct eye contact to be disrepectful (Everett et al., 1983). Therapists from the White majority culture, on the other hand, may interpret the lack of eye contact to imply lack of interest, resistance, or even rudeness.

Behavior that is adaptive in one culture may be considered maladaptive in another culture (Spurlock, 1985). African-American parents, for example, tend to discipline their children more harshly than White parents, but this discipline is not always seen as abusive (Spurlock, 1985). In addition, a Native American cultural value is the shared responsibility for raising children. However, to an individual outside of this culture, it may appear that parents are neglecting children who have been sent to live with nonrelatives (Hull, 1982). In Hispanic culture, traditional norms regarding sex roles that are strictly defined clash with middle-class American norms that allow for more flexibility (Hardy-Fanta & Montana, 1982).

In addition to careful monitoring of nonverbal cues, the therapist should also remain mindful of the ethnic client's perception of the interpersonal dynamics during the sessions. During intake procedures, for example, many mental health providers attempt to gather as much information as early as possible in the form of a series of detailed personal questions. Such an interviewing style may be perceived by many ethnic group members as an overly intrusive interrogation. Consequently, stylistic modifications are advised. For Native Americans, such modifications may include moderate amounts of personal self-disclosure on the part of the professional in order to create an atmosphere of reciprocity (Everett et al. 1983; Katz, 1981; LaFromboise & Rowe, 1983). With Hispanic and Asian clients, therapists (especially young female therapists) may need to inform parents of their credentials in order to foster a heightened sense of ascribed status (Sue & Zane, 1987; Ho, 1992).

Individual Therapy with Children
Because of its problem-solving focus, time-limited nature, and emphasis on strengthening coping skills, Ho recommends short-term ego-supportive psycho-therapy for most ethnic minority children with nonpsychotic disorders (Ho, 1992). Because the main goal of this therapy is solution-focused (i.e., getting needs met adaptively through identification of alternatives and decision making), a trusting relationship between the child and the therapist is crucial to foster motivation for change, strengthen self-esteem, permit role modeling, and promote corrective emotional experiences.

Some ethnic minority children, especially those whose cultures do not sanction open expression of feelings, or those with limited English skills, may not be able to participate verbally to the degree required by the approaches advocated here. In these situations, play therapy may be the only avenue by which a child can communicate conflicts, fantasies, and emotional issues. As Ho (1992) points out, traditional cultures may view therapeutic play as frivolous, a view commonly held by some Asian cultures. As a result, play therapists may first need to educate parents about the value of therapeutic play.

Individual Therapy with Adolescents
Ethnic minority adolescents most often come to the attention of mental health providers as a result of transgressions against societal norms and laws. By the time a referral is initiated, many ethnic minority adolescents have already internalized negative images of themselves. As a result, many adolescents approach therapists with hostility or apathy, both of which are manifestations of the adolescent's struggle to defend against overwhelming powerlessness and hopelessness (Hobbs, 1985). Thus, an initial goal of therapy is to acknowledge these feelings and help the adolescent recognize the value of treatment and take advantage of the opportunity to learn about and change one's self through therapy.

As previously noted, ethnic minority adolescents often experience identity conflicts, particularly in their attempts to develop "bicultural competence." Not exploring ethnic issues during the identity process makes the adolescent vulnerable to a poor self-concept and low self-esteem. Helping the adolescent develop a positive integrated identity will empower him or her and enhance his or her self-concept. Academic intervention efforts should target remediation of social and learning conditions that prevent ethnic minority youth from succeeding academically. Such efforts would not only reduce dropout, but also contribute to reducing delinquency. In addition, for adolescent pregnancy prevention, the focus should be on economic, educational, and social opportunities that make delaying pregnancy a desirable goal. One implication for treatment with teen mothers is that social iosolation must be a target for intervention.

Because of the tendency for many poor ethnic minority adolescents to be involved with multiple agencies in addition to the mental health professional, therapists are cautioned to balance carefully the pull for case management services with the need for in-depth psychotherapy (Hobbs, 1985; Spurlock, 1985). Although the early stages of therapy can be strengthened when therapists demonstrate awareness of and assistance with practical issues, this role should be limited in order to focus on issues such as perceptions of personal power, responsibility, autonomy, and appropriate outlets for the expression of anger and frustration (Hobbs, 1985; Katz, 1981; LaFromboise & Bigfoot, 1988). Social skills training can be a valuable component of therapy in the areas of conflict resolution, anger management, and assertiveness.

Family Therapy

Family therapy offers many unique advantages for serving ethnic children and adolescents that are not easily afforded by individual and group formats (see Chapter 6). Reliance on the extended family as the primary support resource has traditionally characterized ethnic minority families and may represent a more familiar approach to problem solving than other modes of therapy. Family therapy seeks to enhance an individual's interactions with others who can provide support and nurturance, which increases the likelihood that changes can be maintained outside the context of the therapeutic relationship. Any successful attempts to strengthen familial functioning are likely to benefit a child. Particularly salient situations in which family treatment is recommended occur when the child is scapegoated as a result of parental frustrations or feelings of victimization, and when the child and the parents are experiencing generational, acculturation, or cultural conflicts (Ho, 1992).

To demonstrate cultural sensitivity to families, therapists should express personal interest in the family and search for strengths, perhaps by praising the family for its willingness to seek assistance in solving the identified problem. Issues of race should be raised early, especially when the therapist is of a different ethnic or racial background from the family. Conveying to the family that the therapist is not "color-blind" facilitates more open and honest discussion (Grevious, 1985; Ho, 1992; Sykes, 1987). Boyd-Franklin (1989) cautions against attempting extensive data collection and using a genogram with African-American families in the initial interview because many are suspicious of therapists "prying" into their lives. She advises waiting until some degree of trust has been established, which increases the likelihood of getting more detailed and constructive information.

Sykes (1987) advocates using structural family therapy with African-American adolescents. He postulates that this form of therapy is helpful because it focuses less on pathology within the individual and more on alterations in family structure that have resulted from stressful life situations. In addition, this approach is short-term and goal-oriented, and it accounts for the impact of external sources on the family. Cultural sensitivity is also demonstrated by exploring the family's kinship network and inviting relevant individuals to participate in sessions (Boyd-Franklin, 1989). Therapists should bear in mind that many ethnic families include non-blood relatives within the family network, such as friends, neighbors, ministers and deacons, Hispanic godparents, tribal leaders, and elderly members of Asian communities.

Frequently, therapeutic efforts that focus on helping parents to become reestablished into natural helping networks within their communities are the best means by which to help a child or adolescent. These efforts not only can stabilize home life but also can empower the family to solve its own problems (Edwards & Egbert-Edwards, 1990; McGowan & Kohn, 1990; Rodriguez & Zayas, 1990). The therapist may suggest or the family may already be involved with indigenous support systems, such as *curanderos, espiritistas,* and medicine men (see Chapter 9). It may also be helpful to integrate indigenous healers into the therapy or to consult with them with the family's permission.

It is important for the therapist to understand that the roles of family members in ethnic minority cultures may vary. In African-American families, for example, the roles of husband and wife tend to be relatively egalitarian (see Chapter 11), whereas Asian-American and Latin-American husbands tend to be ascribed a more dominant role than their wives. It is also important that the therapist be sensitive to family structure issues (Nagata, 1989). In Asian-American culture, for example, the structure tends to be hierarchical and male-dominated. This can have implications in treatment regarding whom the therapist should address. All communication should be addressed to the father, who is considered the head of the household (Nagata, 1989). In addition, any use of a child as an interpreter during the session should be avoided, as this unbalances the hierarchy of the family by providing the child with more power than the parents, particularly the father (see Chapter 11).

Group Therapy

Having experienced discrimination and oppression within the larger dominant culture, ethnic groups historically have found refuge and survival value in their group (see Chapter 7). In a cohesive group atmosphere, ethnic minority children and adolescents may benefit greatly from the power of collective feedback. In heterogeneous groups composed of people from diverse ethnic and racial backgrounds and varying levels of acculturation, members may learn new communication styles and alternative coping skills, and may experiment with new ways to solve problems through peer modeling and social reinforcement. Ho (1992) suggests that group therapy can be an especially effective modality for the following problems: (1) difficulties with acculturation processes, (2) exploration of ethnic awareness and identity issues, (3) strengthening of bicultural socialization skills, and (4) feelings of isolation and loneliness.

For group therapy with ethnic minority children and adolescents, group composition deserves careful forethought. Generally, groups developed with the goal of ethnic identity exploration should be homogeneous in membership, whereas groups established to lessen racial prejudice and stereotypes should consist of members with different ethnic and racial backgrounds in order to provide an opportunity for positive interracial interaction. An additional group composition parameter is the verbal communication styles of the members. Whereas Asian, Native American, and Hispanic children are generally discouraged from interrupting and are less likely to push to be heard, African-American and White children are typically more aggressive and verbose in a group (Bilides, 1991; Ho, 1992). Similarly, Asian and Latin-American minority youth may feel less comfortable making personal disclosures in the group setting. Given different communication styles and levels of comfort regarding self-disclosure, the group therapist must provide a structure that allows verbally active ethnic minority youth to express themselves and also enables less vocal youth to participate.

Conclusion

As the ethnic minority youth population continues to increase into the next century, it is incumbent upon mental health practitioners to learn effective ways of working with these youth and their families. In order to provide culturally sensitive treatment to ethnic minority children and adolescents, the therapist should be knowledgeable about communication style differences (verbal and nonverbal), family structure and role differences, language and acculturation issues, stereotypes, sociocultural influences, ethnic minority identity development, and how racism and oppression affect the psychological development of ethnic minority youth. The issues of trust, transference, and countertransference are especially crucial in the treatment process of ethnic minority youth.

Further research would be helpful in the area of how ethnic identity status may influence psychopathology in ethnic minority adolescents. All the modalities of treatment discussed in this chapter share a focus on the need to help ethnic minority youth integrate ethnic identity with personal identity and the importance of exploring the perception of limited alternatives. This process can be vital in increasing the youth's self-esteem and self-concept. The therapist can accomplish this by helping ethnic minority youth become educated about their culture, helping them to learn how to counteract negative stereotypes, and empowering them to confront and deal with racism effectively.

References

Abraham, K. G. (1986). Ego-identity differences among Anglo-American and Mexican-American adolescents. *Journal of Adolescence, 9,* 151–166.

Allen-Meares, P. (1989). Adolescent sexuality and premature parenthood: Role of the Black Church in prevention. *Journal of Social Work and Human Sexuality, 8,* 133–142.

Barnes, G. M., & Welte, J. W. (1986). Alcohol consumption of Black youth. *Journal of Studies on Alcohol, 47,* 53–61.

Beauvais, F. B., & LaBoueff, S. (1985). Drug and alcohol abuse intervention in American Indian communities. *International Journal of the Addictions, 20,* 139–171.

Bell, C. C. (1987). Preventive strategies for dealing with violence among Blacks. *Community Mental Health Journal, 23,* 217–228.

Berlin, I. N. (1982). Prevention of emotional problems among Native American children: Overview of developmental issues. *Journal of Preventive Psychiatry, 1,* 319–330.

Berlin, I. N. (1985). Prevention of adolescent suicide among some Native American tribes. *Adolescent Psychiatry, 12,* 77–93.

Berlin, I. N. (1987). Suicide among American Indian adolescents. *Suicide and Life-Threatening Behavior, 17* 218–232.

Bilides, D. (1991). Race, color, ethnicity, and class: Issues of biculturalism in school-based adolescent counseling groups. *Social Work with Groups, 13,* 43–58.

Boyd-Franklin, N. (1989). Five key factors in the treatment of Black families. *Journal of Psychotherapy and the Family, 6,* 53–69.

Caetano, R. (1986). Patterns and problems of drinking among U.S. Hispanics. In T. E. Malone (Ed.), *Report of the Secretary's Task Force on Black and Minority Health: Volume VII: Chemical dependency and diabetes* (pp. 141–186). GPO Publication No. 491-313/44709. Washington, DC: U.S. Government Printing Office.

Centers for Disease Control. (1988). *High-risk racial and ethnic groups—Blacks and Hispanics, 1970–1983.* Atlanta, GA: Author.

Chavez, E. L., Oetting, E. R., & Swaim, R. C. (1994). Dropout and delinquency: Mexican-American and Caucasian non-Hispanic youth. *Journal of Clinical Child Psychology, 23,* 47–55.

Coladarci, T. (1983). High school dropout among Native Americans. *Journal of American Indian Education, 23,* 15–23.

Comas-Díaz, L. (1986). Puerto Rican alcoholic women: Treatment considerations. *Alcohol Treatment Quarterly, 3,* 47–56.

Curtis, P. A. (1990). The consequences of acculturation to service delivery and research with Hispanic families. *Child and Adolescent Social Work, 7,* 147–159.

Dembo, R. (1988). Delinquency among Black male youth. In J. T. Gibbs (Ed.), *Young, Black and male in America: An endangered species* (pp. 174–189). Dover, MA: Auburn House.

Dizmang, L., Watson, J., May P., & Bopp, J. (1974). Adolescent suicide at an Indian reservation. *American Journal of Orthopsychiatry, 44,* 43–50.

Edwards, E. D., & Egbert-Edwards, M. (1990). American Indian adolescents: Combating problems of substance use and abuse through a community model. In A. R. Stiffman & L. E. Davis (Eds.), *Ethnic issues in adolescent mental health* (pp. 285–302). Newbury Park, CA: Sage.

Everett, F., Proctor, N., & Cartmell, B. (1983). Providing psychological services to American Indian children and families. *Professional Psychology: Research and Practice, 14,* 588–603.

Falk, R., Gispert, M., & Baucom, D. H. (1981). Personality factors related to Black teenage pregnancy and abortion. *Psychology of Women Quarterly, 5,* 737–746.

Fitzpatrick, J. P. (1987). *Puerto Rican Americans.* Englewood Cliffs, NJ: Prentice-Hall.

Gibbs, J. T. (1982). Personality patterns of delinquent females: Ethnic and sociocultural variations. *Journal of Clinical Psychology, 38,* 198–206.

Gibbs, J. T. (1984). Black adolescents and youth: An endangered species. *American Journal of Orthopsychiatry, 54,* 6–21.

Gibbs, J. T. (1990). Mental health issues of Black adolescents: Implications for policy and practice. In A. R. Stiffman & L. E. Davis (Eds.), *Ethnic issues in adolescent mental health* (pp. 21–52). Newbury Park, CA: Sage.

Gibbs, J. T., & Huang, L. N. (1989). A conceptual framework for assessing and treating minority youth. In J. T. Gibbs, L. N. Huang, & Associates (Eds.), *Children of color: Psychological interventions with minority youth* (pp. 1–29). San Francisco: Jossey-Bass.

Grevious, C. (1985). The role of the family therapist with low-income Black families. *Family Therapy, 12*, 115–122.

Hardy-Fanta, C., & Montana, P. (1982). The Hispanic female adolescent: A group therapy model. *International Journal of Group Psychotherapy, 32*, 351–366.

Harford, T. C. (1985). Drinking patterns among Black and non-Black adolescents: Results of a national survey. In E. M. Freeman (Ed.), *Social work practice with clients who have alcohol problems* (pp. 276–291). Springfield, IL: Thomas.

Harper, F. D. (1988). Alcohol and Black youth: An overview. *Journal of Drug Issues, 18*, 7–14.

Hauser, S. T. (1972). Adolescent self-image development. *Archives of General Psychiatry, 27*, 537–541.

Heacock, D. R. (1990). Suicidal behavior in Black and Hispanic youth. *Psychiatric Annals, 20*, 134–142.

Ho, M. K. (1992). *Minority children and adolescents in therapy*. Newbury Park, CA: Sage.

Hobbs, S. R. (1985). Issues in psychotherapy with Black male adolescents in the inner city: A Black clinician's perspective. *Journal of Non-White Concerns, 13*, 79–87.

Hope, S. K., & Martin, H. W. (1986). Patterns of suicide among Mexican-Americans and Anglos, 1960–1980. *Social Psychiatry, 21*, 83–88.

Huang, L. N. (1994). An integrative approach to clinical assessment and intervention with Asian-American adolescents. *Journal of Clinical Child Psychology, 23*, 21–31.

Hull, G. H., Jr. (1982). Child welfare services to Native Americans. *Social Casework: The Journal of Contemporary Social Work, 63*, 340–347.

Katz, P. (1981). Psychotherapy with Native adolescents. *Canadian Journal of Psychiatry, 26*, 455–459.

Krisberg, B., Schwartz, I., Fishman, G., Eisikovits, Z., Guttman, E., & Joe, K. (1987). The incarceration of minority youth. *Crime and Delinquency, 33*, 173–205.

Ladner, J. (1972). *Tomorrow's tomorrow: The Black woman*. Garden City, NY: Doubleday.

LaFromboise, T. D., & Bigfoot, D. S. (1988). Cultural and cognitive considerations in the prevention of American Indian adolescent suicide. *Journal of Adolescence, 11*, 139–153.

LaFromboise, T. D., & Rowe, W. (1983). Skills training for bicultural competence: Rationale and application. *Journal of Counseling Psychology, 30*, 389–595.

Liu, W. T., Yu, E. S. H., Chang, C. F., & Fernandez, M. (1990). The mental health of Asian American teenagers: A research challenge. In A. R. Stiffman & L. E. Davis (Eds.), *Ethnic issues in adolescent mental health* (pp. 92–112). Newbury Park, CA: Sage.

Loya, F., Garcia, P., Sullivan, J. D., Vargas, L. A., Allen, N. H., & Mercy, A. (1986). Conditional risks of types of homicide among Anglo, Hispanic, Black, and Asian victims in Los Angeles, 1970–1979. In T. E. Malone (Ed.), *Report of the Secretary's Task Force on Black and Minority Health: Volume V: Homicide, suicide, and unintentional injuries* (pp. 117–133). GPO Publication No. 491-313/44710. Washington, DC: U.S. Government Printing Office.

Maki, M. (1990). Countertransference with adolescent clients of the same ethnicity. *Child and Adolescent Social Work, 7*, 135–145.

Malgady, R. G., Rogler, L. H., & Costantino, G. (1990). Culturally sensitive psychotherapy for Puerto Rican children and adolescents: A program of treatment outcome research. *Journal of Consulting and Clinical Psychology, 58*, 704–712.

Malone, T. E. (1985). *Report of the Secretary's Task Force on Black and Minority Health: Volume I: Executive summary*. GPO Publication No. 487-637/QL3. Washington, DC: U.S. Government Printing Office.

Malone, T. E. (1986a). *Report of the Secretary's Task Force on Black and Minority Health: Volume V: Homicide, Suicide, and Unintentional Injuries*. GPO Publication No. 491-313/44710. Washington, DC: U.S. Government Printing Office.

Malone, T. E. (1986b). *Report of the Secretary's Task Force on Black and Minority Health: Volume VI: Infant mortality and low birth weight*. GPO No. 491-313/44711. Washington, DC: U.S. Government Printing Office.

Marcia, J. E. (1966). Development and validation of

ego identity status. *Journal of Youth and Adolescence, 13,* 419–438.

May, P., & Dizmang, L. (1974). Suicide and the American Indian. *Psychiatric Annals, 4,* 22–28.

McGowan, B. G., & Kohn, A. (1990). Social support and teen pregnancy in the for policy and practice. In A. R. Stiffman & L. E. Davis (Eds.), *Ethnic issues in adolescent mental health* (pp. 189–207). Newbury Park, CA: Sage.

Moncher, M. S., Holden, G. W., & Trimble, J. E. (1990). Substance abuse among Native American youth. *Journal of Consulting and Clinical Psychology, 58,* 408–415.

Myers, H. F. (1989). Urban stress and mental health of Afro-American youth: An epidemiologic and conceptual update. In R. L. Jones (Ed.), *Black adolescents* (pp. 123–152). Berkeley, CA: Cobbs & Henry.

Nagata, D. K. (1989). Japanese American children and adolescents. In J. T. Gibbs, L. N. Huang, & Associates (Eds.), *Children of color: Psychological interventions with minority youth* (pp. 67–113). San Francisco: Jossey-Bass.

Okwumabua, J. O., & Duryea, E. J. (1987). Age of onset, periods of risk, and patterns of progression in drug use among American Indian high school students. *International Journal of the Addictions, 22,* 1269–1276.

Parham, T., & Helms, J. (1985). Attitudes of racial identity and self-esteem of Black students: An exploratory investigation. *Journal of College Student Personnel, 26,* 143–147.

Phinney, J. S. (1989). Stages of ethnic identity development in minority group adolescents. *Journal of Early Adolescence, 9,* 34–49.

Phinney, J. S., & Alipuria, L. L. (1990). Ethnic identity in college students from four ethnic groups. *Journal of Adolescence, 13,* 171–183.

Phinney, J. S., Lochner, B. T., & Murphy, R. (1990). Ethnic identity development and psychological adjustment in adolescence. In A. R. Stiffman & L. E. Davis (Eds.), *Ethnic issues in adolescent mental health* (pp. 53–72). Newbury Park, CA: Sage.

Ramirez, O. (1989). Mexican American children and adolescents. In J. T. Gibbs, L. N. Huang, & Associates (Eds.), *Children of color: Psychological interventions with minority youth* (pp. 224–250). San Francisco: Jossey-Bass.

Rodriguez, O., & Zayas, L. H. (1990). Hispanic adolescents and antisocial behavior: Sociocultural factors and treatment implications. In A. R. Stiffman & L. E. Davis (Eds.), *Ethnic issues in adolescent mental health* (pp. 147–171). Newbury Park, CA: Sage.

Russell, D. M. (1988). Language and psychotherapy: The influence of nonstandard English in clinical practice. In L. Comas-Díaz & E. E. H. Griffith (Eds.), *Clinical guidelines in cross-cultural mental health* (pp. 33–68). New York: Wiley.

Schinke, S. P., Moncher, M. S., Palleja, J., Zayas, L. H., & Schilling, R. F. (1988). Hispanic youth, substance abuse, and stress: Implications for prevention research. *International Journal of the Addictions, 23,* 809–826.

Schinke, S. P., Schilling, R. F., Palleja, J., & Zayas, L. H. (1987). Prevention research among ethnic-racial minority group adolescents. *The Behavior Therapist, 10,* 151–155.

Scott, C. S., Shifman, L., Orr, L., Owen, R. G., & Fawcett, N. (1988). Hispanic and Black American adolescents' beliefs relating to sexuality and contraception. *Adolescence, 23,* 667–688.

Spencer, M. B., & Markstrom-Adams, C. (1990). Identity processes among racial and ethnic minority children in America. *Child Development, 61,* 290–310.

Spurlock, J. (1985). Assessment and therapeutic intervention of Black children. *Journal of the American Academy of Child Psychiatry, 24,* 168–174.

Streitmatter, J. L. (1988). Ethnicity as a mediating variable of early adolescent identity development. *Journal of Adolescence, 11,* 335–346.

Sue, S., & Zane, N. (1987). The role of culture and cultural techniques in psychotherapy: A critique and reformulation. *American Psychologist, 42,* 37–45.

Sykes, D. K., Jr. (1987). An approach to working with Black youth in cross cultural therapy. *Clinical Social Work Journal, 15,* 260–270.

Teicher, J. D. (1979). Suicide and suicide attempters. In J. D. Noshpitz (Ed.), *Basic handbook of child psychiatry: Disturbances of development* (Vol. 2) (pp. 685–697). New York: Basic Books.

Tolmach, J. (1985). "There ain't nobody on my side": A new day treatment program for Black urban youth. *Journal of Clinical Child Psychology, 14,* 214–219.

U.S. Bureau of the Census. (1990). *1990 census of population and housing—Summary tape file 1. Summary population and housing characteristics.* Washington, DC: U.S. Government Printing Office.

U.S. Bureau of the Census. (1992). *1990 census of population, 1990 CP-1-4, General population characteristics.* Washington, DC: U.S. Government Printing Office.

U.S. Congress. (1986). *Indian health care* (OTA-H-290). Washington, DC: U.S. Government Printing Office.

U.S. Department of Health and Human Services. (1984). National Center for Health Statistics. *Monthly Vital Statistics Report* (Vol. 33, No. 3). Washington, DC: Author.

Welte, J. W., & Barnes, G. M. (1987). Alcohol use among adolescent minority groups. *Journal of Studies on Alcohol, 48,* 329–336.

Wissow, L. S., Gittelsohn, A. M., Szklo, M., Starfield, B., & Mussman, M. (1988). Poverty, race, and hospitalization for childhood asthma. *American Journal of Public Health, 78,* 777–781.

Wyche, K. F., & Rotheram-Borus, M. J. (1990). Suicidal behavior among minority youth in the United States. In A. R. Stiffman & L. E. Davis (Eds.), *Ethnic issues in adolescent mental health* (pp. 323–338). Newbury Park, CA: Sage.

Young, T. J. (1988). Substance use and abuse among native Americans. *Clinical Psychology Review, 8,* 125–138.

Chapter 11

Clinical Issues and Intervention with Ethnic Minority Women

ROBIN YOUNG RIVERS

Of the 248,709,873 persons identified in the 1990 census, 127,537,490 or 51.3 percent, are female (U.S. Bureau of Census, 1990). Almost 25 percent of these females are members of ethnic minority groups. More specifically, there are 15,817,802 Black, 10,771,487 Hispanic, 3,701,295 Asian/Pacific Islander, and 1,016,503 Native American/Eskimo/Aleutian females (U.S. Bureau of Census, 1990). A closer inspection of the demographic profiles reveals a number of variations within these ethnic groups. Sex ratios, for example, vary: There are more Black females than Black males and more Hispanic males than Hispanic females. Such patterns reflect different immigration, fertility, and mortality rates among the groups (O'Hare, 1992).

Ethnic minority populations and ethnic minority women, in particular, continue to be underserved and ineffectively served by mental health providers (see Chapters 2, 8, 16 of this book; LaFromboise, Heyle, & Ozer, 1990; Palacios & Franco, 1986; Russo, 1985). Ethnic minority women also bring unique issues and concerns to treatment. Although some of the presenting problems may be similar to those of White women (e.g., depression, anxiety), often the contributing factors are different (e.g., poverty, oppression, acculturation stress). Ethnic minority women, in contrast to White women, experience the unique effects of the interaction of racism and sexism. The psychological well-being of ethnic minority women is affected not only by racism and sexism but oftentimes by the experiences of low socioeconomic status, immigration, acculturation, assimilation, discrimination, and stereotyping.

This chapter will explore the sociocultural history of women in four major racial/ethnic groups: African-American, Native American, Asian-American, and Latin American. The heterogeneity among and between ethnic minority women in these groups must be recognized. Differences in history as well as commonalities in experience with oppression, racism, and discrimination in this country will be discussed. The impact of sociocultural factors (e.g., economic, acculturation, cultural conflict/role strain, stereotypes) on the psychological well-being of ethnic minority women will be delineated, as well as the barriers to treatment. Guidelines for conducting effective psychotherapy with this population will be presented.

Historical Issues

The psychological development and functioning of ethnic minority women has been influenced by their history prior to arrival in the United States, by their history in this country, and by their efforts at acculturation. Each ethnic group has a unique social and cultural history. However, differences exist in the treatment each ethnic group has received during its existence in this country. There continue to be differences in how the majority culture of this country perceives and treats ethnic minority people. However, these differences are better illustrated within a historical context.

Historically, the indigenous peoples of the Americas were conquered by the Europeans, Africans were captured and brought to this country by slave traders, and Asians came as immigrants to the United States. In America, each group was expected to adopt the values of the dominant group (European Americans). Some of these values, through time, became incorporated into the minority groups' own value system. Although some native cultural patterns were retained, disruptions in familial and sex roles were caused by the pressures created by the majority culture for assimilation.

Smith, Burlew, Mosley, and Whitney (1978), describe the ancient African tribal family as characterized by customs and rituals where sex roles were clearly defined. The male was dominant, and the female and children occupied subordinate roles. Although the roles were clearly defined, they appeared to be flexible as husband and wife often shared the daily tasks. This role flexibility was carried over into slavery in America, where both spouses often worked alongside each other in the cotton fields. With the termination of legal slavery, African Americans were then expected to fulfill the roles practiced by the dominant society; that is, African-American males were expected to provide for their families, but they were denied access to educational and occupational resources.

Traditionally, in the family, African-American women have had at least equal status with African-American men (Davenport & Yurich, 1991). African-American women have always worked outside the home and been strong, independent figures within the African-American family. They have not been "traditionally feminine" women who stayed home with their children. However, as African Americans "began to fight for their rights and to participate more fully in this society, they began to take on its values—and these values included male dominance and the traditional role of women" (Rohrbaugh, 1979, p. 250).

It is questionable whether African-American women have ever accepted the "traditional" role of women. While White women tend to evaluate themselves on the basis of the roles of wife and mother, Myers (1980) found from her study of 400 African-American women in Michigan and Mississippi that African-American women do not necessarily evaluate themselves on the basis of any one role. They appear to use several roles as measures of success in order to think well of themselves. She notes that these roles are most often occupational and family maintenance. African-American women tend to value some roles more than others, and some roles are viewed as more important than others for developing and maintaining a positive self-image (Myers, 1980).

For Mexican-American women the situation was different; they have always been ascribed an inferior status to men. With the arrival of the Spanish in Mexico in the sixteenth century came an imperialistic and patriarchal value system with a history of subjugating people of color. Nieto-Gomez (1976) states, "Traditionally, sex through marriage or rape, which are the tools of conquest, have been a means of taking possession of women and land" (p. 227). Women in this culture had long been viewed as property and now came to belong to the man or men who had sexually penetrated them. Both the economic system and the church sanctioned the continued dominance and sexual abuse by the men. The church was used as an ideological force "to maintain social control and subjugation of the Indian woman to her oppression" (p. 228). Women were expected to embrace the concept of *marianisma*, the veneration of the Virgin Mary as the ultimate role model. "Church tradition has directed the women to identify with the emotional suffering of the pure, passive, bystander, the Virgin Mary" (Nieto-Gomez, 1976, p. 228).

From the concept of *marianisma* grew the notion that the woman was to blame for her husband's problems, and *marianisma* convinced the woman to endure injustices committed against her. In addition, this concept inculcated the submission and passivity of women while facilitating and encouraging *machismo* in men. Because the concept has been fostered that the Mexican woman is inferior to the man, it has been reported that the patriarchal structure of Mexican culture works so as to "to instill serious neurosis in the women" (Levine & Padilla, 1980, p. 10). The effect of the patriarchal structure on the Mexican woman is highlighted in the United States today as Chicanas are often torn between the patriarchal values of their Mexican-American culture and the more liberal White/American norms.

This patriarchal structure is also found in Puerto Rican society, where there was a similar history of Spanish conquest. Puerto Rican women tend to experience the same type of conflicts as Chicanas. For Latin American women, in addition to culture conflict, there is significant role strain. Levine and Padilla (1980) note that Hispanic women may use various strategies in an effort to minimize such role strain. Some establish successful compromise in their roles and values. Others reject traditional Hispanic culture completely. In addition, there are those women who never fully resolve the conflict and often exhibit psychological or psychosomatic symptoms.

Confucius had a deleterious effect on the status of Asian women. The philosophy of Confucius subordinated women and ascribed to them an inferior status within the family (Chu & Sue, 1984; Ho, 1990; Yamamoto & Acosta, 1982). Prior to this time, Asian women had been scholars, warriors, and leaders, "but the emergence of his [Confucius'] teachings as the principles of social relationships for all of Asia ensued for women several centuries of status inferiority and imposed incapability" (Fujitomi & Wong, 1976, p. 237). Asian society was patriarchal, patrilineal, and patrilocal, and prearranged marriages were the rule (Homma-True, 1990). Through marriage, the woman became the possession of her husband's family, where she was expected to cater to the demands of all the family members and to attend to menial household tasks. Asian women were socialized to behave submissively as preparation for marriage, and were often denied formal education. The woman worked in both the home and the field and was a servant to her husband, father, and brothers.

Very few women were a part of the large influx of Chinese into the United States in the 1850s because of the constraints of cultural attitudes and the belief that the woman was not to leave her husband's family home for any reason. The passage of the Chinese Exclusion Act in 1882 further precluded the entry of Chinese women to join their husbands. Because the sexual needs of the married or single Chinese male in America were going unsatisfied as a result of laws prohibiting racial integration, Chinese prostitutes were transported to fulfill these needs. In coming to the United States, Chinese men also had transported the traditional Chinese values of female inferiority, and thus Chinese women in the United States "were severely oppressed, reduced to mere slaves and sexual commodities" (Fujitomi & Wong, 1976, p. 242).

The experience of Japanese women was similar to that of the Chinese. Japanese women were also ascribed an inferior status, and marriages tended to be prearranged. For the Japanese woman, her role as a good wife was to sacrifice and be dutiful to her husband first, her children second, and herself last. Asian women who came to the United States found that "American customs permitted greater flexibility and opportunity than did those in their native land" (Rohrbaugh, 1979, p. 251). Today, many Asian-American women are beginning to reject the traditional role, but they are still struggling to achieve equal status and to overcome the inferiority complex inculcated by traditional Asian thinking.

Native American society provides a contrast to the other ethnic minority groups. Historically, African, Latin, and Asian cultures have exhibited a patriarchal/patrilineal structure. However, Native American society has traditionally been matriarchal/matrilineal. In earlier years, Native American women held great political and economic power. According to Rohrbaugh (1979), Native American women had considerable power and status in their tribes at the times Europeans arrived in this country. For example, among the Senecas, women owned and cultivated the land, which they had inherited through their mothers. After marriage, the husband moved into the wife's household, where he lived with the wife's female relatives, their spouses, and their children. The men were responsible for hunting and being warriors. Witt (1976) notes that because of the matrilineal, matriarchal, and matrilocal structure of the Navajos, Navajo women performed a number of roles that were necessary for the survival of the extended family. With the European arrival, a paternalistic and patriarchal value system was imposed upon the Native Americans and the women were stripped of their power and economic function. Many of the women's roles began to be taken over by men. The White man sought to "civilize the Indians" by imposing White/European cultural values and customs on the Native Americans.

Sociocultural Issues

The mental health status of ethnic minority women is often related to sociocultural factors such as economic/financial stress, educational and occupational discrimination, acculturation issues, culture conflict/sex-role conflict, and stereotyping. In addition, ethnic minority women are often subjected to racism, sexism, and oppression, which continue to keep them at the bottom of income, educational, and occupational levels (Greene, 1992; Pyant & Yanico, 1991). All these factors can have a negative impact on women's view of themselves and can produce stress, which may affect their physical health, mental health, and emotional well-being (Watts-Jones, 1990).

Economic/Financial Stress

Minority women tend to suffer from a double stigma in that they are both women and members of a specific racial/ethnic group in a society that devalues both of these characteristics. Minority women may experience a "triple" stigma, for they are also often poor. When ethnic minority women are employed, they are often found in low-wage positions, with limited opportunities for advancement (Helms, 1979). Therefore, as a result of either underemployment or unemployment, ethnic minority women and their families are disproportionately represented among the poverty ranks (O'Hare, 1992). Decreased earnings coupled with high unemployment contribute to the poverty of many minority women.

Poverty, in today's society, has many stressful consequences: lowered social status, inadequate or nonexistent health care, substandard housing, inadequate nutrition, and a generally reduced quality of life (Kerner, Dusenbury, & Mandelblatt, 1993; Ruiz & Padilla, 1977; Watts-Jones, 1990). In addition, stress may be experienced directly as the result of frustration about racism and discrimination in employment. Although the stress of being low income can apply to all poor people, economic and occupational discrimination exacerbates the stress for minority women. Whereas traditionally many majority women have worked out of choice, ethnic minority women have worked because of necessity; for a minority woman, her salary has been needed to supplement that of her mate's as his earnings were less than his White counterpart's (Malson, 1983).

This situation is highlighted by Myers's (1980) assertion that most African-American women cannot afford to stay home, although many would like to, because of the need to supplement the family income. Research has, in fact, indicated that most African-American women expect to work throughout their adult lives (Harrison, 1989; Malson, 1983). The financial stress experienced by other ethnic minority women, as well as African-American women, has also increased as a result of the rise in female-headed households (Ahlburg & De Vita, 1992; O'Hare, 1992; O'Hare, Pollard, Mann, & Kent, 1991). These increases in female-headed households have been due to increased rates of birth to unmarried mothers and increased divorce rates.

As previously mentioned, ethnic minority women tend to receive the lowest wages. Because these women are likely to have earnings that fall below the poverty level, trying to raise and maintain a family is a major source of tension. More specifically, according to the 1990 census, 71.1 percent of Black women had an income of $9,999 or below (U.S. Bureau of Census, 1990). The picture for other ethnic minority women is equally bleak. The income rates for Hispanic, Asian/Pacific Islander, and Native American women below $9,999 were 74.5, 67.5, and 77.0 percent, respectively. Such findings are similar to earlier ones from the 1980 census (Amaro & Russo, 1987; Levine & Padilla, 1980). This bleak economic picture is reflected in the familial poverty rates for Black, Hispanic, Asian/Pacific Islander, and American Indian/Aleutian families, which are 34.2, 23.9, 16.2, and 33.9 percent, respectively according to the 1990 census (U.S. Bureau of Census, 1990).

Educational and Occupational Discrimination

Often as a result of racial discrimination in employment, ethnic minority women are relegated to menial and low-paying jobs (more so than White females and African-American males) (Harrison, 1989; Helms, 1979). Discrimination has also prevented ethnic minority women from obtaining the education they need for better paying jobs. For example, the government-sponsored educational system has offered vocational choices to Native American women that are extremely narrow and sexist, often channeling them into secretarial and domestic roles (LaFromboise, Heyle, & Ozer, 1990). As Witt (1976) states, "Native American females cannot put to use their skills neither off nor on the reservation because reservation life is not conducive to the life of the average Native American homemaker" (p. 252). Essentially, Native American women have been inappropriately educated by the U.S. government and the failure of the educational system to assimilate these females adequately often leads to depression among them.

Acculturation

It has been proposed that the degree of acculturation to United States society produces stress for ethnic minority women. Olmedo and Parron (1981) state, "For Hispanic, Native American, and Asian women, problems related to acculturation to a society that appears prejudicial, hostile, and rejecting place them in a high-risk category for personality disintegration and subsequent need for mental health intervention" (p. 106). Migration and acculturation stress can lead to feelings of depression, loneliness, isolation, and alienation (Curtis, 1990; Sodowsky, Lai, & Plake, 1991), particularly when the extended family (which is a primary source of support) has been disrupted. There may also be spousal or intergenerational conflicts resulting from the faster acculturation of some family members than others. Children tend to acculturate faster than adults. It has been noted that Latin-American and Native American women tend to be less assimilated by American society, whereas Chinese-American women are assimilated faster than Chinese-American men (Leong, 1986).

Culture Conflict and Role Strain

There are other problems related to acculturation, such as value conflict emanating from trying to accommodate to two different cultures, particularly as United States values are often incongruent with the values of minority cultures. Sue and Sue (1972) note that culture conflict appears to be an intimate part of the Asian-American experience. One of the major conflicts for ethnic minority women in the United States is dealing with the significant role strain produced by "culture conflict." Culture conflict causes a great deal of stress for these women as they are expected to acculturate and accommodate to United States society. Culture conflict can lead to sex-role conflict; an identity crisis; and/or feelings of isolation, alienation, or depression. Another problem related to acculturation that produces value conflict for minority women is the acceptance of the American female standard of beauty. Inability to attain this standard because of skin color, facial features, hair texture, and the like produces stress, which can lead to a lowered self-concept and even self-hatred (Neal & Wilson, 1989; Ramseur, 1989).

Stereotypes

Dealing with stereotypes is also a problem for minority women, as stereotypes are often used to justify discrimination. African-American women have variously been labeled "Mammy," "Aunt Jemina," "Sapphire," and "Whore" (Greene, 1992; Helms, 1979; Young, 1989). The predominant image, however, is that of a Superwoman who can handle extraordinary responsibility (Harrison, 1989). This image perpetuates the notion that the African-American woman's lot in life can be ignored because she is able to cope with all of life's difficulties. African-American women also appear to have accepted and internalized this image, and it is constantly promoted as a positive model within the African-American community (Harrison, 1989). Unfortunately, perpetuating and internalizing this image means failing to acknowledge and recognize the stress it engenders resulting from the tremendous amount of energy required to live up to such standards (Harrison, 1989; Lewis, 1989).

Native American women have also been depicted stereotypically. However, Native American women have been plagued by "invisibility." Often, people have difficulty conjuring up an image of her at all. The most predominant image is that of the squaw:

> *The term "Squaw" began as a perfectly acceptable Algonkian term mean-ing "Woman." In time, it became synonymous with "Drudge" and, in some areas, "Prostitute." The squaw is regarded as a brown lump of a drudge, chewing buffalo hide, putting that tipi up and down again and again, carrying heavy burdens along with the dogs while the tribe moves ever onward, away from the pursuing cavalry. (Witt, 1976, p. 249)*

The stereotype of the Native American woman often depicted by Hollywood is that of Pocahontas, a Native American princess. Witt (1976) notes that "the drunken indian, the cadillac indian, lonesome polecat-facelessness—still characterizes Na-tive-American women" (p. 249) as they remain largely invisible.

For the Asian woman, the predominant stereotypic image is one of passivity, sexual attractiveness, and reserve (Chan, 1987). Fujitomi and Wong (1976) note that the pervasiveness of this image creates a continuous struggle for Asian women to develop a more assertive persona and a positive self-image. Asian women are viewed as deferring to males, elders, and authority figures. This image is even accepted among Asian people themselves and is used to subjugate women and prevent them from developing high self-esteem.

The stereotypes for Latin American women include the passive, submissive, male-dominated, all-suffering woman. Additionally, Puerto Rican women have been stereotyped as hysterical, loud, and hot-tempered (Davenport & Yurich, 1991; Gibson, 1983; Palacios & Franco, 1986; Zavala-Martinez, 1987). Some other common stereotypes about Latin Americans are that they are unclean, alcoholic, criminal, deceitful, and unintelligent (Levine & Padilla, 1980). Most ethnic minority people come to accept the existing stereotypes about their women. Ethnic minority women's attempts to overcome such stereotypes can lead to stress. As previously mentioned, they must deal not only with the images applied to them by the larger society but even with those images held by their own people.

In conclusion, the stressful experiences of immigration, acculturation, assimila-tion, and stereotyping, compounded by both racial and sexual discrimination in obtaining education and employment, influence the psychological functioning of ethnic minority women (Soto, 1983; Torres-Matrullo, 1976; Homma-True, 1990). Although there may also be intrapsychic causes such as anxiety or poor coping skills, mental health problems of ethnic minority women tend to be related to extrapsychic factors—racism, sexism, poverty, and discrimination (Yamamoto & Acosta, 1982). Particularly for African-American women, racism usually has more of an impact than sexism (Harrison, 1989; Pyant & Yanico, 1991).

Mental Health Issues

Several researchers have identified sources of stress that pertain to ethnic minority groups: migration, poverty, acculturation, culture conflict, language barriers, and minority group status (Comas-Díaz, 1984; Gibson, 1983; Leong, 1986; Salgado de

Snyder, 1987). For many ethnic minority women, stress emanates from the culture conflict experienced as they try to adapt to United States culture, where sex roles are more liberal (Salgado de Snyder, Cervantes, & Padilla, 1990). Ethnic minority women can be considered "at risk" for mental health problems because of the stresses they experience (del Portillo, 1987; Pyant & Yanico, 1991; Homma-True, 1990). Some of the mental health problems they experience include lowered self-concept/self-esteem, depression and anxiety, alcohol and substance abuse, anger and hostility, psychosomatic symptoms, and psychosis (LaFromboise et al., 1990). To discuss all these problems is beyond the scope of this chapter. Therefore, two issues frequently experienced by ethnic minority women will be examined in more depth.

Self-Concept/Self-Esteem

A significant problem experienced by ethnic minority women is poor self-concept. As Olmedo and Parron (1981) note, "the self-concept of minority women has been greatly affected by racial and ethnic stereotyping, making them feel unacceptable according to White standards of beauty" (p. 106). For this reason, ethnic minority women may develop low self-esteem that leads to racial self-hatred and intense conflicts (Gray & Jones, 1987; Ramseur, 1989). Certain racial/cultural traits are denigrated, and some women may even deny their own ethnicity. This tendency to deny one's ethnicity appears to stem from the pressures of acculturation. Ethnic minority women sometimes use various cosmetics to bleach their skin and hair—that is, to become more White in appearance. However, this practice appears to have declined as a result of the social movement that began in the 1960s. In addition, the stereotypes of some ethnic minority women as passive and submissive, in conjunction with a patriarchal family structure, have contributed to a poor self-concept and low self-esteem in these women.

Myers (1980) posits that better coping leads to increased feelings of self-esteem and asserts that one way African-American women cope is by judging themselves against other African-American women. In addition, she notes that strong family ties and the church have always been a source of support and strength for African Americans. The church and extended family network have generally been supports for all minority groups in America (Ho, 1992). Smith et al. (1978) note that in addition to an inner strength, pride in herself and her race is another quality that contributes to the Black woman's ability to cope successfully. They note that there are at least four characteristics that help the African-American woman "cope with a world that creates much stress for her—inner strength, race- (and self-) pride, concern over femininity, and creativity in problem-solving" (p. 38).

However, Olmedo and Parron (1981) assert that the inner strength of minority women, used as a successful coping strategy, serves to mask the degree of stress they experience. These authors state, "evidence of the severe stress they [minority women] undergo is suggested by studies that show an intimate link between behavior and stress-related life-threatening diseases. Minority women are twice as likely to die from diabetes and three times more likely to die from hypertension than

White women" (p. 106). Not much other data has been reported regarding the coping abilities of other specific ethnic minority women—Latin American, Native American, and Asian-American. Although Levine and Padilla (1980) note that several studies indicate that maintenance of Hispanic values is associated with strong coping abilities. In addition, the authors report that Hispanic females may interact less with the dominant culture than males do, thus reducing some of the stress.

Depression and Anxiety

Most of the research, with the exception of the Epidemiologic Catchment Area (ECA) studies, have found a strong relationship between mental disorders and degree of acculturation of ethnic minorities (Burnam, Hough, Karno, Escobar, & Telles, 1987; Escobar, 1993). Ethnic minority women, in particular, have been found to experience high levels of depression and anxiety as a result of the stress of acculturation (Salgado de Snyder, 1987). In addition, several researchers note that African-American women are at high risk for depression due to the chronic environmental stressors they experience (Pyant & Yanico, 1991; Taylor, Henderson, & Jackson, 1991; Watts-Jones, 1990). High rates of depression have also been noted for immigrant Asian women (Franks & Faux, 1990; Kuo, 1984). In particular, Kuo (1984) found that immigrant Chinese and Filipino women had higher rates of depression than men. LaFromboise et al. (1990) reported high prevalence rates of depression in Native American women due to the intensity of life stressors. Their findings indicated that the prevalence of depression for Native American women within certain communities may be four to six times greater than previous estimates. Internalized feelings of anger related to racism also contribute to depression in some minority women.

For Puerto Rican women, depression appears related to sex-role issues and a patriarchal value system. Studies of Puerto Rican women have found higher rates of depression among island than mainland Puerto Ricans (Comas-Díaz, 1984). An epidemiological study of island Puerto Rican women (Canino et al., 1987) found a significantly higher rate of depressive symptomatology in the women than the men. The prevalence rate was twice as high for depressive disorders and four times greater for dysthymia. The authors offered a sex-role explanation for the gender differences in this study. In Puerto Rican culture, it is culturally expected that the men will have a dominant role while the women will assume a more passive and submissive stance, which appears to contribute to depression.

Levine and Padilla (1980) note that when dealing with Hispanic clients, what are perceived to be psychological symptoms may actually be stress manifested in various ways. Olmedo and Parron (1981) suggest that although depressed ethnic minority women may experience symptoms similar to those of depressed White women, their experience is described differently by clinicians. Ethnic minority women are described as having "poor work habits, being apathetic, driving their husbands away, or lacking in mothering skills" (p. 107). Such attributes are demeaning and could contribute to diminished self-esteem in these women. These authors also note that depression in ethnic minority women is often manifested through drug and alcohol abuse.

In addition to depression, African-American and Latin American women have been found to experience high levels of anxiety (Gray & Jones, 1987; Palacios & Franco, 1986; Zavala-Martinez, 1987). For Puerto Rican women, anxiety is often manifested by psychosomatic symptomatology such as, *nervios* ("nerves") or through an *ataque*. Both of these are stress reactions arising from feelings of anger and powerlessness (Comas-Díaz, 1987; Torres-Matrullo, 1976; Zavala-Martinez, 1987). An *ataque* is a neurotic reaction characterized by psychomotor seizures, often as a result of the stress experienced from attempting to cope in two cultures (Soto, 1983). An *ataque* can last from five to ten minutes, during which time the individual cries or screams, falls to the floor, and swings her arms and/or legs.

Barriers to Treatment

Ethnic minority women tend to have more positive attitudes toward mental health services and use them more frequently than ethnic minority men (Gary, 1987; Neighbors & Howard, 1987). However, a number of barriers may interfere with the effective treatment of ethnic minority women. One barrier for minority women in seeking therapy arises from stereotypical attitudes and sex-role bias. Olmedo and Parron (1981) state that the

> *issues of sex role bias are in many cases compounded for minority women. For example, Asian-American and Mexican-American women are often stereotyped as devoted mothers and wives whose lives revolve entirely around the family. On the other hand, the attributed "inner strength" of Black women is often exaggerated into a "matriarchal dominance stereotype" which distorts their perceived family roles.* (p. 108)

Therefore, ethnic minority women may be reluctant to enter therapy because they see psychology and psychiatry as fields dominated by White males, where stereotypes are perpetuated and the status quo is upheld.

Another cultural barrier pertains to language differences between the ethnic minority female client and the therapist. Language differences can hinder the effectiveness of therapy with ethnic minority clients (see Chapter 2; Martinez, 1988; Russell, 1988) and can take the form of the use of non-Standard English by African Americans or the use of another language by the client (Gibson, 1983; Russell, 1988). Bilingual clients sometimes "maintain independence between the two language systems which can serve to compartmentalize their feelings" (Espin, 1987, p. 497). Several authors note that some bilinguals, when making the translation to English, may exhibit flat affect or appear withdrawn (Espin, 1987; Gibson, 1983; Russell, 1988). In addition, the therapist may have difficulty understanding the English translation from another language (Yamamoto & Acosta, 1982), and it may take the client some time to make the translation so that the therapist understands it clearly. Latin American clients tend to encode experiences with affective meaning in Spanish, so that accurate understanding when translated to English can be problematic (Espin, 1987; Gibson, 1983; Russell, 1988). It has also been suggested that language may be a barrier when working with Native Americans, as their language structure is different (Ho, 1992), making the expression of certain feelings and ideas difficult. In addition, each tribe has its own language, which contributes to the complexity of verbal communication. With Spanish and some Native American and Asian languages, there is not always a direct translation or correspondence with English words (Edwards & Edwards, 1989; Gibson, 1983).

In addition to the language differences between the client and the therapist, some cultures place great emphasis on nonverbal communication. In some cultures, direct eye contact is seen as a form of disrespect (Brower, 1989; Everett, Proctor, & Cartmell, 1989). Other nonverbal behaviors that may have different meanings for ethnic minority and nonminority clients include personal space, body movements, and touching. Differences between the client and the therapist in understanding nonverbal behavior may create a barrier in therapy because they can result in misinterpretation and miscommunication. As a result, the client may feel that she has not been heard or may feel misunderstood and rejected by the therapist.

Guidelines for Effective Therapy

It is important to be aware of the cultural issues discussed in this chapter when providing psychotherapeutic services to ethnic minority women. The awareness of these issues and their impact on the emotional and behavioral functioning of ethnic minority women should help the therapist render more effective services. In working effectively with ethnic minority women, it is important to understand how culture conflict, poverty, low educational and occupational levels, sex bias, race discrimination, and stereotyping contribute to stress and to the psychological functioning of ethnic minority women. In working with ethnic minority clients in general, and ethnic minority women in particular, the therapist must distinguish intrapsychic difficulties (low self-esteem, anxiety, poor coping skills) from extrapsychic conflict (distress caused by social factors such as racism, poverty, and discrimination). Errors in treatment can occur by focusing exclusively on either intrapsychic or extrapsychic problems. It should not be assumed, for example, that all problems emanate from racism. However, the therapist must be aware of the effect of racism on the client. Ethnic minority women will in all likelihood present with a combination of both intra- and extrapsychic issues to be addressed in treatment (see Chapter 5).

One overall goal of treatment with ethnic minority women is to empower them to handle the stresses of their daily lives (Mays, 1986, Zavala-Martinez, 1987). In that process, the therapist should recognize racism and sexism when and where they exist and acknowledge their deleterious effects. The therapist should help the client overcome feelings of powerlessness and helplessness inculcated by racism. It is also important for the therapist to focus on the effects of stereotyping and to discuss ways to counteract stereotypes and negative images of ethnic minority women. This can lead to feelings of empowerment and help the client develop a more positive identity and increased self-esteem. The therapist also should seek to examine his or her own biases regarding women and race and to counter her or his own stereotypes and negative perceptions of ethnic minority women clients. Ethnic minority therapists may have difficulties with racial and sexual bias because they themselves can be as susceptible to these stereotypes as nonminority therapists.

The therapist needs to listen sensitively to the client and not assume that pathology is due exclusively to intrapsychic causes. In general, the therapist should focus on the client's strengths and help the client look at options and choices available to her (del Portillo, 1987). In cross-cultural therapeutic encounters (White therapist and ethnic minority client), the therapist should broach the difference in race in one of the initial sessions (Jones & Seagull, 1989). This lets the client know that racial issues can be discussed in the therapy setting since this can be a salient issue for some ethnic minority women (Greene, 1992).

In working with ethnic minority women, it would also be helpful for the therapist to discuss spirituality issues. As spirituality tends to be a pervasive aspect of minority cultural life and has a great influence on attitudes and beliefs (Gibson, 1983; Yamamoto & Acosta, 1982). It is important for the therapist to understand how spirituality and religious issues may affect the therapy (Yamamoto & Acosta, 1982) and contribute to conflicts experienced by ethnic minority women. Ethnic minority women may experience conflicts related to religion or spirituality especially regarding the role of women, the concept of fatalism, and so on. (Boyd-Franklin, 1987; 1991). In Latin American cultures, Catholicism has had a major influence on the role of women and sex-role attitudes.

In African-American culture as in Latin American culture, the church is typically seen as a major source of support, and spirituality tends to play an important role in the lives of these ethnic minority women (Boyd-Franklin, 1987; 1991). However, some African-American women may experience conflicts regarding their spirituality and being in therapy due to their minister's nonsupport of therapy, a view of therapy as antireligious, the promotion of the concept of a punitive God, or personal issues of shame related to sexuality and morality (Boyd-Franklin, 1991). In addition, it may be helpful at times to involve religious leaders in the client's treatment (Yamamoto & Acosta, 1982) or to refer the client to spiritual guides (see Chapter 9).

It is also important for the therapist to understand extended family issues and their impact on the client (Ho, 1987). Because of the interdependence that tends to characterize ethnic minority families, it may be that the client needs help resolving the interdependent–independent conflict. An attempt should be made to involve the family in treatment so that interventions can be formulated with the family's support and within their cultural framework (see Chapter 6). Interventions should be designed that are consonant with the family's culture, as these are more likely to be carried out. In addition, working with the family provides an opportunity to address issues of culture and sex-role conflict. The therapist may have to facilitate the client's becoming "bicultural"—that is, learning behaviors that are adaptive in both the minority and majority cultures. This may also help to ease conflicts around sex-role and acculturation issues.

It is also important that the therapist assess the availability and quality of the client's support systems. Involving the client with mutually satisfying support systems can lead to an increase in self-esteem for ethnic minority women. Social supports can also serve as effective buffers and mediators of stress (see Chapter 2). In addition, participating with others in organized groups and mutual aid self-help groups, particularly around the issues of racism, social/civic activity, civil rights, and/or sexism, can lead to social change and contribute to the empowerment of the client (Mays, 1986).

For some ethnic minority women, particularly African Americans, it is important to discuss skin color differences, which are sometimes a salient issue within families and ethnic communities (Boyd-Franklin, 1991; Greene, 1992; Neal & Wilson, 1989). Sometimes, within the immediate and extended family, there are wide variations in skin color. Skin color differences within families may create conflicts for the ethnic minority woman because some family members may have been afforded differential treatment within the family based on their skin color. Historically, lighter skinned African Americans also have enjoyed more societal advantages and opportunities than darker skinned African Americans (Neal & Wilson, 1989). In addition, skin color often affects the individual's feelings of attractiveness, which contribute to self-esteem. Therefore, the therapist should assess the significance and impact of skin color in the client's life. Although this is an important issue, it is not always problematic for ethnic minority women.

In working with Latin American women, the therapist must be aware that some experiences will be interpreted differently in Spanish than in English. The therapist should be sensitive to these language differences. It might greatly facilitate communication if the therapist is bilingual (Homma-True, 1990). Other possibilities with Asian-American, Native American, and Latin American cultures include the use of a translator, if necessary, or of bilingual paraprofessionals. In using translators from the family, however, the therapist should be cognizant of family structure issues. Using a child as translator displaces the adult male from the power position in the family, which has a high value in patriarchal family systems (Gibson, 1983). In working with African-American women, it also would be helpful for the therapist to be aware of African-American dialects and certain regional idioms (see Chapter 2; Russell, 1988).

The therapist should be especially attuned to nonverbal cues, such as eye contact, personal space, body movements, and touching, which tend to differ between minority and nonminority clients. Differences in nonverbal cues between ethnic minority men and women will also need to be noted. For some clients, differences in nonverbal cues would depend not only on the client's ethnic background but also on the degree to which she has been assimilated into the majority culture. The awareness of the meanings of nonverbal behavior can help to avoid misunderstanding and misinterpretation.

On a broader level, the therapist should consider interventions that help ethnic minority women seek the education and training needed to increase their standard of living and quality of life. That is, the therapist should be familiar with available programs and opportunities in the local community and should use a multiservice approach (Homma-True, 1990). In addition, the therapist at times may have to be an advocate for the client with social service agencies, government agencies, and private-sector businesses (see Chapter 8; Grevious, 1989). The therapist's efforts on the client's behalf should help to increase and enhance rapport with ethnic minority female clients.

Although this chapter has focused on issues in individual therapy, group therapy has also been found to be a useful therapeutic modality for ethnic minority women (see Chapter 7; Boyd-Franklin, 1987, 1991; Chu & Sue, 1984; Comas-Díaz, 1984; Gibson, 1983; Ho, 1984; Nayman, 1983). Ho (1984) and Chu and Sue (1984) discuss group therapy with Asian Americans. Boyd-Franklin (1991) lists some recurrent themes in group psychotherapy with African-American women, while Comas-Díaz (1984) has identified themes in group therapy with Puerto Rican women. Groups can serve therapeutic, supportive, preventive, and educational purposes (see Chapter 7). The communal, collective, and interdependent nature of ethnic minority cultures tends to lend support to the use of groups. Self-help groups have been reported to be effective for dealing with stress for African-American women (Mays, 1986).

Conclusion

The mental health issues of ethnic minority women tend to be closely tied to societal issues such as acculturation (culture and sex-role conflict), stereotyping, poverty, discrimination, racism, and sexism. Indeed, a salient issue for ethnic minority women is the interaction between racial and sexual discrimination. Another major issue for ethnic minority women is low socioeconomic status, which can contribute to psychological problems. Because of educational and economic discrimination, most minority women continue to have low-paying, low-status jobs and receive menial salaries, often while trying to raise a family. For these women, the tremendous stress emanating from poverty is coupled with the stress generated by trying to overcome stereotypes and the role strain produced by culture conflict, as ethnic minority women attempt to function in two different cultures. However, despite all this, ethnic minority women are coping, and more of their strengths and successes need to be investigated and disseminated. Once therapists have a better understanding of the issues that ethnic minority women bring to therapy as well as an awareness and understanding of their own biases in regard to women and race, they should be able to serve this population more effectively.

References

Ahlburg, D. A., & De Vita, C. J. (1992). New realities of the American family. *Population Bulletin, 47,* 1–44.

Amaro, H., & Russo, N. F. (1987). Hispanic women and mental health: An overview of contemporary issues in research and practice. *Psychology of Women Quarterly, 11,* 393–407.

Boyd-Franklin, N. (1987). Group therapy for Black women: A therapeutic support model. *American Journal of Orthopsychiatry, 57,* 394–401.

Boyd-Franklin, N. (1991). Recurrent themes in the treatment of African-American women in group psychotherapy. *Women & Therapy, 11,* 25–40.

Brower, I. C. (1989). Counseling Vietnamese. In D. R. Atkinson, G. Morten, & D. W. Sue (Eds), *Counseling American minorities: A cross-cultural perspective* (3rd ed.) (pp. 129–143). Dubuque, IA: Brown.

Burnam, M. A., Hough, R. L., & Karno, M., Escobar, J. T., & Telles, C. A. (1987). Acculturation lifetime prevalence of psychiatric disorders among Mexican-Americans in Los Angeles. *Journal of Health and Social Behavior, 28,* 89–102.

Canino, G. J., Rubio-Stipec, M., Shrout, P., Bravo, M., Stolberg, R., & Bird, H. R. (1987). Sex differences and depression in Puerto Rico. *Psychology of Women Quarterly, 11,* 443–459.

Chan, C. S. (1987). Asian-American women: Psychological responses to sexual exploitation and cultural stereotypes. *Women & Therapy, 6,* 33–38.

Chu, J., & Sue, S. (1984). Asian/Pacific Americans and group practice. *Ethnicity in Group Work Practice, 7,* 23–36.

Comas-Díaz, L. (1984). Content themes in group treatment with Puerto Rican women. *Ethnicity in Group Work Practice, 7,* 75–84.

Comas-Díaz, L. (1987). Feminist therapy with mainland Puerto Rican women. *Psychology of Women Quarterly, 11,* 461–474.

Curtis, P. A. (1990). The consequences of acculturation to service delivery and research with Hispanic families. *Child and Adolescent Social Work, 7,* 147–160.

Davenport, D. S., & Yurich, J. M. (1991). Multicultural gender issues. *Journal of Counseling & Development, 70,* 64–71.

del Portillo, C. T. (1987). Poverty, self-concept, and health: Experience of Latinas. *Women & Health, 12,* 229–242.

Edwards, E. D., & Edwards, M. E. (1989). American Indians: Working with individuals and groups. In D. R. Atkinson, G. Morten, & D. W. Sue (Eds), *Counseling American minorities: A cross-cultural perspective* (3rd ed.) (pp. 72–84). Dubuque, IA: Brown.

Escobar, J. I. (1993). Psychiatric epidemiology. In A. C. Gaw (Ed.), *Culture, ethnicity, and mental illness* (pp. 43–73). Washington, DC: American Psychiatric Press.

Espin, O. M. (1987). Psychological impact of migration on Latinas: Implications for psychotherapeutic practice. *Psychology of Women Quarterly, 11,* 489–503.

Everett, F., Proctor, N., & Cartmell, B. (1989). Providing psychological services to American Indian children and families. In D. R. Atkinson, G. Morten, & D. W. Sue (Eds), *Counseling American minorities: A cross-cultural perspective* (3rd ed.) (pp. 53–71). Dubuque, IA: Brown.

Franks, F., & Faux, S. A. (1990). Depression, stress, mastery and social resources in four ethnocultural women's groups. *Research in Nursing & Health, 13,* 283–292.

Fujitomi, S., & Wong, D. (1976). The new Asian-American woman. In S. Cox (Ed.), *Female psychology: The emerging self* (pp. 236–248). Chicago: Science Research Associates.

Gary, L. E. (1987). Attitudes of Black adults toward community mental health centers. *Hospital and Community Psychiatry, 38,* 1100–1105.

Gibson, G. (1983). Hispanic women: Stress and mental health issues. *Women & Therapy, 2,* 113–133.

Gray, B. A., & Jones, B. E. (1987). Psychotherapy and Black women: A survey. *Journal of the National Medical Association, 79,* 177–181.

Greene, B. (1992). Still here: A perspective on psychotherapy with African-American women. In J. C. Chrisler & D. Howard (Eds.), *New directions in feminist psychology* (pp. 13–25). New York: Springer.

Grevious, C. (1989). The role of the family therapist with low-income Black families. In D. R. Atkinson, G. Morten, & D. W. Sue (Eds.), *Counseling American minorities: A cross-cultural perspective* (3rd ed.) (pp. 192–199). Dubuque, IA: Brown.

Harrison, A. O. (1989). Mental health issues of African-American women and adults. In R. L. Jones (Ed.), *Black adult development and aging* (pp. 91–115). Berkeley, CA: Cobb & Henry.

Helms, J. E. (1979). Black women. *The Counseling Psychologist, 8,* 40–41.

Ho, C. K. (1990). An analysis of domestic violence in Asian American communities: A multicultural approach to counseling. *Women & Therapy, 8,* 129–150.

Ho, M. K. (1984). Social group work with Asian/Pacific Americans. *Ethnicity in Group Work Practice, 7,* 49–61.

Ho, M. K. (1987). *Family therapy with ethnic minorities.* Newbury Park, CA: Sage.

Ho, M. K. (1992). *Minority children and adolescents in therapy.* Newbury Park, CA: Sage.

Homma-True, R. (1990). Psychotherapeutic issues with Asian American women. *Sex Roles, 22,* 477–486.

Jones, A., & Seagull, A. A. (1989). Dimensions of the relationship between the Black client and the White therapist. In D. R. Atkinson, G. Morten, & D. W. Sue (Eds.), *Counseling American minorities: A cross-cultural perspective* (3rd ed.) (pp. 200–210). Dubuque, IA: Brown.

Kerner, J. F., Dusenbury, L., & Mandelblatt, J. S. (1993). Poverty and cultural diversity: Challenges for health promotion among the medically underserved. *Annual Review of Public Health, 14,* 355–377.

Kuo, W. H. (1984). Prevalence of depression among Asian-Americans. *The Journal of Nervous and Mental Disease, 172,* 449–457.

LaFromboise, T. D., Heyle, A. M., & Ozer, E. J. (1990). Changing and diverse roles of women in American Indian cultures. *Sex Roles, 22,* 455–476.

Leong, F. T. L. (1986). Counseling and psychotherapy with Asian-Americans: Review of the literature. *Journal of Counseling Psychology, 33,* 196–206.

Levine, E. S., & Padilla, A. M. (1980). *Crossing cultures in therapy: Pluralistic counseling for the Hispanic.* Monterey, CA: Brooks-Cole.

Lewis, E. A. (1989). Role strain in African-American women: The efficacy of support networks. *Journal of Black Studies, 20,* 155–169.

Malson, M. R. (1983). Black women's sex roles: The social context for a new ideology. *Journal of Social Issues, 39,* 101–113.

Martinez, C. (1988). Mexican-Americans. In L. Comas-Díaz & E. E. H. Griffith (Eds.), *Clinical guidelines in cross-cultural mental health* (pp. 182–203). New York: Wiley.

Mays, V. M. (1986). Black women and stress: Utilization of self-help groups for stress reduction. *Women & Therapy, 4,* 67–79.

Myers, L. W. (1980). *Black women: Do they cope better?* Englewood Cliffs, NJ: Prentice-Hall.

Nayman, R. L. (1983). Group work with Black women: Some issues and guidelines. *Journal for Specialists in Group Work, 8,* 31–38.

Neal, A. M., & Wilson, M. L. (1989). The role of skin color and features in the Black community: Implications for Black women and therapy. *Clinical Psychology Review, 9,* 323–333.

Neighbors, H. W., & Howard, C. S. (1987). Sex differences in help seeking among adult Black Americans. *American Journal of Community Psychology, 15,* 403–415.

Nieto-Gomez, A. (1976). A heritage of LaHembra. In S. Cox (Ed.), *Female psychology: The emerging self* (pp. 226–235). Chicago: Science Research Associates.

O'Hare, W. P. (1992). America's minorities—The demographics of diversity. *Population Bulletin, 47*(4), 1–47.

O'Hare, W. P., Pollard, K. M., Mann, T. L., & Kent, K. M. (1991). African Americans in the 1990s. *Population Bulletin, 46,* 1–40.

Olmedo, E. L., & Parron, D. L. (1981). Mental health of minority women: Some special issues. *Professional Psychology, 12,* 103–111.

Palacios, M., & Franco, J. N. (1986). Counseling Mexican-American women. *Journal of Multicultural Counseling and Development, 14,* 124–131.

Pyant, C. T., & Yanico, B. J. (1991). Relationship of racial identity and gender-role attitudes to black women's psychological well-being. *Journal of Counseling Psychology, 38,* 315–322.

Ramseur, H. P. (1989). Psychologically healthy Black adults: A review of theory and research. In R. L. Jones (Ed.), *Black adult development and aging* (pp. 215–241). Berkeley, CA: Cobb & Henry.

Rohrbaugh, J. B. (1979). *Women: Psychology's puzzle.* New York: Basic Books.

Ruiz, R., & Padilla, A. M. (1977). Counseling Latinos. *Personnel and Guidance Journal, 32,* 401–408.

Russell, D. M. (1988). Language and psychotherapy: The influence of Nonstandard English in clinical practice. In L. Comas-Díaz & E. E. H. Griffith (Eds.), *Clinical guidelines in cross-cultural mental health* (pp. 33–68). New York: Wiley.

Russo, N. F. (Ed.). (1985). *A women's mental health agenda.* Washington, DC: American Psychological Association.

Salgado de Snyder, V. N. (1987). Factors associated with acculturative stress and depressive symptomatology among married Mexican immigrant women. *Psychology of Women Quarterly, 11,* 475–488.

Salgado de Snyder, V. N., Cervantes, R. C., & Padilla, A. M. (1990). Gender and ethnic differences in psychosocial stress and generalized distress among Hispanics. *Sex Roles, 22,* 441–453.

Smith, W. D., Burlew, A. K., Mosley, M. H., & Whitney, W. M. (1978). *Minority issues in mental health.* MA: Addison-Wesley.

Sodowsky, G. R., Lai, E. W. M., & Plake, B. S. (1991). Moderating effects of sociocultural variables on acculturation attitudes of Hispanics and Asian Americans. *Journal of Counseling & Development, 70,* 194–204.

Soto, E. (1983). Sex-role traditionalism and assertiveness in Puerto Rican women living in the United States. *Journal of Community Psychology, 11,* 346–354.

Sue, D. W., & Sue, S. (1972). Counseling Chinese-Americans. *Personnel and Guidance Journal, 50,* 637–644.

Taylor, J., Henderson, D., & Jackson, B. B. (1991). A holistic model for understanding and predicting depressive symptoms in African-American women. *Journal of Community Psychology, 19,* 306–320.

Torres-Matrullo, C. (1976). Acculturation and psychopathology among Puerto Rican women in mainland United States. *American Journal of Orthopsychiatry, 46,* 710–719.

U.S. Bureau of Census. (1990). *1990 Census of population and housing—Summary tape file 1. Summary population and housing characteristics.* Washington, DC: U.S. Government Printing Office.

Watts-Jones, D. (1990). Toward a stress scale for African-American women. *Psychology of Women Quarterly, 14,* 271–275.

Witt, S. H. (1976). Native women today: Sexism and the Indian woman. In S. Cox (Ed.), *Female psychology: The emerging self* (pp. 249–259). Chicago: Science Research Associates.

Yamamoto, J., & Acosta, F. X. (1982). Treatment of Asian Americans and Hispanic Americans: Similarities and differences. *Journal of the American Academy of Psychoanalysis, 10,* 585–607.

Young, C. (1989). Psychodynamics of coping and survival of the African-American female in a changing world. *Journal of Black Studies, 20,* 208–223.

Zavala-Martinez, I. (1987). En la lucha: The economic and socioemotional struggles of Puerto Rican women. *Women & Therapy, 6,* 3–24.

Chapter *12*

Interventions with Ethnic Minority Elderly

ROBERT W. GRANT

At the 1993 meeting of the American Association for Geriatric Psychiatry, the keynote lecture was titled "Minority Elderly Mental Health: A Field in Search of a Literature?" (Harper, 1993). This title aptly portrays the dearth of methodologically sound and published research dealing with the mental health of elderly minorities. The study of minority issues as a serious concern is, for most mental health disciplines, only in its third decade. The study of issues relating to the mental health needs of the elderly is of even more recent vintage. Both these areas of study have suffered from inadequate funding. Minority mental health still is underfunded, and only over the last fifteen years or so has significant funding on the national level been devoted to the mental health problems of the elderly.

Demographic Trends

Data available through the 1990 census indicate that ethnic groups are an increasing proportion of the United States population (see Chapter 1 of this book). By 1995, at least five states are expected to have combined ethnic minority populations that are greater than the White population (U.S. Bureau of Census, 1990). By the year 2050, Blacks, Hispanics, Asian/Pacific Islanders, and American Indians/Eskimos/Aleuts will constitute 49.2 percent of the population in this country, with Hispanics (21.1 percent) being the largest ethnic group (U.S. Bureau of Census, 1992a).

Of particular importance is the aging of American society. The 1990 census counted 31.1 million elderly (aged 65 or older), reflecting a 22 percent increase between 1980 and 1990 (U.S. Bureau of Census, 1992b). Ethnic diversity is increasing within the elderly populations (American Society on Aging, 1992). In 1990, 1 in 10 elderly persons were ethnic minorities other than Whites. Of the total elderly population in 1990, about 28.0 million were White, 2.5 million Black, 1.1 million Hispanic, 450,000 Asian/Pacific Islander, and 116,000 American Indian/Eskimo/Aleut. By the year 2050 it is projected that 2 in 10 elderly will be ethnic minorities (U.S. Bureau of Census, 1992a).

By the middle of the twenty-first century there will likely be more people aged 65 or older than persons under 20 years of age. The number of persons aged 80 or over will grow from 6.9 million in 1990 to 25 million by 2050 (U.S. Bureau of Census, 1992a). This increased growth in those 80 or older will be reflected across all ethnic groups. These profound demographic changes are creating enormous challenges for mental health professionals who provide care to minority elderly, and emphasize the importance of the issues faced by those professionals in providing services to these groups.

Problems and Issues Facing Ethnic Minority Elderly

Ethnic minority elderly face a multitude of problems. Some of these difficulties are common to all elderly persons, while others are directly related to race and ethnicity. For many elderly minorities, those issues faced by all older persons are exacerbated by their ethnicity, allowing for the diversity that exists across and within ethnic groups. This section focuses on several problems and issues faced by ethnic elderly, including poverty, dementia, depression, and substance abuse. The role of racism, ageism, and cultural differences is discussed, particularly as they apply to the aforementioned problems. The impact of these issues on intervention and treatment approaches is discussed in the next section.

Poverty among Ethnic Elderly

In 1989, approximately 35 percent of African-American elderly and over 20 percent of Hispanic elderly were poor, as contrasted to 10 percent of White elderly (U.S. Bureau of Census, 1990). With the exception of Japanese elderly, all ethnic minority elderly, as a group, display significantly higher levels of poverty than the majority White elderly (U.S. Bureau of Census, 1990). The well-known repercussions of low income levels are poor nutrition, poor housing, increased stress, and decreased access to health care and other social services (Kerner, Dusenbury, & Mandeblatt, 1993).

The effect of poverty on the availability and use of mental health services by minority elderly is negative, pervasive, and cumulative. As a result of having been employed in low-paying, low-benefit jobs during their working years, minority group members are much less likely to have adequate financial resources and/or health insurance during their later years (American Society on Aging, 1992). The result is that many proven and effective treatments for psychological disorders are simply beyond their means. Psychotherapy is virtually closed to poor ethnic minority elderly by virtue of cost and therapist preference (Acosta, Yamamoto, & Evans, 1982; Hamburg, 1967; Tallent, 1992).

The cost of even medication maintenance or treatment is likely to deter many minority elderly from seeking help, or from compliance with medication regimens. This is especially true of medications such as clozapine (Clozaril) or fluoxetine (Prozac), which are not available generically and which can easily cost a patient several hundred dollars a month. Although Medicare has been instrumental in providing mental health services to the minority elderly, recent increases in Medicare deductibles and cost sharing have resulted in reduced access to care for the poor. This has disproportionately affected minority elderly because of the higher level of poverty and unemployment among minorities in general and aged minorities in particular.

Health of Ethnic Elderly

The socioeconomic factors pointed out in the previous section also contribute substantially to the excess mortality, premature morbidity, and mental and physical disability common to most ethnic minority elderly. At present, there is very little good longitudinal data comparing ethnic minorities to the majority population. There is much more data available regarding African Americans than other groups, but, with the exception of the National Survey of Black Americans (Jackson & Gurin, 1987), little longitudinal data exists that allows us to examines differences over time between ethnic minority populations and the majority population.

Survey reports consistently show most minority elderly having significantly higher morbidity rates than Whites (Morbidity and Mortality Weekly Report, 1986; O'Hare, Pollard, Mann, & Kent, 1991; Siegel & Davidson, 1984). Ill health is one of the greatest stressors for most individuals, and its greater incidence among minority groups leaves them more vulnerable to stress-related psychological disorders, as well as exacerbating the course of such illnesses. This is especially true of elderly minorities in that, as with elders in general, physical illnesses or deficits that might not be a significant factor for younger clients (e.g., a urinary tract infection) may drastically affect the emotional and cognitive status of the elderly individual.

Dementia among Ethnic Elderly

Approximately 15 percent of those over age 65 display some type of dementing disorder, and the figure rises to over 25 percent of those 85 or older (Kaszniak, 1986; Roybal, 1988). Dementia of the Alzheimer type (DAT) is the most common form of dementia, accounting for over 50 percent of the dementias in the aged (Kaszniak, 1986; Neshkes & Jarvik, 1983). Vascular dementias, now known as multi-infarct dementia, are the second most prevalent type of dementia, representing approximately 10 to 20 percent of all cases. Other, much less frequent progressive dementias include those due to Pick's disease, Creutzfeldt-Jakob disease, Huntington's disease, Parkinson's disease, and other neurologic conditions. Reversible dementias can be the result of normal-pressure hydrocephalus, use of over-the-counter or prescription drugs, alcohol, space-occupying lesions, infections, or cardiac/pulmonary insufficiency.

No evidence is available indicating differences in prevalence or incidence of dementing disorders between different racial or ethnic groups. Sociocultural factors may, however, play a significant role in the diagnosis, treatment, and recommendations made to the client and his or her family. Factors that hinder the access of minority elders to health care, such as fewer financial resources, lack of health insurance, and lack of a regular family physician, will obviously affect early diagnosis and treatment. This can be particularly important in cases of reversible dementias, as well as in those such as multi-infarct dementia where prompt treatment may result in cessation or slowing of the dementing process.

Sociocultural factors will also have an effect on the adaptations that the client and his or her caregivers are willing to adopt. Some families, such as those that are relatively recent immigrants to the United States, tend to be unwilling to place their elder members in institutional settings and will keep a demented patient at home even under very difficult circumstances. Cultural factors may also affect issues such as which relative becomes the primary caregiver of a demented elder, or whether particular family members are comfortable helping a demented family member with daily grooming. These factors should be taken into account when formulating plans for care, treatment, or rehabilitation.

Depression among Ethnic Elderly

Depression is the second leading cause of psychiatric hospitalization of the elderly and the most common functional disorder of the aged. Estimates of its prevalence have varied widely (Anthony & Aboraya, 1992), with some researchers claiming prevalence rates of 10 percent for acute depression and up to 30 percent for mild depression (Perlmutter & Hall, 1985). Newer research, using more rigorous diagnostic criteria, has yielded prevalence rates of 2 to 7 percent (Blazer, Hughes, & George, 1987; Klerman et al., 1986). Recent data indicate that approximately 27 percent of the aged experience significant depressive symptoms that do not fit DSM-III-R diagnostic categories (Blazer et al., 1987). Little data exist comparing rates of depression among Whites with those of minority groups. African Americans are the only group for which epidemiological data exists in any detail, and the data suggests that elderly Black females are at much higher risk for depression than older Black males and both male and female White elders (Murrell, Himmelfarb, & Wright, 1983; Stallones, Marx, & Garrity, 1990). Adding particular urgency to the problem of geriatric depression is the finding that elderly males over age 75 have the highest suicide rate of all age groups in our society (Casey, 1991; Roybal, 1988).

What little epidemiological depression data that is available on Hispanic and Asian-American elderly comes primarily from the epidemiological catchment area (ECA) studies in the Los Angeles, California, area (Karno et al., 1987; Stanford & Du Bois, 1992; Yamamoto et al., 1985). Hispanic and Asian-American respondents over

40 years of age also reported high rates of symptoms indicative of dysthymic and depressive disorders. Like African Americans, the Hispanic and Asian American female subjects had higher rates of depression than males. The little data available on Native American elderly is equivocal because of small sample sizes and limitations in the research designs.

In contrast to most cases of dementia, depression can be effectively treated but is often overlooked or unrecognized in the elderly (Casey & Grant, 1993). Elders, especially minority elders, often do not seek treatment because of negative views regarding any type of mental health care. Additionally, depressed elders often present with atypical features when compared to younger depressed patients (e.g., higher incidence of somatic complaints and denial of depressed mood). The treatments most often used are medication, psychotherapy, and electroconvulsive therapy (ECT).

Traditionally, minority group members have been viewed by majority researchers and practitioners as displaying more pathology and psychological disturbance than the majority population. Many of these findings have proved to be the result of racially biased reporting (Thomas & Sillen, 1976) and failure to control for socioeconomic status of the ethnic groups (Markides, 1986). No racial or ethnic differences in prevalence of depression among ethnic minority elderly have been reliably established. What does seem clear is that ethnic and cultural factors affect not only the definition of illness by the elder and their families but also the specific symptom presentation of depression and other disorders (Baker & Lightfoot, 1993; see Chapter 3).

Substance Abuse

Alcohol abuse/dependence is the most common form of substance abuse among minority elders, as well as the aged in general. Many aged minority alcoholics display cognitive deficits resulting from the toxic neurological effects of alcohol. These deficits most often take the form of amnestic deficits and an inability to acquire new knowledge (usually Korsakoff's syndrome or alcoholic dementia). Minority elders with such deficits are obviously difficult to engage in a recovery process, even if motivated. When the alcohol abuse or dependence occurs in combination with the abuse of prescription or over-the-counter drugs, the recovery process becomes even more complicated.

Abuse or dependence on prescription drugs is the second most common form of substance abuse among the minority aged. Relatively little abuse of illegal drugs is found among ethnic minority elders, even in those situations where access to illegal drugs is a relatively simple matter. Polydrug abuse is infrequent among minority elders. A more significant problem is that of the elderly minority patient with a "dual diagnosis" (i.e., a diagnosis of substance abuse as well as a significant psychiatric disorder). As with other so-called dually diagnosed individuals, control of the substance abuse/dependence is usually necessary for treatment of the emotional or psychological disorder to be effective.

Racism, Ageism, and Cultural Differences

Racism, ageism, and cultural differences are the major barriers to mental health services for the ethnic minority aged. Racial stereotyping by majority service providers has historically limited access of minorities to mental health services in general, or has restricted treatment to biologically based models such as medication and ECT (Acosta et al, 1982; Hamburg, 1967; Worthington, 1992). While the accepted shibboleth at present is that the service provider should be sensitive to the cultural characteristics of the client and should adapt the treatment in light of these differences, Worthington (1992) suggests that few practitioners have developed the cultural sensitivity and clinical skills to do so. Aged minority clients not only underutilize available services but also manifest higher dropout rates and less satisfaction with services as a result of inappropriate services (Acosta, 1980; Lorion, 1978; Select Committee on Aging, 1990).

Ageism, or stereotyped beliefs regarding aged individuals, also can result in decreased or inadequate treatment. Many practitioners, despite evidence to the contrary (Gallagher & Thompson, 1982, 1983; Lazarus et al., 1984), still agree with Freud (1904) that the elderly do not possess the reluctant "elasticity of mental processes" for psychoanalysis or, going beyond Freud, for other psychotherapies as well. Practitioners who adhere to such a view will be reluctant to treat the elderly or, at best, will relegate them to treatments that minimize insight and other complex cognitive processes.

Elderly minority clients are often viewed as undesirable patients by younger therapists because they contradict the YAVIS (Y[outhful], A[ttractive], V[erbal], I[ntelligent], and S[uccessful]) (Schofield, 1964) patient in many particulars. They are old and often manifest physical deficits. In most, though not all cases, elderly minority clients possess lower educational levels than the majority population. Some providers feel that their efforts are wasted when applied to those with limited remaining years of life. Aged patients may activate the practitioner's own anxieties regarding old age and death, or may promote countertransference phenomena related to the therapist's own relationships with his or her aged relatives. Finally, the differences in age between the provider and the client may impede the development of an effective treatment relationship.

Specific cultural barriers also prevent many minority aged from effectively accessing the mental health system. Poor facility in the English language is one example of such a barrier, especially for Hispanic and Asian aged who are first-generation immigrants (see Chapter 2). Another is distrust of mental health providers and programs, often as a result of past discrimination by the majority culture. Many minority elderly, due to differences based on ethnicity, cohort, social class, and income, manifest substantially different expectations from the typical majority client in regard to treatment and its course, the role of the therapist, symptom presentation, and the like, which may significantly affect the course of treatment (Baker & Lightfoot, 1993).

Cultural and ethnic factors will affect the presentation of even the most biologically based psychiatric disorder (see Chapter 3). As an example, the content of a schizophrenic's hallucination or a paranoid individual's delusional system will be significantly affected by his or her cultural or ethnic background and beliefs. It can also be important to assess beliefs that differ from those of the majority culture in light of the patient's culture and beliefs. A belief in evil spirits as a cause of mental illness may not be irrational or delusional among certain Native Americans, although traditional majority culture might so view it (see Chapter 9).

Assessment and Diagnostic Issues

The most common experience of service providers in dealing with elderly clients is that they present not with discrete problems but with symptoms that generally have multiple causes. Additionally, the service provider has to consider the issues raised by cultural and ethnic factors. On the one hand this means that many cases present difficult issues of assessment, case conceptualization, and treatment. On the other, it means that cases with this population can be among the most challenging and satisfying to treat successfully. As Margaret Gatz (1989) has cogently stated, "What is interesting about older clients? Actually, the very complexity of the cases is part of the fascination." (p. 84).

Working with ethnic minority elderly clients increases the number of considerations the clinician faces in assessing and treating this population (see Chapter 4). This does not make the task of treating such clients insurmountable, but it does mean that the provider of services must often abandon those assumptions that serve as shortcuts in the assessment process. Indeed, what the minority elderly force us to do if we are to assess and treat them is what we should do for all clients: examine each case carefully and individually because of the multiplicity of factors present.

The application of differential diagnosis criteria to elderly patients usually results in the conclusion that multiple conditions are contributing to the overall clinical picture (e.g., mental illness, declining self-care skills, physical illness or frailty, and cognitive deficits). One result is that multiple treatments are often necessary and concurrent. Emotional illness and symptoms may result from stressors in any area: social, emotional, biological, cognitive, or sensory. A familiar scenario to most professionals serving the aged population is that of an adequately functioning individual who suffers some physical or emotional trauma, such as a broken hip or the loss of a spouse, and, within a short period of time, begins to display significant deficits in cognition and self-care skills. One way to conceptualize this process is to visualize the elderly client as one who has lost much of the excess capacity to cope with insults in functional and adaptive aspects of life. Such a person is much more vulnerable to experiences that may overwhelm his or her adaptive capacity.

Another issue facing practitioners treating minority elders is that of case conceptualization and treatment choice. The mental health provider must maintain an acute awareness of how cultural factors and the social environment can affect the presentation and behavior of minority individuals, and at the same maintain a positive attitude regarding treatment outcome even though the larger social environment in which the client must function is unchanged (Thomas & Sillen, 1976). The problems presented by a minority client may mainly be a product of an oppressive and discriminatory environment (Baker & Lightfoot, 1993) or result of a biochemical aberration and wholly internal to the individual, or they may represent the interaction of environmental stimuli on an emotional vulnerability specific to that individual. To be able to recognize and conceptualize such situations adequately requires that the treating professional be cognizant of both the cultural perspective of the client and the manner in which the environment may affect the functioning of that client.

Much of this assessment process obviously involves differential diagnosis. As mentioned previously, cultural factors may affect the presenting symptoms displayed by the client (see Chapter 3). Whereas depressed elders generally report many somatic symptoms, depressed Hispanic clients of all ages, for example, generally report many somatic symptoms, and Hispanic elders may hence report more physical symptoms than depressed Whites (Ramos-McKay, Comas-Díaz, & Griffith, 1988). This phenomenon is not limited to Hispanics but is common among ethnic groups who are not psychologically minded and acculturated (Gaw, 1993).

In general, assessment issues with minority elderly are different from those with younger clients. Typically, most tests of functioning for the aged population use measures that are very close to the actual performance or construct that they are supposed to measure. Thus, there is less chance that cultural factors could interfere as intervening variables. In choosing a test of cognitive functioning, it is important to realize that tests such as the Wechsler Memory Scale (Wechsler, 1945) or the Mini Mental State Exam (Folstein, Folstein, & McHugh, 1975) that rely on a composite single score as an index of impairment can be misleading. An individual may show a significant and large deficit on one or two tasks, but may still achieve an adequate score if he or she scores well on all the others.

Tests that allow one to isolate and examine particular areas of functioning are much to be preferred, as they easily reveal areas of deficient functioning that may be circumscribed and not readily elicited in most situations. Tests such as this include the Wechsler Memory Scale—Revised (Wechsler, 1987) and the Neurobehavioral Cognitive Status Exam (Kiernan, Mueller, Langston, & Van Dyke, 1987). As noted before, little evidence exists that cultural factors influence performance on these tests. Whether examiner bias influences the interpretation of the results is an area that has not been empirically explored. Bias is less likely to have an effect because the scoring criteria are behaviorally specific, but examiner bias is still a danger. Examiner bias is more likely to have an effect when the minority elderly client presents with a purely functional psychiatric disorder.

Examination of the older client usually involves some form of *functional assessment* (American Geriatric Society Public Policy Committee, 1989). Functional assessment usually involves measuring an individual client's capacities and competencies in important life areas such as cognitive functioning, physical and functional health, and behavioral competencies in terms of self-care and social functioning. M. Powell Lawton's (1985) highly regarded work on this topic furnishes a description of the domains that are usually assessed. Again, the individual examiner must be careful that culturally based assumptions do not lead to errors in evaluating the ethnic minority client's competency. The prudent examiner should evaluate all the responses and behavior of minority aged clients in light of their cultural, ethnic, racial, and socioeconomic background.

Intervention and Treatment Approaches

Elderly individuals are more vulnerable to life stressors of all types and will display psychiatric symptoms when overly stressed biologically, socially, or psychologically. Ethnic minority elders, in comparison to the majority elderly, are apt to enter old age with fewer resources in terms of finances and health status and with greater social stress. Financial considerations and cultural differences are the most common barriers to mental health utilization and effective treatment for minority elderly. Cultural and ethnic attitudes and expectations of the minority elder and his or her social support system can significantly affect the effectiveness of medical, psychological, or social interventions.

Many older clients consider any type of mental health treatment as stigmatizing or as a sign of personal weakness. They seldom seek help from mental health providers and may resist referral by physicians, family members, or caretakers (Lebowitz & Niederehe, 1992). This is especially true of the minority elder, who may distrust majority providers and institutions as a result of previous discriminatory or oppressive experiences. Other barriers to seeking help are communication difficulties (whether due to sensory or language obstacles), problems with physical access to the provider or agency resulting from physical disability or transportation problems, and problems with generating the necessary finances. All of these barriers will disproportionately affect minority elderly as compared to the majority population of elderly.

Dementia

As previously mentioned, most dementias are progressive and irreversible. The first step, however, should always be a complete medical examination to determine if the cognitive dysfunction is a reversible type (e.g., due to drugs or to normal-pressure hydrocephalus). A complete medical examination is also necessary because physical and emotional stress due to illness or injury may cause an elderly patient to display cognitive deficits that will often remit as his or her medical condition improves. With progressive dementias, intervention most often takes the form of educating and assisting the family in the expected progression of the disease and in arranging appropriate care (whether at home or in an institution).

Mental health providers should be sensitive to the manner in which cultural differences and customs may affect a family or caregiver's decision-making process regarding the patient's future care and placement. Interventions are most often focused on controlling the more disruptive behaviors that occur in many demented individuals. Behavioral techniques are often quite effective in managing such behaviors (Fisher & Carstensen, 1990). The biopsychosocial management of such individuals includes reduction of stress in their environment; maintenance of familiar and orienting objects, caregivers, and situations; management of sensory input so as to not overload the patient's reduced adaptive capacities; and maintenance of a medication regimen by caregivers (if medication is deemed necessary).

Depression

Elders have the highest rate of completed suicide of any age group in our society, largely as a result of the strikingly high rate of elderly White males. Elders in general, including minority elders, tend to use quite lethal methods and hence show a high ratio of completed to attempted suicides, and the rate appears to be rising (Casey, 1991). Any elder, therefore, who complains of depression or shows significant depression should be carefully evaluated for suicidal ideation, suicidal plan, and availability of means. It is important to keep in mind that the minority elderly, like elders in general, often present with denial of depressed mood and an atypically higher incidence of somatic complaints. Many other groups of patients will also present with physical complaints in response to emotional stress, but such reactions appear to be more common and prominent in the elderly (Raskin & Rae, 1981; Raskin & Sathonanthan, 1979).

The treatment of depression in the elderly often involves constraints not present in the treatment of younger patients. As with other age groups, antidepressant medication is often very effective, particularly for those suffering from severe depression. However, many antidepressant medications produce side effects that many elderly patients and their families are unwilling or unable to tolerate (Hurwitz, 1969; Learoyd, 1972). Sedation, confusion, urinary retention, tachycardia, constipation, dry mouth, orthostatic hypotension, and blurred vision are some of the more common side effects. Orthostatic hypotension is particularly dangerous because it often contributes to falls, which can result in serious injury to the elderly person.

As a result of the distrust that many minority groups have of majority practitioners and institutions, it is often difficult to persuade patients and their families to adhere to a medication regimen, especially when unpleasant side effects occur. Electroconvulsive therapy is a generally safe and effective procedure for the aged. Its use is limited, however, because it is generally used only with hospitalized patients, who represent a small percentage of the depressed elderly. More significantly, the political and legal climate in many parts of the United States greatly inhibits the use of ECT, and for this reason ECT is less used in the United States than in many other countries (Small, Small, & Milstein, 1986). As the use of antidepressant medication may be contraindicated because of serious side effects, and ECT is often inadvisable because of medicolegal problems, psychotherapy has become a valued alternative form of treatment for geriatric depression.

Several different forms of psychotherapy have been demonstrated to be effective in the treatment of geriatric depression (Gatz, Popkin, Pino, & VandenBos, 1985). Overall, the research data indicate that geriatric depression can be successfully treated with various forms of psychotherapy, including psychodynamic, behavioral, cognitive-behavioral, and interpersonal therapies (Gallagher & Thompson, 1982, 1983; Gallagher et al., 1981; Horowitz, Marmar, Weiss, DeWitt, & Rosenbaum, 1984; Steuer et al., 1984). Antidepressant medications are often used along with these different therapeutic interventions.

Depressed minority elders with mild cognitive deficits may often be successfully treated with psychotherapy (Casey & Grant, 1993; Teri & Gallagher, 1989). However, special care should be taken to establish a positive therapeutic relationship and to ensure that the therapy is meeting the client's needs as he or she conceives them. Failure to address successfully the problems that the client defines is but one of many reasons that minority clients may judge therapy to be ineffective or may leave therapy prematurely (Acosta, 1980; Baker & Lightfoot, 1993; Sue, 1981). Many of the recommendations for working with older persons are similar to those for conducting psychotherapy with ethnic minorities.

Substance Abuse

Treatment of alcohol abuse or dependence in the elderly is difficult. There exist complications not often seen in young clients, including cognitive deficits resulting from the use of alcohol (see Chapter 13). Those deficits that are temporary will decrease with abstinence, but those that are permanent may require continual intervention by the minority elder's family. Successful cessation of drinking behavior may require hospitalization or may depend on the caregiver's ability to restrict the client's access to alcohol.

Many minority elders are entrenched in an extended family system that gives them significant social supports and resources to help them in their recovery from alcohol abuse or dependence. Others, for cultural or historical reasons (e.g., elderly Chinese men who emigrated to this country early in this century), may be isolated and may need significant support and structure from the treating professionals, treating institutions, and from groups like Alcoholics Anonymous (AA). Elders without significant cognitive deficits can often be treated in conventional alcohol treatment programs. Many of these treatment programs (e.g., AA) depend heavily on peer group help and support, so it is especially important that the aged minority client be involved with individuals and organizations that can relate to and support him or her in a culturally relevant manner. Many elderly Asians, for example, may find the common AA practice of *public* confession of abuse or dependence and intoxicated behavior shameful and distressing. In such a community, AA meetings will have to be altered in both form and content to meet the needs and cultural desires of the local population.

In general, once diagnosed, elderly clients should be detoxified and enrolled in an appropriate substance abuse treatment program. Efforts should be made to involve the client in groups and organizations that are similar to his or her usual cultural milieu. If hospitalization proves necessary, it should be provided by individuals familiar with (or preferably from) his ethnic group. The substance abuse should also be considered in light of cultural influences (for example, alcohol abuse is likely to be considered and judged quite differently by first-generation Russian immigrants than by first-generation immigrants from a Muslim country such as Iraq).

Other Disorders Experienced by Ethnic Elderly

Most of the other disorders of the aged (e.g., personality disorders, pain disorders, sexual disorders) can be addressed by traditional psychological methods and techniques. However, many of the symptoms presented may vary because of cultural factors. The perception and expression of pain is often influenced by cultural variables. Similarly, cultural attitudes toward sexual behavior and gender roles may significantly affect the presenting symptoms or course of therapy of a sexual disorder. Many of the more severe disorders, such as acute schizophrenia, psychotic or severely regressed depression, or acute mania will require hospitalization and biological therapy. There exists little evidence that the course of the disease or the response to treatment in these conditions are related to cultural factors, although such factors, as previously mentioned, can influence the presenting symptoms and have significant effects on the development of a therapeutic and trusting relationship.

Guidelines for Working with Ethnic Minority Elderly

The most important advice for those working with the ethnic minority elderly is that they need to be well informed regarding the cultural milieu from which their client comes and to have some understanding of its relationship to the majority culture. They should assume little and should test clinical judgments by requesting information and views from the client. Some professional organizations are beginning to offer education and training on minority and aging issues, and these should be utilized by the provider. It is also important to realize that one cannot be an expert on all minority cultures, and that the most appropriate and ethically sound decision may be to seek consultation or even referral to someone more experienced with a particular group, when confronted by an unfamiliar situation or culture.

Interventions directed at ethnic minority elderly, as previously mentioned, must recognize the diversity within ethnic groups and often have to be broad based, multilevel, and directed at the multiple conditions contributing to the presenting problem. Appropriate interventions may involve a variety of professionals and agencies. However, psychotherapy with ethnic elderly patients can be very effective, especially when dealing with depression or similar affective or anxiety disorders. Some specific recommendations and modifications for psychotherapeutic interventions with ethnic minority elderly are detailed next.

1. *Ensure that the patient understands the therapy process.* Elderly and ethnic minority patients often have negative and unrealistic views regarding the content and process of psychotherapy. Practitioners should not assume that the ethnic minority client has knowledge of the therapy process and of the roles of therapist and client, but should explore these areas with the client and educate the client to the degree necessary before embarking on the therapy itself (Root, 1989). Professional jargon should be kept to a minimum, and the goals and methods of therapy should be explained in an uncomplicated, commonsense manner that helps the patient view therapy as an effective and understandable way of dealing with one's problems.

2. *Be more active in the therapy process.* Minority elders demand a more active stance of their therapist and may view a passive stance as reflecting a lack of interest in their problems. Elderly patients with a severe depression will not be able to bring much energy to the therapy process, especially during the early stages, and the therapist may have to furnish much of the necessary energy to the therapeutic process.

3. *Employ all available resources in treatment.* The biopsychosocial model implies that treatment is directed toward a number of areas. Consequently, referral to sources that furnish biological and social interventions in addition to psychological interventions are often made. Examples include medical interventions, physical therapy, help in the home, and the use of natural support systems in the community (George, 1992; McShane, 1987). Often the minority elderly will require assistance and advice in accessing the many social institutions and public agencies with which they must deal.

4. *Involve the family and other social supports in treatment.* The term *family* should be interpreted loosely and inclusively to include multiple generations, extended family, informal social networks of friends, and supportive institutions such as the church (Starrett, Todd, Decker, & Walters, 1989; Stokesberry, 1985; see Chapter 6). Many of these caregivers and institutions may also require some education about the treatment process but will reward the effort by supporting and maintaining therapy gains.

Minority elders who are in treatment often need ancillary services for a multitude of physical, social, legal, or economic problems. The therapist should at least be able to refer a client to the appropriate agency or provider. If necessary, one should be ready to help the client negotiate bureaucratic or environmental hurdles and gain access to necessary services. This also is in the best interest of the therapist, as the client's progress in treatment will likely be hindered by these additional stressors or problems, and the client will likely view these "practical" problems as a first priority, as opposed to, say, psychotherapy. Insight can be useful, but having a roof over one's head or adequate treatment when physically ill is a more basic need.

When racial or ethnic factors or attitudes are influencing the course of therapy, they should be brought out in the open and explored with the client. This may be uncomfortable for both the therapist and the client, but to ignore it would be as disastrous and unprofessional as refusing to recognize or deal with any other transference issue or disguised emotion. If the professional has not dealt internally with issues that are sure to arise in the treatment of the minority elderly (e.g., aging, death, racism, cultural stereotyping), it will prove impossible to provide effective treatment for this group of clients.

References

Acosta, F. X. (1980). Self-described reasons for premature termination of psychotherapy by Mexican American, Black American, and Anglo-American patients. *Psychological Reports, 47*, 435–443.

Acosta, F. X., Yamamoto, J., Evans, L. A. (1982). *Effective psychotherapy for low-income and minority patients.* New York: Plenum Press.

American Geriatric Society Public Policy Committee. (1989). Comprehensive geriatric assessment. *Journal of the American Geriatric Society, 37*, 473–474.

American Society on Aging. (1992). *Serving elders of color: Challenges to providers and the aging network.* San Francisco: Author.

Anthony, J. C., & Aboraya, A. (1992). The epidemiology of selected mental disorders in later life. In J. E. Birren, R. B. Sloane, & G. D. Cohen (Eds.), *Handbook of mental health and aging* (2nd ed.) (pp. 27–73). San Diego, CA: Academic Press.

Baker, F. M., & Lightfoot, O. B. (1993). Psychiatric care of ethnic elders. In A. C. Gaw (Ed.), *Culture, ethnicity, and mental health* (pp. 517–532). Washington, DC: American Psychiatric Press.

Blazer, D., Hughes, D. C., & George, L. K. (1987). The epidemiology of depression in an elderly community population. *Gerontologist, 27*, 281–287.

Casey, D. A. (1991). Suicide in the elderly: A two-year study of death certificate data. *Southern Medical Journal, 84*, 1185–1187.

Casey, D. A., & Grant, R. W. (1993). Cognitive therapy with depressed elderly inpatients. In J. H. Wright, M. E. Thase, A. T. Beck, & J. W. Ludgate (Eds.), *Cognitive therapy with inpatients* (pp. 295–314). New York: Guilford.

Fisher, J. E., & Carstensen, L. L. (1990). Behavior management of the dementias. *Clinical Psychology Review, 10*, 611–629.

Folstein, M. F., Folstein, S. E., & McHugh, P. R. (1975). "Mini-Mental State": A practical method for grading the cognitive state of patients for the clinician. *Journal of Psychiatric Research, 12*, 189–198.

Freud, S. (1950). On psychotherapy. *Collected papers* (Vol. 1) (pp. 249–263). London: Hogarth Press. (Original work published 1904).

Gallagher, D. E., & Thompson, L. W. (1982). Differential effectiveness of psychotherapies for the treatment of major depressive disorder in older adult patients. *Psychotherapy: Theory, Research, and Practice, 27*, 482–490.

Gallagher, D. E., & Thompson, L. W. (1983). Effectiveness of psychotherapy for both endogenous and non-endogenous depression in older adult outpatients. *Journal of Gerontology, 38*, 707–712.

Gallagher, D. E., Thompson, L. W., Baffa, G., Piatt, C., Ringering, L., & Stone, V. (1981). *Depression in the elderly: A behavioral treatment manual.* Los Angeles: University of Southern California.

Gatz, M. (1989). Clinical psychology and aging. In M. Storandt & G. R. VandenBos (Eds.), *The adult years: Continuity and change* (pp. 81–114). Washington, DC: America Psychological Association.

Gatz, M., Popkin, S., Pino, C. D., & VandenBos, G. R. (1985). Psychological interventions with older adults. In J. E. Birren & K. W. Schaie (Eds.), *Handbook of the psychology of aging* (2nd ed.) (pp. 775–785). New York: Van Nostrand Reinhold.

Gaw, A. C. (1993). Psychiatric care of Chinese Americans. In A. C. Gaw (Ed.), *Culture, ethnicity and mental illness* (pp. 245–280). Washington, DC: American Psychiatric Press.

George, L. K. (1992). Community and home care for mentally ill older adults. In J. E. Birren, R. B. Sloane, & G. D. Cohen (Eds), *Handbook of mental health and aging* (2nd ed.) (pp. 793–813). San Diego: Academic Press.

Hamburg, D. A. (1967). *Report of ad hoc committee on central fact-gathering data.* New York: American Psychanalytic Association.

Harper, M. (1993, February). *Minority elderly mental health: A field in search of a literature?.* Paper presented at the meeting of the American Association for Geriatric Psychiatry, New Orleans, LA.

Horowitz, M. J., Marmar, C., Weiss, D. S., DeWitt, K. N., & Rosenbaum, R. (1984). Brief psychotherapy of grief reactions. *Archives of General Psychiatry, 41,* 439–448.

Hurwitz, N. (1969). Predisposing factors in adverse reactions to drugs. *British Medical Journal, 1,* 536–539.

Jackson, J. S., & Gurin, G. (1987). *National survey of Black Americans—1979–1980.* Ann Arbor, MI: Interuniversity Consortium for Political and Social Research.

Karno, M., Hough, R. L., Burnam, M. A., Escobar, J. I., Timbers, D. M., Santana, F., & Boyd, J. H. (1987). Lifetime prevalence of specific psychiatric disorders among Mexican Americans and non-Hispanic Whites in Los Angeles. *Archives of General Psychiatry, 44,* 695–701.

Kaszniak, A. W. (1986). The neuropsychology of dementia. In I. Grant & K. Adams (Eds.), *Neuropsychological assessment of neuropsychiatric disorders* (pp. 172–220). New York: Oxford University Press.

Kerner, J. F., Dusenbury, L., & Mandeblatt, J. S. (1993). Poverty and cultural diversity: Challenges for health promotion among medically underserved. *Annual Review of Public Health, 14,* 355–377.

Kiernan, R. J., Mueller, J., Langston, J. W., & Van Dyke, C. (1987). The neurobehavioral cognitive status examination: A brief but differentiated approach to cognitive assessment. *Annals of Internal Medicine, 107,* 481–485.

Klerman, G. L., Lavori, P. W., Rice, J., Reich, T., Endicott, J., Andreason, N. C., Keller, M. B., & Hirschfeld, R. M. A. (1986). Birth-cohort trends in rates of major depressive disorder among relatives of patients with affective disorder. *Archives of General Psychiatry, 47,* 689–693.

Lawton, M. P. (1985). Functional assessment. In L. Teri & P. M. Lewinsohn (Eds.), *Geropsychological assessment and treatment* (pp. 39–84). New York: Springer.

Lazarus, L. W., Groves, L., Newton, N., Gutmann, D., Ripeckyj, A., Frankl, R., Grunes, J., & Havasy-Galloway, S. (1984). Brief psychotherapy with the elderly: A review and preliminary study and outcome. In L. Lazarus (Ed.), *Psychotherapy with the elderly* (pp. 15–35). Washington, DC: American Psychiatric Press.

Learoyd, B. (1972). Psychotropic drugs and the elderly patient. *Medical Journal of Australia, 1,* 1131–1133.

Lebowitz, B. D., & Niederehe, G. (1992). Concepts and issues in mental health and aging. In J. E. Birren, R. B. Sloane, & G. D. Cohen (Eds.), *Handbook of mental health and aging* (2nd ed.) (pp. 3–26). San Diego: Academic Press.

Lorion, R. P. (1978). Research on psychotherapy and behavior change with the disadvantaged: Past, present and future directions. In S. L. Garfield & A. E. Bergin (Eds.), *Handbook of psychotherapy and behavior change* (2nd ed.) (pp. 903–938). New York: Wiley.

Markides, K. S. (1986). Minority status, aging, and mental health. *International Journal of Aging and Human Development, 23,* 285–300.

McShane, D. (1987). Mental health and North American Indian/Native communities: Cultural transactions, education, and regulation. *American Journal of Community Psychology, 15,* 95–116.

Morbidity and Mortality Weekly Report. (1986). Perspectives in disease prevention and health promotion: Report of the secretary's Task Force on Black and Minority Health. *Journal of the American Medical Association, 255,* 3347–3348.

Murrell, S. A., Himmelfarb, S., & Wright, K. (1983). Prevalence of depression and its correlates in older adults. *American Journal of Epidemiology, 117,* 173–185.

Neshkes, R. E., & Jarvik, L. F. (1983). Pharmacologic approach to the treatment of senile dementia. *Psychiatric Annals, 13,* 14–30.

O'Hare, W. P., Pollard, K. M., Mann, T. L., & Kent, K. M. (1991). African Americans in the 1990s. *Population Bulletin, 46,* 1–40.

Perlmutter, M., & Hall, E. (1985). *Adult development and aging.* New York: Wiley.

Ramos-Mckay, J. M., Comas-Díaz, L., & Rivera, L. A. (1988). Puerto Ricans. In L. Comas-Díaz &

E. H. H. Griffith (Eds.), *Clinical guidelines in cross cultural mental health* (pp. 204–232). New York: Wiley.

Raskin, A., & Rae, D. S. (1981). Psychiatric symptoms in the elderly. *Psychopharmacology Bulletin, 16,* 23–25.

Raskin, A., & Sathonanthan, G. (1979). Depression in the elderly. *Psychopharmacology Bulletin, 15,* 14–16.

Root, M. P. P. (1989). Guidelines for facilitating therapy with Asian American clients. In D. R. Atkinson, G. Morten, & D. W. Sue (Eds.), *Counseling American Minorities* (3rd ed.) (pp. 116–128). Dubuque, IA: Brown.

Roybal, E. R. (1988). Mental health and aging. *American Psychologist, 43,* 189–194.

Schofield, W. (1964). *Psychotherapy: The purchase of friendship.* Englewood Cliffs, NJ: Prentice-Hall.

Select Committee on Aging. (1990). *Implementation of the older Americans act of 1987: The aging network.* Committee Publication 101–768. Washington, DC: U.S. Government Printing Office.

Siegel, J. S., & Davidson, M. (1984). *Demographic and socioeconomic aspects of aging in the United States.* Washington, DC: U.S. Bureau of the Census, Current Population Reports, Series P-23, No. 138. Washington, DC: U.S. Government Printing Office.

Small, I. F., Small, J. G., & Milstein, V. (1986). Electroconvulsive therapy. In P. A. Berger & H. K. Brodie (Eds.), *American handbook of psychiatry: Vol. 8, Biological psychiatry* (pp. 999–1028). New York: Basic Books.

Stallones, L., Marx, M. B., & Garrity, F. F. (1990). Prevalence and correlates of depressive symptoms among older U.S. adults. *American Journal of Preventive Medicine, 6,* 295–303.

Stanford, E. P., & Du Bois, B. C. (1992). Gender and ethnicity patters. In J. E. Birren, R. B. Sloane, & G. D. Cohen (Eds.), *Handbook of mental health and aging* (2nd ed.) (pp. 99–117). San Diego: Academic Press.

Starrett, R. A., Todd, A. M., Decker, J. T., & Walters, G. (1989). The use of formal helping networks to meet the psychological needs of Hispanic elderly. *Hispanic Journal of Behavioral Sciences, 11,* 259–273.

Steuer, J. L., Mintz, J., Hammen, C. L., Hill, M. A., Jarvik, L. F., McCarley, T., Motike, P., & Rosen, R. (1984). Cognitive behavioral and psychodynamic group psychotherapy in treatment of geriatric depression. *Journal of Consulting and Clinical Psychology, 52,* 180–189.

Stokesberry, J. (1985). New policy issues in Black aging: A state and national perspective. *Journal of Applied Gerontology, 4,* 28–34.

Sue, D. W. (1981). *Counseling the culturally different.* New York: Wiley.

Tallent, N. (1992). *The practice of psychological assessment.* Englewood Cliffs, NJ: Simon & Schuster.

Teri, L., & Gallagher, D. (1989). Cognitive behavioral interventions for depressed patients with dementia of the Alzheimer's type. In T. Sunderland (Ed.), *Depression in Alzheimer's disease: Component or consequence* (pp. 413–416). New York: Grune & Stratton.

Thomas, A., & Sillen, S. (1976). *Racism and psychiatry.* Seacaucus, NJ: Citadel Press.

U.S. Bureau of the Census. (1990). *Statistical abstract of the United States: 1990* (110th ed.). Washington, DC: U.S. Government Printing Office.

U.S. Bureau of Census. (1992a). *Current population reports, P 25-1092: Population projections of the United States by age, sex, race, and Hispanic origin: 1992–2050.* Washington, DC: U.S. Government Printing Office.

U.S. Bureau of Census. (1992b). *Current population reports, P 23-178: Sixty-five plus in America.* Washington, DC: U.S. Government Printing Office.

Wechsler, D. A. (1945). A standardized memory scale for clinical use. *Journal of Psychology, 19,* 87–95.

Wechsler, D. (1987). *Wechsler Memory Scale-Revised manual.* New York: Psychological Corporation.

Worthington, C. (1992). An examination of factors influencing the diagnosis and treatment of Black patients in the mental health system. *Archives of Psychiatric Nursing, 6,* 195–204.

Yamamoto, J., Machizawa, S., Araki, F., Reece, S., Steinberg, A., Leung, J., & Cater, R. (1985). Mental health of elderly Asian Americans in Los Angeles. *American Journal of Social Psychiatry, 1,* 37–46.

C h a p t e r **13**

Intervention and Treatment of Ethnic Minority Substance Abusers

PAMELA JUMPER THURMAN
RANDALL SWAIM
BARBARA PLESTED

The problem of alcohol and other drug abuse in the United States has been firmly established as a matter of great concern (Bratter & Forrest, 1985; Helzer, 1987). Three factors need to be considered in a discussion of alcohol and other drug abuse: physiological, sociological, and psychological (Lawson & Lawson, 1989). Physiological studies have indicated a genetic factor for some forms of substance abuse (Cotton, 1979), sociological research has demonstrated the influence of family and peers on abuse of alcohol and other drugs (Cahalan, 1970; Glynn, 1981; Oetting & Beauvais, 1987), and psychological factors have been found to play a role in alcohol abuse (Lawson, Peterson, & Lawson, 1983) and in the chronic abuse of drugs such as cocaine, barbiturates, and heroin (Craig, 1982; Spotts & Shontz, 1982).

It is clear that there are multiple pathways leading to substance abuse (Bry, McKeon, & Pandina, 1982; Maddahian, Newcomb, & Bentler, 1988; Newcomb, Maddahian, & Bentler, 1986). Early childhood traits such as the "difficult child syndrome" and hyperactivity have been associated with alcohol and substance abuse as well as later-appearing antisocial behaviors. Social factors such as family dysfunction, parental modeling of use, and use by peers have been identified as risk factors for the development of substance use. The combined and additive nature of these risk factors may be responsible for the development and emergence of substance abuse (Swaim, 1991). The interaction of these risk factors with genetic, psychological, and sociological factors may help explain variations in substance use as well as patterns of protective factors that may prevent others from initiating use or developing abusive patterns of substance use.

Just as the etiology of this problem may vary greatly across individuals, treatment strategies need to be individualized as well so that they address those risk factors that are unique to specific clients. To some degree, this uniqueness should be considered across larger groups such as ethnic minorities who vary in their history, experiences, socioeconomic characteristics, values, beliefs and behaviors (see Chapters 1 and 2). However, the treatment needs of the individual, whether a member of an ethnic minority or not, must always be assessed and taken into account.

In the last decade, health risk behavior in various ethnic groups has gained the active attention of researchers, treatment providers, and policymakers (Orlandi, Weston, & Epstein, 1992). Some results indicate that minority populations are at higher risk for alcohol and other drug abuse than the general population (U.S. Department of Health and Human Services, 1985). However, it is important to note that many earlier studies on substance abuse in ethnic communities focused on negative aspects rather than resiliency factors, and data were often obtained from sources where minorities were likely to be overrepresented (e.g., emergency room facilities, public treatment programs). Most studies have compared ethnic minorities to Whites, often using one sample or the study of one group to generalize to the entire ethnic population. This has unfortunately led to stereotypes and negative assumptions regarding the nature and extent of alcohol and other drug abuse among minority groups.

Current research indicates that Whites generally tend to use alcohol and most drugs at higher rates than African Americans, Hispanics, or Asians, whereas studies on youth have found that Whites and Native Americans have the highest rates of lifetime and annual prevalence and the highest rates of heavy use of alcohol (Bachman et al., 1991; Rebach, 1992). Results from four years of survey data conducted on over 200,000 eighth and twelfth grade students indicated that Native American, Mexican-American, and White youth had higher lifetime prevalence rates for a number of substances compared to Black and Asian youth.

May (1986) indicates that 50 to 90 percent of Native American youth, depending on the tribe, have experimented with alcohol. One in every seven Indian eighth graders is currently using inhalants (Beauvais, 1992). Rates of frequent heavier drinking seem to be highest among Whites, followed by Hispanics, then African Americans (Caetano, 1984). Asian Americans generally demonstrate lower rates of alcohol use than Whites, Native Americans, or Hispanics (Kitano, Lubben, & Chi, 1988).

Diversity within Native American, Latino, African-American, and Asian-American groups makes it hazardous to generalize from a particular subgroup to the larger group. For example, differences exist between rural, reservation, and urban Indians; among tribes; and even within tribes. The same is true for Asian Americans, Latinos, and African Americans (see Chapter 1). The terms *Native American* and *Alaska Native, African American, Latino,* and *Asian American* vary in usage and reflect the richness of hundreds of various subcultures and perspectives (see the Preface).

This chapter will focus on the nature and extent of alcohol and other drug abuse among the aforementioned ethnic groups. The historical factors, epidemiology, and correlates of substance abuse for these groups will be presented briefly. (For a more extensive survey, see Austin & Gilbert, 1989; Beauvais, 1992; Brown & Tooley, 1989; DeLaRosa, Khalsa, & Rouse, 1990; Herd, 1985; Sue, 1987; Watts & Wright, 1983.) The chapter will also discuss interventions and culturally specific treatment modalities, as well as recommendations and suggestions for the treatment provider working with specific ethnic groups.

Nature and Extent of Alcohol and Other Drug Abuse

African Americans

Historical Factors
African Americans make up the largest ethnic minority group in the United States, with 28.9 million people or 12.1 percent of the total population (U.S. Bureau of Census, 1990). It would appear likely that research in the area of alcohol and other drug use, patterns, problems, and treatment within this population would be plentiful due to the number of African Americans. However, only minimal information is available on this group. Few African Americans were included in the drug and alcohol surveys of the 1960s and 1970s.

At the time of the Civil War, the temperance movement was closely associated with the antislavery movement. This may have had a major influence on Blacks, who, at that time, demonstrated very low rates of alcohol-related problems (Herd, 1985). After the Civil War, however, many changes occurred. With their new-found freedom, Blacks began to migrate more and to build small communities. Fewer Blacks associated with the temperance movement as it became more racist. This may have had the effect of increasing their drinking behavior. As free men and women, Blacks also had greater opportunity to purchase and use alcohol. Although clearly these were not the only contributing factors, drinking among Blacks did begin to increase. More recent studies indicate that African Americans do experience problems with alcohol and other drug abuse (King, 1982).

Epidemiology
National surveys indicate that African-American youth between 14 and 17 years of age use alcohol to a lesser degree than their White counterparts and have fewer alcohol-related consequences (Brown & Tooley, 1989). For African-American males over 30, however, the picture begins to change. The heavy drinking rate within this group is approximately 32 percent, compared to 20 percent for White males (Freeman, 1992). Likewise, there were substantial differences between Black men and White men with regard to binge drinking (4 percent versus 1.6 percent), symptoms of physical dependence (29.5 percent versus 9.9 percent), and symptoms of loss of

control (17.2 percent versus 11.2 percent) (Herd, 1985). African-American women report fewer alcohol-related problems than their White counterparts, and they report higher abstinence rates (46 percent versus 34 percent of White women).

There are few alcohol and other drug abuse studies on African-American youth. One study (Globetti, Alsikafi, & Morse, 1980) on African-American high school females reflected a strong abstinence tradition, with 65 percent of the girls indicating that they were nondrinkers. Among the drinkers, only 24 percent drank frequently, 35 percent drank seldom, and 32 percent occasionally. The National Household Survey on Drug Abuse also found differences in drinking behavior between African-American and White youth (National Institute on Drug Abuse, 1988). African-American youth age 12 to 17 reported use of alcohol at least once in 38.8 percent of the sample compared to 60.7 percent of Whites and 44.1 percent of Latinos. Similar responses were found in use during the past year and the past month. African-American females reported lower use rates (17.9 percent) than did African-American males (23.8 percent). These data may reflect underreporting due to higher dropout rates and unrepresentative samples. It is possible to conclude tentatively, however, that alcohol use among African-American youth is less than that of White youth, but that, after the age of 30, drinking-related problems increase for males.

Correlates

Too often, African Americans, even more so than other ethnic populations, are treated as a monolithic group, with important regional and demographic differences overlooked or ignored. Of particular note are the differences in socioeconomic status that exist among African Americans (see Chapters 1 and 2). Socioeconomic status has been a focus of several studies (Clifford & Jones, 1988; Watts & Wright, 1983). Alcohol use has been related to factors such as unemployment and poverty across all ethnicities (Yee & Thu, 1987; Harvey, 1985; Beauvais & LaBoueff, 1985). Such studies make a strong case that the stress of coping with poverty, unemployment, discrimination, and inadequate housing could contribute to substance abuse. Certainly, living in these communities and knowing that there is such limited opportunity for economic and social advancement could have significant impact on the decision to use. It is imperative that additional correlate studies be undertaken in an effort to explain and prevent substance abuse among African Americans.

Native Americans and Alaska Natives

Historical Factors

According to figures released by the U.S. Census Bureau, there are approximately 2 million Native Americans and Alaska Natives in the United States. Census data also indicate a very youthful population—a median age of 26.3 years compared to 34.0 years for Whites (U.S. Bureau of Census, 1992). There are approximately 300 federal reservations and 500 federally recognized tribes in the United States, including some 200 Alaska Native village groups (Klein, 1993). Although most reservations and tribes are concentrated in a few states, Native Americans can be found in every state (see Chapter 1).

Frequently there is the tendency to view Native Americans and Alaska Natives as a homogeneous group—as "Indians" whose customs, beliefs, and traditions are very similar. Native Americans and Alaska Natives, however, are a highly diverse group of people, not only with individual and family differences, but with tribal differences that vary greatly from location to location and often even within the same general areas. Differences exist in appearance, clothing, customs and ceremonies, practices, family roles, child-rearing practices, beliefs, and attitudes. Each tribe, band, or village maintains a unique perception of the world both inside and outside its particular area. Even within the same geographic locality, differences exist. Some Native Americans or Alaska Natives are very traditional in their beliefs, maintaining tribal languages, ceremonies, and customs. Others may be more contemporary, retaining some Native American traditions while maintaining a successful orientation to non-Native American society as well.

One striking similarity shared by all Native Americans and Alaska Natives is federal or governmental control over tribal/Native issues as well as control over many individual decisions. There have been major federal attempts at assimilation, removal of Native Americans and Alaska Natives from homelands, sterilization, and relocation programs. Pamela Kalar (1991) states: "Cultural insensitivity, voracious greed, paternalism and the bitter fruits of inept lawmaking have compounded the inequities suffered by Native peoples on and off the reservation" (p. 10). Often it is forgotten or overlooked that these "First Americans" were not given voting citizenship until 1924 in most states and until 1946 in Arizona and New Mexico.

Another encounter with the White majority culture shared by most Native groups is the boarding school experience. From the late 1800s to the 1960s, church-affiliated boarding schools literally terrorized many Native children. They were punished, often severely, for speaking their own language; were humiliated in front of their peers; and received extreme haircuts in an effort to assimilate them to the White Christian culture. Such experiences, as well as those mentioned previously, have had a profound impact on the ethnic identity of Native groups and their view of majority culture.

Recent legislative actions have returned some power to Native American and Alaska Native nations through measures such as the Self-Determination Act, the Indian Education Act, and the Indian Child Welfare Act. It is believed that such events have finally begun to empower Indian people to the extent that many Native American and Alaska Natives have involved themselves politically in major decision-making issues. It is significant to note, however, that although there have been some political successes, sadly, few economic successes have occurred. Many Native families still experience poor nutrition, live in substandard housing, and lack the resources necessary to give their children choices for positive opportunities. Their experiences with assimilation, their lack of access to many of society's benefits, and the prejudice they experience place Natives at high risk for substance abuse.

Epidemiology

Given the tribal and village differences that exist, it is not surprising that alcohol and drug use among Natives varies tremendously from one group to the next (May,

1982). May (1986) cites some tribes as having fewer drinking adults (30 percent) than the United States population (67 percent), whereas other tribal groups have more (69–80 percent). Some believe the rates may be underestimated as a result of deaths occurring for reasons such as alcohol-related injury, suicide, or homicide in which the use of alcohol goes unreported.

A large proportion of the Native American and Alaska Native population, as previously mentioned, is young. It has been established that Native American youth use almost every type of drug with greater frequency than non-Native American youth and that the age of first involvement with alcohol is younger for Native American children. The rates of drug use and involvement can be two to three times higher for Native American youth than for Anglo youth (Beauvais, 1992). Inhalants are also problematic for Native American and Alaska Native youth. They are often the first drug used, and prevalence rates for reservation Native Americans are almost three times those of their White counterparts.

Oetting and Beauvais (1983) have developed a classification system of drug use that ranks youth in three categories, from essentially no use to continued heavy use. Group one consists of low-risk non-users, young people who have tried a drug but are not currently using any drug. The second group is made up of moderate-risk users, youth who get drunk once a month or more and who may use some marijuana. The third group includes high-risk users, youth who use marijuana more than once or twice a week or who use other drugs at least once a month. High-risk users are those who are currently using drugs and/or alcohol in such a way they may incur some physical or emotional harm from that use. Using this system, since 1977 the high-risk users' group has not changed substantially. Between 17 and 20 percent of reservation youth continue to use drugs at a rate sufficient to place them at high risk (Beauvais, 1992).

Correlates

Recent research in the area of risk factors for substance-abusing Native American youth has cited use by peers, weak family bonding, poor school adjustment, weak family sanctions against drugs, positive attitudes toward alcohol use, and risk of school dropout (Swaim, Oetting, Thurman, Beauvais, & Edwards, 1993; Swaim, Thurman, Beauvais, Oetting, & Wayman, 1993). Other studies have reported that substance abuse behavior among Native Americans may be influenced by cultural values and norms (May, 1986). Yet another risk factor that accounts for high use rates among Native American youth is low educational achievement and employment opportunity. School dropouts report rates of substance use far in excess of those of students who remain in school (Chavez, Edwards, & Oetting, 1989).

When Native American youth begin to reach adulthood, they find few chances of securing decent jobs, limited educational opportunities, and scant resources for improving their situation. Even though the abuse of substances may be well established by dropouts by the time they leave school, the lack of opportunity they will face in obtaining adequate employment may contribute to the maintenance or exacerbation of their use of alcohol and/or drugs (Oetting, 1992; Oetting & Beauvais, 1990). Unfortunately, limited economic opportunity and other negative community factors such as prejudice and violence are prevalent in disadvantaged minority neighborhoods (Oetting, 1992).

Latinos

History
Morales (1984) traces some of the historical factors that form the background for use and abuse of substances among Hispanics. The abuse of alcohol can be traced back to the Aztecs of the fifteenth century, ancestors of present-day Mexican Americans. To control excessive drinking, they established elaborate mechanisms of social control that prescribed those conditions when drinking was sanctioned, primarily ceremonial and religious occasions. No more than five gourds of alcohol were to be consumed on these occasions, and there were severe penalties for breaking these societal rules (Paredes, 1975).

Prejudice and stereotypes regarding Hispanic substance use have historically resulted in arrests and imprisonment of this group at rates that exceed their relative population within the country. For example, in 1914 it was reported that "the excessive use of liquor is the Mexican's greatest moral problem. With few exceptions both men and women use liquor to excess" (McEuen, 1914, p. 13). Examination of Los Angeles police records in 1913 revealed the effect of such prejudicial thinking. A total of 24.3 percent of all arrests for drunkenness were of Mexicans, compared to their share of the population in Los Angeles of only 5 percent. Overrepresentation of Mexicans within the California state prison system from 1918 to 1930 was primarily the result of arrests for violation of the "State Poison Act," mostly for marijuana use. In 1931 the California State Narcotics Committee stated that marijuana use was widespread among Mexicans. During this period, however, there were only sixty-three arrests of Mexicans for narcotics violations.

Epidemiology
Several recent empirical studies and reviews of the literature have reported that drug and alcohol use and abuse are substantial problems within the Latino population (Austin & Gilbert, 1989; Bachman et al., 1991; De La Rosa et al., 1990; National Institute on Drug Abuse, 1987). The very rapid recent growth of Latinos within the United States population (39 percent between 1980 and 1989, compared to 7.5 percent for the non-Latino population) (Carter & Wilson, 1991) underscores the need to address the problem of substance use within this ethnic/racial group.

Most studies of alcohol use indicate that rates of use are either similar to or slightly below those of White non-Hispanics, but higher than rates for Blacks or Asians (Gilbert, 1989). Bachman et al., (1991) found a similar pattern for illicit drug use among Hispanic high school seniors, with the exception of high rates of cocaine use among Hispanic males. Chavez and Swaim (1992a) conducted a national probability study of eighth- and twelfth-grade Mexican-American students and found that rates of use for a number of substances was higher for Mexican Americans at the eighth-grade level. This pattern was reversed, however, among twelfth-grade students, with White non-Hispanic seniors reporting higher rates than their

Mexican-American counterparts. The reversal in rates of use between the two racial groups is likely due to the higher rate of drug use among school dropouts and the higher rate of school dropout among Mexican Americans (Swaim, Oetting, Chavez, & Beauvais, 1993).

One key factor that needs to be taken into account when considering Latino substance use is the gender disparity in rates of use. Differences in rates of use between males and females is often larger than differences observed in other racial groups. Among Mexican Americans, substantial differences in alcohol use have been noted, a disparity that tends to increase with age. There is some evidence, however, that these gender differences, especially for alcohol, may be decreasing as a result of higher levels of use among young Hispanic females (Austin & Gilbert, 1989; Chavez & Swaim, 1992b; Gilbert, 1987). The greater gender disparity in rates of use among Hispanics suggests the need for gender-focused interventions (Gilbert & Alcocer, 1988).

Correlates

Risk and protective factors for alcohol and drug use for Latinos are similar to those found among other adolescents (Gilbert, 1989). However, the relative strength of different factors and their interactive effects may vary when Latino and White non-Hispanic adolescents are compared (Felix-Ortiz & Newcomb, 1992). Important family variables predictive of substance use among Latinos include quality of the family relationship and parental drinking. Use of alcohol by peers is a strong predictor of Latino adolescent alcohol use. Coombs, Paulson, and Richardson (1991) found that peer variables were the most influential in predicting drug and alcohol abuse for both Hispanic and Anglo children and adolescents. However, such findings may be spurious because of differences in the predictor variables used in the Hispanic and Anglo groups.

Asian Americans

Historical Factors

Asian Americans and Pacific Islanders currently make up 2.9 percent of the United States population and number approximately 7.3 million (U.S. Bureau of Census, 1990). They, too, are a diverse and fast-growing group of people, primarily because of their high immigration rates. In fact, since the 1980 census, the number of Asian Americans and Pacific Islanders has more than doubled (see Chapter 1 for a more detailed description of the ethnic subgroups).

Although minimal literature exists discussing the effects of immigration and acculturation into Western society of these groups, there is evidence that at some periods in Chinese history alcohol consumption has been very high and at other times very low (Lee, 1987). As with American Indians, the extended family is important in Asian society. Elders control family resources in the Asian homeland and therefore are better able to control the behavior of younger family members (Johnson & Nagoshi, 1990). However, the power of these elders becomes weaker in

U.S. society and may be a significant influence in the increasing alcohol use among some Asian-American groups.

Epidemiology

As with other ethnic groups, discussions of substance use among Asian Americans is difficult because of the diversity involved. Like American Indians and Alaska Natives and Hispanics, Asian Americans can not be aggregated into a single population. In fact, more than 20 Asian-American groups have been identified by the U.S. Bureau of the Census (Zane & Sasao, 1992). Variations occur in the drinking patterns of Chinese, Japanese, Koreans, and Filipinos (Kitano & Chi, 1985). These authors report that there exists a relatively high proportion of heavy drinkers among Japanese and Filipino men. Those men most likely to drink are under the age of 45, with higher social status.

In a telephone survey of a Japanese community, results indicated that there were reported frequencies of 73 percent for lifetime alcohol use and 61 percent for thirty-day prevalence use (Sasao, 1989). These figures reflect greater usage than levels found for the United States general public. Important differences were found between American-born and Japan-born Japanese. For example, Japan-born Japanese exhibited higher rates of refusal to participate and demonstrated less knowledge and social concern about substance abuse. They were also less likely to view alcohol use as a substance abuse problem.

Use of the term *Asian-American* to describe this heterogeneous group is inappropriate. It is necessary to examine carefully the Asian-American differences in substance use patterns and to be cautious with generalizations. Little research literture is available on such topics as drinking patterns and alcohol consumption rates for Asian-American females. Across Japanese, Chinese, and Filipino groups, however, the rate appears to be consistently lower for females compared to males (Ahern, 1985). More research is needed given the diversity and the rapid growth of this population.

Correlates

Johnson and Nagoshi (1990) give a very thorough account of the sociocultural influences affecting Asian Americans and alcohol consumption. They argue that the social-psychological variables that vary across Asian-American groups have not been fully assessed and probably have important sociocultural/environmental bases. This is likely very true, as there are documented substantial differences in alcohol consumption across these groups that may not be adequately explained through some of the discrepant findings in existing physiological models (Sue, 1987).

Treatment Utilization

Most research indicates that minorities are less likely to seek treatment and also less likely to complete a treatment regimen (Sue, 1987), yet they are often overrepresented in federally funded treatment facilities. Asians in particular as well as African Americans are reported as very unlikely to enter treatment (Sue, 1987). Much of this reluctance may be attributed to a mistrust of the mental health system (Sue, 1981). Such distrust is also found in the use of substance abuse programs; in fact, rather than using traditional forms of treatment, some Blacks have turned to spirituality in an effort to abstain from alcohol. African Americans have reported that they stopped drinking prior to entering the treatment program and reported the reason for this abstinence as their return to spirituality (Brisbane, 1987).

African Americans made up 27 percent of the clients admitted to federally funded drug abuse treatment centers in 1980. Of these, 12 percent were under the age of 18 (Gibbs, 1984). It was not clear, however, whether these admissions were for alcohol, cocaine, or heroin treatment. Less information is available regarding treatment utilization for American Indians, although an early study reported a significant relationship between societal involvement and treatment outcomes for Navajo Indians. Those with a stake in primarily traditional Indian society had a 72 percent treatment success rate. Those with no stake in either traditional Indian society or Caucasian society evidenced only a 23 percent success rate. Those with the highest treatment success rate (74 percent) had a stake in both traditional and Caucasian society (Ferguson, 1976).

Hispanics also tend to use health and mental health services at lower rates than other racial/ethnic groups (Angel, 1985). However, they are overrepresented in their use of alcohol services (Butynski, Record, & Yates, 1985), and the majority of these clients are male adults (Santiestevan & Santiesteva, 1984). Data primarily on Mexican-Americn alcohol treatment clients indicates that they are also more likely to be married, to be less well educated, to be employed, and to have higher incomes than other clients (Engmann, 1976). But they are similar in age to other clients (Butynski et al., 1985), with most falling between ages 25 and 44. There is also some evidence that Mexican Americans are more likely than White non-Hispanics to self-refer or be referred by a close relative, factors that are predictive of good treatment outcomes (Schuckit, Schwei, & Gold, 1986).

Hispanics are less likely to use detoxification services (Butynski et al., 1985). Gilbert and Cervantes (1986) suggest that this may be due to lower levels of severe dependency, lower rates of withdrawal, or more attempts at withdrawal without medical supervision. Mexican Americans are also less likely to use residential services. Gilbert and Cervantes (1986) propose that this is likely due to the different profile of the residential client, who usually has a longer history of high-level abuse and is more likely to have had multiple admissions, to be separated or divorced, to be living alone, and to be unemployed. Mexican-American clients are more likely to remain within stable family systems. Another contributing factor, however, may be the limited number of culturally focused residential programs for Hispanics.

Based on the 1980 census, Hispanics accounted for 6.4 percent of the total United States population and for 20.5 percent of drug treatment admissions based on client treatment surveys. Although Hispanics are overrepresented in these settings, Moore and Mata (1981) report that Hispanics are likely to perceive drug treatment programs as inaccessible because the settings are perceived as being oriented toward White and Black clients. Data from the 1985 National Drug and Alcoholism Treatment Utilization Survey (National Institute on Drug Abuse, 1988) indicates that only 10.5 percent of all drug treatment units provided specialized programs for Hispanics.

Treatment Strategies

Although treatment is believed to be effective in the reduction of substance abuse, disagreement is the usual state of affairs when the recommended intervention strategy for a specific case is discussed. There is considerable agreement, however, that a multidisciplinary approach is most effective and that family variables are a major key to the treatment of all populations, including African-American, Latino, American Indian/Alaska Native, and Asian-American substance abusers. Such an approach begins to address the multiple pathways leading to substance abuse.

The other critical variable that is most often mentioned is the alteration of substance-focused peer relationships. Unfortunately, very few empirical studies have tested alcohol or drug treatment, incorporating peers into the intervention. In research studies of adolescent substance use, however, use of illicit drugs or alcohol by peers has been the most consistently reported risk factor. A recent study by Dinges and Oetting (1993) illustrated this point. Among those adolescents who reported no use of drugs, very few of their friends reported use. Among those who reported use of specific drugs, however, over 90 percent of their friends used those same drugs.

Rogler, Malgady, Costantino, and Blumenthal (1987) identified three means of providing culturally sensitive mental health services to Hispanics, which also have application to substance abuse populations. These included increasing the accessibility of services through such means as use of bilingual/bicultural staff participation and development of treatment environments in which ethnic/cultural values and norms were honored. Another component of culturally sensitive treatment included matching ethnic clients with treatment modalities that are consonant with their perceived values, such as providing more behaviorally oriented or crisis intervention services rather than traditional insight-oriented therapy, particularly for less acculturated clients (Ruiz, 1981). A final approach directly incorporates cultural values into the therapeutic modality (e.g., utilizing cultural concepts like *machismo*, *respeto*, or *familism*, which are either restructured or used to therapeutic advantage).

Delgado (1988) stresses the importance of both a culture-specific intake and culture-specific intervention in the treatment of alcohol abuse. The intake should consist of five guiding principles: (1) development of an understanding of the role of alcohol and drugs within the family, (2) assessment of the degree of ethnic identity or acculturation, (3) language preference, (4) assessment of the adolescent's social network, and (5) previous treatment experience. Assessment of all of these dimensions should guide the intervention strategies and techniques used with the client (see Chapters 2 and 4).

Retention is one key problem in adolescent treatment services. Many who initially present for treatment drop out after only one or a few sessions. Retention is likely to be improved during the intake process if the client's experience is one in which their cultural experience is valued and understood. Szapocznik and his colleagues (1988) reported on a strategic, structural family systems approach in which the technique of joining was utilized and those interactions that were likely to prevent retention were restructured. The effects of these interventions were dramatic, resulting in a 77 percent completion rate compared to a 25 percent completion rate for a control condition.

Among various intervention strategies, family therapy is one form of treatment that has been emphasized in a number of studies of ethnic minority substance use. Panitz, McConchie, Sauber, and Fonseca (1983) emphasize the crucial element of family variables in both the etiology and the treatment of Latino alcoholism. Included in their recommendation is the important component of distinguishing between pathological and ideal *machismo*. The positive aspects of *machismo* are encouraged, in contrast to pathological *machismo* in which peer groups of males exert pressure on others to consume increasing amounts of alcohol to demonstrate one's masculinity.

Moncher, Holden, Schinke, and Palleja (1990) also suggest that the concept of *familism*, the complex interaction among Hispanic family members wherein identity and esteem are established, may be more applicable to Hispanic than to non-Hispanic families. They describe a complex and difficult case in which a Puerto Rican adolescent male was treated for substance abuse using multiple methods of structural family therapy, functional family therapy, cognitive-behavioral therapy, and case management. They indicate that use of *compadrazgo*, the extended kinship ties between godparents or *padrinos* and godchildren or *ahijados* can be utilized in which both family and extended family members can learn to provide reinforcement for positive behaviors such as the avoidance of substance abuse.

Gilbert and Cervantes (1986) also emphasizes the importance of the extended family in treating Hispanic alcoholism and notes that disintegration of the family begins with distal relationships and then works toward the nuclear family. One of the primary goals of family therapy, then, may be to reestablish extended family ties that have been broken during the course of the alcoholism. Inclusion of supportive treatment or referral to Al-Anon for spouses may be indicated because of the high proportion of Hispanic clients who remain in intact families.

Szapocznik et al. (1989) have developed a comprehensive prevention and intervention approach to Hispanic adolescent substance use and other problem behaviors, utilizing a strategic structural family systems approach. They identify three familial risk factors that are likely to lead to later problem behavior in adolescents: (1) current family maladaptive interactions (i.e., enmeshed or overinvolved maternal relationships combined with distant, excluded paternal relationships, as well as poor conflict resolution skills); (2) intergenerational conflict (i.e., the conflict that occurs developmentally as children move into adolescence); and (3) intercultural conflict (i.e., a problem that may be unique to migrating families in which youth acculturate more rapidly than adults, setting the stage for conflict to emerge over cultural values and behaviors). Family Effectiveness Training is aimed at correcting maladaptive family interactions and strengthening the family by increasing its flexibility in dealing with both developmental and cultural conflicts. Its psychoeducational format, which includes both didactic and experiential components, has been demonstrated to be superior to control conditions in improving family functioning and reducing problem behaviors in adolescents on the basis of both parental and self-report (Szapocznik et al., 1989).

Moore (1992) also supports the use of family therapy with African Americans. She noted that one cause for resistance in therapy may be familial. In the families' attempts to protect their children from treatment programs under the jurisdiction of Whites, Black parents sometimes participate in the maintenance of the problem. Family therapy is also congruent with the Native American community, in that many people have clan systems that are still active today. Extended family systems are important to this population, and inclusion of family in the therapeutic process is paramount to treatment success. The family system is also of primary importance to the psychosocial functioning of Pacific Islanders (Sue & Morishima, 1982). This group of families and their extended kinship have been recognized as an important protective factor against many health and mental health problems (Hsu, 1973).

Barrett, Simpson, and Lehman (1988) reported on results from four treatment programs that targeted drug and alcohol use, school problems, and legal involvement among Mexican-American adolescents that might also cross the cultural barrier to other populations. Although the findings were based only on the first three months of participation, reduction of these problems was found to relate to the development of positive peer relationships, reduction in peer drug use, family support, program participation, and religious background.

Although it was used for treatment of behavioral problems rather than substance use, one culturally based method for Puerto Rican children and adolescents incorporated the use of *cuentos* (Puerto Rican folktales) in which the characters served as therapeutic models (Malgady, Rogler, & Costantino, 1990). Adult hero and heroine role models were used with the adolescents. This culturally congruent treatment showed evidence of effectiveness in reducing anxiety and increasing social judgment in participants. Adaptations of this method could be made for use in substance abuse treatment. Freeman (1992) also utilizes storytelling with young African-American males. She uses family and cultural storytelling techniques to gain insight into engaging children and youth for prevention and treatment of substance abuse problems.

Spirituality is also a recognized tool in the treatment of ethnic minorities. In fact, a strong multidisciplinary team might include a spiritual leader reflective of the community culture. Elders and youth might also be included recognizing the special roles that both play in the community. Likewise, medicine wheels, sweat lodges, talking circles, sundance preparation, and other traditional activities are used in some treatment centers to facilitate the healing process. Spiritual leaders, shamans, and medicine men or women are consulted by family members as well as by treatment professionals for inclusion in the therapeutic curriculum (see Chapter 9).

Knox (1985) argues that spirituality is a tool that can be used effectively in the treatment of the Black alcoholic and the family and should be explored in the assessment process. The sources of hope and strength should be examined, as well as the meaning of spirituality and the diversity of beliefs and practices of the family. Trotter and Chavira (1978) describes the role of *curanderos*, traditional folk healers, who have historically been consulted for the treatment of substance abuse problems, particularly alcohol abuse, among Latino families. *Curanderos* identify specific etiologies, and cures for alcohol abuse and make distinctions between problem drinking and alcohol addiction. Cures may consist of counseling, herbal cures, or administration of *Haba de San Ignacio*, a preparation similar to disulfiram, both of which produce nausea and vomiting when mixed with alcohol. Less acculturated Latinos, particularly older females, may be likely to consult traditional folk healers but often use traditional methods to supplement, rather than replace, medical approaches.

Guidelines for Working in Ethnic Communities

Development of culturally sensitive and appropriate treatment interventions requires a careful and thorough scrutiny of the specific population. A solid first step would be the recruitment of staff who are members of the targeted population or are familiar with the culture. At a minimum, recruited staff must be culturally sensitive—able to consider age, gender, socioeconomic status, access to opportunities, degree of acculturation, availability of social supports, cultural values and norms, spirituality, and family system. It is often beneficial to look within oneself and examine one's own values before confronting someone whose cultural values, traditions, and customs may be quite different.

Because of the diversity between and within ethnic populations, it is also necessary to develop an understanding of the target group that resides in the service delivery area (Orlandi et al., 1992). Although it is difficult to generalize across groups, it is often helpful to review the literature. More important, local statistics related to substance abuse behaviors should be examined. Often this type of examination requires both an emotional and an intellectual commitment on the part of the service provider. It is important not to be caught in stereotypes, positive or negative. For example, all Native Americans are not noble warriors, nor are they all "drunken Indians."

The need for multicultural consideration can extend to inclusion of diverse community members on advisory boards and task forces (see Chapter 8). These experts can help plan inservice training, service delivery, and policy format. They also have the opportunity to serve as role models for other community members while building a mutual understanding of the cultural issues between the participants. Such efforts also empower local ethnic communities to deal with the risk factors that can contribute to alcoholism and drug abuse.

Historically, the focus has been on assimilation—integrating the various ethnic populations into the "American" way of life. Current thinking, however, focuses on efforts to help the dominant society understand the values and needs of the minority community. It is no longer acceptable to look upon the traditions of the various ethnic communities as dysfunctional. Instead, one is asked to seek out the strengths and resiliency that these traditions contribute to the ethnic groups. Finally, despite the many challenges that nearly all cultures have experienced at one time or another, they have survived. Many have maintained their cultural traditions even though the losses have been devastating, and they continue to demonstrate the extraordinary capacity to heal and grow.

References

Ahern, F. M. (1985). Alcohol use and abuse among four ethnic groups in Hawaii: Native Hawaiians, Japanese, Filipinos, and Caucasians. In *Alcohol use among U.S. ethnic minorities.* NIAAA Research Monograph No. 18. DHHS Publication No. (ADM) 89-1435 pp. 3–50). Rockville, MD: National Institute on Alcohol Abuse and Alcoholism.

Angel, R. (1985). The health of the Mexican-American population. In R. O. de la Garza, F. D. Bean, C. M. Bonjean, R. Romo, & R. Alvarez (Eds.), *The Mexican-American experience: An interdisciplinary anthology* (pp. 410–426). Austin: University of Texas Press.

Austin, G., & Gilbert, M. J. (1989). Substance abuse among Latino youth. *Prevention Research Update, 3,* 1–26. Los Alamitos, CA: Southwest Regional Educational Laboratory.

Bachman, J. G., Wallace, J. M., O'Malley, P. M., Johnston, L. D., Kurth, C. C., & Neighbors, H. W. (1991). Racial/ethnic differences in smoking, drinking, and illicit drug use among American high school seniors, 1976–89. *American Journal of Public Health, 81,* 372–377.

Barrett, M. E., Simpson, D. D., & Lehman, W. E. K. (1988). Behavioral changes of adolescents in drug abuse intervention programs. *Journal of Clinical Psychology, 44,* 461–473.

Beauvais, F. (1992). Trends in Indian adolescent drug and alcohol use. *American Indian and Alaska Native Mental Health Research Journal, 5,* 1–12.

Beauvais, F., & LaBoueff, W. (1985). Drug and alcohol abuse intervention in American Indian Communities. *International Journal of the Addictions, 20,* 139–171.

Bratter, T. E., & Forrest, G. G. (Eds.). (1985). *Alcoholism and substance abuse: Strategies for clinical intervention.* New York: Free Press.

Brisbane, F. L. (1987). Divided feeling of Black alcoholic daughters. *Alcohol Health and Research World, 11,* 48–50.

Brown, F., & Tooley, J. (1989). Alcoholism in the Black Community. In G. W. Lawson & A. W. Lawson (Eds.), *Alcoholism and substance abuse in special populations* (pp. 115–128). Rockville, MD: Aspen.

Bry, B. H., McKeon, P., & Pandina, R. J. (1982). Extent of drug use as a function of number of risk factors. *Journal of Abnormal Psychology, 91,* 273–279.

Butynski, W., Record, N., & Yates, L. (1985). *State resources and services for alcohol and drug abuse problems.* Fiscal year 1984. DHHS 461 357 20444. Washington, DC: U.S. Government Printing Office.

Caetano, R. (1984). Ethnicity and drinking in Northern California: A comparison among Whites, Blacks, and Hispanics. *Alcohol and Alcoholism, 19,* 31–44.

Cahalan, D. (1970). *Problem drinkers: A national survey.* San Francisco: Jossey-Bass.

Carter, D. J., & Wilson, R. (1991). *Ninth annual status report: Minorities in higher education.* Washington, DC: American Council on Education.

Chavez, E. L., Edwards, R. W., & Oetting, E. R. (1989). Mexican-American and White American dropouts' drug use, health status, and involvement in violence. *Public Health Reports, 104,* 594–604.

Chavez, E. L., & Swaim, R. C. (1992a). An epidemiological comparison of Mexican-American and

White non-Hispanic eighth- and twelfth-grade students' substance use. *American Journal of Public Health, 82,* 445–447.

Chavez, E. L., & Swaim, R. C. (1992b). Hispanic substance use: Problems in epidemiology. In J. Trimble, C. Bolek, & S. Niemcryk (Eds.), *Ethnic and multicultural drug abuse: Perspectives on current research* (pp. 211–230). New York: Haworth

Clifford, P. R., & Jones, W., Jr. (1988). Alcohol abuse, prevention issues, and the Black community. *Evaluation and the Health Professions, 11,* 272–277.

Coombs, R. H., Paulson, M. J., & Richardson, M. A. (1991). Peer vs. parental influence in substance use among Hispanic and Anglo children and adolescents. *Journal of Youth and Adolescence, 20,* 73–88.

Cotton, N. S. (1979). The familial incidence of alcoholism: A review. *Journal of Studies on Alcohol, 46,* 98–116.

Craig, R. J. (1982). Personality characteristics of heroin addicts: Review of empirical research 1976–1979. *International Journal of the Addictions, 17,* 227–248.

De La Rosa, M. R., Khalsa, J. H., & Rouse, B. A. (1990). Hispanics and illicit drug use: A review of recent findings. *International Journal of the Addictions, 25,* 665–691.

Delgado, M. (1988). Alcoholism treatment and Hispanic youth. *Journal of Drug Issues, 18,* 59–68.

Dinges, N. M., & Oetting, E. R. (1993). Similarity in drug use patterns between adolescents and their friends. *Adolescence, 28,* 253–266.

Engmann, D. J. (1976). *Alcoholism and alcohol abuse among the Spanish-speaking population in California: A needs and services assessment.* Sacramento: California Commission on Alcoholism for the Spanish-speaking.

Felix-Ortiz, M., & Newcomb, M. D. (1992). Risk and protective factors for drug use among Latino and White adolescents. *Hispanic Journal of Behavioral Sciences, 14,* 291–309.

Ferguson, F. N. (1976). Stake theory as an explanatory device in Navajo alcoholism treatment response. *Human Organization, 35,* 65–78.

Freeman, E. (1992). The use of storytelling techniques with young African American males: Implications for substance abuse prevention. *Journal of Intergroup Relations, 19,* 53–72.

Gibbs, J. T. (1984). Black adolescents and youth: An endangered species. *American Journal of Orthopsychiatry, 54,* 6–20.

Gilbert, M. J. (1987). Alcohol consumption patterns in immigrant and later generation Mexican-American women. *Hispanic Journal of Behavioral Sciences, 9,* 299–314.

Gilbert, M. J., (1989). Alcohol use among Latino adolescents: What we know and what we need to know. *Drugs and Society, 3,* 39–57.

Gilbert, M. J., & Alcocer, A. M. (1988). Alcohol use and Hispanic youth: An overview. *Journal of Drug Issues, 18,* 33–48.

Gilbert, M. J., & Cervantes, R. C. (1986). Alcohol services for Mexican-Americans: A review of utilization patterns, treatment considerations, and prevention activities. *Hispanic Journal of Behavioral Sciences, 8,* 191–223.

Globetti, G., Alsikafi, M., & Morse, R. (1980). Black female high school students and the use of beverage alcohol. *International Journal of Addictions, 15,* 189–200.

Glynn, T. J. (1981). From family to peer: A review of transitions of influence among drug-using youth. *Journal of Youth and Adolescence, 10,* 363–383.

Harvey, W. B. (1985). Alcohol abuse and the Black community: A contemporary analysis. *Journal of Drug Issues, 15,* 81–91.

Helzer, J. E. (1987). Epidemiology of alcoholism. *Journal of Consulting and Clinical Psychology, 55,* 284–292.

Herd, D. (1985). The epidemiology of drinking patterns and alcohol-related problems among U.S. Blacks. In *Alcohol use among U.S. Ethnic Minorities.* NIAAA Research Monograph No. 18. DHHS Publication No. (ADM)89-1435 pp. 3–50). Rockville, MD: National Institute on Alcohol Abuse and Alcoholism.

Hsu, F. L. K. (1973). Kinship is the key. *Center Magazine, 6,* 4–14.

Johnson, R. C., & Nagoshi, C. T. (1990). Asians, Asian-Americans, and alcohol. *Journal of Psychoactive Drugs, 22,* 45–52.

Kalar, P. (1991). *Issues to consider: The American Indian and the media.* New York: National Conference of Christians and Jews.

King, L. M. (1982). Alcoholism: Studies regarding Black Americans, 1977–1980. In *Special Populations Issues. Alcohol and Health Monograph 4,*

DHHS Pub. No. (ADM) 82-1193, 385–410. Rockville, MD: National Institute on Alcohol Abuse and Alcoholism.

Kitano, H. L., & Chi, I. (1985). Asian Americans and alcohol: The Chinese, Japanese, Koreans, and Filipinos in Los Angeles In D. Spiegler, D. Tate, S. Aitken, & C. Christian (Eds.), *Alcohol use among U.S. ethnic minorities* (pp. 373–382). Rockville, MD: National Institute on Alcoholism and Alcohol Abuse.

Kitano, H. L., Lubben, J. E., & Chi, I. (1988). Predicting Japanese American drinking behavior. *The International Journal of the Addictions, 23,* 417–428.

Klein, B. T. (Ed.) (1993). *Reference encyclopedia of the American Indian* (6th ed.) (pp. 35–39). West Nyack, NY: Todd Publications.

Knox, D. H. (1985). Spirituality: A tool in the assessment and treatment of Black alcoholics and their families. *Alcoholism Treatment Quarterly. 2,* 31–44.

Lawson, G. W., & Lawson, A. W. (1989). *Alcoholism and substance abuse in special populations.* Rockville, MD: Aspen.

Lawson, G., Peterson, J., & Lawson, A. (1983). *Alcoholism and the family: A guide to treatment and prevention.* Rockville, MD: Aspen.

Lee, J. A. (1987). Chinese, alcohol, and flushing: Sociohistorical and biobehavioral conditions. *Journal of Psychoactive Drugs, 19,* 319–327.

Maddahian, E., Newcomb, M. D., & Bentler, P. M. (1988). Risk factors for substance use: Ethnic differences among adolescents. *Journal of Substance Abuse, 1,* 11–23.

Malgady, R. G., Rogler, L. H., & Costantino, G. (1990). Culturally sensitive psychotherapy for Puerto Rican children and adolescents: A program of treatment outcome research. *Journal of Consulting and Clinical Psychology, 58,* 704–712.

May, P. A. (1982). Substance abuse and American Indians: Prevalence and susceptibility. *International Journal of the Addictions, 17,* 1185–1209.

May, P. A. (1986). Alcohol and drug misuse prevention programs for American Indians: Needs and opportunities. *Journal of Studies on Alcohol, 47,* 187–195.

McEuen, W. W. (1914). *Survey of the Mexican in Los Angeles.* Los Angeles: University of Southern California, Department of Economics and Sociology.

Moncher, M. S., Holden, G. W., Schinke, S. P., & Palleja, J. (1990). Behavioral family treatment of the substance abusing Hispanic adolescent. In E. L. Feindler & G. R. Kalfus (Eds.), *Adolescent behavior therapy handbook* (pp. 329–349). New York: Springer.

Moore, S. E. (1992). Cultural sensitivity treatment and research issues with Black adolescent drug users. *Child and Adolescent Social Work Journal, 9,* 249–260.

Moore, J., & Mata, A. (1981). *Women and heroin in Chicano communities.* Unpublished manuscript.

Morales, A. (1984). Substance abuse and Mexican-American youth: An overview. *Journal of Drug Issues, 14,* 297–311.

National Institute on Drug Abuse. (1987). *Use of selected drugs among Hispanics: Mexican-Americans, Puerto Ricans, and Cuban-Americans, Findings from the Hispanic Health and Nutrition Examination Survey.* DHHS Pub. No. (ADM) 87-1527. Washington, DC: U.S. Government Printing Office.

National Institute on Drug Abuse. (1988). *National household survey on drug abuse: Main findings 1985.* DHHS Publication No. (ADM)88-1565. Washington, DC: U.S. Government Printing Office.

Newcomb, M. D., Maddahian, E., & Bentler, P. M. (1986). Risk factors for drug use among adolescents: Concurrent and longitudinal analyses. *American Journal of Public Health, 76,* 525–531.

Oetting, E. R. (1992). Planning programs for prevention of deviant behavior: A psychosocial model. In J. Trimble, C. Bolek, & S. Niemcryk (Eds.), *Ethnic and multicultural drug abuse: Perspectives on current research* (pp. 313–344). Binghamton, NY: Harrington Park.

Oetting, E. R., & Beauvais, F. (1983). A typology of adolescent drug use: A practical classification system for describing drug use patterns. *Academic Psychology Bulletin, 5,* 55–69.

Oetting, E. R., & Beauvais, F. (1987). Peer cluster theory, socialization characteristics and adolescent drug use: A path analysis. *Journal of Counseling Psychology, 34,* 205–213.

Oetting, E. R., & Beauvais, F. (1990). Orthogonal cultural identification theory: The cultural identification of minority adolescents. *International Journal of the Addictions, 25,* 655–685.

Orlandi, M. A., Weston, R., & Epstein, L. G. (1992). (Eds.), *Cultural competence for evaluators: A guide for alcohol and other drug abuse prevention practitioners working with ethnic/racial communities*. Rockville, MD: U.S. Department of Health and Human Services.

Panitz, D. R., McConchie, R. D., Sauber, S. R., & Fonseca, J. A. (1983). The role of *machismo* and the Hispanic family in the etiology and treatment of alcoholism in Hispanic American males. *American Journal of Family Therapy, 11,* 31–42.

Paredes, A. (1975). Social control of drinking among the Aztec Indians of Mesoamerica. *Journal of Studies on Alcohol, 36,* 1139–1153.

Rebach, H. (1992). Alcohol and drug use among American minorities. In J. Trimble, C. Bolek, & S. Niemcryk (Eds.), *Ethnic and multicultural drug abuse: Perspectives on current research* (pp. 23–58). Binghamton, NY: Haworth.

Rogler, L. H., Malgady, R. G., Costantino, G., & Blumenthal, R. (1987). What do culturally sensitive mental health services mean? The case of Hispanics. *American Psychologist, 42,* 565–570.

Ruiz, R. (1981). Cultural and historical perspectives in counseling Hispanics. In D. W. Sue (Ed.), *Counseling the culturally different: Theory and practice* (pp. 186–215). New York: Wiley.

Santiestevan, H., & Santiestevan, S. (Eds.). (1984). *The Hispanic almanac.* Washington, DC: Hispanic Policy Development Project.

Sasao, T. (1989). *Patterns of substance use and health practices among Japanese Americans in southern California.* Paper presented at the third annual conference of the Asian American Psychological Association, New Orleans, LA.

Schuckit, M. A., Schwei, M. G., & Gold, E. (1986). Prediction outcome in outpatient alcoholics. *Journal of Studies on Alcohol, 2,* 151–155.

Spotts, J. V., & Shontz, F. C. (1982). Ego development, dragon fights, and chronic drug abusers. *International Journal of the Addictions, 17,* 945–976.

Sue, D. W. (1981). *Counseling the culturally different: Theory and practice.* New York: Wiley.

Sue, D. W. (1987). Use and abuse of alcohol by Asian Americans. *Journal of Psychoactive Drugs, 19,* 57–66.

Sue, S., & Morishima, J. K. (1982). *The mental health of Asian Americans.* San Francisco: Jossey-Bass.

Swaim, R. C. (1991). Childhood risk factors and adolescent drug and alcohol abuse. *Educational Psychology Review, 3,* 363–398.

Swaim, R. C., Oetting, E. R., Chavez, E. L., & Beauvais, F. (1993). *The effect of dropout status on estimates of adolescent substance use among ethnic groups.* Unpublished manuscript.

Swaim, R. C., Oetting, E. R., Thurman, P. J., Beauvais, F., & Edwards, R. W. (1993). American Indian adolescent drug use and socialization characteristics: A cross-cultural comparison. *Journal of Cross Cultural Psychology, 24,* 53–70.

Swaim, R. C., Thurman, P. J., Beauvais, F., Oetting, E. R., & Wayman, J. (1993). *Indian adolescent substance use as a function of number of risk factors.* Manuscript submitted for publication.

Szapocznik, J., Perez-Vidal, A., Brickman, A. L., Foote, F. H., Santisteban, D., & Hervis, O. (1988). Engaging adolescent drug abusers and their families in treatment: A strategic structural systems approach. *Journal of Consulting and Clinical Psychology, 56,* 552–557.

Szapocznik, J., Santisteban, D., Rio, A., Perez-Vidal, A., Santisteban, D., & Kurtines, W. M. (1989). Family effectiveness training: An intervention to prevent drug abuse and problem behaviors in Hispanic adolescents. *Hispanic Journal of Behavioral Sciences, 11,* 4–27.

Trotter, R. C., & Chavira, J. A. (1978). Discovering new models for alcohol. Counseling in minority groups. In B. Velimirov (Ed.), *Modern medicine and medical anthropology in the United States-Mexico border population* (pp. 164–171). Washington, DC: Pan American Health Organization.

U.S. Bureau of the Census. (1990). *Statistical abstract of the United States: 1990 (110th Edition).* Washington, DC: U.S. Government Printing Office.

U.S. Bureau of the Census. (1992). *1990 census of population, 1990 CP-1-4, General population characteristics.* Washington, DC: U.S. Government Printing Office.

U.S. Department of Health and Human Services. (1985). *Report of the Secretary's Task Force on Black and Minority Health.* DHHS Pub. No. (ADM) 85-487. Washington, DC: U.S. Government Printing Office.

Watts, T. D. & Wright, R. Jr. (Eds.). (1983). *Black alcoholism: Toward a comprehensive understanding.* Springfield, IL: Thomas.

Yee, B. W. K., & Thu, N. D. (1987). Correlates of drug use and abuse among Indochinese refugees: Mental health implications. *Journal of Psychoactive Drugs. 19,* 77–83.

Zane, N., & Sasao, T. (1992). Research on drug abuse among Asian Pacific Americans. In J. Trimble, C. Bolek, & S. Niemcryk (Eds.), *Ethnic and multi-cultural drug abuse* (pp. 181–209). Binghamton, NY: Harrington Park.

Chapter *14*

Ethnic Minority Physical Health: Issues and Interventions

CAROL M. CUMMINGS
DANA D. DEHART

According to the report from the Task Force on Minority Health (U.S. Department of Health and Human Services [DHHS], 1985) the general health of ethnic group members in the United States is poorer, with few exceptions, than that of Whites. Recent reports from the Centers for Disease Control (CDC) in Atlanta and the National Center for Health Statistics, show that while some of the gaps in White and ethnic health are closing, others are widening. In 1991, for example, the CDC reported that life expectancy among African Americans was again declining from its peak during the 1970s. Deaths due to tuberculosis (TB); cancers of the breast, cervix, and prostate gland; acquired immunodeficiency syndrome (AIDS); and homicide are increasing for the United States population, especially among young ethnic teens and adults (Centers for Disease Control, 1991, 1993a).

This chapter is directed toward helping mental health practitioners become aware of the serious physical health issues faced by ethnic clients, and toward assisting mental health practitioners in understanding the relationship between physical health and psychosocial well-being. We shall address topics such as the incidence and prevalence of illness among specific ethnic groups. The role of individual risk behavior, group behavior based on cultural norms and peer pressures, cultural perceptions of health care, and traditional beliefs about health will also be discussed. Other important foci include the impact of poverty and other forces in society, such as racism, sexism, heterosexism, and institutional barriers (Kerner, Dosenbury, & Mandelblatt, 1993).

The first section of this chapter looks at chronic disease incidence and base rates for acute illness among ethnic groups. The second section covers some of the causal factors for illness, such as individual risk behavior and life-style patterns. Within this psychosocial framework, we examine group behavior that may contribute to risk-taking activities or perpetuate risky behavior. We also discuss organizational, institutional, environmental, and societal forces affecting ethnic people's access to health services, to resources for prevention, and to educational information pertaining to physical health. Throughout this section, we focus largely on the human immunodeficiency virus (HIV) and AIDS literature that has begun to emerge in the last decade. We conclude with an integration and synopsis of intervention at the individual, group, organizational, and environmental levels.

Physical Health of Ethnic Groups: Incidence, Prevalence, and Base Rates

The Task Force on Minority Health (U.S. Department of Health and Human Services, 1985) has published a report that identifies a number of disparities between the health status of ethnic groups and Whites in the United States. Of all major causes of death combined—including heart disease, stroke, cancer, infant mortality, homicide, accidents, cirrhosis, and diabetes—African Americans show a 1.5 percent greater likelihood of dying compared to Whites. Of particular significance is the fact that African-American males show greater than 6 to 1 ratio with White males of dying from homicide, and African-American females show more than 4 to 1 ratio over White females for such deaths.

The Task Force report also discusses "excess deaths," which are defined as age-adjusted death rates in excess of the number who would have died had their rates been equal to (not greater than) death rates among Whites. Excess deaths among Hispanics are attributed primarily to motor vehicle accidents and homicide. Almost half of excess deaths among Native Americans are due to unintentional injuries, and homicide accounts for approximately 10 percent of Native American excess deaths. Cirrhosis accounted for 11 percent of male and 20 percent of female excess deaths among Native Americans, indicating that alcohol abuse is one of the major causes of early death for this group (see Chapter 13). Excessive use of alcohol may also lead to risky sexual behavior for exposure to HIV (Leigh & Stall, 1993).

Asians/Pacific Islanders are reported by the Task Force to be the healthiest overall racial/ethnic group in the United States. This group shows virtually no excess deaths in the 1985 report, yet specific health problems do exist among various groups within Asian communities. When compared to Whites in Hawaii, Native Hawaiians experienced excess deaths from heart disease, cancer, diabetes, infant mortality, and accidents. Hawaiians displayed especially high excess death rates from stomach and lung cancers. Analysis of data for the three major Asian ethnic groups, Chinese, Japanese, and Filipinos, showed no substantial excess death for a majority of causes, with the exception of female suicide, relative to White females. Differences in socioeconomic status, culture, and life-style, as well as less smoking and alcohol consumption, may explain lower relative mortality among these populations.

In the United States today, the fastest growing health issues in ethnic communities are the infectious diseases, including TB and HIV/AIDS. Between 1985 and 1992, TB rates rose by 26 percent among African Americans, 75 percent among Hispanics, and 47 percent among Asians and Pacific Islanders, while rates dropped among Whites and Native Americans. In the short span between 1990 and 1992, HIV rates among Blacks increased by 19 percent, and rates among American Indians and Alaskan Natives increased by 35 percent, as compared to the relative stability of HIV incidence among Whites, Asians, and Hispanics (Centers for Disease Control, 1993a). Although the HIV rates for Hispanics have been stable, they are high compared to those for Whites.

Of the 315,390 U.S. AIDS cases reported through June 1993, almost half (49 percent) represent ethnic minority persons; this percentage is in stark contrast to the 21 percent of United States citizens who are ethnic minority group members (Centers for Disease Control, 1989, 1993a). Asians and Native Americans represent very small proportions of the total AIDS cases (less than 1 percent each). African Americans, however, are overrepresented in almost every currently acknowledged HIV risk group in the United States (Centers for Disease Control, 1993b). Among adolescent and adult female AIDS cases reported through June 1993, 53 percent are African Americans. Hispanic men, women, and children represent and 17 percent of the United States AIDS cases reported through June 1993 (Centers for Disease Control, 1993b).

Finally, while life expectancy in general has been increasing over the mid-twentieth century, available data indicate that ethnic–White differences remain. In 1991, White male life expectancy was 73.4 years, as compared to 65.6 years for African-American males (U.S. Bureau of Census, 1993; U.S. Department of Health and Human Services, 1991). Native American and Hispanic male life expectancies reflected similar patterns, whereas Asian male life expectancy tended to be greater than that of White males. In general, women were reported as having greater life expectancy than males, but disparities between ethnic and White females were roughly analogous to disparities between males (U.S. Department of Health and Human Services, 1985).

Data indicate that excess deaths are correlated with education, socioeconomic status, culture, and life-style differences (Kerner et al., 1993). It cannot be overemphasized that health differences among ethnic groups in the United States largely reflect poor quality of life for people of color, who are identifiable as being low in status, low in power, and low in income. These social conditions adversely affect nutrition, housing, and education, which in turn can become chronic stressors. Although data on some ethnic groups are sparse or incomplete, it is clear that some environmental factors have an impact on ethnic group health, and that a comprehensive response requires social, economic, and life-style changes.

Physical Health Issues and Interventions

The following sections focus on four levels of functioning: individual, group, organizational/ institutional, and environmental. Individual attitudes, beliefs, and life-styles will be reviewed at the first level. At the group level, the role of social networks will be discussed. The organizational/institutional level will focus on the health care system. Finally, on the environmental level, the role of living conditions and societal forces will be discussed. Examples will be drawn from the literature on HIV/AIDS, since a well-developed body of knowledge exists in this area that illustrates the issues at each of these levels despite the fact that there has been limited success in addressing this condition (Kelly, Murphy, Sikkema, & Kalichman, 1993).

Individual Level: Attitudes, Beliefs, and Life-Style

No attitude, belief, or behavior arises independently of a social context. Thus, when we speak of health-related issues at the individual level, we are to some extent discussing concerns that derive from cultural and societal circumstances. Although these forces are typically thought of as external/environmental effects, they are also linked to intrapersonal experiences. The issues we have chosen to approach in this section pertain to themes of autonomy, efficacy, and role fulfillment. Whether the phenomena discussed originate in the environment or within the individual, these psychosocial factors intersect in the domain of physical being and physical health.

Religious ideals, social mores, and living conditions may play a significant role in the HIV risk behavior of ethnic groups in the United States. Many Hispanics, for instance, are practicing Catholics. The Catholic Church's condemnation of birth control and abortion may influence decisions to use condoms and may deter seropositive Latinas from terminating pregnancies (Jue & Kain, 1989). These women, feeling they have no choice but to bear the child, may gamble with the 50 to 65 percent probability that the infant, too, will be HIV positive (Peckham, Sentuvia, & Ades, 1987). The child, seropositive or not, will soon lose a parent; this issue sometimes eludes consideration by the mother and health care providers.

Many factors, such as socioeconomic status, political orientation, and relationship maintenance, may also influence whether pregnancies are continued and whether pre- and postnatal care is sought. Women in underserved communities may not be aware of or have access to services that can promote good decision making regarding disease prevention, birth control, and obstetrics. Empirical research, for instance, estimates that about one-third of African-American women take no measures to reduce their own risk of HIV infection (Jemmott & Jemmott, 1991; Mays & Cochran, 1988). Furthermore, pregnant African-American women are less likely than White women to have prenatal care in the early stages of pregnancy, and fewer Blacks than Whites choose to have abortions (U.S. Department of Health and Human Services, 1986).

Ethnic women may view HIV as a lower order concern in a hierarchy of needs and risks (Mays & Cochran, 1988). They may believe that insistence on safer sex could jeopardize relationships that sustain emotional and physical support. In African-American communities, sex-ratio imbalances and low marriage rates may render relationships less secure, and females in these communities may feel pressured into sexual compliance (Mays & Cochran, 1988). In one survey, almost half of the women felt that their sexual partners would disapprove of condom use (Jemmott & Jemmott, 1991). In some Hispanic cultures, modesty, self-sacrifice, and sexual naivete may be requisite indicators of female virtue (Fernandez, Ruiz, & Bing, 1993; Jue & Kain, 1989), and authorization for condom use is thought to be the man's decision (Mays & Cochran, 1988). The Latina who defies these mores by suggesting condom use may risk condemnation, abandonment, or abuse (Carballo-Diéguez, 1989; Jue & Kain, 1989; Mays & Cochran, 1988).

In working with women who have been socialized into complaisant roles, the mental health professional may have to prepare the client to deal with the reactions of her significant other and the stressors entailed by assertive sexual communication. The client is unlikely at first to appreciate the logic that if she is rejected for suggesting condom use, she has merely lost an oppressor. The mental health professional may work toward empowerment of these women by helping the client realize her autonomy and right to make decisions regarding her own body.

Women are not the only persons whose HIV-risk behavior may be affected by social conditions. The HIV risk of men also hinges on systems of belief and cultural experience. A number of researchers, for instance, have suggested that the concept of *machismo* (e.g., protector, breadwinner, manly) is still prevalent in some Hispanic communities (Carballo-Diéguez, 1989; Fernandez et al., 1993; Jue & Kain, 1989; Mays & Cochran, 1988; Peterson & Marin, 1988; Singer, 1992). For men who subscribe to this traditional role, infidelity and promiscuity may be equated with virility, and sexual urges are viewed as difficult to control, requiring periodic discharge as opportunities present themselves (Carballo-Diéguez, 1989).

These norms to which some Hispanic men adhere can be discordant with safer sexual ideals. The mental health professional, however, can work within the framework of *machismo* to encourage safer sexual behavior without undermining the client's sense of role fulfillment (Peterson & Marin, 1988; Singer, 1992). Traditional Hispanic concepts of *machismo, respeto* (interpersonal respect), *responsabilidad* (responsibility), and *comunidad* (social solidarity) all possess elements of interpersonal concern and care for others (Carballo-Diéguez, 1989; Peterson & Marin, 1988; Singer, 1992). The clinician or service provider may promote safer sexual behavior by focusing on the client's role as protector of the family and community (Fernandez et al., 1993; Jue & Kain, 1989; Peterson & Marin, 1988).

In many ethnic communities, sexually ambivalent males who engage in situational homosexuality (i.e., in prison or under the influence of drugs) or who take the "masculine" (insertive) role in homosexual encounters may not perceive themselves as homosexual and thereby may discount the HIV risk associated with certain behaviors (Carballo-Diéguez, 1989; Jue & Kain, 1989; Peterson & Marin, 1988; Thomas, So'Brien van Putten, & Chen, 1991). These men may resent being regarded as gay by the mental health professional (Carrier & Magana, 1992; Morales, 1990; Peterson & Marin, 1988). Additionally, some mental health practitioners will find themselves working with the wives and partners of these bisexual men. These women are at heightened HIV risk and may be subject to emotional trauma and denial upon discovering a partner's bisexuality.

The AIDS epidemic centers around youthful persons who face the progressive debilitation of a terminal illness while simultaneously facing social messages of hatred, exclusion, and abandonment. The mental health professional can offer strength, support, and empowerment throughout the phases of diagnosis, adjustment, and full-blown AIDS. Instead of using a medical or physiologically based model of health promotion, mental health professionals may wish to concentrate on factors such as efficacy beliefs, negotiation skills, self-esteem, and normative pressures, all of which are likely to be influenced by environmental conditions and cultural scripts (Quimby, 1992; Mays, 1988). Changed behaviors may be facilitated by innovation within the psychosocial context of the person's life.

Thus, health promotion includes evaluation and/or alteration of the individual's behavioral and belief systems. Although either belief systems or behavior might be modified independently of the other, conjoint adjustment of beliefs and behavior has an intuitive appeal. Health beliefs concerning personal vulnerability and efficacy, however, tend to be resistant to change, remaining relatively stable over the course of a lifetime (D. S. Gochman, September 1993, personal communication). To promote healthy behavior, the mental health professional should reframe HIV prevention and other health issues in a context that is personally and culturally relevant to the client. The clinician or service provider may explore issues that are most important to the client and may help the client understand how health-promoting behavior can protect or enhance that which is valued.

American HIV/AIDS education campaigns have typically utilized individualistic messages, urging persons to protect *themselves* from HIV. For some persons, especially those from ethnic backgrounds, messages that emphasize concern for *others* may be more effective. Mental health professionals might also encourage persons to look beyond immediate circumstances toward long-term risks and benefits of behavior; carelessness and instantaneous gratification on the client's part might be exchanged for purposeful action and hopefulness. Elevating the client's sense of being able to control her or his own life and outcomes, as well as to help others who share her or his condition, makes it infinitely easier to engage the client in self-care. The client will be more creative in attending to health issues and concerns, and less dismayed by the formal and sometimes "unfriendly" structure of the health care system.

Group Level: Social Networks and Belonging

Identification and belonging are important for most ethnic group members. Ethnic groups in United States society tend to feel alienated within and stigmatized by the larger culture. As a result, they may be more inclined to engage in health risk behaviors, especially when such behaviors are connected with a sense of belonging. Group behavior, such as needle sharing, shooting at "galleries," and skin-to-skin rather than protected sexual contact, can foster a sense of unconditional acceptance to persons who lack acceptance from the rest of society. Although fostering a sense of belonging is a good thing, belonging in a group where risk taking is a consequence of membership is not good. Thus, the clinician facing these obstacles in therapy needs to foster the client's emotional well-being without encouraging health-threatening behaviors.

Group membership is especially important for certain stigmatized group members. African-American gays and other persons of dual-minority status, for instance, may be forced to choose between alliance with a Black community or with a gay community (Morales, 1990). The Centers for Disease Control (1993b) in Atlanta report that about 20 percent of the gay or bisexual men with AIDS in the United States are African American. Because a distinct Black gay subculture does not exist in many communities, African-American gays often identify primarily with Black culture, sometimes as bisexual, as an alternative to becoming absorbed by White gay culture (Jue & Kain, 1989; Morales, 1990). African-American women represent one-third of female AIDS cases in the United States whose primary HIV risk was sex with a bisexual male (Centers for Disease Control, 1993b).

The isolation of African-American gays from the larger gay subculture may limit their access to HIV/AIDS information that is readily available to White gays (Peterson & Marin, 1988). The excessive stigma associated with homosexuality in Black communities may deter some African Americans, gay and straight, from even accepting HIV/AIDS literature (Jue & Kain, 1989; Peterson & Marin, 1988). Accordingly, researchers have indicated that African-American gays are notably deficient in HIV/AIDS knowledge; they have lower risk knowledge levels than African-American injectable drug users (Peterson & Marin, 1988).

Group membership may also predispose individuals to risks not otherwise prevalent. Hispanic migrant workers, for example, often reside in male-dominated housing projects and have left wives or partners in Mexico. Unwilling to frequent public places to meet women, many migrant workers use the services of prostitutes (Carrier & Magana, 1992). Survey research has indicated that interaction between migrant workers and prostitutes often involves serial intercourse (a number of men and a single prostitute) and seldom involves condom use (Carrier & Magana, 1992). The HIV risk of these immigrant males is further compromised by high rates of sexually transmitted diseases, which makes HIV transmission more probable (Carrier & Magana, 1992).

Another example of risky group behavior is that of injectable drug use. Despite HIV/AIDS messages directed toward injectable drug users (IDUs), needle sharing persists, and intravenous transmission of HIV continues to occur. Poor IDUs, unable to obtain syringes, may use "shooting galleries," where needle sharing is common (Jue & Kain, 1989). Yet the decision to share syringes is not solely a function of poverty and needle availability. Mays and Cochran (1988) note that sharing "works" sometimes denotes bonding among "running buddies" who use drugs. Those IDUs who are most in need of social validation may be more likely to engage in this form of behavior.

Ethnic minority IDUs, because of the importance of "belonging," may be particularly susceptible to these risky behaviors. Ethnic minority IDUs, however, may face additional stressors stemming from racial discrimination, poverty, and deprivation. By way of ascribed "subculture" status, ethnic minority IDUs may feel they have no access to the resources of White society; these persons may suffer overwhelming feelings of alienation and may grasp at the opportunity to use available syringes. Accordingly, researchers have indicated that Black and Hispanic IDUs are more likely to share syringes than are White IDUs (Des Jarlais, Friedman, & Hopkins, 1985). Of the 73,610 United States AIDS cases that can be directly attributed to injectable drug use through June 1993, 51 percent are African American and 28 percent are Hispanic (Centers for Disease Control, 1993b).

Belonging and maintaining social connections may become integral aspects of living with HIV. Many ethnic minority groups extol the family as a primary social unit and necessary means for support (see Chapter 6). If they are in close contact with family members, some clients may wish for family members to meet the mental health practitioner, and persons from ethnic cultures may take affront to a professional's declining such a request (Jue & Kain, 1989). When interaction with client family members is involved, the mental health professional will need to clarify with the client which aspects of the client's life-style or illness are free for discussion and which should remain confidential (Jue & Kain, 1989).

Although family supports may be valued by the client, not all persons have the luxury of familial support in times of illness. Many Asians and Hispanics, for instance, may have migrated to the United States without family in search of economic opportunities or to avoid the ravages of political oppression and war (see Chapter 1). Native Americans whose families live on reservations may be unable to stay with family once medical needs exceed the capabilities of local health services, as is often the case with HIV/AIDS. If the client's personal or family base is a reservation or community without adequate medical facilities, particular attention should be devoted to establishing alternative means of medical and social support.

Familial support may also be deficient among ethnic gays with HIV/AIDS. Gays who have not "come out" to family may fear rejection if the family were to discover the individual's seropositive status. Other gays who have come out may have already been exiled by their family. In such a context, concealing a homosexual life-style may be difficult and painful for the individual; yet coming out is also likely to be traumatic and often involves the extended as well as the nuclear family (Morales, 1990). In certain Asian cultures, a male child's homosexuality is viewed as the end of the family and as a sign that his parents have failed (Aoki, Ngin, Mo, & Ja, 1989). The son's failure to perpetuate his lineage may bring shame not only to the family but to the community as a whole (Aoki et al., 1989; Carrier, Nguyen, & Sue, 1992). For Hispanic or Asian clients, ingrained values of social obligation may necessitate the family's physical acceptance of and care for all ill child, but this physical support does not necessitate emotional support. Emotional commitment to the seropositive family member may be lacking, and alternative means of psychological support will need to be established (Jue & Kain, 1989).

While 81 percent of adult male Native Americans and Alaskan Natives with AIDS engage in some degree of same-sex eroticism (Centers for Disease Control, 1993b), the social rejection that typifies coming out in other cultures may not be an issue for gay Native Americans. In certain Native American tribes, concepts of gender are not dichotomized. A "third sex," sometimes called a *berdache*, exists. The *berdache* may function as a "sexual outlet" for men and women who are without access to sex (men whose wives are pregnant, women without partners) (Tafoya, 1989). Men who have sex with a *berdache* may not consider themselves to be gay or bisexual, nor are they considered gay within their tribes.

Thus, kinship networks and other social affiliations may play a role in HIV risk behavior and in the support or condemnation of the seropositive individual. Individual differences may govern the client's responses to offered support or social rejection. Some persons may feel extreme loss if rejected by the cohesive family or community, whereas other persons may generally eschew unsolicited support, relying instead on personal strength and autonomy (Fernandez et al., 1993; Jue & Kain, 1989). The mental health professional might help clients establish the desired balance between dependence and independence, in which supports do not undermine personal esteem or impede the individual's ability to engage in self-care.

Organizational/Institutional Level: Interaction with the Health Care System

At some time or other in their history in the United States, ethnic groups have experienced some type of organizational and institutional barriers to needed health and mental health services. Poverty and lack of resources allocated to underserved groups may be the most important barriers (Kerner et al., 1993). Both of these barriers stem from failure of United States institutions to recognize and support needy groups because such constituencies lack political resources. Less stable groups such as migrants, homeless persons, prison inmates, racially alienated gays and those who live in poverty, are at greatest risk to experience these barriers. Ethnic group members are disproportionately represented among these groups (Snell, 1993; Fernandez et al., 1993; Quimby, 1992).

The segmented political organization of ethnic group members has recently been noted as an impediment to HIV/AIDS-prevention efforts. White gays and lesbians, for example, were able to approach the HIV epidemic from within preexisting activist organizations (Quimby, 1992). These organizations were unified by a strong commitment to gay and lesbian issues, and group members were accustomed to social and political resistance in response to these issues. In contrast, ethnic organizations are often affiliated with community churches, and some members may have experienced aversion or ambivalence in dealing with a purportedly "gay" epidemic. Given the United States history of discriminating against ethnic minorities, some groups may have been wary of HIV/AIDS information propagated by Whites. Many ethnic persons felt that advocacy of condom use and of needle exchange programs was genocidal (Jue & Kain, 1989; Mays & Cochran, 1988; Quimby, 1992; Thomas et al., 1991).

These organizational and institutional factors not only influence prevention efforts and risk behavior but also affect use of the health care system in general. Eric Bailey's (1991) report on African-American use of ethnomedicine noted that African Americans retained many such practices from traditional West African health beliefs because ethnomedicinal practices were thought to be most effective. Reasons for continuing to utilize these herbal and folk remedies included communication problems with Europeans and fear of European physicians. Historically, in the course of the development of European medicine, Blacks were used for experiments and sacrificed (Jones, 1981; Krieger, 1987; Clark, 1989). Such brutal practices are long remembered, and fears were passed down through generations, so that some African-American clients are not easily persuaded to seek out Western medical treatments if traditional alternatives are salient.

Barriers to care vary across populations. Native Americans, for instance, face several unique institutional barriers. They continue to be subject to government laws and regulations that are products of treaties (LaFromboise, 1988). City-dwelling Native Americans are often denied access to federal benefits because city residences are not "on or near" Indian reservations (Tafoya, 1989). Instead, the government rewards reliance on Indian Health Services (IHS), usually located in close proximity to reservations. Yet IHS facilities commonly lack resources available to privately owned medical institutions, and Native Americans who use IHS may receive care that is insufficient for detecting or combatting various chronic illnesses.

Recent statistics indicate that a small number of Native American AIDS cases have been diagnosed through the IHS (Metler, Conway, & Stehr-Green, 1991). This may indicate a high degree of misdiagnosis by the IHS or may reflect the geographic removal of IHS facilities relative to urban epicenters where seroconversion among Native Americans may be more prevalent (Metler et al., 1991). Also, Tafoya (1989) has suggested that some Native Americans may be less likely to seek treatment until the final stages of illness, at which point the White hospital may be sought as a "place to die." Tafoya notes that the average life span for some tribe members after HIV diagnosis is only six weeks, indicating a large degree of AIDS progression prior to diagnosis.

Interaction with the health delivery system in this country may be further complicated for persons who are unfamiliar with American patterns of health-seeking behavior. Home remedies and family care may be relied on as an alternative to entering into what may be perceived as a highly unusual institutionalized medical setting. Some clients may more readily utilize services if self-referrals, home assessment, drop-in sessions, and other forms of flexibility sensitive to client scheduling and transportation are feasible (Gonzales, Hays, Bond, & Kelly, 1991; Singer, 1992). Members of some ethnic groups may perceive therapy itself to be awkward or peculiar (Jue & Kain, 1989) and these persons may be reluctant to share the intimate details of their lives with someone who is not even a family member (Peterson & Marin, 1988).

To alleviate discomfort and distrust of the clinical setting, service providers might initially focus on establishing trust, ensuring confidentiality, and demonstrating relevance of treatment (Jue & Kain, 1989). The practitioner may do this by clarifying implied goals and promptly addressing the client's extant issues with a problem-solving approach (Jue & Kain, 1989; McGoldrick, Pearce, & Giordano, 1982). Clinicians or service providers may, for instance, offer information about resources and benefits, serve as a liaison or advocate for the client, and direct the individual to appropriate supplementary services such as substance abuse programs, domestic violence programs, and child care facilities (Gonzales et al., 1991; Jue & Kain, 1989).

The mental health professional may also take the role of an educator, conveying pertinent information about health issues such as HIV transmission, HIV testing, and AIDS. As educators, mental health professionals need to present information in concrete, explicit terms in order to ensure clarity of messages (Peterson & Marin, 1988). When therapists are bilingual or use translators, sensitivity to variations in dialect is important (Carballo-Diéguez, 1989); if clients have difficulty understanding or interpreting the mental health professional, talk-oriented therapy and interventions will not be as effective (Gonzales et al., 1991).

Whenever possible, the client's cultural beliefs should be integrated in the treatment process (Kerner et al., 1993). Traditional healing methods and beliefs about death and life may be markedly different across populations (see Chapter 9). Mental health professionals should be sensitive to cultural variations within ethnic groups, facilitating the client's pursuits of religious and social values and practices. If the seropositive individual wishes in participate in religious rites that seem unusual or inconsequential to the mental health professional, special care should be taken not to demean the client's beliefs or to discourage the client from engaging in activities that may promote psychological healing around her or his condition (Carballo-Diéguez, 1989).

Incorporating cultural values, such as the traditional Hispanic values of interpersonal respect, *personalismo,* and *confianza,* into the therapeutic context may greatly facilitate the client's participation in guided health self-care. *Personalismo* describes the importance of supportive and reliable face-to-face interactions as a foundation for social relations, while *confianza* refers to the maintenance of a trusting and open bond between individuals (Singer, 1992). If these values can be implemented in the health care setting, the client's use of and continued involvement with the service provider or clinician may be more likely.

Empowering ethnic communities within the health care system has been partially addressed by the Task Force on Minority Health (DHHS, 1985). Their community surveys showed that the most successful health programs included "community involvement" and outreach, such as community activists sitting on the policy boards of health service agencies, and service providers rendering services and education within community centers and public events. Successful programs also frequently reported having a focus on comprehensive services, including prevention and health promotion. Also important is the agency's ability to facilitate and advocate for improved access to health services and cultural sensitivity to the groups being served, such as bilingual and culturally sensitive staff, as well as having ethnic service providers.

Environmental Level: Living Conditions and Societal Forces

Poverty, limited resources, and lack of political power among ethnic groups leads to inadequate educational, occupational, nutritional, and preventive-health-care opportunities (Kerner et al., 1993). Later in life, these factors can contribute to chronic conditions, increased morbidity, and early mortality. With regard to HIV/AIDS, inaccessible or inadequate services may delay ethnic group members from discovering seropositivity until the later stages of infection (Jue & Kain, 1989). This delayed awareness, in conjunction with community conditions of poverty, crime, and substance abuse, puts ethnic minority persons and their partners at greater risk for personal compromise from HIV infection (Thomas et al., 1991). African Americans, for example, have an average life expectancy of only 8 months after HIV diagnosis, as compared to a 22-month expectancy for Whites (Mays, 1989).

Health research, using a socioenvironmental perspective, has shown that chronic social stressors and resulting emotional conditions can also threaten immune system functioning, and can influence prevalence of chronic illness. Dressler, Dos Santos, and Viteri (1986) have found that being of ethnic status and having fewer psychosocial resources is associated with higher blood pressures in ethnic persons. Dressler, Mata, Chavez, Viteri, and Gallagher (1986) also found that arterial blood pressure was lower among Mexicans who had higher social support levels. Dressler, Dos Santos, Gallagher, and Viteri (1987) found that blood pressures increase with development and modernization in Brazil. Eyer and Sterling (1977) used archival data to show that stress-related mortality was related to social organization, such as a capitalist economy; and Baker (1987) showed that attitudes, life events, and depression are correlated with cancer mortality and other ailments.

Compounding the problems of quality of life for ethnic persons is the problem of learned helplessness. *Learned helplessness* refers to feelings to powerlessness with respect to one's social and personal conditions. The social and political conditions experienced by ethnic groups may hinder the development of perceived efficacy and coping skills. Repeatedly faced with frustrating social experiences, efforts to alter conditions may seem futile (Fernandez et al., 1993). The sense of helplessness can accompany not only a particular client's resistance to self-help health approaches, but can also be reflected in community-wide helplessness and resistance to seeking change.

Economic development and political structure play an important role in the quality of life and health issues. However, because of learned helplessness toward these forces and social structures, these problems have come to be viewed as too enormous to change. Nevertheless, in recent decades the United States has seen massive social movements grow out of smaller concerns, which, through consciousness raising and community outreach, have come to be seen as national issues. One example is the civil rights movement, once thought to be the problem of Black peoples, which later came to be viewed as an American race problem. Just as HIV/AIDS was once viewed as the hemophiliac and gay-White-male disease, community awareness campaigns and outreach have increasingly enlightened women, ethnic communities, heterosexuals, injectable drug users, teenagers, and other groups concerning their increasing exposure to the virus and their own mortality. These efforts have helped such groups to view HIV/AIDS as a national issue.

To correct the perceptions that people cannot change and systems cannot be changed, ethnic persons and communities must be empowered to take personal control and to see social and political links to their quality of life. Therefore clinicians and service providers need to address empowerment with the client by focusing on these external, environmental forces as one of the key elements of change. Vulnerability of ethnic groups to health problems in the United States must be viewed primarily as a structural issue involving institutional and systemic tendencies to ignore quality of life for ethnic groups. The prevalence of chronic and acute illness among ethnic groups in mid- to late adulthood, like infant mortality, cannot be addressed solely through efforts to achieve change in individual life-style or behaviors. These issues must be addressed as lifelong social problems, through structural change in institutions, and through activism and social change.

Clients' motivation to address personal physical health needs through the medical system and through self-care is often diminished when they are ill. Service providers may play an important role in clients' empowerment within the health care system by acting as agents themselves on behalf of clients and by encouraging and educating clients in their own advocacy. This issue is key due to the high prevalence of internalized oppression, which is the client's sense that the very real racism and sexism encountered within the health system is all-powerful and will prevent the client's needs from being met. Service providers can help clients to engage in more assertive behavior with respect to getting questions answered and services rendered.

Summary and Conclusions

In the face of escalating numbers of affected ethnic group members, chronic and acute disease may be viewed and addressed as a composite of forces ranging from individual, to group (social and family), to institutional, and to environmental issues (Green & Kreutler, 1990). We have argued, using HIV/AIDS as an example, that these four levels are affected not only by psychosocial well-being but also by overall quality of life. Primary and tertiary interventions must address all four levels, including efforts to change the larger society, social policies, and government. Psychosocial well-being (Level I) is critically affected by a sense of belonging, self-efficacy, a sense of empowerment, internalized hatred or prejudice, and learned helplessness. These in turn can effect changes in physical well-being by affecting whether clients seek out health services, diagnoses, and early treatment. Thus, working with the impact of stigma has become the target of the clinician's work at the individual level.

Moreover, the individual level has a critical impact on all other levels. Among these, the strength of group or peer pressure on the client is affected by the client's internalized sense of belonging and acceptance within a family or social group (Level II). A sense of self-efficacy and empowerment, in turn, affects clients' Level III behavior or willingness to interact with service providers, advocating for themselves or for others within institutions such as the health care or social welfare systems. Finally, Level IV behavior, advocating for changes in the environment, social system, and society at large, are affected by internalized hatred or prejudice, fear and hopelessness.

Countering illness or "dis-ease" within poor and ethnic communities of color entails a four-level response. The client must become involved in his or her own treatment of all levels. Clinicians too must become involved as role models of social change activism for the sake of their clients and society as a whole. With recognition of the importance of a holistic approach to health, it has become clear that to the extent therapists themselves are involved in social change and health promotion activities (by promoting self-care and developing clients' sense of responsibility for self and community health), they become better advocates and role models for change in their clients.

References

Aoki, B., Ngin, C. P., Mo, B., & Ja, D. Y. (1989). AIDS prevention models in Asian-American communities. In V. M. Mays, G. W. Albee, & S. F. Schneider (Eds.), *Primary prevention of AIDS: Psychological approaches* (pp. 290–308). Newbury Park, CA: Sage.

Bailey, E. (1991). Hypertension: An analysis of Detroit African American health care treatment patterns. *Human Organization, 50,* 287–296.

Baker, G. H. B. (1987). Invited review: Psychological factors in immunity. *Journal of Psychosomatic Research, 31,* 1–10.

Carballo-Diéguez, A. (1989). Hispanic culture, gay male culture, and AIDS: Counseling implications. *Journal of Counseling and Development, 68,* 26–68.

Carrier, J. M., & Magana, J. R. (1992). Use of ethnosexual data on men of Mexican origin for HIV/AIDS prevention programs. In G. Herdt & S. Lindenbaum (Eds.), *The time of AIDS: Social analysis, theory, and method* (pp. 243–258). Newbury Park, CA: Sage.

Carrier, J. C., Nguyen, B., & Su, S. (1992). Vietnamese American sexual behaviors and HIV infection. *Journal of Sex Research, 29,* 547–560.

Centers for Disease Control. (1989, May). AIDS and Human Immunodeficiency Virus infection in the United States: 1988 Update. *Morbidity and Mortality Weekly Report, 38,* 18.

Centers for Disease Control. (1991, January). *HIV/AIDS surveillance, year end edition: United States AIDS cases reported through December 1990.* Atlanta: Department of Health and Human Services.

Centers for Disease Control. (1993a, February). *HIV/AIDS surveillance, year end edition: United States AIDS cases reported through December 1992.* Atlanta: Department of Health and Human Services.

Centers for Disease Control. (1993b, July). *HIV/AIDS surveillance report, second quarter edition (Vol. 5, no. 2): United States AIDS cases reported through June 1993.* Atlanta: Department of Health and Human Services.

Clark, K. (1989). *Motherwit: An Alabama midwife's story (As told by Onnie Lee Logan).* New York: E. P. Dutton.

Des Jarlais, D. C., Friedman, S. R., & Hopkins, W. (1985). Risk reduction for acquired immunodeficiency syndrome among intravenous drug users. *Annals of Internal Medicine, 103,* 755–759.

Dressler, W. W., Dos Santos, J. E., & Viteri, F. E. (1986). Blood pressure, ethnicity and psychosocial resources. *Psychosomatic Medicine, 48,* 509–519.

Dressler, W. W., Mata, A., Chavez, A., Gallagher, P. N., & Viteri, F. E. (1986). Social support and arterial blood pressure in a Central Mexican community. *Psychosomatic Medicine, 48,* 338–350.

Dressler, W. W., Dos Santos, J. E., Gallagher, P. N., & Viteri, F. E. (1987). Arterial blood pressure and modernization in Brazil. *American Anthropologist, 80,* 398–409.

Eyer, J., & Sterling, P. (1977). Stress-related mortality and social organization. *Review of Radical Political Economy, 11,* 1–44.

Fernandez, F., Ruiz, P., & Bing, E. (1993). The mental health impact of AIDS on ethnic minorities. In A. C. Gaw (Ed.), *Culture, ethnicity, and mental illness* (pp. 573–586). Washington, DC: American Psychiatric Association.

Gonzales, L. R., Hays, R. B., Bond, M. A., & Kelly, J. G. (1991). Community mental health. In M. Hersen, A. E. Kazdin, A. S. Bellack (Eds.), *Clinical psychology handbook* (pp. 735–758). New York: Pergamon Press.

Green, L. W., & Kreutler, M. W. (1990) Health promotion as a public health strategy for the 1990s. *Annual Review of Public Health, 11,* 319–334.

Jemmott, L. S., & Jemmott, J. B. (1991). Applying the Theory of Reasoned Action to AIDS risk behavior: Condom use among Black women. *Nursing Research, 40,* 228–234.

Jones, J. H. (1981). *Bad blood: The Tuskeegee syphilis experiment—A tragedy of race and medicine.* New York: Free Press.

Jue, S., & Kain, C. D. (1989). Culturally sensitive AIDS counseling. In C. Kain (Ed.), *No longer immune: A counselor's guide to AIDS* (pp. 131–148). Alexandria, VA: American Association for Counseling and Development.

Kelly, J. A., Murphy, D. A., Sikkema, K. J., & Kalichman, S. C. (1993). Psychological interventions to prevent HIV infection are urgently needed: New priorities for behavioral research in the second decade of AIDS. *American Psychologist, 48,* 1023–1034.

Kerner, J. F., Dusenbuzy, L., & Mandeblatt, J. S.

(1993). Poverty and cultural diversity: Challenges for health promotion among medically underserved. *Annual Review of Public Health, 14,* 355–377.

Krieger, N. (1987). Shades of difference: Theoretical underpinnings of the medical controversy on Black/White differences in the United States, 1830–1870. *International Journal of Health Services, 17,* 259–278.

LaFromboise, T. D. (1988). American Indian mental health policy. *American Psychologist, 43,* 388–397.

Leigh, B. C., & Stall, R. (1993). Substance use and risky sexual behavior for exposure to HIV: Issues in methodology, interpretation, and prevention. *American Psychologist, 48,* 1035–1045.

Mays, V. M. (1988). Section introduction. *American Psychologist, 43,* 948.

Mays, V. M. (1989). AIDS prevention in Black populations: Methods of a safer kind. In V. M. Mays, G. W. Albee, & S. F. Schneider (Eds.), *Primary prevention of AIDS: Psychological approaches* (pp. 264–279). Newbury Park, CA: Sage.

Mays, V. M., & Cochran, S. D. (1988). Issues in the perception of AIDS risk and risk reduction activities by Black and Hispanic/Latina women. *American Psychologist, 43,* 949–957.

McGoldrick, M., Pearce, J., & Giordano, J. (Eds.). (1982). *Ethnicity and family therapy.* New York: Guilford Press.

Metler, R., Conway, G. A., & Stehr-Green, J. (1991). AIDS surveillance among American Indians and Alaska Natives. *American Journal of Public Health, 81,* 1469–1471.

Morales, E. S. (1990). Ethnic minority families and minority gays and lesbians. *Marriage & Family Review, 14,* 217–239.

Peckham, C. S., Sentuvia, Y. D., & Ades, A. E. (1987). Obstetric and perinatal consequences of human immunodeficiency virus (HIV) infection: A review. *British Journal of Obstetrics and Gynecology, 94,* 403–407.

Peterson, J. L., & Marin, G. (1988). Issues in the prevention of AIDS among Black and Hispanic men. *American Psychologist, 43,* 871–877.

Quimby, E. (1992). Anthropological witnessing for African Americans: Power, responsibility, and choice in the age of AIDS. In G. Herdt & S. Lindenbaum (Eds.), *The time of AIDS: Social analysis, theory, and method* (pp. 159–184). Newbury Park: Sage.

Singer, M. (1992). AIDS and U.S. ethnic minorities: The crisis and alternative anthropological responses. *Human Organization, 51,* 89–95.

Snell, T. (1993). *Bureau of justice statistics: Correctional populations in the United States, 1991.* Washington, DC: U.S. Department of Justice.

Tafoya, T. (1989). Pulling the coyote's tale: Native American sexuality and AIDS. In V. M. Mays, G. W. Albee, & S. F. Schneider (Eds.), *Primary prevention of AIDS: Psychological approaches* (pp. 280–289). Newbury Park, CA: Sage.

Toomey, K. E., Oberschelp, A. G., & Greenspan, J. R. (1989). Sexually transmitted diseases and Native Americans: Trends in reported gonorrhea and syphilis morbidity, 1984–1988. *Public Health Reports, 104,* 566–572.

Thomas, S. B., So'Brien van Putten, J. M., & Chen, M. S. (1991). *A program planning and evaluation manual for HIV education programs: A primer for ethnic and racial minority community based organizations.* Columbus: Ohio Department of Health.

U. S. Bureau of the Census. (1993). *Statistical abstract of the United States: 1993* (113th ed.). Washington, DC: U.S. Government Printing Office.

U.S. Department of Health and Human Services. (1985). *Report of the Secretary's Task Force on Black and Minority Health.* Volume I, Executive Summary.

U.S. Department of Health and Human Services. (1986). *Health status of the disadvantaged: Chartbook 1986* (DHHS Publication No. HRSA HRS-P-DV86-2). Washington, DC: U.S. Government Printing Office.

U.S. Department of Health and Human Services. (1991). *Health status of minorities and low-income groups: Third edition.* Washington, DC: U.S. Government Printing Office.

Intervention and Treatment for Ethnic Minority Homeless Adults

NORWETTA G. MILBURN
TERRLYN L. CURRY

Homelessness is a pressing social problem that seems to be a growing and persistent characteristic of United States society despite the attention that has been focused on it at the local, state, and federal levels (U.S. Conference of Mayors, 1987). In the last ten years, homelessness—epitomized by the sight of a woman pushing a shopping cart filled with all her possessions, or a man asking for spare change or standing at an intersection with a sign that says "Homeless. Will work for food"—has become so prevalent in major United States metropolitan areas that some people have become immune or desensitized to these images (Toro & McDonnell, 1992).

Homelessness will not go away anytime soon. Mental health professionals and human service providers need to be cognizant not only of its presence but of its complexity as well. In particular, the numbers and types of homeless adults who are ethnic minorities, the problems they experience, the treatments and interventions that have been used to address these problems (including the difficulties that have been associated with these treatments and interventions), and the steps that can be taken to address the needs of minority homeless adults must be carefully considered.

Numbers and Types of Minority Homeless Adults

The homeless population in the United States is diverse (Kiesler, 1991), except that almost all homeless people are poor. The heterogeneity of the homeless population is obvious when various subgroups of homeless people are considered, including families (usually a mother and her children), single men and women, runaway and "throwaway" adolescents, elderly adults, people who are mentally ill, substance abusers, and people with infectious diseases such as AIDS or tuberculosis (Bassuk, Rubin, & Lauriat, 1986; Breakey et al., 1989; Cohen, 1989; Milburn & Booth, 1990; Susser, Goldfinger, & White, 1990; Robertson, 1991; Rotheram-Borus, Koopman, & Ehrhardt, 1991). This chapter will focus on minority homeless adults and will differentiate them, whenever possible, by gender to discuss their characteristics and needs and the treatments and interventions that have been employed to meet those needs.

African Americans or Hispanic (Latino) Americans, are represented in disproportionate numbers in the homeless population in the United States (Farr, Koegel, & Burnam, 1986; Ladner, Crystal, Towber, Callendar, & Calhoun, 1986; Morse & Calsyn, 1985–1986; Rossi, Wright, Fischer, & Willis, 1987; Roth, Bean, Lust, & Saveanu, 1985; U.S. Conference of Mayors, 1987). The importance of the race and ethnicity of homeless people was initially raised by Martin (1986). She observed, in studies targeted at the homeless mentally ill, that disproportionate numbers of minority people were represented in those samples and suggested that this finding should be given greater attention in program development, public policy, and research on homeless mentally ill people.

Table 15-1 presents an overview of a number of studies of homeless adults, organized by the region of the country where they were conducted and by the gender of the samples. This compilation of studies is not exhaustive but does include many of the studies that have been conducted on homeless adults within the past few years, provided data on the racial composition of their samples, and is an illustrative representation of studies of homeless adults. The findings of most of the major studies are reported only once. Therefore, one reference is noted for studies that have multiple reports on a given sample, such as some of the work of Bassuk and her colleagues (Bassuk, Rubin, & Lauriat, 1986). These studies were conducted in urban areas and, for the most part, targeted adults in shelter settings.

The racial composition reported for these samples suggests that at least half of the participants in most of these studies were minority men and women. Exceptions are the study by Hagen and Ivanoff (1988) that was conducted in Albany, New York, and the study by Bassuk, Rubin, and Lauriat (1984) that was conducted in Boston. Usually the minority representation in these studies consisted of African Americans or Hispanic (Latino) Americans (Davis & Winkleby, 1993: Milburn & Booth, 1990; Mills & Ota, 1989; Shinn, Knickman, & Weitzman, 1991). African Americans are often the most prevalent minority group, but studies that were done in the West often included some Native Americans in their samples. McChesney (1986) noted that 6 percent of her sample and Robertson and Cousineau (1986) observed that 11 percent of their sample were Native American. Asian Americans are seldom reported in homeless samples because the actual numbers appear to be small and they may fall into the "other" category noted in some studies (D'Ercole & Struening, 1990).

These studies suggest that minority status is a vulnerability factor for homeless-

TABLE 15-1   Studies of Homeless Adults

Study	Site	N	Racial/Ethnic Composition
Data on Homeless Women			
Shinn et al. (1991)	New York, NY	704	55% Black 32% Puerto Rican 7% Other Hispanic 4% White 2% Other
D'Ercole & Struening (1990)	New York, NY	147	67% Black 14% White 12% Hispanic 7% Other
Milburn & Booth (1990)	Washington, DC	146	85% Black 10% Puerto Rican 1% Other Hispanic 2% White 2% Other
Breakey et al. (1989)	Baltimore, MD	528	66% Non-White 34% White
Rafferty et al. (1989)	New York, NY	277	74% Black 22% Hispanic 4% Other
Bassuk & Rosenberg (1988)	Boston, MA	49	67% Non-White 33% White
Hagen & Ivanoff (1988)	Albany, NY	51	25% Non-White 75% White
Bassuk et al. (1986)	Boston, MA	80	45% Black 48% White 6% Hispanic 1% Other
Johnson & Krueger (1989)	St. Louis, MO	240	77% Black 23% White
Mills & Ota (1989)	Detroit, MI	87	90% Black 7% White 3% Other
Wood et al. (1990)	Los Angeles, CA	196	57% Black 30% White 8% Hispanic 6% Other
Robertson & Cousineau (1986)	Los Angeles, CA	283	49% White 26% Black 15% Hispanic 11% Native American
McChesney (19860	Los Angeles, CA	80	55% Black 33% White 9% Hispanic 3% Native American

Study	Site	N	Racial/Ethnic Composition[a]
Data on Homeless Men			
Davis & Winkleby (1993)	California	1205	22% Black 50% White 28% Foreign-born Hispanic 12% Native-born Hispanic
Breakey et al. (1989)	Baltimore, MD	298	63% Non-White 37% White
Fischer et al. (1986)[b]	Baltimore, MD	51	47% Non-White 53% White
Data on Homeless Men and Women			
Bassuk et al. (1984)[c]	Boston, MA	78	22% Black 1% Hispanic 77% White
Lipton et al. (1983)[d]	New York, NY	90	39% Black 14% Hispanic 47% White
Belcher (1989)[e]	Midwest	132	42% Black 58% White

[a]Racial/ethnic categories that were used by the author(s) are indicated.
[b]This sample was 94.1% male.
[c]This sample was 83% male.
[d]This sample was 75% male.
[e]This sample was 55% male.

ness. In part, as noted previously, this finding is expected because homeless people are poor, and minorities are also represented in disproportionate numbers among the poor in United States society (see Chapter 1). In addition, other risk factors for homelessness may occur more frequently among minority adults than nonminority adults. For example, among women, these risk factors are being pregnant, the recent birth of a child, previous homelessness, disruptive experiences during childhood such as physical or sexual abuse or living in a foster home, and disruptive experiences during adulthood such as physical or sexual abuse (Knickman & Weitzman, 1989; Shinn et al., 1991). It is not known to what degree these risk factors are greater among minority women than nonminority women, but these factors must be considered in any attempt to identify women at risk for homelessness.

Even though minorities are disproportionately represented in studies of homeless adults, there is a dearth of information on the specific sociocultural, behavioral, and psychological characteristics of minority homeless adults. These data could provide further information on ethnic and racial differences in vulnerability factors. Notable exceptions include work by First, Roth, and Arewa (1988), Kreuger, Stretch, and Johnson (1987), Knickman and Weitzman (1989), and Davis and Winkleby (1993).

First et al. (1988) found that homeless African-American adults in Ohio, in comparison to nonminority homeless adults, were slightly younger, had a slightly higher educational level, were homeless for fewer days, tended to cycle in and out of homelessness, were less likely to be currently earning income, and "had fewer psychiatric symptoms" and more "behavioral disturbances." Kreuger et al. (1987) reported on racial differences in the etiological characteristics of homeless women with children in St. Louis, Missouri. Characteristics that contributed to homelessness among these families were inadequate kinship support, lack of affordable housing, loss of tenancy, income instability, family disruptions, geographic mobility, and deinstitutionalization. In addition, they found that African-American homeless women, prior to becoming homeless, had often been precariously housed, doubling up with either family or friends. When this multiple family situation was no longer feasible, these women became homeless.

Examining ethnic and housing status differences, Knickman and Weitzman (1989) found homeless African-American women were more likely to be pregnant and to have parents on public assistance than other homeless women, who were primarily Hispanic (Latino) American. More important, when homeless African-American women were compared to poor, nonhomeless African-American women, more homeless African-American women had multiple moves within the past year, were pregnant, had had a baby within the past year, had parents on public assistance, or had experienced social disruptions.

Davis and Winkleby (1993) identified racial and ethnic differences in childhood and adulthood risk factors for homeless men. They observed African-American homeless men were better educated and held more nonprofessional white-collar jobs (e.g., technical and service jobs) than did European American and Hispanic (Latino) American homeless men. African-American homeless men also reported a lower prevalence of alcohol and drug abuse, overnight psychiatric hospitalization, placement in foster care, and physical and sexual abuse than did European American homeless men.

Foreign-born Hispanic (Latino) American homeless men, on the other hand, reported the lowest levels of education and the highest employment in nonskilled blue-collar jobs. This group, however, was the least likely to report drug and alcohol abuse and psychiatric hospitalization. Native-born Hispanic (Latino) homeless men, compared to European-American homeless men, reported lower rates of adverse childhood events, drug abuse, and psychiatric hospitalization. Compared to the other three ethnic groups, this group reported the most alcohol abuse. Native-born Hispanic (Latino) Americans were the most likely to report sleeping outdoors, African Americans the least likely. European Americans and native-born Hispanic (Latino) Americans were the most likely to have been homeless on more than one occasion and to have been homeless for more than one year.

Others have also found that minority homeless adults are less likely than European-American homeless adults to have mental health problems. Crystal, Ladner, and Towber (1986), for example, compared African-American, Hispanic (Latino) American, and European-American shelter users ($N = 7,578$) in New York City and found that mental health problems were more prevalent among European

Americans (30.6 percent) than African Americans (22.9 percent) or Hispanic (Latino) Americans (23.9 percent).

While generalizations from these studies must be made with caution because of methodological differences, the findings suggest that: (1) minority homeless adults seem to have less psychiatric impairment, such as substance abuse and a history of psychiatric hospitalization, than nonminority homeless adults; (2) the characteristics of ethnic minority homeless adults vary somewhat, with African Americans reporting higher levels of educational attainment than other ethnic groups, Hispanic (Latino) American men reporting more episodes of homelessness and homelessness of longer duration than other ethnic minority men, and African-American women reporting more often that they were currently pregnant or came from families on public assistance than Hispanic (Latino) women; and (3) the paths to homelessness differ somewhat by ethnicity and race among women, with African-American women moving into homelessness because of prior doubling up with family or friends and European-American women moving into homelessness because of geographic relocation with a spouse (or significant other).

Issues and Problems in Working with Homeless Ethnic Minorities

Before treatments and interventions for homeless ethnic minority adults are discussed, some issues inherent in working with the homeless population must be addressed. Among these issues are the following: (1) the role of stressful life events and social supports in homelessness; (2) barriers experienced by ethnic minorities as reflected in service providers' racial, ethnic, and class attitudes, structural constraints, and language differences; and (3) the inability of the ethnic homeless person to meet his or her basic needs.

Many of the aforementioned studies suggest that one appropriate way to conceptualize these risk factors is as stressors. In other words, stress (stressful life events) is one of the major risk factors associated with homelessness. Stress is a result of threatening circumstances, inadequate assistance from psychological and social resources sought to address these circumstances, and the perception of and adaptation to these circumstances (Belle, 1984; Milburn & D'Ercole, 1991). A number of the risk factors associated with homelessness among women, many of whom are ethnic minorities, include stressful life events such as physical or sexual abuse experienced as a child or adult, the recent birth of a child, a prior experience of homelessness, and precarious housing patterns (doubling up with family and friends or multiple moves). Many of these events are not unusual among poor minority women (Belle, 1984); unfortunately, these events can result in homelessness for many of these women for several reasons.

Social supports that were once available to help combat these stressors are frequently not available (see Chapter 2). For some, the social supports may not be readily available or may not be what is necessary to meet the individual's needs

(Hirsch, 1980; McLanahan, Wedemeyer, & Adelberg, 1981). Additionally, for many of these women, who are characterized by family and friends as "strong and able to handle anything," involvement in a social support group can lead to additional stress if these women must respond to the problems of members of their support group as well as to their own problems (Stack, 1974). The failure of coping methods and insufficient or ineffective assistance from service providers can also lead to homelessness.

Homeless minority men also experience stressful life events such as growing up in poverty and probable experiences of discrimination in the labor and housing markets that can lead to homelessness (Davis & Winkleby, 1993). As noted earlier, African-American men who are homeless as a group, are less psychiatrically impaired, are more educated, and have more job skills than European-American men who are homeless (Davis & Winkleby, 1993; First et al., 1988). This finding suggests that the stress of discrimination contributes to homelessness in this group. Conceptualizing homelessness within the context of a stress paradigm enables clinicians and service providers to consider treatment approaches and interventions that take into account subjective and objective experiences of homeless adults, including how they assess and cope with events that lead to homelessness or exacerbate their homeless condition (Milburn & D'Ercole, 1991).

Added to these stressful events are barriers that inhibit homeless adults from receiving appropriate services. These barriers are the second set of issues, and they pertain to the provision of treatments and services for ethnic minority populations in general. The indivudual's race, ethnicity, and class difference can become barriers for this population, especially if the service provider makes little effort to understand their experiences. Belle (1984), for example, points out that many clinicians have negative stereotypes about low-income and ethnic minority women. Such attitudes can prompt poor ethnic minority women to fail to seek treatment, refuse treatment when offered, or discontinue treatment after a limited number of visits.

Belle (1984) suggests additional barriers experienced by low-income and minority women that are particularly relevant for homeless ethnic minority women. Among these barriers are the cost of services, lack of transportation to and from services, inadequate child care, and fear that one's child will be placed in foster care if parent–child problems are revealed to social service agencies. Such structural barriers and perceptions on the part of the service recipient convey the message that service agencies are inaccessible or even a place to be avoided.

For many ethnic minorities, language is another barrier to receiving treatment. Some individuals who seek treatment and services may speak a language or dialect that differs from that of the clinician or service provider. These differences may lead to confusion, frustration, and an inappropriate diagnosis. In addition, the lack of professionals who are a part of the individual's ethnic culture may result in an unwillingness to seek or accept services. Moreover, many of the professionals serving in these capacities are unaware of the special needs of ethnic minorities and fail to offer services that are appropriate for these individuals. These special needs must be considered when assessing, diagnosing, and treating individuals from various ethnic minority groups. Intervention techniques and treatment modalities should be consistent with values, experiences, and traditions that are relevant to a given culture.

Finally, there is a set of issues that pertain to the provision of treatments and services for ethnic minority homeless adults. Research on the ethnic minority homeless population indicates that they are more concerned with having their basic needs met (e.g., food, clothing, shelter) than with just receiving assistance for other necessities (e.g., alcohol, mental health, or physical health treatment). For example, Linn and Gelberg (1989) noted that while two southern California communities found good health to be a top priority among the homeless population in general, homeless ethnic minorities emphasized the need for permanent housing.

Inadequate income contributes to the inability of ethnic minority homeless adults to afford and maintain permanent housing. Consequently, homeless minorities not only want permanent housing but also desire employment that provides a suitable income to obtain housing and address their varied needs. Rossi (1988) in a study of homeless people in Chicago, in which African Americans (53 percent) and Native Americans (5.1 percent) were highly represented, found that 18 percent of the individuals surveyed had no income during the previous month, half had incomes below $100, and the average monthly income was $168. As he suggests, these incomes do not by any means provide an adequate or reasonable standard of living in Chicago or in most other United States cities. Moreover, many homeless minority adults want to be employed if given the opportunity (First et al., 1988; Roberts-Gray, Wenzel, Baumann, & Grigsby, 1991).

Interventions and Treatments Directed at Homeless Ethnic Minorities

In light of the growing problems of homelessness and the diversity with the homeless population, the federal government in recent years has sought to explore and understand the needs of the homeless population, as is evident by its funding of numerous studies exploring such issues {see *Two Generations of NIMH-Funded Research on Homelessness and Mental Illness: 1982–1990* (National Institute of Mental Health, 1991)}. More recently, *Outcasts on Main Street: Final Report of the Federal Task Force on Homelessness and Severe Mental Illness* (Interagency Council on Homelessness, 1992) identified numerous service needs (e.g., housing, basic health care, and treatment for substance abuse and mental illness) for the homeless population in general and the severely mentally ill homeless in particular. Yet, few of these studies and others reported in the literature have focused on the intervention and treatment of ethnic minorities.

One may argue that if minorities are disproportionately represented among the homeless population and these studies have focused on the needs of the homeless population, then the findings of these studies should apply to homeless ethnic minorities. In some ways, this assumption is valid. Many of the services, treatments, and interventions identified in these studies are appropriate for ethnic minorities (e.g., housing, case management, medical assessment, and drug prevention and treatment programs) (Roberts-Gray et al., 1991). In other ways, however, this assumption is invalid and misleading. For example, service providers sometimes fail to consider the diversity of the population when delivering services, or they may lack assessment instruments that are sensitive to differences within ethnic minority groups, or they may be unaware of the various risk factors for ethnic minority homelessness that may require the development of multifaceted and individualized interventions (Davis & Winkleby, 1993; Welch & Toff, 1987).

Carter (1991) examining treatment of African-American homeless mentally ill persons, observes that "psychiatric disorders have biological, psychological, social, and situational components" (p. 316). He concludes that when treatment modalities include nonpsychiatric techniques and therapists are familiar with the world of homeless mentally ill African Americans, the individual can be treated successfully. Although Carter speaks here only of African Americans, this same philosophy can be applied when treating homeless individuals from other ethnic groups.

While some programs are not specifically designed for prevention, treatment, and intervention for homeless ethnic minorities, the number of minorities represented in these programs is overwhemingly high. Examination of these programs provides some insight into the availability of services for this population and what modifications need to be made in order to provide appropriate prevention and treatment for homeless ethnic minorities, in light of the previous discussion of the unique characteristics and experiences of ethnic homeless groups.

One such program is the Diagnostic and Rehabilitation Center (DRC) of Philadelphia. According to Comfort, Shipley, White, Griffith, and Shandler (1990), the DRC provides services for substance abuse recovery to homeless mentally ill persons and seeks to break the cycle of drug and public welfare dependency which often leads to homelessness. The DRC conducted a pilot study of the program and found 92 percent of the participants were African-American homeless women. Among the services offered are residential programs that provided training in daily living skills; therapeutic treatment for substance abuse addiction, which included substance abuse education, financial stabilization, access to medical care and housing, building support systems, group therapy, and referral for job placement; and intensive case management which assisted the individual in access to services within the community. This project demonstrates the multiple needs of homeless addicted women, evaluates services for homeless addicted women, and monitors participant utilization.

Other studies have investigated treatment and intervention programs targeted to the general homeless population and not just those who have specific problems, such as substance abuse. Cohen (1989) discusses strategies that are necessary to encourage homeless adults to seek and accept treatment that are also useful for the engagement of homeless ethnic minorities. Homeless individuals should be offered services voluntarily in order to give them some control over their environment. They should be provided services that meet their own perceived needs (e.g., clean clothes, a hot meal) and thus serve as an incentive to accept services. They should be empowered to exert more external control and responsibility and should be exposed to group activities to encourage strong social relationships. All these factors are crucial to providing treatment and intervention to the homeless population but are particularly relevant to homeless ethnic minorities.

Studies indicate that ethnic minority homeless adults are a heterogeneous group (Davis & Winkleby, 1993; Knickman & Weitzman, 1989) and require a range of services, treatments, and interventions that are targeted toward their individual needs. Some of the risk factors for homelessness among women, such as physical and sexual abuse experienced as a child or adult, include negative stressful life events that have been the focus of prevention and treatment programs (D'Ercole & Struening, 1990; Sullivan, Tan, Basta, Rumptz, & Davidson, 1992). Interventions that address various issues of physical and sexual abuse have been developed, but few programs consider sexual and physical abuse in the context of minority status. Little is known about how minority homeless women view and cope with physical or sexual abuse. More needs to be known about the informal coping strategies they employ, the formal mechanisms they use, and the effectiveness of these strategies. These issues need to be incorporated into programs targeted at minority homeless women who have been victimized.

Other risk factors that were identified by Shinn et al. (1991), such as being pregnant and the recent birth of a child, are consistent with data showing racial differences in entry into single parenthood that need to be considered in programs. For instance, African-American women, on average, become single mothers because they never marry. European-American women, on average, become single mothers because they become divorced or separated (Garfinkel & McLanahan, 1986). Consequently, programs targeted at addressing poverty among homeless women and children must be multifaceted and consider different approaches, including developing mechanisms to identify noncustodial parents and require them to provide child support.

Although programs that address treatment and intervention for ethnic minority homeless adults are sorely lacking, efforts are now being made to address some of these problems. In New York City, Women in Need, Inc., is specifically designed to target the needs of homeless ethnic minorities. The program offers a range of services to homeless women and children, primarily African Americans and Hispanic (Latino) Americans. Treatment and intervention offered to participants include substance abuse treatment, acupuncture for stress or other conditions, housing, respite child care for children, and educational and employment opportunities (Ridlen, Asamoah, Edwards, & Zimmer, 1990). Again, this program is one of the few specifically designed to meet the needs of homeless ethnic minorities, and staff training in engagement, outreach, service delivery, and the like is provided in order to meet the needs of participants more effectively. Even in this specialized program, difficulties in serving the needs of ethnic minorities arise. As Ridlen et al. (1990) note, 40 percent of the population served is Hispanic (Latino) American, and efforts to find bilingual staff have been unsuccessful.

Guidelines for Interventions for Homeless Ethnic Minority Adults

Despite the paucity of research findings on treatment and intervention for homeless ethnic minority adults, social and clinical experiences provide several sets of guidelines for improving treatment outcomes for these clients. These guidelines move from broad societal-level interventions that require changes in public policy and involve political mechanisms, such as the legislative process, that are not often used by clinicians, to specific service delivery–level interventions that can be readily employed by clinicians. The issues and problems in working with homeless ethnic minorities that were raised previously suggest a multifaceted approach is needed to address their plight adequately, in terms of both the needs that must be attended to and the levels of intervention that must be considered. The guidelines that follow take such an approach. They include interventions that incorporate a stress, resource, and coping perspective and that focus on situational factors related to homelessness; interventions aimed at attitudinal and structural barriers to attaining services; and interventions that target the basic needs of ethnic minority homeless adults. Other levels of intervention include opportunities for ethnic minority homeless adults to articulate and address their basic needs and to implement services that tear down attitudinal and situational barriers. Multiple-level guidelines enable service providers to suggest the means for restructuring societal and situational factors that contribute to homelessness and to help develop programs that provide resources for ethnic minority homeless adults to cope with their situations.

Societal-Level Intervention Guidelines

- Develop more appropriate and accessible housing, including transitional housing in neighborhoods with resources such as public transportation, shopping, recreational, child and day care, and health facilities.
- Identify and provide access to existing jobs, and develop new jobs that pay decent living wages.
- Encourage and support local churches and community organizations to provide food, clothing, temporary shelter, and emergency financial support (e.g., low-interest loans) to individuals who are at risk for becoming homeless (e.g., are about to be evicted) as well as homeless individuals.
- Encourage professional organizations, including both minority and nonminority associations (e.g., Association of Black Psychologists, National Association of Black Social Workers, American Psychological Association, National Association of Social Workers), to lobby local, state, and federal governments regarding the plight of the homeless.

Program-Level Intervention Guidelines

- Provide advocacy for clients in which, at the very least, case management is provided wherein clients are helped in negotiating the social service delivery system, mental health system, health system, legal system, and educational system (Cohen, 1989; Susser et al., 1990).
- Provide demystification for clients in which they learn how their symptoms are assessed and classified. They should be taught what psychiatric and psychological labels mean. In addition, they should be taught how to express themselves so that service providers will be responsive to them (Cohen, 1989; Susser et al., 1990).
- Provide education so that clients learn how to generalize their skills in order to negotiate larger service delivery systems effectively (Cohen, 1989; Susser et al., 1990).
- Provide current and frequently updated information on job availability (e.g., a job announcement bulletin board) within treatment settings.
- Develop outreach programs that provide information on money management, health maintenance, child care, and other topics for individuals who are at risk of homelessness as well as those who are homeless.
- Develop informational discussion programs for neighborhood residents that address the issues of NIMBY ("Not In My Back Yard") and housing for homeless individuals. These programs should be designed to address the rational and irrational concerns of neighborhood residents about homeless individuals residing in their communities. This is particularly important for the placement of ethnic minority homeless individuals, who may be unduly stigmatized and perceived as undesirable neighbors because of their race or ethnicity and housing status.

Service Delivery-Level Intervention Guidelines

- Develop intervention techniques and treatment modalities that incorporate values, experiences, and traditions that are relevant within a given culture.
- Negotiate entry very carefully into the settings where homeless people can be found. Pay attention to the organizational climate of the setting to gauge receptivity to treatment. Relationships must be established before treatment can be provided, both with staff and with clients (Cohen, 1989; Susser et al., 1990).
- Provide services to homeless adults that are based on a needs assessment that includes the most "needy." It is often easier to provide services to clients who are better functioning and not take into account less functional clients as well as clients who have been rejected elsewhere (Susser et al., 1990). This approach, however, would leave out most homeless adults.

- Provide multiple services to homeless adults in addition to traditional mental health services (Ridlen et al., 1990). Traditional mental health services may not be relevant until basic needs are met. One can think of this in terms of Maslow's hierarchy of needs, starting with the most basic needs and then moving to higher order needs. For homeless adults, the most basic need that must be addressed in all programs is housing.
- Develop volunteer mechanisms for clinicians to provide pro bono mental health treatment at a shelter or program for homeless individuals.

This is by no means an exhaustive list of recommendations. They are provided as a starting point for service providers and clinicians who are interested in addressing the needs of ethnic minority homeless adults. Of particular importance is the recognition that homeless ethnic persons have many needs and that addressing them requires interventions at several different levels in a timely, appropriate, and effective manner.

Future Research Directions

Research findings on homeless ethnic minorities have been largely cross-sectional and descriptive. This research, as well as the few epidemiologic studies that have been carried out, have not focused specifically on the significance of ethnic minority status. Very little intervention research of an experimental or quasi-experimental nature has been conducted to examine the effectiveness of treatments and programs for homeless ethnic minorities. Therefore, future research should consider several issues and directions that will contribute to the development of appropriate services for this population.

More needs to be known about the relationship to homelessness of ethnic minority status and factors such as acculturation, role expectations, belief systems and attitudes, and values. Additional comparative studies of minority and nonminority homeless adults are required to identify personal and situational factors that are unique to minority homeless adults. These investigations, however, should include situational and personal factors that are particularly salient to ethnic minorities. A better understanding of the contribution to homelessness of situational factors, such as discrimination in the housing or job market, is needed because previous research has primarily examined personal factors such as educational attainment and age (First et al., 1988).

Longitudinal research is also warranted to examine how ethnic minority adults move in and out of homelessness. Intervention research that addresses risk factors for homelessness among minority women, such as physical and sexual abuse, is also necessary. The findings from these kinds of studies can enable service providers to understand better and meet more effectively the needs of ethnic minority homeless adults and to contribute to the alleviation of homelessness.

References

Bassuk, E. L., & Rosenberg, L. (1988). Why does family homelessness occur? A case control study. *American Journal of Public Health, 78,* 783–788.

Bassuk, E. L., Rubin, L., & Lauriat, A. (1984). Is homelessness a mental health problem? *American Journal of Psychiatry, 14,* 1546–1550.

Bassuk, E. L., Rubin, L., & Lauriat, A. S. (1986). Characteristics of sheltered homeless families. *American Journal of Public Health, 76,* 1097–1101.

Belle, D. (1984). Inequality and mental health: Low income and minority women. In L. E. Walker (Ed.), *Women and mental health policy* (pp. 135–150). Beverly Hills, CA: Sage.

Belcher, J. R. (1989). On becoming homeless: A study of chronically mentally ill persons. *Journal of Community Psychology, 17,* 173–175.

Breakey, W., Fischer, P., Kramer, M., Nedstadt, G., Romanoski, A., Ross, A., Royall, R., & Stine, O. (1989). Health and mental health problems of homeless men and women in Baltimore. *Journal of the American Medical Association, 262,* 1352–1357.

Carter, J. H. (1991). Chronic mental illness and homelessness in Black populations: Prologue and prospects. *Journal of National Medical Association, 83,* 313–317.

Cohen, M. B. (1989). Social work practice with homeless mentally ill people: Engaging the client. *Social Work, 34,* 505–509.

Comfort, M., Shipley, T. E., White, K., Griffith, E. M., & Shandler, I. W. (1990). Family treatment for homeless alcohol/drug-addicted women and their preschool children. *Alcoholism Treatment Quarterly, 7,* 129–147.

Crystal, S., Ladner, S., & Towber, R. (1986). Multiple impairment patterns in the mentally ill homeless. *International Journal of Mental Health, 14,* 61–73.

Davis, L. A., & Winkleby, M. A. (1993). Sociodemographic and health-related risk factors among African-American, Caucasian, and Hispanic homeless men: A comparative study. *Journal of Social Distress and Homelessness, 2,* 83–102.

D'Ercole, A., & Struening, E. (1990). Victimization among homeless women: Implications for service delivery. *Journal of Community Psychology, 18,* 141–152.

Farr, R., Koegel, P., & Burnam, A. (1986). *A study of homelessness and mental illness in the skid row areas of Los Angeles.* (Report prepared for the National Institute of Mental Health). Los Angeles: Los Angeles County Department of Mental Health.

First, R. J., Roth, D., & Arewa, B. D. (1988). Homelessness: Understanding the dimensions of the problem for minorities. *Social Work, 33,* 120–124.

Fischer, P. J., Shapiro, S., Breakey, W. R., Anthony, J. C., & Kramer, M. (1986). Mental health and social characteristics of the homeless: A survey of mission users. *American Journal of Public Health, 76,* 519–524.

Garfinkel, I., & McLanahan, S. S. (1986). *Single mothers and their children: A new American dilemma.* Washington, DC: Urban Institute.

Hagen, J. L., & Ivanhoff, A. M. (1988). Homeless women: A high risk population. *Affilia, 3,* 19–33.

Hirsch, B. J. (1980). Psychological dimensions of social networks: A multi-method analysis. *American Journal of Community Psychology, 8,* 159–171.

Interagency Council on Homelessness. (1992). *Outcasts on Main Street: Report of the Federal Task Force on Homelessness and Severe Mental Illness.* Washington, DC: U.S. Department of Health and Human Services.

Johnson, A. K., & Kreuger, L. W. (1989). Toward a better understanding of homeless women. *Social Work, 34,* 537–540.

Kiesler, C. A. (1991). Homeless and public policy priorities. *American Psychologist, 46,* 1245–1252.

Knickman, J. R., & Weitzman, B. C. (1989). *A study of homeless families in New York city: Risk assessment models and strategies for prevention.* New York: New York University, Health Research Program.

Kreuger, L. W., Stretch, J. J., & Johnson, A. K. (1987, June). *Ethnic differentials among the homeless seeking shelter placement of traumatized families.* Paper presented at the annual meeting of the National Association of Social Work Minorities Issues conference, Washington, DC.

Ladner, S., Crystal, S., Towber, R., Callendar, B., & Calhoun, J. (1986). *Project future: Focusing, understanding, targeting and utilizing resources for the homeless mentally ill, elderly, youth substance abusers and employable.* (Report prepared for the National Institute of Mental Health). New York: City of New York, Human Resource Administration.

Linn, L. S., & Gelberg, L. (1989). Priority of basic needs among homeless adults. *Social Psychiatry and Psychiatric Epidemiology, 24,* 23–29.

Lipton, F., Sabatini, A., & Katz, S. (1983). Down and out in the city: The homeless mentally ill. *Hospital and Community Psychiatry, 34,* 817–821.

Martin, M. (1986). *The implications of NIMH-supported research for homeless mentally ill racial and ethnic minority persons.* Unpublished manuscript, Hunter College, New York.

McChesney, K. Y. (1986). New findings on homeless families. *Family Professional, 1,* 165–174.

McLanahan, S. S., Wedemeyer, N. V., & Adelberg, T. (1981). Network structure, social support, and psychological well-being in the single-parent family. *Journal of Marriage and the Family, 73,* 601–612.

Milburn, N. G., & Booth, J. (1990). Sociodemographic, homeless state, and mental health characteristics of women in shelters: Preliminary findings. *Urban Research Review, 12,* 1–4.

Milburn, N., & D'Ercole, A. (1991). Homeless women: Moving toward a comprehensive model. *American Psychologist, 46,* 1161–1169.

Mills, C., & Ota, H. (1989). Homeless women with minor children in the Detroit Metropolitan area. *Social Work, 34,* 485–489.

Morse, G., & Calsyn, R. J. (1985–1986). Mentally disturbed homeless people in St. Louis: Needy, willing, but underserved. *International Journal of Mental Health, 14,* 74–94.

National Institute of Mental Health. (1991). *Two generations of NIMH-funded research on homelessness and mental illness: 1982–1990.* Rockville, MD.

Rafferty, Y., & Rollins N. (1989, August). *The impact of homelessness on children: No time to lose.* Paper presented at the annual meeting of the American Psychological Association, New Orleans, LA.

Ridlen, S., Asamoah, Y., Edwards, H. G., & Zimmer, R. (1990). Outreach and engagement for homeless women at risk of alcoholism: Family treatment for homeless alcohol/drug-addicted women and their preschool children. *Alcoholism Treatment Quarterly, 7,* 99–109.

Roberts-Gray, C., Wenzel, S. L., Baumann, D., & Grigsby, C. (1991, June). *Team case management for homeless persons in job training.* Paper presented at the meeting of the Society for Community Action and Research, Phoenix, AZ.

Robertson, M. J. (1991). Homeless women with children: The role of alcohol and other drug abuse. *American Psychologist, 46,* 1198–1204.

Robertson, M. J., & Cousineau, M. R. (1986). Health status and access to health services among the urban homeless. *American Journal of Public Health, 76* 561–563.

Rossi, P. H. (1988). Minorities and homelessness. In G. D. Sandefur & M. Tienda (Eds.), *Divided opportunities* (pp. 87–115). New York: Plenum Press.

Rossi, P. H., Wright, J. D., Fischer, G. A., & Willis, G. (1987). The urban homeless: Estimating composition and size. *Science, 285,* 1336–1341.

Roth, D., Bean, J., Lust, N., & Saveanu, T. (1985). *Homelessness in Ohio: A study of people in need.* Columbus: Ohio Department of Mental Health.

Rotheram-Borus, M. J., Koopman, C., & Ehrhardt, A. A. (1991). Homeless youths and HIV infection. *American Psychologist, 46,* 1188–1197.

Shinn, M., Knickman, J. R., & Weitzman, B. C. (1991). Social relationships and vulnerability to becoming homeless among poor families. *American Psychologist, 46,* 1180–1187.

Stack, C. (1974). *All our kin: Strategies for survival in a Black community.* New York: Harper & Row.

Sullivan, C. M., Tan, C., Basta, J., Rumptz, M., &

Davidson, W. S. II (1992). An advocacy intervention program: Initial evaluation. *American Journal of Community Psychology, 20,* 309–332.

Susser, E., Goldfinger, S. M., & White, A. (1990). Some clinical approaches to the homeless mentally ill. *Community Mental Health Journal, 26,* 463–480.

Toro, P. A., & McDonnell, D. M. (1992). Beliefs, attitudes, and knowledge about homelessness: A survey of the general public. *American Journal of Community Psychology, 20,* 53–80.

U.S. Conference of Mayors. (1987). *The continued growth of hunger, homelessness and poverty in America's cities in 1986.* Washington, DC: Author.

Welch, W. M., & Toff, G. (1987). Service needs of minority persons who are homeless and homeless mentally ill. *Proceedings of the Third of Four Knowledge Development Meetings on Issues Affecting Homeless Mentally Ill Persons.* Washington, DC: George Washington University.

Wood, D., Valdez, R. B., Hayashi, T., & Shen, A. (1990). Homeless and housed families in Los Angeles: A study comparing demographic, economic, and family function characteristics. *American Journal of Public Health, 80,* 1049–1052.

Chapter *16*

Ethnic Minority Intervention and Treatment Research

Stanley Sue
Chi-Ah Chun
Kenneth Gee

This chapter deals with research issues concerning ethnic minority interventions and treatment. It specifically focuses on (1) conceptual and methodological research issues, (2) psychotherapeutic outcome and process findings, and (3) applications of research to treatment and mental health practices. To aid students and practitioners who want to learn more about how to conduct research on ethnic minorities, as well as practitioners interested in using research in their work, we have attempted not only to present issues and research findings but also to suggest how to use these findings. Those who work with ethnic minority populations must be aware of the issues and be able to translate these issues into research and clinical practice.

Ethnic minority research in psychotherapy has had a relatively short history. Most psychotherapy research initiated about half a century ago examined the question of whether psychotherapy was effective. In time, questions were raised concerning what kinds of treatment were effective and what kinds of treatment were appropriate with what kinds of therapists, clients, and situations (for a history of psychotherapy including ethnicity and treatment, see Freedheim, 1992). The client variable of ethnicity was only of peripheral interest, for a variety of reasons: lack of interest in ethnicity on the part of researchers, lack of available funding for ethnic research, the belief among some that psychotherapy was unimportant because massive social and political interventions were needed in order to address race and ethnic relations, and difficulties in conducting ethnic research. Over time, the situation has changed, as reflected in the growing interest in ethnic research, greater availability of funding opportunities, and realization that although massive interventions are needed, so are efforts to help individual clients. Research contributions have increased, and the numbers of researchers who are themselves members of ethnic groups has helped to provide insider perspectives. Despite the fact that ethnic research has been an exciting area and its contributions have been highly important, a number of conceptual and methodological issues continue to confront the field.

Conceptual Considerations

Many conceptual issues arise in the field of ethnic research: What is the definition of ethnicity (or race)? How can we conceptualize observable ethnic differences? Are Western and traditional concepts of human beings really applicable to culturally different groups?

Definition of Ethnicity

In research and practice, ethnicity has been used to convey group membership according to race or ethnic background. Ethnic groups such as African Americans are often compared with Whites on utilization of services and treatment outcomes. Although such comparisons are meaningful in a broad sense, they often violate a more strict sense of the concept of ethnicity. The strict sense of the concept refers to a social-psychological sense of "peoplehood" in which members of a group share a unique social and cultural heritage. Yet we often fail to ascertain whether members of particular ethnic groups really share cultural features. Data are many times based on self-identification: If we want to conduct a study of clients and we combine self-identified Latino Americans into one group, we have no assurance that the clients are "ethnically" Latino. Some may have similar backgrounds, experiences, and attitudes, whereas others may be quite different. For example, Puerto Rican Americans who have recently arrived on the mainland may not share the same sense of ethnicity as fourth-generation Mexican Americans. Yet, in research, they are often conceptualized as all being Latino Americans. This problem also exists when we compare ethnics to "Whites," who are themselves quite diverse.

How can we address this problem? At times, the broad concept of ethnicity is important to use, especially if we want to establish parameters for ethnic comparisons. In this case, however, researchers should acknowledge the limitations in aggregating diverse individuals into an ethnic category. Another way of addressing the problem is to begin studying individual differences among members of an ethnic group. For example, Helms (1984) has studied whether African Americans prefer to see a therapist who is racially similar. She has found that African Americans who accept an African-American identity and who are skeptical of White values are most likely to want a therapist of the same race. Those at other stages of identity development are less likely to exhibit a racial preference. The value of the research is not solely in its demonstration that African Americans differ from one another.

The specification of the individual difference variables that are important in explaining research results is also important.

Conceptualization of Differences

In the past, studies have revealed behavioral differences among ethnic groups. For instance, Malzberg (1959) found differences in utilization rates of mental facilities in New York between African Americans and Whites. The problem with this study was that other demographic differences, such as gender and social class, that could be confounded with ethnicity were not controlled. Problems like this one are obvious. Less obvious is how the very concept of ethnicity is confounded with another important phenomenon—namely, minority group status.

We often attribute differences between ethnic groups to cultural factors. For example, traditional Chinese values are contrasted with Western values in order to explain why Chinese Americans may tend to show certain attitudinal or personality differences from White Americans. In essence, the two cultures are conceptualized as being orthogonal or independent variables, while in reality, the two are interactive and not independent (Sue, 1983). Chinese Americans have had a long history in the United States. Because they are members of a minority group who have experienced prejudice and discrimination, their attitudes and behavior may be a product not only of Chinese culture but also of their history and experiences in this country. In studying ethnic minority groups, researchers should be aware that minority group status is intertwined with the concept of ethnicity and should attempt to study the interactions between culture and minority group status.

Applicability of Western Theories

Disciplines such as psychology, psychiatry, social work, and nursing, are highly developed in Western societies in terms of their empirical, methodological, and theoretical contributions. An issue raised by many cross-cultural and ethnic minority researchers concerns the applicability and validity of theories developed in the West to non-Western societies or cultures. The issue is exemplified in the *etic-emic* distinction. The term *etic* refers to culture-general concepts or theories, whereas *emic* is defined as a culture-specific phenomenon. This important distinction can be illustrated as follows: Let us assume a psychotherapist finds that catharsis (e.g., having clients express pent-up emotions directly) relieves tension and depressive feelings. For the principle of catharsis to be *etic* or universal in nature, it should be applicable to different cultural groups. If it is not, then the principle is *emic*—perhaps specific only to the cultural group from which the client came.

A common error in research and in people's everyday thinking is to believe that one's concepts, practices, or principles are universal in nature (Brislin, 1993). A parent who believes that all children are better off in an atmosphere of parental permissiveness, a teacher who advocates that the best way to learn is through competition among all students, or a psychotherapist who assumes that nondirective techniques are effective with all clients may be confusing *emics* for *etics* to the extent that these truisms are confined to particular cultures. Of course, theory is necessary in any science. Rather than discarding theoretically based research, one may use cross-cultural or ethnic investigations to test whether proposed theories are applicable to different groups.

In clinical practice, some researchers and clinicians believe that current psychotherapeutic practices based on Western modes of treatment may be culturally inappropriate with certain members of ethnic minority groups. They advocate more culturally responsive forms of treatment. It is important to have treatment approaches consistent with clients' cultural lifestyles. However, the concept of "culturally responsive" interventions often consists only of vague notions of being culturally sensitive and knowledgeable about the client's culture. There is a need to specify more carefully what the concept of culturally responsive therapy means and to test the effectiveness of these interventions, as discussed later.

Methodological Considerations

Conducting research on ethnic minority groups is difficult. Researchers often have difficulty finding and selecting an appropriate sample to study, choosing a good research design and controlling for confounding variables, and finding valid measures. It is important to be familiar with these methodological difficulties, not only to improve future research designs but also to understand better the contributions and limitations of past research findings.

Research Participants

Although ethnic minority populations are rapidly increasing, researchers still face difficulties in finding adequate and representative samples to study. These difficulties include the relatively small size of the populations and the unwillingness of some ethnic minorities (e.g., illegal immigrants in the United States) to become research subjects. For example, large-scale epidemiological studies of the prevalence of mental disorders have been conducted among Americans (Myers et al., 1984). Yet, these studies have failed to include sufficient numbers of ethnic groups such as Native Americans and Asian Americans, so that accurate prevalence rates for these groups have not been found. Similarly, it is frequently difficult to study the effectiveness of treatment for Asian Americans at a particular mental health center because Asian Americans tend to avoid such services.

These difficulties in finding adequate samples may have two unfortunate consequences. First, researchers may simply be unable to find a representative sample of ethnic minority populations. Rather than studying the population of Native Americans, they may confine their investigation to urban rather than reservation Native Americans, or to students rather than those in the community at large. Second, investigators may lump diverse groups together in order to achieve adequate sample sizes. In the past, research compared Whites with the broad category of non-Whites. Even today, research on "Latinos" or "Hispanics" combines many diverse groups—Mexican Americans, Puerto Ricans, immigrants from Cuba, El Salvador, and elsewhere. Asian-American research includes as subjects Chinese, Japanese, Koreans, Pilipinos (many Asian-American researchers now use this term rather than *Filipino*), Vietnamese, and other groups. The problem is that focusing on a particular segment of the ethnic population limits the generalizability of findings. Forming a large aggregate group (e.g., Latino Americans) often fails to reveal the individual differences within the aggregate group. This problem of limited generality and of failure to consider individual differences also exists in studies of the "White" population. However, it is especially true for ethnic minority populations, which are small in numbers and exhibit considerable cultural and experiential variations.

Research that focuses on a particular segment or on an aggregate group can have important value. Researchers need to draw conclusions that are appropriate to the samples under study and to the research questions being addressed. Furthermore, greater efforts and funds should be expended to overcome some of the problems inherent in studying small and culturally diverse populations. For such populations, researchers must often spend a great deal of time and research funds to find adequate numbers of subjects and to achieve a representative sample. For example, conducting a representative survey of urban Native Americans is far more problematic than conducting a similar survey of urban Whites.

Research Designs and Confounding Variables

Psychological research has available a wide range of research designs and strategies. Research emphasizing experimental, correlational, field, longitudinal, analogue, and other approaches have been used in ethnic minority research. In devising research strategies, however, investigators have often had to consider the availability of sample sizes of ethnics. This is apparent in clinical and counseling studies. For example, a researcher who wants to study whether ethnic similarity between therapist and clients affects treatment outcomes may not be able to find sufficient numbers of ethnic clients and therapists. Consequently, the researcher may use an analogue approach in which students, rather than actual clients and therapists, play the roles of clients and therapists. There are obvious limitations in analogue studies. The external validity and generality of findings can be questioned. But such compromises in research ideals must sometimes be made because of practical realities.

Many researchers have used ethnographic techniques and qualitative methods in ethnic research. Ethnographic studies involve more descriptive-analytic techniques to study aspects of culture or the effects of culture, especially as viewed by members of that culture. Often used by anthropologists, ethnography is primarily descriptive, identifying important aspects of culture, categorizing phenomena, and exploring relationships between cultural variables and behavior. It is frequently used to establish research parameters for further investigations. For example, before comparing how different cultural groups fare in psychotherapy, we may first wish to study ethnographically how these groups generally respond to those healers already in their cultures in order to understand cultural practices in the different groups and their familiarity with and reactions to Western psychotherapists.

In any research design, it is important to be able to control for confounding variables. As mentioned previously, ethnicity is a broad variable, encompassing many features. Because ethnicity is often associated not only with culture but also with variables such as social class, investigators have often argued whether observed differences between, say, African Americans and Whites are really a matter of race or of social class. Research designs must obviously control for social class, as well as other demographic and social variables, before attributing differences to ethnicity or race. It is important to note that the "disadvantaged" status of ethnic minority groups cannot simply be attributed to social class differences. Although we know that certain groups such as African Americans, Native Americans, and Latino Americans have lower educational and income levels than do Whites, being a member of an ethnic minority group may involve other disadvantages that are important to study

Valid Measures

Validity refers to whether tests or assessment instruments accurately measure what they purport to measure. Researchers often have difficulty finding valid measures to use with different cultural groups. Take, for example, this item from the MMPI: "I feel blue." For people in U.S. society who are familiar with English idioms, this statement refers to feeling depressed or sad. But recent immigrants or those with limited English proficiency may not understand the meaning of "blue" in this context and may interpret the item as literally referring to the color blue.

Brislin (1993) identifies two major problems that are pertinent to our discussion of measures. First, concepts may not be equivalent across cultures. He notes that the concept of intelligent behavior is not equivalent in the United States and among the Baganda of East Africa. In the United States, one sign of intelligence is quickness in mental tasks, in East Africa, by contrast slow, deliberate thought is considered a part of intelligence. Obviously, tests of intelligence devised in the two cultures would differ, and individuals taking the tests could be considered intelligent on one measure but not the other. As another example, consider the concept of sincerity. In the United States, sincerity refers to being truthful, genuine, and straightforward—not to enacting roles. For Japanese, however, the sincere individual is one who acts in accordance with role expectations, not subjective personal feelings (DeVos, 1978).

Scalar or metric equivalence refers to whether scores on assessment instruments are really equivalent in cross-cultural research. For example, many universities use the Scholastic Aptitude Test (SAT), which has a verbal and quantitative component, as a criterion for admission. Many members of ethnic minority groups score lower on the SAT than do Whites. Do the test scores accurately assess academic potential, achievements, and ability to succeed? SAT scores moderately predict subsequent university grades. However, Sue and Abe (1988) found that the ability of the SAT score to predict success varies according to ethnicity and the components of the SAT.

Whereas the SAT verbal component was a good predictor of university grades for Whites, the SAT quantitative portion was a good predictor of grades for Asian-American students. Thus, Asian-American and White students who have the same total SAT score (combining verbal and quantitative subscores) may perform quite differently on grades, depending on the subscores. Researchers must study the conceptual and scalar equivalence of tests when working with ethnic minority groups. The use of multiple measures is also important to see if the measures provide consistent findings.

The conceptual and methodological issues and the short history of ethnic minority research have had several consequences. Research has had to proceed carefully in order to take into consideration the difficulties in ethnic research. Accordingly, much of the research is exploratory because of the lack of baseline information and the uncertain applicability of Western theories. Nevertheless, as we shall see, much of the research has been pioneering and exciting. The work has also provided insight into the applicability of existing theories and methods to use in cross-cultural studies. Keeping in mind the conceptual and methodological issues that have been raised, we would now like to review the substantive research on psychotherapy with ethnic minority groups.

Psychotherapy Research

Is psychotherapy effective with members of ethnic minority groups? This question is probably better stated as: "Under what conditions is psychotherapy helpful to members of ethnic minority groups?" Critics of psychotherapy with ethnic groups rarely challenge the value of psychotherapy or psychological interventions. What they do often challenge are the outcomes of psychotherapy when traditional psychotherapeutic practices do not consider the culture and minority group experiences of ethnic minority clients. Some critics may also advocate for prevention and for social, political, and economic changes rather than psychotherapy. But few would argue that psychotherapy cannot be effective with ethnic minority group clients.

In our review, we examine several issues: (1) Do ethnic minority groups use mental health services? (2) How long do ethnic clients remain in treatment? (3) What are the findings of research on psychotherapy outcomes? Although research has provided some insights into the answers to these questions, we need much more research to enable us to draw stronger conclusions. Our analysis is based on a recent review of psychotherapy research by one of the authors (see Sue, Zane, & Young, 1994).

Utilization of Mental Health Services

Investigations on utilization of mental health services by ethnic minorities have repeatedly found that African Americans and Native Americans tend to overutilize, whereas Asian Americans and Latino Americans tend to underutilize mental health services (Beiser & Attneave, 1982; Brown, Stein, Huang, & Harris, 1973; López, 1981; Mollica, Blum, & Redlich, 1980; O'Sullivan, Peterson, Cox, & Kirkeby, 1989; San Francisco Department of Mental Health, 1982; Scheffler & Miller, 1989; Snowden & Cheung, 1990; Sue, 1977). These patterns of utilization of the four major ethnic groups vary little from inpatient to outpatient settings and among various types of service facilities (e.g., community mental health facilities, state and county mental hospitals, Veterans Administration medical centers, general hospitals, and private psychiatric hospitals). According to the findings of a recent study by O'Sullivan et al. (1989), the utilization pattern of some groups appears to be changing. Their study, which was a follow-up study to the Sue (1977) study in Seattle, has found that, although African Americans and Native Americans continued to overutilize, Asian Americans and Latino Americans no longer underutilized services. More studies are needed to confirm these findings.

Many different explanations have been offered by investigators for the presence of ethnic differences in service utilization. Unfortunately, few were based on research findings, and most were speculative (Sue et al., 1994). Snowden and Cheung (1990) have attributed the group utilization differences to the group differences in socioeconomic status, rates of psychopathology, help-seeking tendencies, and therapists' diagnostic bias and involuntary hospitalization (especially in the case of African Americans). It is imperative that more research be conducted because these differences have serious implications for determining the mental health needs of these groups and the effectiveness of the currently available treatments for them.

Some caution should be taken in interpreting these findings. First, there may be some inconsistencies in service utilization patterns between findings from national surveys that include those who have not sought treatment at mental health facilities and findings from treated samples from community, state, or county mental health facilities. Neighbors (1985) found that in his national survey of adult African Americans, only a relatively small number of African Americans reported that they used mental health services for psychological problems. Yet, the studies cited earlier on utilization patterns demonstrated that African Americans *overutilized* services. Second, in a review article by Rogler et al. (1983), Puerto Ricans in New York had significantly higher rates of psychiatric admissions, use of outpatient psychiatric services, and community mental health facilities than did non-Latino Whites. Only recently have Puerto Ricans showed relatively low rates of admission. This points to the fact that utilization patterns or statistics change and need to be monitored over time. Third, we have used the terms *underutilization* and *overutilization* loosely to refer to whether groups differ in use compared to their relative population figures. A group may have a low percentage of users simply because it has a low prevalence of mental disorders. Similarly, groups that statistically overutilize services may not be overutilizing if the prevalence of disorders in that group is high. In this case, statistically defined under- and overutilization are discrepant with definitions based on need for services. Because we do not know enough about the prevalence of mental disorders among ethnic minority populations, most studies have employed a statistical definition as indicators of utilization. It should be noted, however, that indirect indicators of well-being suggest that Asian Americans and Latino Americans are not extraordinarily well adjusted. Thus, their underutilization may reflect actual low use rather than low needs for services.

Length of Treatment

Another commonly used method of examining the impact or effectiveness of psychotherapy for ethnic minorities is investigating the length of treatment. The assumption behind this type of research is that an effective therapy can keep clients in treatment, whereas an ineffective therapy will be terminated prematurely by clients. In fact, studies have consistently shown that the longer clients stay in treatment, the more change occurs (Luborsky, Chandler, Auerbach, Cohen, & Bachrach, 1971; Pekarik, 1986).

Findings on length of treatment of ethnic minority clients are inconsistent. Length of treatment has been measured either as the average number of sessions or the dropout rate after the first session of treatment. Sue (1977) investigated the dropout rate of African Americans, Native Americans, Asian Americans, and Latin Americans in Seattle. He found all groups of ethnic minorities to have significantly higher dropout rates after the first session than White Americans. In the follow-up study in Seattle, O'Sullivan et al. (1989) found no consistent differences in dropout rates between ethnic and White groups. In a recent study of the outpatient facilities in Los Angeles County (Sue, Fujino, Hu, Takeuchi, & Zane, 1991), only African Americans had a higher dropout rate from treatment after the first session than White Americans. Latino Americans did not differ from White Americans and Asian Americans had even a lower dropout rate than White Americans. Therefore, Asian Americans had the highest average number of sessions, followed by White and Latino Americans. African Americans had the lowest average number of treatment sessions. The inconsistency between the findings of the different studies may be due to variations in region, service system, and time period (Sue et al., 1994), or it may be an indication of some recent improvement in our mental health system's cultural responsiveness.

One study of different ethnic groups has provided some insight into factors associated with length of treatment. The Los Angeles County study (Sue et al., 1991) revealed that among African Americans, Asian Americans, Mexican Americans, and Whites, two factors were related to number of sessions across all groups: income and ethnic match between clients and therapists. Being poorer and not having an ethnically similar therapist predicted a lower number of treatment sessions. Having a psychotic diagnosis was also associated with fewer sessions in all groups except Mexican Americans. Thus, in this study, poor clients were more likely to average fewer sessions than were clients with higher incomes. The finding that having a therapist of the same ethnicity results in more sessions is interesting, although the reasons for this finding are unclear. Perhaps ethnic match tends to increase interpersonal attraction or influence of therapists.

Treatment Outcome Research

The paucity of treatment outcome studies on ethnic minorities makes it difficult to draw any definitive conclusions about the effectiveness of psychotherapy with ethnic groups. We need many more studies that rigorously examine treatment effects using (1) within– and between–ethnic group comparisons, (2) sufficient sample sizes, (3) different forms of treatment, (4) a variety of cross-culturally valid outcome measures, (5) follow-up strategies that can shed light on the stability of treatment effects over time, and (6) adequate methodological designs so that researchers can control for confounding variables or alternative explanations for findings. The few studies that are available often provide conflicting findings for all major ethnic groups. In none of the studies, however, did ethnic minorities consistently fare better than White Americans. Ethnic minorities tended at best to have similar treatment outcomes to White Americans.

Treatment outcome literature on African Americans seems to indicate that African Americans do not fare better than other ethnic clients, including White Americans, and that they may even have worse outcomes (Sue et al., 1994). Earlier studies on African Americans have revealed no racial differences from White Americans (Lerner, 1972). Jones (1978; 1982) has repeatedly found that African-American clients showed similar rates of improvement to those of White Americans regardless of the ethnicity of their therapists. In more recent studies, however, the treatment outcomes of African Americans were poorer than the outcomes of White Americans and sometimes even poorer than the outcomes of other ethnic minority groups in drug treatment programs and in Los Angeles County mental health facilities (Brown, Joe, & Thompson, 1985; Sue et al., 1991). In no study were the outcomes of African Americans superior to those of White Americans and other ethnic minority groups.

Less is known about the effectiveness of psychotherapy for Native Americans (Manson, Walker, & Kivlahan, 1987; Neligh, 1988). Most mental health–related programs intended for Native Americans have focused on treatment and prevention programs for substance abuse. Query (1985) compared the outcomes of White and Native American adolescents in an inpatient chemical dependency treatment program at a North Dakota State Hospital. He found that Native American adolescents were overrepresented in the unit compared to their population figure. Furthermore, during the six months after discharge, significantly more Native American adolescents than White American adolescents had either thought of or attempted suicide. Overall, the treatment was more effective on White American adolescents than Native Americans. Prevention programs for Native Americans have been more successful in producing positive changes, especially in bicultural competence skills (LaFromboise, Trimble, & Mohatt, 1990; Schinke et al., 1988). Given the few findings, discussion of treatment outcome of Native Americans should wait until more research is conducted.

Outcome studies on Asian Americans, compared to other ethnic minority groups, have found more positive results. In Zane's study of the effectiveness of psychotherapy with Asian-American clients in a community-based mental health clinic in Richmond, California (1983), Asian-American clients showed significant improvement on both client self-report and therapist-rated outcome measures. Southeast Asian Americans have also been successfully treated for depression and posttraumatic stress disorder through psychotherapy and psychopharmacotherapy (Mollica et al., 1990; Kinzie & Leung, 1989). Compared to other ethnic groups, Asian Americans did not differ on posttreatment Global Assessment Score (GAS) from White Americans, even after controlling the pretreatment GAS scores (Zane & Hatanaka, 1988). Sue et al. (1991) have also found that Asian and White Americans had similar outcomes (in the same study, African Americans had worse outcomes than White Americans). In terms of clients' satisfaction with the therapy, however, Asian Americans have been found to be much less satisfied with service or progress of the therapy than were White Americans (Lee & Mixon, 1985; Zane, 1983; Zane & Hatanaka 1988). Asian Americans in Lee and Mixon's study have rated both the counseling experience and the therapists as less effective.

Much of the treatment outcome research on Latino Americans has examined the effects of "culturally sensitive" treatment programs that can effectively meet the mental health needs of Latinos (Rogler, Malgady, Costantino, & Blumenthal, 1987). These culturally sensitive treatments have aimed to improve the accessibility of services to Latinos (e.g., by providing flexible hours or by placing the treatment facility in a Latino community), employing bicultural/bilingual staff, and selecting, modifying, or developing therapies that either utilize or are most appropriate for Latino cultural customs, values, and beliefs (e.g., involving indigeneous healers or religious leaders in the community in treatment, or increasing participation of family members in treatment). Research suggests that these treatments may increase service utilization, length of treatment, and clients' satisfaction with treatment and may decrease premature termination of treatment (Rogler, Malgady, & Rodriguez, 1989; Sue et al., 1994). How do Latinos fare in mainstream mental health services? When compared to other ethnic groups in mainstream treatments, Mexican Americans in one study were most likely to improve with treatment (Sue et al., 1991). However, having ethnic matches between therapist and client (a Mexican-American therapist with a Mexican-American client) was associated with better treatment outcomes than were mismatches. The research suggests that interventions involving culturally sensitive approaches produce more positive changes than interventions that do not consider cultural factors.

Treatment outcome research on ethnic groups can be characterized as sparse and targeted to many different aspects of psychotherapy. Under such circumstances, there is a need for more systematic research in order to address more fully the issue of effectiveness of both the mainstream and ethnic-specific treatment plans for ethnic minorities. Such research can help us identify treatment elements that are universally effective and those that are culture-specific.

Process Research

Our review has emphasized treatment outcome research. However, we would like to mention that a number of investigators have examined treatment process variables. Research has been conducted on client preferences for the ethnicity of thera-pists. In many cases, studies have shown that ethnic clients tend to prefer or to view more positively ethnically similar therapists (Atkinson, 1983; Dauphinais, Dauphi-nais, & Rowe, 1981; López, López, & Fong, 1991; Sattler, 1977), although other investigations have questioned these findings or have questioned whether therapist ethnicity is a very important variable relative to other therapist variables (Acosta & Sheehan, 1976; Furlong, Atkinson, & Casas, 1979; LaFromboise & Dixon, 1981). Preferences for an ethnically similar therapist appears to be a function of individual differences, such as a client's ethnic identity, gender, trust of Whites, and level of acculturation (Bennett & BigFoot-Sipes, 1991; Helms & Carter, 1991; Parham & Helms, 1981; Ponce & Atkinson, 1989; Ponterotto, Alexander, & Hinkston, 1988; Watkins & Terrell, 1988). Thus, research suggests that many ethnic clients prefer ethnically similar therapists but that other variables mediate the preferences.

Ratings of therapist competence or preferences for a therapist are also influ-enced by the nature of psychotherapy. Therapists who intimately self-disclose to African-American clients elicit more intimate self-disclosures than do therapists who do not intimately self-disclose (Berg & Wright-Buckley, 1988); those who acknowledge and deal with cultural issues raised by therapists are perceived to be more culturally competent than are therapists who avoid such issues (Pomales, Claiborn, & LaFromboise, 1986). Culturally sensitive therapists or those who are trained to deal with cultural issues (Dauphinais et al., 1981; Gim, Atkinson, & Kim, 1991; LaFromboise et al., 1990; Wade & Bernstein, 1991) are also judged to be more competent or more favorable. Some studies have found that Asian Americans and Latino Americans prefer directive over nondirective therapists (Atkinson, Maruyama, & Matsui, 1978; Pomales & Williams, 1989; Ponce & Atkinson, 1989).

Rather than focusing on therapists, some researchers have examined the bene-fits of culture-specific forms of treatment—that is, therapies or modification of treatment approaches designed especially for certain ethnic groups. Family-network therapy, extended family therapy, or other forms of treatment that inte-grate traditional cultural healing practices or cultural aspects have been advocated by some (Comas-Díaz, 1981; Costantino, Malgady, & Rogler, 1986; LaFromboise, 1988; Lee, 1982; Manson et al., 1987; Szapocznik et al., 1989). Although systematic studies of the effectiveness of these culturally based forms of treatment are limited, they appear to be valuable, according to practitioners.

Application of Research Findings to Treatment

Some skepticism has been expressed over the value of research in affecting practice. As noted by Beutler (1992), many practitioners and clinicians do not read research reports, do not find reports helpful, or fail to use research findings in their practice. Nevertheless, Beutler also noted that research has had an impact on the practice of psychotherapy over the course of time. Although a single piece of research may have no had direct impact, the cumulative effect of many studies has been impor-tant. How can we apply the research findings and writings of different scholars to psychotherapeutic practice? Some general recommendations follow.

First, ethnicity, culture, and minority group status are important concepts for psychotherapists who work with ethnic minority clients. The available evidence suggests that therapists should be prepared to deal with these concepts and issues with their clients. While cultural issues may not be salient to all ethnic clients in all situations, therapists who are uncomfortable with these issues may not be able to deal with the issues if they do arise. Therapists should become knowledgeable about the cultural background of ethnic clients and should be adept at working in cross-cultural situations.

Second, having available a therapist of the same ethnicity as the client may be advantageous. While ethnic matches are not necessary for positive outcomes, at times certain clients may prefer or work better with an ethnically similar therapist. Having bilingual and bicultural therapists is vital to clients who are recent immigrants and are not fully proficient in English. The problem is that ethnic clients often have little choice, unless we train more ethnic minority, bilingual, and bicultural therapists.

Third, therapists who are unfamiliar with the cultural backgrounds of their clients may want to consult with mental health professionals who are knowledgeable of the clients' culture. Receiving training in working with culturally diverse clients is also recommended. It is difficult to be fully proficient in working with many diverse groups. Assistance should be sought in the assessment or treatment of any client whose cultural background or life-style is unfamiliar to the therapist or markedly different from that of the therapist.

Fourth, culture-specific treatment should be available to ethnic clients, especially those who are unacculturated or who hold very traditional ethnic values that are discrepant from Western values. As mentioned previously, many researchers have argued that such treatment is valuable and beneficial.

Fifth, for clients who are unfamiliar with Western psychotherapy, some sort of pretherapy intervention may be important. Before therapy, clients should receive some knowledge of what psychotherapy is, what roles clients and therapists adopt, what to expect in treatment, and how treatment can affect mental disorders. Similarly, efforts should be made to educate community groups on how to recognize emotional disturbance, what to do with someone who is disturbed, what mental health services are, and how to use such services. Issues of confidentiality, client rights, and the like should also be presented to the community. These strategies increase the likelihood that ethnic clients will better understand treatment and reduce feelings of strangeness in the client role.

This chapter has reviewed some of the conceptual and methodological issues facing researchers who study ethnic minority groups. Despite the many problems encountered in ethnic research, psychotherapy research has been growing and has provided some preliminary ideas on helpful strategies to use in providing mental health services to these groups. Much more research is needed that go beyond the descriptive level of discovering ethnic differences in therapy outcome and to begin to identify cultural elements that are important in psychotherapy. The existence of a critical need for more and better ethnic minority research does not imply that current ethnic investigators have failed to make important contributions. Indeed, the relatively small number of ethnic and cross-cultural investigators have made many pioneering contributions despite the obstacles encountered in ethnic minority research. These contributions are the basis for the next generation of research.

What directions should future research take? Beyond the recommendations for conducting more research and methodologically stronger research (in terms of adequate sample sizes, representative samples, valid measures, rigorous research designs, etc.), it is meaningful for future research to be targeted to certain issues. First, research should be devoted to uncovering how cultural elements influence treatment processes and outcomes among ethnic minorities. Second, the application of these cultural elements in devising culture-specific treatment programs needs to be investigated. Third, ethnic minority groups show much within-group variation, and effective therapeutic strategies for a highly acculturated ethnic minority client may differ from those for a recent immigrant. Research on individual differences is needed in order to overcome stereotypes that particular treatment tactics are effective with all members of a certain ethnic minority group. Fourth, because of the multicultural nature of our society, therapists will be increasingly exposed to clients from different ethnic groups. An important research direction is to discover those psychotherapeutic skills that enable therapists to work effectively with a diverse clientele and to find means of training therapists to develop effective skills.

References

Acosta, F. X., & Sheehan, J. G. (1976). Preferences toward Mexican American and Anglo American psychotherapists. *Journal of Consulting and Clinical Psychology, 44*, 272–279.

Atkinson, D. R. (1983). Ethnic similarity in counseling psychology: A review of research. *The Counseling Psychologist, 11*, 79–92.

Atkinson, D. R., Maruyama, M., & Matsui, S. (1978). Effects of counselor race and counseling approach on Asian Americans' perceptions of counselor credibility and utility. *Journal of Counseling Psychology, 25*, 76–85.

Beiser, M., & Attneave, C. L. (1982). Mental disorders among Native American children: Rates and risk periods for entering treatment. *American Journal of Psychiatry, 139*, 193–198.

Bennett, S. K., & BigFoot-Sipes, D. S. (1991). American Indian and white college student preferences for counselor characteristics. *Journal of Counseling Psychology, 38*, 440–445.

Berg, J. H., & Wright-Buckley, C. (1988). Effects of racial similarity and interviewer intimacy in a peer counseling analogue. *Journal of Counseling Psychology, 35*, 377–384.

Beutler, L. (1992). Leading clinical practice. *The Scientist Practitioner, 2*, 10–19.

Brislin, R. (1993). *Understanding culture's influence on behavior.* New York: Harcourt Brace Jovanovich.

Brown, B. S., Joe, G. W., & Thompson, P. (1985). Minority group status and treatment retention. *International Journal of the Addictions, 20*, 319–335.

Brown, T. R., Stein, K. M., Huang, K., & Harris, D. E. (1973). Mental illness and the role of mental health facilities in Chinatown. In S. Sue & N. Wagner (Eds.), *Asian-Americans: Psychological perspectives* (pp. 212–231). Palo Alto, CA: Science & Behavior Books.

Comas-Díaz, L. (1981). Effects of cognitive and behavioral group treatment on the depressive symptomatology of Puerto Rican women. *Journal of Consulting and Clinical Psychology, 49*, 627–632.

Costantino, G., Malgady, R. G., & Rogler, L. H. (1986). Cuento therapy: A culturally senstitive modality for Puerto Rican children. *Journal of Counseling and Clinical Psychology, 54*, 639–645.

Dauphinais, P., Dauphinais, L., & Rowe, W. (1981). Effects of race and communication style on Indian perceptions of counselor effectiveness. *Counselor Education and Supervision, 21*, 72–80.

DeVos, G. (1978). *Selective permeability and reference group sanctioning: Psychological continuities in role degradation.* Paper presented at the seminar on Comparative Studies in Ethnicity and Nationality, University of Washington, Seattle.

Freedheim, D. K. (1992). *History of psychotherapy.* Washington, DC: American Psychological Association.

Furlong, M. J., Atkinson, D. R., & Casas, J. M. (1979). Effects of counselor ethnicity and attitudinal similarity on Chicano students' perceptions of counselor credibility and attractiveness. *Hispanic Journal of Behavioral Science, 1*, 41–53.

Gim, R. H., Atkinson, D. R., & Kim, S. J. (1991). Asian-American acculturation, counselor ethnicity and cultural sensitivity, and ratings of counselors. *Journal of Counseling Psychology, 38*, 57–62.

Helms, J. E. (1984). Toward a theoretical explanation of the effects of race on counseling: A Black and White model. *Counseling Psychologist, 12*, 153–164.

Helms, J. E., & Carter, R. T. (1991). Relationships of White and Black racial identity attitudes and demographic similarity to counselor preferences. *Journal of Counseling Psychology, 38*, 446–457.

Jones, E. E. (1978). Effects of race on psychotherapy process and outcome: An exploratory investigation. *Psychotherapy: Theory, Research, and Practice, 15*, 226–236.

Jones, E. E. (1982). Psychotherapists' impressions of treatment outcome as a function of race. *Journal of Clinical Psychology, 38*, 722–731.

Kinzie, J. D., & Leung, P. (1989). Clonidine in Cambodian patients with post-traumatic stress disorder. *Journal of Nervous and Mental Disease, 177*, 546–550.

LaFromboise, T. D. (1988). American Indian mental health policy. *American Psychologist, 43*, 388–397.

LaFromboise, T. D., & Dixon, D. N. (1981). American Indian perception of trustworthiness in a counseling interview. *Journal of Counseling Psychology, 28*, 135–139.

LaFromboise, T. D., Trimble, J. E., & Mohatt, G. V. (1990). Counseling intervention and American Indian tradition: An integrative approach. *The Counseling Psychologist, 18*, 628–654.

Lee, E. (1982). A social systems approach to assessment and treatment for Chinese American families. In M. McGoldrick & J. Giordano (Eds.), *Ethnicity and family therapy* (pp. 527–551). New York: Guilford Press.

Lee, W. M. L., & Mixson, R. J. (1985). *An evaluation of counseling services by college students of Asian and Caucasian ethnicity.* Unpublished manuscript.

Lerner, B. (1972). *Therapy in the ghetto: Political impotence and personal disintegration.* Baltimore: Johns Hopkins University Press.

López, S. (1981). Mexican-American usage of mental health facilities: Underutilization reconsidered. In A. Baron, Jr. (Ed.), *Explorations in Chicano psychology* (pp. 139–164). New York: Praeger.

López, S. R., López, A. A., & Fong, K. T. (1991). Mexican Americans' initial preferences for counselors: The role of ethnic factors. *Journal of Counseling Psychology, 38*, 487–496.

Luborsky, L., Chandler, M., Auerbach, A. H., Cohen, J., & Bachrach, H. M. (1971). Factors influencing the outcome of psychotherapy: A review of quantitative research. *Psychological Bulletin, 75*, 145–408.

Malzberg, B. (1959). Mental disease among Negroes: An analysis of the first admissions in New York State, 1949–1951. *Mental Hygiene, 43*, 422–459.

Manson, S. M., Walker, R. D., & Kivlahan, D. R. (1987). Psychiatric assessment and treatment of American Indians and Alaska Natives. *Hospital and Community Psychiatry, 38*, 165–173.

Mollica, R. F., Blum, J. D., & Redlich, F. (1980). Equity and the psychiatric care of the Black patient, 1950–1975. *Journal of Nervous and Mental Disease, 168*, 279–286.

Mollica, R. F., Wyshak, G., Lavelle, J., Truong, T., Tor, S., & Yang, T. (1990). Assessment symptom change in Southeast refugee survivors of mass violence and torture. *American Journal of Psychiatry, 147*, 83–88.

Myers, J. K., Weissman, M. M., Tischler, G. L., Holzer, C. E., Leaf, P. J., Orvaschel, H., Anthony, J. C., Boyd, J. H., Burke, J. D., Kramer, M., & Stoltzman, R. (1984). Six-month prevalence of psychiatric disorder in three communities: 1980 to 1982. *Archives of General Psychiatry, 41,* 959–967.

Neighbors, H. W. (1985). Seeking professional help for personal problems: Black Americans' use of health and mental health services. *Community Mental Health Journal, 21,* 156–166.

Neligh, G. (1988). Major mental disorders and behavior among American Indians and Alaska Natives. In *Behavioral health issues among American Indians and Alaska Natives: Explorations on the frontiers of the biobehavioral sciences.* American Indian and Alaska Native Mental Health Research. Monograph *1,* 116–159.

O'Sullivan, M. J., Peterson, P. D., Cox, G. B., & Kirkeby, J. (1989). Ethnic populations: Community mental health services ten years later. *American Journal of Community Psychology, 17,* 17–30.

Parham, T. A., & Helms, J. E. (1981). The influence of Black students' racial identity attitudes on preferences for counselor's race. *Journal of Counseling Psychology, 28,* 250–257.

Pekarik, G. (1986). The use of termination status and treatment duration patterns as an indicator of clinical improvement. *Evaluation and Program Planning, 9,* 25–30.

Pomales, J., Claiborn, C. D., & LaFromboise, T. D. (1986). Effects of Black students' racial identity on perceptions of White counselors varying in cultural sensitivity. *Journal of Counseling Psychology, 33,* 57–61.

Pomales, J., & Williams, V. (1989). Effects of level of acculturation and counseling style on Hispanic students' perceptions of counselor. *Journal of Counseling Psychology, 36,* 79–83.

Ponce, F. Q., & Atkinson, D. R. (1989). Mexican-American acculturation, counselor ethnicity, counseling style, and perceived counselor credibility. *Journal of Counseling Psychology, 36,* 203–208.

Ponterotto, J. G., Alexander, C. M., & Hinkston, J. A. (1988). Afro-American preferences for counselor characteristics: A replication and extension. *Journal of Counseling Psychology, 35,* 175–182.

Query, J. M. N. (1985). Comparative admission and follow-up study of American Indians and Whites in a youth chemical dependency unit on the North Central Plains. *International Journal of the Addictions, 20,* 489–502.

Rogler, L. H., Cooney, R. S., Costantino, G., Earley, B. F., Grossman, B., Gurak, D. T., Malgady, R., & Rodriguez, O. (1983). *A conceptual framework for mental health research on Hispanic populations.* Bronx, NY: Fordham University, Hispanic Research Center.

Rogler, L. H., Malgady, R. G., Costantino, G., & Blumenthal, R. (1987). What do culturally sensitive mental health services mean?: The case of Hispanics. *American Psychologist, 42,* 565–570.

Rogler, L. H., Malgady, R. G., & Rodriguez, O. (1989). *Hispanics and mental health: A framework for research.* Malabar, FL: Krieger.

San Francisco Department of Mental Health. (1982). *Community mental health services report.* San Francisco: Author.

Sattler, J. M. (1977). The effects of therapist–client racial similarity. In A. S. Gurman & A. M. Razin (Eds.), *Effective psychotherapy: A handbook of research* (pp. 252–290). Elmsford, NY: Pergamon Press.

Scheffler, R. M., & Miller, A. B. (1989). Demand analysis of mental health service use among ethnic subpopulations. *Inquiry, 26,* 202–215.

Schinke, S. P., Orlandi, M. A., Botvin, G. J., Gilchrist, L. D., Trimble, J. E., & Locklear, V. B. (1988). Preventing substance abuse among American-Indian adolescents: A bicultural competence skills approach. *Journal of Counseling Psychology, 35,* 87–90.

Snowden, L. R., & Cheung, F. K. (1990). Use of inpatient mental health services by members of ethnic minority groups. *American Psychologist, 45,* 347–355.

Sue, S. (1977). Community mental health services to minority groups: Some optimism, some pessimism. *American Psychologist, 32,* 616–624.

Sue, S. (1983). Ethnic minority issues in psychology: A reexamination. *American Psychologist, 38,* 583–592.

Sue, S., & Abe, J. (1988). *Predictors of academic achievement among Asian American and White students.* New York: The College Board.

Sue, S., Fujino, D. C., Hu, L. T., Takeuchi, D. T., & Zane, N. W. S. (1991). Community mental health services for ethnic minority groups: A test of the cultural responsiveness hypothesis. *Journal of Counseling Psychology, 59,* 533–540.

Sue, S., Zane, N., & Young, K. (1994). Research on psychotherapy with culturally diverse populations. In A. E. Bergin & S. L. Garfield (Eds.), *Handbook of psychotherapy and behavior change* (4th ed.) (pp. 783–817). New York: Wiley.

Szapocznik, J., Rio, A., Murray, E., Cohen, R., Scopetta, M., Rivas-Vazquez, A., Hervis, O., Posada, V., & Kurtines, W. (1989). Structural family versus psychodynamic child therapy for problematic Hispanic boys. *Journal of Counseling and Clinical Psychology, 57,* 571–578.

Wade, P., & Bernstein, B. (1991). Culture sensitivity training and counselor's race: Effects on Black female clients' perceptions and attrition. *Journal of Counseling Psychology, 38,* 9–15.

Watkins, C. E., Jr., & Terrell, F. (1988). Mistrust level and its effects on counseling expectations in Black client–White counselor relationships: An analogue study. *Journal of Counseling Psychology, 35,* 194–197.

Zane, N. (1983, August). *Evaluation of outpatient psychotherapy for Asian and Non-Asian American clients.* Paper presented at the American Psychological Association Conference, Anaheim.

Zane, N., & Hatanaka, H. (1988, October). *Utilization and evaluation of a parallel service delivery model for ethnic minority clients.* Paper presented at the Professional Symposium: Recent Trends and New Approaches to the Treatment of Mental Illness and Substance Abuse, Oklahoma Mental Health Research Institute.

Chapter *17*

Education and Training Issues for Intervention with Ethnic Groups

JOSEPH F. APONTE
JIM CLIFFORD

Over the last several decades there have been significant changes in the number and distribution of ethnic populations, immigration and migration patterns, and ethnic population characteristics. These changes have significant implications for the training of mental health service practitioners (see Chapter 1). It is predicted that members of ethnic groups will constitute one-third of the U.S. population by the turn of the century and almost half the population by 2050 (U.S. Bureau of Census, 1992). It is incumbent on all graduate and professional programs in the mental health disciplines, and psychology in particular, to incorporate ethnically diverse content and training into their programs in order to be responsive to present and future population changes (Myers, 1992; Myers, Wohlford, Guzman, & Echemendia, 1991).

Along with these acknowledged increases in ethnic populations, there has been increased attention directed at the education and training of psychologists to work with ethnic groups. A number of national training conferences have underscored the importance of training in this area (American Psychological Association, 1987; Bourg, Bent, McHolland, & Stricker, 1989; Brammer et al., 1988; Dong, Wong, Callao, Nishihara, & Chin, 1978; Gary & Weaver, 1991; Stricker et al., 1990). These conferences have strongly recommended that the curricula devoted to ethnic groups be increased. Such efforts have been supported by the American Psychological Association (APA), including the Committee on Accreditation (Aponte, 1992).

Although the impetus for focusing on ethnic populations has been present over the last two decades, those efforts that have been put forth have led to only limited success (Bernal, 1992; Bernal & Padilla, 1982; Puente et al., 1993). The purpose of this chapter is to (1) review the current status of education and training of psychologists to work with ethnic populations; (2) identify the issues and barriers encountered in educating and training efforts; (3) present a number of models and strategies for enhancing the ethnic education and training of students and professionals; and (4) identify guidelines that can be of use to graduate and professional programs in developing ethnic curricula.

Current Status of Education and Training

To have a full understanding of the issues, problems, and barriers to educating and training psychologists to work with ethnic groups, it is important to identify the number of ethnic students and faculty currently in graduate and professional schools and to describe the curriculum, courses, and training experiences in graduate and professional programs. The discussion that follows is based primarily on data provided by the Office of Demographic, Employment, and Educational Research, and the Office of Ethnic Minority Affairs of the American Psychological Association (APA) and published surveys of training programs.

Number of Graduate Students and Faculty

The number of ethnic students in graduate programs is often directly related to the number of ethnic faculty in the programs. A recent report by Wicherski and Kohout (1992) indicates that minority representation on graduate psychology faculties has shown little improvement over the past decade. White faculty in psychology programs remained at between 93 and 95 percent from 1981 to 1991, and, correspondingly, the percentage of African-American psychology faculty held steady at about 3 percent over that ten-year period (see Table 17-1). Hispanics and Asian Americans have each consistently made up 1 to 2 percent of psychology faculty, and Native American faculty account for less than 1 percent of all psychology faculty. Ethnic faculty are clearly underrepresented in psychology departments in comparison to the number of ethnic persons in the general population (see Chapter 1).

The future prospects for recruiting new psychology faculty also looks dismal. Recent data indicate that only 11.3 percent of all psychology doctoral graduates were ethnic students (Guzman & Messenger, 1991). This represents only a slight increase in the number of doctoral students over the past decade (Atkinson, 1983; Bernal, 1990; 1992; Russo, Olmedo, Stapp, & Fulcher, 1981). Such figures become even more startling in light of the fact that the percent of new doctoral graduates in psychology who wish to pursue an academic career has been declining over the last ten years (Wicherski & Kohout, 1992). In fact, the percentage of all Ph.D.'s who were

TABLE 17-1   Percentage of Faculty by Race/Ethnicity in U.S. Graduate
Departments of Psychology by Academic Year

| Survey Year | 1981– | 1983– | 1986– | 1989– | 1992– |
Sample Size	1982	1984	1987	1990	1992
Race:					
White	95	94	94	93	93
Black	3	3	2	3	3
Hispanic	1	1	1	1	2
Asian	1	1	1	2	2
Native American	<1	<1	<1	<1	<1
Not Specified	1	1	1	1	<1

Source: Surveys of graduate departments of psychology, 1981–1982 through 1993–1993, American
Psychological Association and Council of Graduate Departments of Psychology.

working in academic settings has recently declined for all ethnic groups (Jones,
Goertz, & Kuh, 1992).

Recent data indicate that changes in the rate of graduate school enrollment have
varied by ethnic group. From 1976 to 1986, graduate school enrollment for Blacks
decreased, while enrollments increased for Hispanics and Asian Americans, and
remained the same for Native Americans (Brown, 1988; Jones et al., 1992). Fewer
Blacks are in general obtaining doctorates in all fields (Jenkins, 1992; Thurgood &
Weinman, 1990). Such trends were reflected in psychology, with graduate school
enrollments remaining overall at 12 percent (Kohout & Pion, 1990). Undergraduate
enrollments have shown patterns similar to the graduate profiles, indicating that
the pipeline from undergraduate to graduate school and then to faculty status, while
improving for Hispanics and Asian Americans, has decreased for African Americans, thus making the future prospects for more African-American faculty rather
bleak.

Overall, ethnic representation in psychology, as reflected in psychology doctoral enrollments, psychology doctoral recipients, APA members with Ph.D.'s, and
psychology faculty in graduate departments, has not changed significantly in the
past decade (Howard et al., 1986; Pion, Bramblett, & Wicherski, 1987; Pion, Bramblett, Wicherski, & Stapp, 1985; Russo et al., 1981; Stapp, Tucker, & VandenBos,
1985). Most of the data suggest, at best, that any increase of ethnic persons in the
field of psychology has been at a rate that continues to fall further behind the rate
of increase of ethnic groups in the U.S. population, and, at worst, appears to be flat
or decreasing in the face of increasing ethnic group populations (Bernal, 1990).

Available Curriculum Courses and Training Experiences

Over the years, a number of surveys on ethnic courses and training experiences in
doctoral and internship programs have been conducted. Early studies found that
the courses and training experiences offered on ethnicity were sparse and typically
not required of all students (American Psychological Association, 1982; Bernal &

Padilla, 1982; Boxley & Wagner, 1971; Wyatt & Parham, 1985). Results from more recent surveys acknowledge some measurable progress, with approximately 60 percent of APA clinical programs having a course on ethnic mental health issues, and 25 percent requiring one such course for graduation (Bernal, 1992).

Significant changes from the earlier Bernal and Padilla (1982) survey are that there are several programs with specialized curricula and training experiences specifically designed to prepare psychologists for working with ethnic populations (Arredondo, 1985; Bernal, 1990), and programs that have made special efforts to recruit and retain ethnic students (Collins, Green, & Chaney, 1992; Myers, Taylor, & Davila, 1992). Among those programs identified and described by Bernal are the California School of Professional Psychology at Los Angeles, Colorado State University, Oklahoma State University, University of Maryland, and New York University Medical Center. The offerings of these programs vary from ethnic content and training experiences being embedded throughout the curriculum to specialized tracks within the programs to prepare students to work with ethnic populations.

Although, as previously noted, some gains have been made in the curricula, courses, and training experiences directed specifically at working with ethnic group members, 40 percent of the programs have no course offerings in this area, and the vast majority of the programs apparently do not consider such training important enough to require such a course for graduation (Bernal, 1992). There is as yet no agreement as to the training models, structure, sequence, and content of courses and training experiences for teaching students to work effectively with ethnic populations, nor is there continuity in ethnic training between doctoral training programs and internship settings (LaFromboise & Foster, 1992).

Ridley (1985) has identified five imperatives that speak to the importance of including ethnic and cultural content and training experiences in graduate programs. These imperatives are (1) professional participation, the underrepresentation of ethnic psychologists in the profession; (2) ethical, the need for competent services to be provided to ethnic populations as exemplified by the APA code of ethics; (3) cultural-context, the importance of culture in all treatment interventions; (4) scholarly, the need to correct inadequate or incorrect information about ethnic groups; and (5) legal, having the necessary qualifications to provide services to ethnic populations as exemplified by state licensing laws. Before considering the approaches to training people to work with ethnic populations, it is useful to consider the barriers to incorporating such training into training programs.

Education and Training Issues and Barriers

An analysis of the barriers to implementing content and training experiences into graduate and professional programs can be organized around several independent yet interlocking levels (Aponte & Clifford, 1993; Hammond & Yung, 1993): (1) societal and community level; (2) institutional level (e.g., university or college in which the psychology training program is housed) and departmental or program level (e.g., where the actual clinical, counseling, or school psychology training occurs); and (3) individual level (e.g., instructional level through which an understanding and knowledge and skills in working with ethnic populations is imparted to graduate students). A discussion of each of these levels follows.

Societal and Community Level Barriers

The societal and national arena appear to be far removed from the day-to-day ethnic course offerings and training. Yet, the economic and political climate can have a direct impact on ethnic training (Diaz, 1990). Jones (1985) pointed out how the Reagan administration budget cuts had a detrimental impact on training support for ethnic groups. In addition, during times of shrinking academic budgets competing for limited economic resources, a tendency exists to amplify both fears of things different as well as reinforcing peoples attraction to the familiar (Hemstone & Jaspars, 1982; Judd & Park, 1988; Park & Rothbart, 1982). As such, universities, colleges, departments, and programs may find themselves in either a status quo or a retrenchment mode with respect to these novel and nontraditional areas of study.

Beliefs, attitudes, and actions, rather than being directed at being supportive of ethnic groups, have been directed against them, in some cases resulting in the rolling back or undermining of the civil rights gains of the 1960s and 1970s. When strong interest and incentives (both positive and negative) for addressing ethnic issues wax and wane at the societal and national levels, the impact eventually trickles down to the university level. Such incentives are often necessary to ensure implementation of required changes in universities, departments, and programs (Casas, 1985; LaFromboise & Foster, 1992; Ridley, 1985). Certain beliefs and attitudes result in a negative climate for the inclusion of ethnic issues in curricula and contribute to the declining ethnic enrollment in psychology programs (Wyatt & Parham, 1985).

Institutional, Departmental, and Program Barriers

Universities and colleges often mirror the prevailing values, beliefs, and attitudes of society and the community in which they reside. They may reflect these in racist attitudes and in the standards, policies, and procedures these institutions use (Payne, 1984). The criteria used, efforts made, and successes achieved by institutions in recruiting ethnic faculty and graduate students will influence the climate for offering courses on cultural diversity within these institutions. Artificial barriers such as the use of Graduate Record Examination (GRE) cutoff scores that have little relationship to success in graduate school performance hamper progress in this area (Astin, 1982; Casas, 1985; Diaz, 1990). Administrative obstacles such as excessive application fees can make it difficult for some ethnic students to apply to graduate school.

Departments and programs also reflect the values, beliefs, and attitudes of the universities and colleges in which they reside. They add a different dimension in that they are of crucial importance in making decisions that will have a more direct impact on ethnic persons and on the training of psychology graduate students to work with ethnic populations. Departments and programs make decisions about (1) recruitment, promotion, and tenure of ethnic faculty; (2) recruitment, retention, and graduation of ethnic students; and (3) the content and training experiences provided. Their general climate and openness to cultural diversity is reflected in each of these decisions.

It is not unusual, for example, for departments and programs to have more stringent requirements and standards than the graduate schools and colleges in which they are housed because of the large number of psychology majors and applicant pool candidates. To select students below the 1200–1300 total Quantitative and Verbal Graduate Record Examination (GRE) scores and to use nontraditional admission procedures appears to "lower standards" (Cases, 1985). While departments and programs are aware of the limited validity and predictability of GRE scores and accept minority students below the 1200–1300 range, this can lead to the perception that ethnic students are not meeting "minimum standards" and are of inferior quality, when in fact they can compete with the White graduate students and do equally well in the program.

Ethnic faculty, as previously mentioned, continue to be underrepresented in psychology departments and training settings, with little change over the last decade in the percentage of minority faculty (Bernal, 1990; Ricardo & Holden, 1994). Those departments and programs that have minority faculty often assign these ethnic faculty to teach the "cultural diversity" course. Such administrative and curriculum decisions have the impact of encapsulating the course and exposing students to limited content and role models in the area, even if it is a required course. Often the "cultural diversity" course is not required, and those students who could benefit most do not take the course.

Ethnic faculty are typically asked to work with ethnic students under the supposition that these students will work better with them in comparison to their White colleagues. Nor is it unusual for ethnic faculty to be on "minority committees" that have as their mandate the recruitment and retention of ethnic graduate students (Olmedo, 1990). Such efforts are important in having ethnic faculty serve as role models and mentors, and in increasing awareness of diversity issues within departments and programs (Aponte, 1990). However, such activities also have the effects of undermining the responsibility and minimizing the role of White faculty and students in their commitment to multiculturalism and placing an undue burden on ethnic faculty members and jeopardizing their chances for promotion and tenure (Suinn & Witt, 1982).

Plans to address student and faculty recruitment and retention tend to be more common at the university level than within the psychology departments per se. As of mid-1990, nearly 40 percent of psychology departments had no departmental plan for attracting ethnic group students, and 30 percent had no such plan at the university level (Guzman & Messenger, 1991). Worse yet, nearly 75 percent of psychology programs had no plan for ethnic group faculty retention. Such university-level ethnic group faculty retention programs have yet to be established at over 55 percent of universities containing a psychology program.

Individual-Level Barriers

At the individual level, a number of forces are present that also can have a detrimental impact on training people to work with ethnic populations. From the field of social psychology, it is known how people operate in social situations to maintain their misguided and distorted views of others. The work of Festinger (1957) regarding cognitive dissonance and Sweeney and Gruber (1984) around selective avoidance and exposure is germane to this discussion. Such research has demonstrated that people tend to seek information that will confirm their current world view and actively tend to avoid information that is potentially at odds with this view, especially where controversial and sensitive issues are involved (Bodenhausen & Wyer, 1985; Fisk & Taylor, 1984). Such processes can operate to maintain racist attitudes.

Also contributing to barriers at the individual level are several phenomena that have emerged from research on cognition and memory processes. This research has identified a number of mechanisms such as attribution error, self-serving bias, actor–observer effects, and selective recall that can have an effect on one's attitudes and behaviors toward ethnic groups (Jellison & Greene, 1981; Loftus, 1983; Reeder, 1982; Safer, 1980). Such phenomena can lead people to make more internal than external attributions regarding the difficulties experienced by ethnic persons, to see themselves as having a more positive view toward ethnic persons than may actually be the case, and to promulgate the assumption that they can "handle better" the situational difficulties experienced by ethnic persons.

When curricula are built into training programs, the content may ignore the cultural heritage of ethnic groups; depict them as inferior, powerless, passive, and unmotivated; and present these groups as experiencing a plethora of moral, social, and psychological problems (King, Moody, Thompson, & Bennett, 1983). The strengths inherent in ethnic families may be minimized or completely disregarded, with the White nuclear family being held up as the standard of comparison. Ethnic persons may be presented as homogeneous groups without recognizing the vast differences that may exist in the backgrounds, experiences, and psychological makeup that exists across and within African Americans, Hispanics, Asian Americans, and Native Americans (see Chapter 1).

The predominant view in the content of courses is a Eurocentric perspective. Other views, such as Afrocentric perspectives, are either ignored or viewed with disdain. Emphasis on an "Anglo" point of view diminishes the understanding and appreciation of racial, cultural, and language values in our training programs (Arredondo-Dowd & Gonsalves, 1980). Trimble, Mackey, LaFromboise, and France (1983) argue that psychology's tradition of ignoring the relevance of culture to understanding and helping people is a major obstacle to a multicultural curriculum and training. Associated frequently with these notions is the assumption that ethnic populations (particularly recent immigrants) should "Americanize" and assimilate into this country. This idea shows little respect for a variety of cultures and the values, beliefs, attitudes, and behaviors that characterize them.

Several other obstacles may emerge at the individual level. These may include racist values and attitudes of instructors, supervisors, and trainees, and fear of "overidentification" with the ethnic client, and the lack of hope for ethnic clients (Barbarin, 1984; Evans, 1985). Racist attitudes may be reflected in erroneous beliefs and negative attitudes about ethnic groups (Smits & Patterson, 1976). The fear of overidentification can result in reduced empathy with ethnic faculty, students, and clients. The lack of hope for ethnic groups may manifest itself in limited expectations for change, improvement, success, and growth in ethnic faculty, students, and clients. All these factors have the effect of distancing faculty and students from ethnic persons and maintaining misguided and distorted views of each other.

Enhancing Ethnic Education and Training

It is essential to address the barriers in order to incorporate ethnic education and training effectively into graduate and professional programs. Addressing such barriers requires an assessment of their nature and extent at the institutional, departmental, program, and individual levels (Aponte & Clifford, 1993). The intercultural sensitivity model developed by M. J. Bennett (1986) provides a useful framework for assessing these barriers. The use of needs assessment approaches that have been developed in the program evaluation field can serve as the tools through which relevant data on these barriers can be collected (Aponte, 1983).

Framework for Assessing Intercultural Sensitivity

M. J. Bennett (1986) has proposed an approach to training for intercultural sensitivity that can be useful in the process of assessing how ethnic populations are viewed. He identified six stages (Denial, Defense, Minimization, Acceptance, Adaptation, and Integration) that vary from ethnocentric to ethnorelativistic positions, as one moves from the Denial to Integration stages on a developmental continuum. At each of these stages, the person has a particular view of how cultural differences are construed, which subsequently has an impact on their sensitivity to diverse groups and how they communicate with these groups.

At the early stages in the developmental continuum, the person or group assumes a parochial position to the differences between themselves and ethnic persons, evaluates these differences negatively, and later assumes a universalist position in minimizing differences between themselves and ethnic groups (M. J. Bennett, 1986). Later stages on the continuum involve acceptance of differences between Whites and ethnic groups, adaptation to these differences, and integration of these differences into one's world view of ethnic persons. Though not explicitly stated, it is assumed that the stage in which one finds oneself can be affected by the situational context.

The stage of intercultural sensitivity can be identified through a variety of mechanisms. At the departmental and programmatic level, for example, the existence of ethnic faculty and graduate students, the existence of structures such as "diversity committees," and specific course offerings on diversity provide some clues to the intercultural sensitivity stage. Detailed perusal of course content can reveal how ethnic groups are regarded. At the individual level, identification of administrators, faculty, and students' beliefs, attitudes, racial identity (Sabnani, Ponterotto, & Borodovsky, 1991), and behaviors toward different ethnic groups by means of survey, key informant, and nominal group needs assessment procedures (Aponte, 1983) could provide a picture of their stage of development.

The proposed analysis of intercultural sensitivity is directed at multiple levels (e.g., university, department, program, faculty, students). Each of these levels is discrete yet interconnected; changes directed at each level are assumed to affect all levels. Changes in university and departmental policies and procedures, for example, can have an impact on all faculty and students. Conversely, changes in the values, beliefs, and attitudes of students and faculty can have an impact on the department and university. Such changes can occur through retreats, workshops, and inservice training of administrators, faculty, and staff, and through the use of expert consultants.

Changing the values, attitudes, and beliefs of administrators, staff, faculty, and students is only one step in the process of developing and implementing ethnic content and training experiences into graduate and professional programs. The previously identified barriers, some of which are institutional and organizational, need to be addressed. Recruiting, hiring and promoting ethnic faculty, and recruiting and retaining ethnic graduate students is essential to providing a critical mass that ensures that ethnic issues and content are addressed in training programs. Universities, departments, and programs need to make a commitment and provide the necessary financial support to hire, recruit, and support ethnic faculty and graduate students.

Education and Training Models and Methods

J. M. Bennett (1986) has identified several models for cross-cultural training that provide a framework for organizing courses and training experiences. According to Bennett, cross-cultural training can be divided into three broad models, Orientation, Training, and Education, with each model having a different focus, content, and process. For example, the process for the Orientation model would be intellectual, that of the Training model experiential, and that of the Education model a combination of intellectual and experiential. Each component of each model can be linked to specific education and training strategies.

A number of specific education and training strategies (see Table 17-2) for working with ethnic groups have also been identified by scholars in the field (Copeland, 1982; LaFromboise & Foster, 1992). These strategies can be divided into six categories: (1) culture-specific events such as presentations and colloquium on ethnicity; (2) workshops involving one- to three-day training experiences on ethnicity; (3) interdisciplinary approaches (taking courses in other related disciplines); (4) separate courses designed to cover ethnicity issues; (5) the area of concentration approach, in which a variety of didactic courses and practicum experiences in

TABLE 17-2   Strategies for Incorporating Ethnic Content and Experiences into Graduate and Professional Training Programs

Training Strategies	Description of Strategy	Training Model Emphasized
Cultural specific events approach	Presentations and colloquium	Orientation model
Workshop approach	Extended training experienced	Training model
Interdisciplinary approach	Courses in related disciplines	Orientation model
Separate courses approach	Courses with specific ethnic content	Orientation model
Area of concentration approach	Organized courses and training experiences	Education model
Integration approach	Ethnic content embedded in all courses	Orientation model

working with ethnic groups is provided; and (6) the integration approach, in which content and experiences on ethnicity are imbedded in all core courses.

Each of these specific education and training strategies can be grouped under the three models previously identified by J. M. Bennett (1986). For example, culture-specific events can be placed in the Orientation model, the workshop approach in the Training model, and the area of concentration approach under the Education model. Each strategy varies in its focus, content, and process. Of particular importance is the process component—that is, how much of the process is intellectual, experiential, or a combination of the two. Too often, the emphasis is placed on ethnic content, and this may not even be well presented. Training programs need to have a balance of content and experiential learnings.

Education and Training Components

What are the education and training components that must be considered in designing an ethnically relevant curriculum? Ridley (1985) has proposed a three-dimensional model that can be used as a framework for such a task. The three dimensions of this model are (1) population target (e.g., African Americans, Hispanics, Asian/Pacific Islanders, Native Americans, Panhuman population); (2) intervention target (e.g., individual, family, group, community); and (3) curriculum (e.g., theory, research, practice). The Panhuman population category refers to those universally applied variables that enhance cross-cultural understanding (Ridley, 1985).

It may not be possible to incorporate all elements of this model into training programs. For some programs, it is best to focus on those ethnic groups that are in close proximity to the training program. Programs in South Florida or Southwest Texas, for example, could specialize in training graduate students to work with Hispanic populations. However, such programs should be designed so that the knowledge and skills acquired in working with these populations could be extrapolated to other ethnic groups. Such a transfer of knowledge and skills is particularly important with the changing demographic profile of this country (see Chapter 1) and the mobility of professionals across the country.

Training all graduate students in a variety of intervention strategies is desirable in general, and in particular for students who eventually will be working with ethnic populations. At times, family and group interventions are called for in working with ethnic groups (see Chapters 6 and 7). On other occasions community interventions utilizing prevention and consultation efforts are appropriate (see Chapter 8). Unfortunately, not all of these intervention strategies are equally developed, either general or specifically with ethnic groups, nor are all programs equipped to provide such training. Only recently have researchers and practitioners in family, group, and community approaches begun to pay attention to ethnic populations.

Integrating ethnic theory, research, and practice is fundamentally important (Bernal, Bernal, Martinez, Olmedo, & Santisteban, 1983; LaFromboise & Foster, 1992; Ridley, 1985). In general, programs struggle to integrate these three components, and to integrate ethnic content and experiences is even more difficult, in part because of the limited empirical psychological research on ethnic populations. There are too few researchers studying ethnic populations and variables. In existing empirical studies, the sample sizes are often too small and unrepresentative, the measures and instruments biased, the research designs inappropriate, and the findings erroneously interpreted.

Specific curriculum, course, and training experiences for training students to work with ethnic groups have been described in the literature (Anderson, Bass, Munford, & Wyatt, 1977; Green, 1981; López et al., 1989; McDavis & Parker, 1977; Mio & Morris, 1990; Parker, Bingham, & Fukuyama, 1985; Payne, 1984). Such descriptions typically present a sequence of courses and training experiences that provide a historical and cultural context for ethnic populations, delineate the types of problems and issues encountered by these groups, and discuss and train students to provide appropriate and effective interventions to address these problems and issues. The importance of mentorship, particularly for ethnic students, has also been pointed out by a number of scholars (Aponte, 1990; Atkinson, Neville, & Casas, 1991).

The need to deal with therapists' beliefs and attitudes toward ethnic groups and difficult client–therapist interactions has been noted by a number of writers (Barbarin, 1984; Evans, 1985; Hunt, 1987). Such training requires moving beyond "knowing that" to "knowing how" to work with ethnic groups (Johnson, 1987). This type of knowledge requires experiential training which allows for an exploration of one's own beliefs, attitudes, behavior, and interactions with ethnic persons. The Triad Training Model developed by Pedersen (1978), the Multiethnic Counselor Education Curriculum developed by Johnson (1987), the Culture Shock Model of Merta, Stringham, and Ponterotto (1988), and the computer-based client simulation program developed by Lichtenberg, Hummel, and Schaffer (1984) serve such a purpose.

Education and Training Guidelines

The importance of educating and training graduate students and psychologists to work with ethnic populations no longer should be an issue. As has been noted in this chapter and elsewhere in this book, the changing demographic profile and needs of African Americans, Hispanics, Asian/Pacific Islanders, and Native Americans demand that curriculum, courses, and training experiences be designed and changed so as to train all students effectively to work with these groups. For those psychologists who have completed their formal academic education, such training can be achieved through continuing education courses, workshops, and training experiences.

As is evident from this chapter, incorporating ethnic content and training experiences cannot be achieved without addressing the barriers to such efforts at multiple levels: societal, community, university, department, program, and individual (Aponte & Clifford, 1993). Such an effort requires a process of rigorous self-examination and evaluation that may require forming committees, task forces, or bringing in outside consultants. From this process a commitment to training in this area needs to emerge. Although the training goals, objectives, models, and methods can vary, there are a number of guidelines that should be followed in achieving these goals.

It is imperative that the goals and objectives of such an education and training effort be clearly articulated and documented in writing (Ridley, 1985). The development of such goals and objectives needs to be as broad based as possible (e.g., community, university, college, department, program). Involvement of individuals from these multiple levels ensures a broad base of commitment to such efforts, allows for a channeling of limited resources and energy into this area, begins to identify individuals who can serve as research and clinical mentors, and identifies training opportunities outside and inside the institution as placement sites for working with ethnic populations (LaFromboise & Foster, 1992).

Efforts to recruit and retain ethnic faculty and graduate students need to continue (Bernal, 1992; Blount, Frank, & Calhoun, 1992; Jenkins, 1992; Myers, Taylor, & Davila, 1992; Puente et al., 1993; Ricardo & Holden, 1994; Ridley, 1985). Such efforts are required at various levels within the university (Olmedo, 1990). Continued pressure from outside the university through professional organizations such as the APA Committee on Accreditation (Aponte, 1992), funding sources (such as National Institute of Mental Health) through state laws and licensing and certification boards also needs to occur. Recruitment of ethnic students needs to assume a long-term perspective, with students being encouraged and supported to enter psychology as early as elementary and middle school (Jenkins, 1992; Turnbull, 1986).

Even if the recruitment and promotion of ethnic faculty is reasonably successful, there will not be enough ethnic faculty and service providers to meet the needs of ethnic populations (Myers, 1992). The knowledge and skills of all faculty and practitioners will need to be enhanced in order to meet these training and service needs. To accomplish this task it will be necessary to build in "a system of rewards and incentives" in order to encourage faculty to improve their cross-cultural knowledge and skills (Ridley, 1985). Such efforts could take the form of departments paying for continuing education courses and workshops, or bringing in expert consultants to provide inservice training for the faculty.

Departments and training programs need to develop a comprehensive and coherent plan for educating and training students to become "culturally proficient" to work with ethnic populations (Bernal, 1992). Such training involves a number of elements including a set of attitudes that values diverse cultures. Programs need to embrace the concept of *affirmative diversity*—that is, affirming the value of human diversity (Jones, 1990). In addition, training needs to incorporate ethnic content that directly relates to the basic clinical skills taught in all programs, and the coordination of ethnically relevant didactic and practicum experiences (LaFromboise & Foster, 1992). Mechanisms for incorporating research findings and new knowledge on ethnic groups also need to be incorporated into programs (Wong, Kim, Lim, & Morishima, 1983).

Training all students to be culturally proficient calls for a required series of courses and training experiences. Although this can be achieved in a number of ways, one effective way is through the integration approach (Chunn, Dunston, & Ross-Sheriff, 1983; Copeland, 1982; LaFromboise & Foster, 1992; Ridley, 1985). This approach involves integrating cultural content in every course in the department. It involves all faculty; bridges theory, research, and practice; and incorporates intellectual and experiential components into the training. Achieving such a goal is impossible without educating and training existing faculty and supervisors on ethnic issues.

Departments of psychology periodically need to review their ethnic training goals and objectives (Ridley, 1985). Such a process should include an assessment of barriers impeding progress toward those goals and objectives. The evaluation can be carried out by governance groups or relevant committees (e.g., ethnic committee, curriculum committee) within the department. Once obstacles are identified, then action should be taken to change the situation. The evaluation can also be competency-based. A number of writers have addressed the specific competencies required to work with ethnic populations (Arrendondo, 1985; Copeland, 1983; Ivey, 1977; LaFromboise, Coleman, & Hernandez, 1991).

The changes that have occurred in the field to date have been limited, and the importance of taking a broad and long-term perspective in educating and training psychologists to work with ethnic populations has been underscored in this chapter. Such a perspective involves changing beliefs, attitudes, and behaviors at multiple levels; increasing the number of ethnic faculty and students; and changing and developing curriculum that allows ethnic content to be embedded in the theoretical, research, and practice components of training programs. The task may appear onerous; nevertheless, the profession needs to accelerate its efforts if it is to train culturally competent ethnic and White psychologists to meet the needs of ethnic populations in the year 2000.

References

American Psychological Association. (1982). *Survey of graduate departments of psychology.* Washington, DC: Author.

American Psychological Association. (1987). Resolutions approved by the National Conference on Graduate Education in Psychology. *American Psychologist, 42,* 1070–1084.

Anderson, G., Bass, B. A., Munford, P. R., & Wyatt, G. E. (1977). A seminar on the assessment and treatment of Black patients. *Professional Psychology, 8,* 340–348.

Aponte, J. F. (1983). Need assessment: The state of the art and future directions. In R. A. Bell, M. Sundel, J. F. Aponte, S. A. Murrell, & E. Lin (Eds.), *Assessing human service needs: Concepts, methods, and applications* (pp. 285–302). New York: Human Sciences Press.

Aponte, J. F. (1990, August). *Mentoring ethnic minority students and faculty: Issues and recommendations.* Paper presented at the Ninety-eighth annual convention of the American Psychological Association, Boston.

Aponte, J. F. (1992). The role of APA accreditation in enhancing cultural diversity in graduate and professional training programs. In S. D. Johnson, Jr., & R. T. Carter (Eds.), *The 1992 Teachers College Winter Roundtable Conference Proceedings: Addressing cultural issues in an organizational context* (pp. 73–90). New York: Columbia University.

Aponte, J. F., & Clifford, J. P. (1993). Incorporating ethnically diverse content and training into predominately White graduate and professional programs: Dealing with inertia and resistance. In S. D. Johnson, Jr., R. T. Carter, E. I. Sicalides, & T. R. Buckley (Eds.), *The 1993 Teachers College Winter Roundtable Conference Proceedings: Training for cross-cultural competence* (pp. 22–26). New York: Columbia University.

Arredondo, P. (1985). Cross-cultural counselor education and training. In P. Pedersen (Ed.), *Handbook of cross-cultural counseling and therapy* (pp. 281–289). Westport, CT: Greenwood Press.

Arredondo-Dowd, P. M., & Gonsalves, J. (1980).

Preparing culturally effective counselors. *Personnel and Guidance Journal, 58,* 657–661.

Astin, A. (1982). *Minorities in American higher education.* San Francisco: Jossey-Bass.

Atkinson, D. R. (1983). Ethnic minority representation in counselor education. *Counselor Education and Supervision, 23,* 7–19.

Atkinson, D. R., Neville, H., & Casas, A. (1991). The mentorship of ethnic minorities in professional psychology. *Professional Psychology: Research and Practice, 22,* 336–338.

Barbarin, O. A. (1984). Racial themes in psychotherapy with Blacks: Effects of training in the attitude of Black and White psychiatrists. *American Journal of Social Psychiatry, 4,* 13–20.

Bennett, J. M. (1986). Models of cross-cultural training. *International Journal of Intercultural Relations, 10,* 117–134.

Bennett, M. J. (1986). A developmental approach to training for intercultural sensitivity. *International Journal of Intercultural Relations, 10,* 179–196.

Bernal, G., Bernal, M. E., Martinez, A. C., Olmedo, E. L., & Santisteban, D. (1983). Hispanic mental health curriculum for psychology. In J. C. Chunn II, P. J. Dunston, & F. Ross-Sheriff (Eds.), *Mental health and people of color: Curriculum development and change* (pp. 65–94). Washington, DC: Howard University Press.

Bernal, M. E. (1990). Ethnic mental health training: Trends and issues. In F. C. Serafica, A. I. Schwebel, R. K. Russell, P. D. Isaac, & L. B. Meyers (Eds.), *Mental health of ethnic minorities* (pp. 249–274). New York: Praeger.

Bernal, M. E. (1992, May). *Status of minority training in psychology: A decade of progress.* Invited address, Rocky Mountain Psychological Association Meeting, Boise, Idaho.

Bernal, M. E., & Padilla, A. M. (1982). Status of minority curricula and training in clinical psychology. *American Psychologist, 37,* 780–787.

Blount, R. L., Frank, N. C., & Calhoun, K. C. (1992). The recruitment and retention of minority students. *The Clinical Psychologist, 45,* 1–3.

Bodenhausen, G. V., & Wyer, R. S. (1985). Effects of stereotypes on decision making and information processing strategies. *Journal of Personality and Social Psychology, 48,* 267–282.

Bourg, E. F., Bent, R. J., McHolland, J., & Stricker, G. (1989). Standards and evaluation in the education and training of professional psychologists: The National Council of Schools of Professional Psychology Mission Bay Conference. *American Psychologist, 44,* 66–72.

Boxley, R., & Wagner, N. (1971). Clinical psychology training programs and minority groups: A survey. *Professional Psychology, 2,* 75–81.

Brammer, L., Alcorn, J., Birk, J., Gazda, G., Hurst, J., LaFromboise, T., Newman, R., Osipow, S., Packard, T., Romero, D., & Scott, N. (1988). Organizational and political issues in counseling psychology: Recommendations for change. *The Counseling Psychologist, 16,* 407–422.

Brown, S. V. (1988). *Increasing minority faculty: An elusive goal.* Princeton, NJ: Educational Testing Service.

Casas, J. M. (1985). The status of racial- and ethnic-minority counseling. A training perspective. In P. Pedersen (Ed.), *Handbook of cross cultural counseling and therapy* (pp. 267–273). Westport, CT: Greenwood Press.

Chunn, J., Dunston, P., & Ross-Sheriff, F. (1983). *Mental health and people color: Curriculum development and change.* Washington, DC: Howard University Press.

Collins, F. L., Jr., Green, V., & Chaney, J. M. (1992). Clinical psychology training for American Indians. *The Clinical Psychologist, 45,* 35–44.

Copeland, E. J. (1982). Minority populations and traditional counseling programs: Some alternatives. *Counselor Education and Supervision, 21,* 187–193.

Copeland, E. J. (1983). Cross-cultural counseling and psychotherapy: A historical perspective, implications for research and training. *The Personnel and Guidance Journal, 62,* 10–15.

Diaz, E. (1990). Barriers to minorities in the field of psychology and strategies for change. In G. Stricker, E. Davis-Russell, E. Bourg, E. Duran, W. R. Hammond, J. McHolland, K. Polite, & B. E. Vaughn (Eds.), *Toward ethnic diversification in psychology education and training* (pp. 77–88). Washington, DC: American Psychological Association.

Dong, T., Wong, H., Callao, M., Nishihara, A., & Chin, R. (1978). National Asian American Psychology Training Conference. *American Psychologist, 33,* 691–692.

Evans, D. A. (1985). Psychotherapy and Black patients: Problems of training, trainees, and trainers. *Psychotherapy: Theory, Research and Practice, 22,* 457–460.

Festinger, L. (1957). *A theory of cognitive dissonance,* Evanston, IL: Row Peterson.

Fisk, S. T., & Taylor, S. E. (1984). *Social cognition.* Reading, MA: Addison-Wesley.

Gary, L. E., & Weaver, G. D. (Eds.). (1991). *A multidisciplinary national conference on clinical training for services to mentally ill ethnic minorities. Proceedings.* Washington, DC: Howard University, Institute for Urban Affairs and Research.

Green, L. (1981). Training psychologists to work with minority clients: A prototype model with Black clients. *Professional Psychology, 12,* 732–739.

Guzman, L. P., & Messenger, L. C. (1991). *Recruitment and retention of ethnic minority students and faculty: A survey of doctoral programs in psychology.* Washington, DC: American Psychological Association.

Hammond, W. R., & Yung, B. (1993). Minority student recruitment and retention practices among schools of professional psychology: A national survey and analysis. *Professional Psychology: Research and Practice, 24,* 3–12.

Hemstone, A., & Jaspars, J. (1982). Explanations for racial discrimination: The effect of group decision on intergroup attributions. *European Journal of Social Psychology, 12,* 1–16.

Howard, A., Pion, G. M., Gottfredson, G. D., Flattau, P. E., Oskamp, S., Pfaffin, S. M., Bray, D. W., & Burnstein, A. G. (1986). The changing face of American psychology: A report from the Committee on Employment and Human Resources. *American Psychologist, 41,* 1311–1327.

Hunt, P. L. (1987). Black clients: Implications for supervision of trainees. *Psychotherapy, 24,* 114–119.

Ivey, A. E. (1977). Cultural expertise: Toward a systematic outcome criteria in counseling and psychological education. *The Personnel and Guidance Journal, 55,* 296–302.

Jellison, J. M., & Green, J. (1981). A self-presentation approach to the fundamental attribution error: The norm of internality. *Journal of Personality and Social Psychology, 40,* 643–649.

Jenkins, J. O. (1992). The recruitment of Black students at psychology departments of predominantly White institutions of higher education. *The Clinical Psychologist, 45,* 45–49.

Johnson, S. D., Jr. (1987). Knowing that versus knowing how: Toward achieving expertise through multicultural training and counseling. *The Counseling Psychologist, 15,* 320–331.

Jones, J. M. (1985). The sociopolitical context of clinical training in psychology: The ethnic minority case. *Psychotherapy: Theory, Research, and Practice, 22,* 453–456.

Jones, J. M. (1990). Invitational address: Who is training our ethnic minority psychologists, and are they doing it right? In G. Stricker, E. Davis-Russel, E. Bourg, E. Duran, W. R. Hammond, J. McHolland, K. Polite, & B. E. Vaughn (Eds.), *Toward ethnic diversification in psychology education and training* (pp. 17–34). Washington, DC: American Psychological Association.

Jones, J. M., Goertz, M. E., & Kuh, C. V. (Eds.). (1992). *Minorities in graduate education: Pipeline policy and practice.* Princeton, NJ: Educational Testing Service.

Judd, C. M., & Park, B. (1988). Outgroup homogeneity: Judgments of variability at the individual and group levels. *Journal of Personality and Social Psychology, 54,* 778–788.

King, L. M., Moody, S., Thompson, O., & Bennett, M. (1983). Black psychology reconsidered: Notes toward curriculum development. In J. C. Chunn II, P. J. Donston, F. Ross-Sheriff (Eds.), *Mental health and people of color* (pp. 3–22). Washington, DC: Howard University Press.

Kohout, J., & Pion, G. (1990). Participation of ethnic minorities in psychology. In G. Stricker, E. Davis-Russel, E. Bourg, E. Duran, R. Hammond, T. McHolland, K. Polite, & B. Vaughn (Eds.), *Toward ethnic diversity in psychology education and training* (pp. 153–165). Washington, DC: American Psychological Association.

LaFromboise, T. D., Coleman, H. L. K., & Hernandez, A. (1991). Development and factor structure of the Cross-Cultural Counseling Inventory—Revised. *Professional Psychology Research and Practice, 22,* 380–388.

LaFromboise, T. D., & Foster, S. L. (1992). Cross-cultural training: Scientist-practitioner model and methods. *The Counseling Psychologist, 20,* 472–489.

Lichtenberg, J. W., Hummel, T. J., & Shaffer, W. F. (1984). Client 1: A computer simulation for use in counselor education and research. *Counselor Education and Supervision, 24,* 155–167.

Loftus, E. F. (1983). Silence is not golden. *American Psychologist, 38,* 564–572.

López, S. R., Grover, K. P., Holland, D., Johnson, M. J., Kain, C. D., Kanel, K., Mellins, L. A., & Rhyne, M. C. (1989). Development of culturally sensitive psychotherapists. *Professional Psychology: Research and Practice, 20,* 369–376.

McDavis, R. J., & Parker, M. (1977). A course on counseling ethnic minorities: A model. *Counselor Education and Supervision, 17,* 146–149.

Merta, R. J., Stringham, E. M., & Ponterotto, J. G. (1988). Simulating cultural shock in counselor trainees: An experiential exercise for cross-cultural training. *Journal of Counseling and Development, 66,* 242–245.

Mio, J. S., & Morris, D. R. (1990). Cross-cultural issues in psychology training programs: An invitation for discussion. *Professional Psychology: Research and Practice, 21,* 434–441.

Myers, H. F. (1992). Overview and historical perspectives on ethnic minority clinical training in psychology. *The Clinical Psychologist, 45,* 5–12.

Myers, H. F., Taylor, S., & Davila, J. (1992). The recruitment and training of ethnic minority clinical psychologists in a multicultural context: The UCLA program. *The Clinical Psychologist, 45,* 23–33.

Myers, H. F., Wohlford, P., Guzman, L. P., & Echemendia, R. J. (Eds.), (1991). *Ethnic minority perspectives on clinical training and services in psychology.* Washington, DC: American Psychological Association.

Olmedo, E. L. (1990). Minority faculty development: Issues in retention and promotion. In G. Stricker, E. Davis-Russell, E. Bourg, E. Duran, E. R. Hammond, J. McHolland, K. Polite, & B. E. Vaughn (Eds.), *Toward ethnic diversification in psychology education and training* (pp. 95–104). Washington, DC: American Psychological Association.

Park, B., & Rothbart, M. (1982). Perception of outgroup homogeneity and levels of social categorization: Memory for the subordinate attributes of in-group and out-group members. *Journal of Personality and Social Psychology, 42*, 1051–1068.

Parker, W. M., Bingham, R. P., & Fukuyama, M. (1985). Improving cross-cultural effectiveness of counselor trainees. *Counselor Education and Supervision, 24*, 349–352.

Payne, C. (1984). Multicultural education and racism in American schools. *Theory into Practice, 23*, 124–131.

Pedersen, P. (1978). Four dimensions of cross cultural skill in counselor training. *The Personnel and Guidance Journal, 56*, 480–484.

Pion, G. M., Bramblett, J. P., Jr., & Wicherski, M. (1987). *Graduate departments of psychology 1986–87: Report of the annual APA/COGDOP department survey.* Washington, DC: American Psychological Association, Office of Demographic, Employment, and Educational Research.

Pion, G., Bramblett, P., Wicherski, M., & Stapp, J. (1985). *Summary report of the 1984–85 survey of graduate departments of Psychology.* Washington, DC: American Psychological Association.

Puente, A. E., Blanch, E., Canoland, D. K., Denmark, F. L., Laman, C., Lutsky, N., Reid, P. T., & Schiayo, R. S. (1993). Toward a psychology of variance: Increasing the presence and understanding of ethnic minorities in psychology. In T. V. McGovern (Ed.), *Handbook for enhancing undergraduate psychology* (pp. 71–92). Washington, DC: American Psychological Association.

Reeder, G. D. (1982). Let's give the fundamental attribution error another chance. *Journal of Personality and Social Psychology, 43*, 341–344.

Ricardo, I. B., & Holden, E. W. (1994). Multicultural training in pediatric and clinical child psychology predoctoral internship programs. *Journal of Clinical Child Psychology, 23*, 32–39.

Ridley, C. R. (1985). Imperatives for ethnic and cultural relevance in psychology training programs. *Professional Psychology: Research and Practice, 16*, 611–622.

Russo, N. F., Olmedo, E. L., Stapp, J., & Fulcher, R. (1981). Women and minorities in psychology. *American Psychologists, 36*, 1315–1363.

Sabnani, H. B., Ponterotto, J. G., & Borodovsky, L. G. (1991). White racial identity development and cross-cultural counselor training: A stage model. *The Counseling Psychologist, 19*, 76–102.

Safer, M. A. (1980). Attributing evil to the subject, not the situation: Student reaction to Milgram's film on obedience. *Personality and Social Psychology Bulletin, 6*, 205–208.

Smits, S. J., & Patterson, D. L. (1976). The psychologist's role in the prevention and reduction of prejudice. *Professional Psychology, 7*, 84–93.

Stapp, J., Tucker, A. M., & VandenBos, G. R. (1985). Census of psychological personnel: 1983. *American Psychologist, 40*, 1317–1351.

Stricker, G., Davis-Russell, E., Bourg, E., Duran, E., Hammond, W. R., McHolland, J., Polite, K., & Vaughn, B. E. (Eds.). (1990). *Toward ethnic diversification in psychology and training.* Washington, DC: American Psychological Association.

Suinn, R. M., & Witt, J. C. (1982). Survey on ethnic minority faculty recruitment and retention. *American Psychologist, 37*, 1239–1244.

Sweeney, P. D., & Gruber, K. L. (1984). Selective exposure: Voter information preferences and the Watergate affair. *Journal of Personality and Social Psychology, 46*, 1208–1221.

Thurgood, D. H., & Weinman, J. M. (1990). *Summary report, 1989; Doctorate recipients from United States universities.* Washington, DC: National Academy Press.

Trimble, J. E., Mackey, D. H., LaFromboise, T. D., & France, G. A. (1983). American Indians, psychology and curriculum development. In J. C. Chunn II, P. J. Dunston, & F. Ross-Sheriff (Eds.), *Mental health and people of color: Curriculum development and change* (pp. 43–64). Washington, DC: Howard University Press.

Turnbull, W. W. (1986). Involvement: The key to retention. *Journal of Developmental Education, 10*, 6–11.

U.S. Bureau of Census (1992). *Current population reports, P25-1092, Population projections of the United States by age, sex, race, and Hispanic origin: 1992–2050.* Washington, DC: U.S. Government Printing Office.

Wicherski, M., & Kohout, J. (1992). *1990–91 Characteristics of graduate departments of psychology.* Washington, DC: American Psychological Association.

Wong, H. Z., Kim, L. T., Lim, D. T., & Morishima, J. K. (1983). The training of psychologists for

Asian and Pacific American Communities. In J. C. Chunn II, P. J. Dunston, & F. Ross-Sheriff (Eds.), *Mental health and people of color* (pp. 23–41). Washington, DC: Howard University Press.

Wyatt, G. E., & Parham, W. D. (1985). The inclusion of culturally sensitive course materials in graduate school and training programs. *Psychotherapy: Theory, Research, and Practice, 22,* 461–468.

Chapter *18*

Common Themes and Future Prospects

JULIAN WOHL
JOSEPH F. APONTE

The need for this book arises from the fact that great change in the ethnic character and culture of the clientele for psychological services is underway, with the rate of such change promising to accelerate dramatically in the next few decades (see Chapter 1). Appreciation of the problems involved and the skills required to cope with this transformation has made intervention and treatment of ethnic populations a topic in all disciplines conventionally identified as the "mental health" or "helping" professions. As the chapters of this book amply demonstrate, a variety of theoretical views can be brought to bear in formulating means of defining and solving problems. Virtually every chapter acknowledges that, in addition to psychological causes, the broader context of economic, political, and social forces plays a critical etiological role in the problems of clients.

The need to provide effective mental health services and treatment to ethnic groups has begun to be acknowledged by administrators, service providers, clinicians, and researchers as an ongoing issue (Cheung & Snowden, 1990; Korchin, 1980; Padilla, Ruiz, & Alverez, 1975; Sue, 1988). Ethnic persons have characteristically been underserved in the mental health system, have received inappropriate or inadequate services, and have received ineffective treatment (Acosta, Yamamoto, & Evans, 1982; Jackson, 1983; Leong, 1986; Lorion & Felner, 1986; Roll, Millen, & Martinez, 1980). The need for mental health services for and training to treat these populations will also continue to increase in the 1990s as political, socioeconomic, and societal forces continue to put these groups at risk.

In acknowledging the need to expand and modify training in the mental health fields to respond to cultural and ethnic diversity (as discussed in Chapter 17), psychology links itself to the recognition by the broader society of changes in the cultural makeup of the United States. We are experiencing and will continue to experience increasing representation of people whose ethnic roots are not European. African-American, Latino, and Asian-American groups may not accept the traditional expectations to assimilate or Americanize themselves. These groups may reject the earlier idea of integration or accept only a restricted view of it while emphasizing instead their own culturally unique identities. Native Americans, squeezed by their history in an acculturation–identity vise, also struggle to extricate and redefine themselves.

For the larger society, the danger in this revaluation of and adjustment to ethnic diversity is an increase in the animosity and conflict that, on a more brutal and violent scale, has erupted in many other pluralistic societies around the world, such as the former Soviet Union, the remains of Yugoslavia, India, and Northern Ireland. In these countries we see how violence and destruction can develop in societies contending with nationalistic, religious, and ethnic differences. One of the dangers of an uncritical national embrace of "multiculturalism" as an ideology, coupled with the denial of any positive unifying national identity to balance it, might well be a further fragmentation in United States society, and an increase in intergroup tensions and conflict.

The struggle to achieve balance between diversity and assimilation to the larger society is mirrored in the personal struggles of many individual members of ethnic groups. As noted in various chapters, they are caught between the pull of their cultural identity and the force of acculturation. This struggle may take the form of intrapersonal, intergenerational, and intergroup tensions and conflicts. In a small way, clinicians who work with clients to achieve this needed balance are dealing with a critical social problem as well as with the personal agony of clients.

In the mental health field we usually deal not with the larger societal issues directly, but with a narrower multicultural issue: the fact that we must intervene clinically in the lives of people whose ethnic and cultural characteristics differ from those of the traditional clients of mental health professions. This idea constitutes the central point of departure for this book. The authors begin there and move outward in many directions as they struggle with this problem. Despite the differences in theoretical viewpoints, specific subject matter, and modes of intervention presented, many of the same questions and problems repeatedly emerge. In this concluding chapter, we try to identify the major themes and issues most frequently found in this book. This will be followed by a discussion of the directions in which the field is moving, ideas about where it should be going, and suggestions about how to get there.

Political and Scientific Perspectives

Any student of the literature on intervention with ethnic groups in the United States will observe that most of the contributors (including the editors of and contributors to this book) have more than a dispassionate attitude toward their subject matter.

Either they are members of ethnic groups themselves and have directly experienced discrimination and oppression, or their moral outrage at the injustice historically or currently experienced by these groups propelled them toward this work. Exceptions exist, of course, but for the most part we believe that mental health professionals bring intense personal commitment to their work on interethnic and intercultural intervention.

This passion is reflected in the often-stated argument that the problems of ethnic populations require more than just conventional clinical interventions and practices. Because they often result from social and economic discrimination, the real attack on these problems must be on their societal roots. This argument says that inequity and injustice created by the social and political structure can be rectified only by changing that structure. To target individuals, placing the locus of troubles within their psychologies and asking them to change, would be to "blame the victim." This conceptualization expresses the political perspective on the sociopsychological difficulties of ethnic groups mentioned by Jones and Korchin (1982) as one of two contrasting frameworks in the field of ethnic mental health.

The political approach, imbued with moral passion and righteous anger, highlights issues of equity, fairness, and rights. In contrast is what Jones and Korchin refer to as a "cross-cultural" view (1982, pp. 3–4), a scientific framework that declares that differences in attitudes, values, and behavior among different cultural groups need to be studied and understood. Psychological functioning is comprehensible only if we understand the culture in which it is embedded. Designing effective interventions requires an understanding of the cultural context of the clients' difficulties. Both perspectives are reflected in the pages of this book. A passionate desire to improve the social position and a wish for effective political change to achieve fairer societal treatment for the groups in question pervades the text. At the same time, emotional commitment is tempered by the embrace of a scientific-clinical framework that demands a degree of detachment and a thoughtful and critical attitude.

Common Themes

We have found it convenient to divide our treatment of thematic ideas into three categories:

1. *Context* or framework, consisting of factors which determine the situation within which the intervention occurs
2. Issues more or less directly tied to the *client*
3. Issues most directly linked to the *service provider*. The distinctions between categories are not sharp. They overlap generously, and they potentially interact with each other.

Contextual Issues

This broadest of the categories refers to and includes all of the antecedent conditions and circumstances that determine the presentation of the client, as well as those situational factors that influence, define, and control the treatment process itself. They can include political, social, economic, and historical forces that have affected a particular client's ethnic group and thus, indirectly, the client, along with actual experiences of the client that stem from, and psychologically are linked directly to, membership in that group. A good example is ethnicity, which is a powerful factor in the client's life and therefore a controlling influence in the presentation of the client (see Chapter 3). Because of the importance of ethnicity to the client and possibly because of their own sensitivity on the subject, service providers need to be aware of the emotional power of this issue for the client.

Another important contextual factor is the history experienced by ethnic groups of racial abuse, discrimination, and oppression. These experiences appear to be more frequent and overt over the last decade after a period in which they were covert and hidden. Such experiences also are often reflected in contacts with community, social, and governmental organizations that lead to frustration with these institutions. These experiences can promote varying degrees of distrust, from skepticism, through suspicion, to outright hostility toward mental health agencies and service providers.

Deriving in considerable part from that discrimination history is the fact that ethnic minorities are found disproportionately to be of low socioeconomic status (see Chapters 1 and 2). Ethnic children and adolescents, women, and the elderly are overrepresented at these lower levels. They are frequently poor, have relatively less formal education, suffer employment and housing problems, and have little hope for improvement of these circumstances. The latter state, hopelessness, represents a specific kind of functioning rooted in this socioeconomic contextual feature that can have a detrimental impact on all ethnic groups.

It must be recognized, however, that not all ethnic group members are impoverished. As noted in Chapter 1, there is variability in socioeconomic status both across and within ethnic groups. Selective migration has accounted for some ethnic group members doing well, and over the last two decades the socioeconomic status of some segments of ethnic groups have improved. Some individuals who have grown up in impoverished circumstances have also exhibited remarkable resiliency in being able to function well psychologically and make contributions to their community and society (McCubbin & McCubbin, 1988).

Frustration at the failure of the majority mainstream institutions and systems to redress grievances or function fairly for them can also breed a sense of powerlessness in ethnic group members. For this reason, empowering people has become a common issue in their treatment at the individual, familial, group, and community levels. At all these levels a goal of treatment is (as for all clients regardless of ethnicity) personal empowerment—that is, to develop and nurture those inner resources that enable clients to function and act more effectively. But equally important is the recognition that for ethnic clients social and political action may be necessary pathways to overcoming powerlessness and hopelessness.

Starting from their own cultural traditions, and perhaps intensified by the discrimination tradition, ethnic groups have evolved strong, collaborative social support systems. Family (nuclear, extended, and transgenerational) seems to play a more important supportive function than majority service providers might expect on the basis of their own backgrounds (see Chapters 2 and 6). Beyond the family are various religious, social, and community organizations. Such support systems function as effective buffers and mediators of stress. Intervention agents need to appreciate and take into account this important aspect of ethnic culture (see Chapters 8 and 9).

A final contextual feature encompasses a class of cultural differences between the average White, majority, mainstream, North American service provider and clients who are either African American, Latino, Asian American, or Native American. These differences involve cognitive styles, values, beliefs, and attitudes. Conceptions of personality functioning, psychopathology, assessment, and treatment are products of our European-American cultural tradition, embodying its philosophy of science, notions of cause and effect, and values. They will not automatically be comprehended and accepted as legitimate aspects of helping, and they may conflict with conceptions of providing help, that stem from substantially different world views that are part of ethnic cultural traditions. World view differences between client and service provider can be a major barrier to intercultural understanding, communication, and effective service.

Client Factors

An individual client will undoubtedly share many of the contextual features characterizing ethnic groups in general, and many characteristics associated with a specific ethnic group. In our concern with problems of the large units we refer to as "ethnic minorities," we must not forget that the client (unless it is an institution) is always an individual person, notwithstanding instances when individuals are seen collectively, as in group and family therapy. The pithy axiom of Kluckhohn and Murray retains validity more than forty-five years after its publication: "Every man is in certain respects: (1) like all other men, (2) like some other men, and (3) like no other man" (1948, p. 35). Diversity flourishes within each ethnic group and no ethnic clients, any more than nonethnic clients or practitioners passively accept that they are identical to all other members of their group.

Although we have noted that economic hardship disproportionately besets ethnic groups in general, socioeconomic variation within groups also is a fact (see Chapter 1). Heterogeneity in employment, income, education, and housing means that intervention agents and practitioners need to treat clients as individuals on those dimensions rather than simply assume that all their ethnic clients are impoverished. Recognizing such variations in socioeconomic status also allows service providers to seek out and distinguish those issues that are a by-product of discrimination and prejudice from those that are due to economic circumstances.

Ethnic clientele can find their way into the mental health system through a number of complex routes. Economically disadvantaged ethnic groups, particularly immigrants, may not utilize the mental health system because they have access to family, indigenous networks, and other help-giving organizations and structures (Rogler, 1993; Rogler & Cortes, 1993). Some cultural groups also tend to somatize distress (Angel & Guarnaccia, 1989; Rogler, 1989) and therefore may present themselves to physicians, public health officials, and emergency rooms. Their use of these pathways can block or delay their receiving mental health services (Alegria et al., 1991).

A second major variation within ethnic groups that is vital for their adaptation, and therefore for practitioners to appreciate, is the degree of acculturation to the majority culture around them (see Chapter 2). Acculturation can have sociopolitical complications within an ethnic group that result in the criticism or condemnation of a member who has violated some criterion limit on assimilation by having gone "too far" toward the majority group. But unless the ethnic group member is to function only within the confines of the ethnic group world, some degree of acculturation is unavoidable. Ethnic group members must be able to function in each of two cultures and switch back and forth as circumstances require. For many, striking a balance between assimilation and the maintenance of cultural ethnic identity can be a core psychological issue.

Related to the questions of acculturation, assimilation, and ethnic identity are an array of language issues. For immigrants, learning the language of a new society will enhance their potential ability to function effectively in that society. For the second and third generations, language differences between themselves and their parents and grandparents can produce generational cultural tensions. Native-born persons whose original English is nonstandard or a dialect confront the same adaptation issues. To function maximally in the majority culture, they are best served by standard English; but to maintain the bond with their own tradition, they will want to remain fluent in the original dialect or nonstandard English. As with immigrant peoples, bicultural adaptation means bilingual competence and the ability to switch appropriately.

Service Provider Issues

The major problems of nonminority clinicians with ethnic clients fall in the realms of personal reactions, cultural sophistication, and professional-technical competence (American Psychological Association, 1992, 1993). Personal prejudices, stereotypes, unconscious or semiconscious derogatory attitudes, and irrational ideas about members of an ethnically different group can corrupt, contaminate, and destroy the provider's efforts to be of service. Although it is emphasized most with respect to psychotherapy, clinicians in general are advised throughout this book to scrutinize themselves and excise, or at least understand and control, their own biases.

From a purely technical viewpoint, practitioners need to recognize the limits of appropriate application of assessment techniques and the need for normative data on the population represented by their clients (see Chapter 4). Similarly, they must bear in mind that some psychotherapeutic methods may be culturally unsuitable for some ethnic clients. The editors of this book agree that clinicians require the personal flexibility that would permit them to modify their methods and adapt them to the culturally based conceptions of the client. To do so, however, calls for both the professional competence and the cultural sensitivity that would inform them when adjustment is needed.

Perhaps the broadest guidance for clinicians is that they become "cross-cultural." They are asked to understand the cultural roots and cultural boundedness of their methods, theories, and concepts of assessment, pathology, personality, intervention, and communicative habits, as well as normative assumptions, values, and beliefs about other people in the world. When they appreciate these different world views, their contributions to the majority culture, and the disparity between themselves and their clients, they are equipped to become culturally sensitive practitioners. When appropriate skills are built upon this sensitivity, then competency can be achieved.

Changes in the Field of Psychology

The need for changes in the field of psychology that will make practitioners more sensitive, responsive, and effective with ethnic populations has been underscored in this book. Changes in psychology can come about through two main sources. One of these is internal to the discipline, as reflected in professional organizations and national education and training conferences. The second source of change is external and consists of external pressures from entities such as the federal government that have the power to influence psychology and other related mental health fields by controlling funding for research and training. A brief review of each of these forces follows.

Forces Internal to Psychology

Professional organizations such as the American Psychological Association (APA) are important in determining the direction of the field. APA has recently begun to address diversity issues by increasing ethnic participation in the organization and by developing structures (e.g., divisions, committees, and offices) to address ethnic issues (Comas-Díaz, 1990). But while ethnic membership has increased over the last two decades, the percentage of ethnic representation within the association has remained about the same and is not reflective of the general population. The prospects for change are not optimistic given the limited number of ethnic students enrolled in graduate and professional programs (see Chapter 17).

Historically, national conferences have been another internal vehicle for instituting change in the field of psychology. Over the last four decades, there have been six major conferences in psychology, beginning with the Conference on Training in Clinical Psychology held in Boulder, Colorado, in 1949, during which the basic framework of the scientist-practitioner training model was put forth for psychology. Of these six conferences, the last two have been the most relevant for ethnic groups (Comas-Díaz, 1990). These are the National Conference on Levels and Patterns of Professional Training in Psychology (Vail conference) held in Vail, Colorado, in 1973

(Korman, 1976), and the National Conference on Graduate Education (Utah Conference) held in Salt Lake City, Utah, in 1987 (Bickman, 1987).

Both the Vail conference and the Utah conference passed a number of resolutions of importance to ethnic groups. The importance of training students to work with diverse populations in a pluralistic society were particularly emphasized in each conference (Comas-Díaz, 1990). In addition to emphasizing the importance of ethnic student recruitment and retention, the Utah Conference passed a number of resolutions on ethnic faculty recruitment and promotion (American Psychological Association, 1987). These resolutions were clearly aimed at increasing the number of ethnic psychologists in the discipline.

Forces External to Psychology

The involvement of the federal government in ethnic research, education and training, and service delivery issues had its origins during the 1960s. During these socially and politically turbulent times, racism began to be viewed as a public health problem that had a devastating impact on the psychological well-being and functioning of ethnic groups and that called for governmental action (Williams, 1975). In the early 1970s, ethnic professional organizations also began to pressure the federal government to take action and involve ethnic persons in decision-making roles (Parron, 1990). These forces lead to the creation of the National Institute of Mental Health (NIMH) Center for Minority Group Mental Health Programs.

Among the accomplishments of the NIMH Minority Group Mental Health Programs were: (1) provision of research initiatives and funds for studying ethnic mental health concerns; (2) creation of the Minority Fellowship Program (MFP), which provided financial support for graduate and professional students and was administered through five mental health professional associations (including APA); and (3) development of centers designed to create a sound empirical base for studying mental health issues of Blacks, Hispanics, Asian Americans/Pacific Islanders, and Native Americans. As of 1994, there are five ethnic research centers (Parron, 1990; D. L. Parron, personal communication, January 1994).

In 1985, NIMH was reorganized and a concerted effort made to include funding for research on ethnic populations and investigations by ethnic researchers in each of the newly created research divisions—Clinical Research, Basic Sciences, and Biometry and Applied Sciences (Parron, 1990). These changes tended to move research on ethnic populations into the mainstream of NIMH activities. While research funding for studies focusing on ethnic populations has increased over the last decade (D. L. Parron, personal communication, January 1994), much of the funding has shifted to high-priority areas specified by NIMH, including children, elderly people, and substance abusers (Parron, 1990). These are noteworthy and important areas for all groups and for ethnic groups in particular. However, as noted by several of the authors in this book, the pace of research directed at especially vulnerable populations (e.g., children and adolescents, women, the elderly), and contemporary problems (e.g., substance abuse, health problems, homelessness) has not been as fast as it should be.

Future Changes and Prospects

The mental health field, and psychology in particular, have been in a state of flux over the last two decades. APA has reorganized (American Psychological Association, 1988) and the American Psychological Society (APS) has been created. As noted previously in this chapter, some of these changes have been driven by internal forces, others by external events. Changes are expected to continue over the next decade. For purposes of discussion, these can be categorized under the headings of research, intervention and treatment, and education and training trends. The salient issue is how ethnic populations will be affected by these trends and how they can influence each of these complex arenas.

Research Trends

Although the quantity and quality of research on ethnic populations has been called into question (Graham, 1992; Loo, Fong, & Iwamasa, 1988; see Chapter 16), re-searchers are beginning to acknowledge that culture and ethnicity are of central importance to the delivery of mental health services, the assessment of mental health, and the treatment of ethnic clientele. Researchers also are beginning to take a multilevel approach that recognizes the role of culture and societal forces at the individual, group, and community levels. Most of the research to date has focused on only one level at a time, not fully recognizing nor investigating how each level compounds the difficulties of providing effective mental health services to ethnic populations, and confounds research efforts to grasp more fully the role of culture and societal forces in this complicated treatment process.

The difficulties with the concepts of culture, race, and ethnicity and importance of making distinctions between them have been underscored by a number of individuals (Betancourt & López, 1993; Yee, Fairchild, Weizmann, & Wyatt, 1993; Zuckerman, 1990). Betancourt and López (1993) argue that mainstream and cross-cultural investigators need to define these concepts more rigorously, measure them effectively, examine specific hypotheses, and incorporate the results within a theoretical framework. These researchers believe that both mainstream and cross-cultural psychology can assist each other in the study of culture and ethnicity and thereby advance both fields.

An integral part of research efforts also needs to be the investigation and identification of those factors that contribute to psychological dysfunction and healthy psychological functioning in ethnic individuals. Coie et al. (1993) have proposed a conceptual framework for developing a "science of prevention" that focuses on the role of *risk factors* and *protective factors* in the functioning of individuals. Such a focus is particularly relevant to ethnic populations because of the environmental and social stressors in their life (see Chapters 1 and 2) and the role of community, social networks, and family in their psychological well-being (see Chapters 6, 7, and 8).

According to Coie and his associates (1993), the "science of prevention" involves a systems perspective, emphasizes the transactions between individuals and their environments, focuses on short- and long-term process and outcome variables, and is capable of generating explanatory and predictive models of behavior. Preventive sciences research is designed to yield insights into the causes of psychological disorders and into factors that can prevent these disorders from occurring or contribute to the recovery from these disorders. A direct treatment approach is required when preventive efforts are not implemented or are not effective.

At the assessment and diagnosis level, Rogler (1993) has argued that psychiatric diagnosis needs to consider three hierarchical levels, including ". . . the role of culture in symptom assessment, the configuration of symptoms into disorders, and the diagnostic situation" (p. 407). Others within this book have pointed out succinctly how symptom presentations vary across and within groups (see Chapter 3), how certain syndromes can be found in groups such as Hispanics, Asians, and American Indians (see Chapter 9), and how the assessment process must be sensitive to and incorporate culturally relevant norms, items, and interpretations (see Chapter 4). Not to take culture into consideration at all levels in the process introduces cumulative errors into the final diagnosis (Rogler, 1993).

At the treatment level, research efforts have focused on either the client, the therapist, or the interaction between the two. Such a focus, as previously pointed out, has been found in this book. According to Helms (1990), the client-as-problem (CAP) or the therapist-as-problem (TAP) research has included several themes. The CAP perspective locates the difficulty of clinical work in the client, which emerges in two general forms in the "cultural scar hypothesis" and the "acting-out client phenomenon" (Helms, 1990, p. 172). The TAP perspective assumes that the impediments to therapeutic progress is largely due to the therapist's cultural insensitivity or prejudice. It has not been until recently that ethnic research has focused on the interaction between the two (Sue, Fujino, Hu, Li-Tze, & Takeuchi, 1991).

Future research also needs to focus on identifying those characteristics of traditional approaches (e.g., psychodynamic, behavioral, cognitive behavioral, phenomenological, interpersonal, eclectic) that apply to all cultures (Atkinson, Morten, & Sue, 1989). Research also needs to move beyond identifying these conceptual and common factor elements (Frank & Frank, 1991) to identifying conceptual frameworks and specific strategies and techniques that apply to specific ethnic groups (Jenkins & Ramsey, 1983; Sue, Zane, & Young, 1994). The specific strategies and techniques are determined in part by patient predisposing variables—for example, diagnosis, personality characteristics, and environmental circumstances (Beutler & Clarkin, 1990)—and equally by cultural characteristics of the ethnic group.

Intervention and Treatment Trends

Ethnic communities and clients often require multilevel and multimodal interventions and treatment strategies because of the complexity of needs and issues they face (Atkinson et al., 1989; Ponterotto, 1987; Vega & Murphy, 1990). Such a view has been reflected in a number of chapters in this book, including those on individual psychotherapy (Chapter 5), family approaches (Chapter 6), group methods (Chapter 7), community interventions (Chapter 8), and traditional folk and healing methods (Chapter 9). Within each of these approaches, a continuous theme, as previously pointed out in this chapter, is differentiating between those issues and processes that are internal to the individual and those that require action directed at the group, community, and society (Atkinson et al., 1989).

Several future changes in the delivery of mental health services can have an impact on ethnic populations. As noted in Chapter 8, managed health care has become the primary vehicle through which health care in general, and mental health services in particular, are being delivered. It is anticipated that such efforts to reduce service rates and the amount of service provided will continue even with the creation of a universal system of health care. Although more ethnic persons would be covered through universal health care, the types of services may be limited in order to contain costs and may still be inappropriate and ineffective as the treatment options diminish or if the services continue to be insensitive to those ethnic persons they serve.

Another change is the development of clinical practice guidelines for delivering mental health services (Clinton, McCormick, & Besteman, 1994). These guidelines have taken a variety of different forms. The Agency for Health Care Policy and Research (AHCPR) in the U.S. Department of Health and Human Services, for example, has been developing clinical practice guidelines for a variety of physical conditions and recently has been developing guidelines for the diagnosis and treatment of depression (Muñoz, Hollon, McGrath, Rehm, & VandenBos, 1994; Rush, 1993; Rush, Trivedi, Schriger, & Petty, 1992). These guidelines are designed to help health care providers recognize, diagnose, and treat depression (Schulberg & Rush, 1994). The inherent danger of trying to force culturally different patients into an inappropriate and ineffective framework can be reduced by including working with diverse populations as part of the guidelines training.

Progress is being made in incorporating cultural variables in the diagnosis of psychiatric disorders (Fabrega, 1992). A number of researchers and practitioners have been working on enhancing the cultural sensitivity and cross-cultural suitability of the new version of the American Psychiatric Association Diagnostic and Statistical Manual, fourth edition (DSM-IV) (Mezzich, Fabrega, & Kleinman, 1992; Mezzich et al., 1992). This has led to the inclusion of Appendix I in DSM-IV, which provides information on how clinicians can evaluate and report the impact of an individual's cultural context (American Psychiatric Association, 1994). The inclusion of cultural variables in psychiatric disorders and the identification of culture-bound syndromes in DSM-IV will begin to provide a cultural context for the diagnosis and treatment of a number of disorders.

A number of practitioners and researchers have also recently voiced concern about the competencies and skills needed to work with ethnic populations (Atkinson et al., 1989; Malgady, Rogler, & Costantino, 1987; Root, 1985; Sue et al., 1982; Zuniga, 1988). To help service providers deliver psychological services to ethnic and culturally diverse populations, guidelines have been developed by the Board of Ethnic Minority Affairs Task Force on the Delivery of Services to Ethnic Minority Populations (American Psychological Association, 1993). These guidelines provide a framework for recognizing the role of ethnicity and culture in the assessment and treatment process, as well as specific admonitions for appreciating and respecting cultural differences between the client and service provider.

Education and Training Trends

The need to educate and train researchers and practitioners to work with ethnic populations and issues has been recognized over the last two decades. The importance of this need has been reflected in the structures within APA created to address ethnic concerns, through the resolutions of the recent national training conferences (see Chapter 17), and through recent government and NIMH initiatives (Wohlford, 1992). These efforts have been designed either to encourage majority practitioners and researchers to work with and address ethnic and cultural issues, or to increase the number of ethnic graduate students, academicians, practitioners, and researchers. These efforts, as pointed out in this book, have achieved only limited success.

A pressing need still exists to train more ethnic psychologists (Myers, Echemendia, & Trimble, 1991), yet there is a clear realization that many of the services and much of the research focusing on ethnic populations will be carried out by White practitioners and researchers (Bernal, 1992). Such a realization underscores the importance of all graduate students being trained to work with ethnic and culturally diverse populations. Yet, over the past two decades there has been only limited success in achieving this goal (Bernal, 1990; 1992). Most programs do not have required courses and training experiences that focus on ethnic populations. Few programs come close to training students to be "culturally proficient" (Bernal, 1992). Past and recent graduates may find themselves inadequately prepared to work with culturally diverse populations. Both practitioners and researchers may thus be forced either not to work with these groups at all or to work with them without proper training and experience.

To address these education and training issues in the future, psychology will need to step forward to ensure that there is an increased pool of students and professionals in the field and that all graduate and professional students are trained to work with ethnic populations (Aponte & Clifford, 1993; Puente et al., 1993). Graduate and professional programs will also need to ensure that all students are exposed to ethnic content and trained to work with diverse populations (American Psychological Association, 1992). Such efforts will also be required in the other mental health disciplines in order to ensure their competency to work with ethnic populations.

As detailed in Chapter 17, a number of steps can be taken to train psychologists to work with ethnic populations. These steps are applicable to other mental health disciplines as well. The ethical, cultural context, legal, demographic, and scholarly imperatives identified by Ridley (1985) require that cross-cultural training be included in professional training programs. Such training can be strongly encouraged through internal program initiatives, as discussed in Chapter 17, and through external initiatives such as strengthening accreditation criteria around cultural diversity (Aponte, 1992).

Concluding Comments

Each and every ethnic person is not in need of mental health services. Many ethnic persons function very well despite the racism, discrimination, and oppression they experience. The issues and difficulties in providing services and treating African Americans, Latinos, Asian Americans, and Native Americans who need treatment do not reside with these groups. The difficulty inheres in the treatment systems, agencies, and people who manage them and provide the services. This book presents a wide-ranging survey of facts about ethnic populations, their increasing size, the concomitant increased need for services, and the interventions and treatment strategies for working with them.

This book also points out the historical failure of the mental health system and service providers to respond adequately to the needs of ethnic populations, and the relatively recent, belated efforts to acknowledge these deficiencies and to change. Efforts to change research, practice, and training advance in fits and starts, with these changes being driven by internal and external forces. The chapters identify these forces and display the difficulties and highlight gaps in knowledge and skills. Yet, despite incomplete knowledge and barriers to service delivery and treatment, positive suggestions for effective understanding and work with these ethnic populations are offered in each chapter.

Notwithstanding sincere efforts to recruit into the professions members of these groups, it remains clear that for many years to come the main source of service will be mainstream, White service providers and clinicians. This means that an overriding requirement is to build cultural and ethnic training into our educational and training systems and change the values and practices of these systems so that they embrace it as a positive necessity and not grudgingly accept it as a necessary evil. Such efforts need to occur in conjunction with addressing the racism, discrimination, and oppression (which all ethnic groups face regardless of their socioeconomic status) in the larger society.

References

Acosta, F. X., Yamamoto, J., & Evans, L. A. (1982). *Effective psychotherapy for low-income minority patients.* New York: Plenum Press.

Alegria, M., Robles, R., Freeman, D. H., Vera, M., Jimenez, A. L., Rios, C., & Rios, R. (1991). Patterns of mental health utilization among island Puerto Rican poor. *American Journal of Public Health, 81,* 875–879.

American Psychiatric Association. (1994). *Diagnostic and statistical manual of mental disorders* (4th ed.). *(DSM-IV).* Washington, DC: Author.

American Psychological Association. (1987). Resolutions approved by the National Conference on Graduate Education in Psychology. *American Psychologist, 42,* 1070–1084.

American Psychological Association. (1988). *A plan for the reorganization of the American Psychological Association.* Washington, DC: Author.

American Psychological Association. (1992). Ethical principles of psychologists and code of conduct. *American Psychologist, 47,* 1597–1611.

American Psychological Association. (1993). Guidelines for providers of psychological services to ethnic, linguistic, and culturally diverse populations. *American Psychologist, 48,* 45–48.

Angel, R., & Guarnaccia, P. (1989). Mind, body, and culture: Somatization among Hispanics. *Social Science Medicine, 28,* 1229–1238.

Aponte, J. F. (1992). The role of APA accreditation in enhancing cultural diversity in graduate and professional training programs. In S. D. Johnson, Jr., & R. T. Carter (Eds.), *The 1992 Teachers College Winter Roundtable Conference Proceedings: Addressing cultural issues in an organizational context* (pp. 73–80). New York: Columbia University.

Aponte, J. F., & Clifford, J. P. (1993). Incorporating ethnically diverse content and training into predominately White graduate and professional programs: Dealing with inertia and resistance. In S. D. Johnson, Jr., R. T. Carter, E. I. Sicalides, & T. R. Buckley (Eds.), *The 1993 Teachers College Winter Roundtable Conference Proceedings: Training for cross-cultural competence* (pp. 22–26). New York: Columbia University.

Atkinson, D. R., Morten, G., & Sue, D. W. (1989). *Counseling American minorities: A cross-cultural perspective* (3rd ed.). Dubuque, IA: Brown.

Bernal, M. E. (1990). Ethnic mental health training: Trends and issues. In F. C. Serafica, A. I. Schwebel, R. K. Russell, P. D. Isaac, & L. B. Meyers (Eds.), *Mental health of ethnic minorities* (pp. 249–274). New York: Praeger.

Bernal, M. E. (May, 1992). *Status of minority training in psychology: A decade of progress.* Invited address, Rocky Mountain Psychological Association Meeting, Boise, Idaho.

Betancourt, H., & López, S. R. (1993). The study of culture, ethnicity, and race in American psychology. *American Psychologist, 48,* 629–637.

Beutler, L. E., & Clarkin, J. F. (1990). *Systematic treatment selection: Toward targeted therapeutic interventions.* New York: Brunner/Mazel.

Bickman, L. (1987). Graduate education in psychology. *American Psychologist, 42,* 1041–1047.

Cheung, F. K., & Snowden, L. R. (1990). Community mental health and ethnic minority populations. *Community Mental Health Journal, 26,* 277–291.

Clinton, J. J., McCormick, K., & Besteman, J. (1994). Enhancing clinical practice: The role of practice guidelines. *American Psychologists, 49,* 30–33.

Coie, J. D., Watt, N. F., West, S. G., Hawkins, J. D., Asarnow, J. R., Markman, H. J., Ramey, S. L.,

Shure, M. B., & Long, B. (1993). The science of prevention: A conceptual framework and some directions for a national research program. *American Psychologist, 48,* 1013–1022.

Comas-Díaz, L. (1990). Ethnic minority mental health: Contributions and future directions of the American Psychological Association. In F. C. Serafica, A. T. Schwebel, R. K. Russell, P. D. Isaac, & L. B. Myers (Eds.), *Mental health of ethnic minorities* (pp. 275–301), New York: Praeger.

Fabrega, H., Jr. (1992). Diagnosis interminable: Toward a culturally sensitive DSM-IV. *Journal of Nervous and Mental Disease, 180,* 5–7.

Frank, J. D., & Frank, J. B. (1991). *Persuasion and healing: A comparative study of psychotherapy* (3rd ed.). Baltimore: Johns Hopkins University Press.

Graham, S. (1992). Most of the subjects were White and middle class: Trends in published research on African Americans. *American Psychologist, 47,* 629–639.

Helms, J. E. (1990). Three perspectives on counseling and psychotherapy with visible racial/ethnic group clients. In F. C. Serafica, A. J. Schwebel, R. K. Russell, P. D. Isaac, & L. B. Myers (Eds.), *Mental health of ethnic minorities* (pp. 171–201). New York: Praeger.

Jackson, A. (1983). Treatment issues for Black patients. *Psychotherapy: Theory, Research, and Practice, 20,* 143–151.

Jenkins, T. O., & Ramsey, G. A. (1983). Minorities. In M. Hersen, A. E. Kazdin, & A. S. Bellack (Eds.), *The clinical psychology handbook* (pp. 724–740), New York: Pergamon Press.

Jones, E. E., & Korchin, S. J. (Eds.). (1982). *Minority mental health.* New York: Praeger.

Kluckhohn, C., & Murray, H. A. (Eds.). (1948). *Personality in nature, society, and culture.* New York: Knopf.

Korchin, S. J. (1980). Clinical psychology and minority problems. *American Psychologist, 35,* 262–269.

Korman, M. (1976). *Levels and patterns of professional training in psychology.* Washington, DC: American Psychological Association.

Leong, F. T. L. (1986). Counseling and psychotherapy with Asian Americans: A review of the literature. *Journal of Counseling Psychology, 33,* 192–206.

Loo, C., Fong, K. T., & Iwamasa, G. (1988). Ethnicity and cultural diversity: An analysis of work published in community psychology journals, 1965–1985. *Journal of Community Psychology, 16,* 332–349.

Lorion, R. P., & Felner, R. D. (1986). Research on psychotherapy with the disadvantaged. In S. L. Garfield & A. E. Bergin (Eds.), *Handbook of psychotherapy and behavior change* (3rd ed.) (pp. 739–775). New York: Wiley.

McCubbin, H. I., & McCubbin, M. A. (1988). Typologies of resilient families: Emerging roles of social class and ethnicity. *Family Relations, 37,* 247–254.

Mezzich, J. E., Fabrega, H., & Kleinman, A. (1992). Cultural validity and DSM-IV. *Journal of Nervous and Mental Disease, 180,* 4.

Mezzich, J. E., Kleinman, A., Fabrega, H., Good, B., Johnson-Powell, G., Lin, K. M., Manson, S., & Parron, D. (1992). *Cultural proposals for DSM-IV*. Submitted to the DSM-IV Task Force by the Steering Committee, NIMH-Sponsored Group on Culture and Diagnosis.

Muñoz, R. F., Hollon, S. D., McGrath, E., Rehm, L. P., & VandenBos, G. R. (1994). On the AHCPR depression in primary care guidelines: Further considerations for practitioners. *American Psychologists, 49,* 42–61.

Myers, H. F., Echemendia, R. J., & Trimble, J. E. (1991). The need for training ethnic minority psychologists. In H. F. Myers, P. Wohlford, L. P. Guzman, & R. J. Echemendia (Eds.), *Ethnic minority perspectives on clinical training and services in psychology* (pp. 3–11), Washington, DC: American Psychological Association.

Padilla, A. M., Ruiz, R. A., & Alverez, R. A. (1975). Community mental health services to Spanish-speaking surnamed population. *American Psychologist, 30,* 892–905.

Parron, D. L. (1990). Federal initiatives in support of mental health research on ethnic minorities. In F. C. Serafica, A. I. Schwebel, R. K. Russell, P. D. Isaac, & L. B. Myers (Eds.), *Mental health of ethnic minorities* (pp. 302–309). New York: Praeger.

Ponterotto, J. G. (1987). Counseling Mexican Americans: A multimodel approach. *Journal of Counseling and Development, 65,* 308–312.

Puente, A. E., Blanch, E., Candland, D. K., Denmark, F. L., Lawman, C., Lutsky, N., Reid, P. T., & Schiavo, R. S. (1993). Toward a psychology of variance: Increasing the presence and understanding of ethnic minorities in psychology. In T. V. McGovern (Ed.), *Handbook for enhancing undergraduate education in psychology* (pp. 71–92). Washington, DC: American Psychological Association.

Ridley, C. R. (1985). Imperatives for ethnic and cultural relevance in psychology training programs. *Professional Psychology: Research and Practice, 16,* 611–622.

Rogler, L. H. (1989). The meaning of culturally sensitive research in mental health. *American Journal of Psychiatry, 146,* 296–303.

Rogler, L. H. (1993). Culturally sensitizing psychiatric diagnosis: A framework for research. *Journal of Nervous and Mental Disease, 181,* 401–408.

Rogler, L. H., & Cortes, D. E. (1993). Help-seeking pathways: A unifying concept in mental health care. *American Journal of Psychiatry, 150,* 554–561.

Roll, S., Millen, L., & Martinez, R. (1980). Common errors in psychotherapy with Chicanos: Extrapolation from research and clinical practice. *Psychotherapy: Theory, Research and Practice, 17,* 158–168.

Root, M. P. P. (1985). Guidelines for facilitating therapy with Asian American clients. *Psychotherapy, 22,* 349–356.

Rush, A. J. (1993). Clinical practice guidelines: Good news, bad news, or no news? *Archives of General Psychiatry, 50,* 483–490.

Rush, A. J., Trivedi, M. H., Schriger, D., & Petty, F. (1992). The development of clinical practice guidelines for the diagnosis and treatment of depression. *General Hospital Psychiatry, 230,* 230–236.

Schulberg, H. C., & Rush, A. J. (1994). Clinical practice guidelines for managing major depression in primary care practice: Implications for psychologists. *American Psychologists, 49,* 34–41.

Sue, S. (1988). Psychotherapeutic services for ethnic minorities: Two decades of research findings. *American Psychologist, 43,* 301–308.

Sue, D. W., Bernier, J. E., Durran, A., Feinberg, L., Pedersen, P., Smith, E. J., & Vasquez-Nuttall, E. (1982). Position paper: Cross cultural counseling competencies. *The Counseling Psychologists, 10,* 45–52.

Sue, S., Fujino, D. C., Hu, Li-tze, & Takeuchi, D. T. (1991). Community mental health services for ethnic minority groups: A test of the cultural responsiveness hypothesis. *Journal of Consulting and Clinical Psychology, 59,* 533–540.

Sue, S., Zane, N., & Young, K. (1994). Research on psychotherapy with culturally diverse populations. In A. Bergin & S. Garfield (Eds.), *Handbook of psychotherapy and behavior change* (4th ed.) (pp. 783–817). New York: Wiley.

Williams, B. S. (1975). Discrimination. In E. J. Lieberman (Ed.), *Mental health: The public health challenge* (pp. 208–211). Washington, DC: American Public Health Association.

Wohlford, P. (1992). Patterns of NIMH support of clinical training for ethnic minorities. *The Clinical Psychologist, 45,* 13–21.

Vega, W. A., & Murphy, J. W. (1990). *Culture and the restructuring of community mental health.* New York: Greenwood.

Yee, A. H., Fairchild, H. H., Weizmann, F., Wyatt, G. E. (1993). Addressing psychology's problems with race. *American Psychologist, 48,* 1132–1140.

Zuckerman, M. (1990). Some dubious premises in research and theory on racial differences. *American Psychologist, 45,* 1297–1303.

Zuniga, M. E. (1988). Assessment issues with Chicanas: Practical implications. *Psychotherapy, 25,* 288–293.

Name Index

Subject Index

Abortion, 237
Acculturation, 34–35
  and Asian Americans, 102, 186–187
  assimilation, as outcome of, 23
  and Chinese Americans, 102
  cross-cultural model, 20–22
  definition of, 21–22
  and ethnic classification, 23–24
  ethnic minorities, impact on, 27, 102, 170, 306
  and group therapy, 118
  and Hispanic Americans, 102, 186–187
  and homelessness, 262
  and immigrants, 27, 302
  integration, as outcome of, 23
  and language, 24–26
  marginalization, as outcome of, 23
  as moderator variables, 22–32, 59–60
  and Native Americans, 59, 102, 186–187
  segregation, as outcome of, 23
  separation, as outcome of, 23
  and sojourners, 27
  and women, 186–187
Acquired Immune Deficiency Syndrome (see AIDS)
Activism, 242, 245–246
African Americans, 1–2, 4, 6–7
  acculturation of, 26
  and AIDS/HIV, 236, 237–238, 240–241, 243, 245
  and Black Identity Development Model, 23
  child rearing, practices of, 172
  and community mental health centers, 130, 136–137
  depression among, 45, 170, 203
  and desegregated schools, 31
  and Developmental Inventory of Black Consciousness, 24
  family therapy for, 174–175
  and homelessness, 251–255, 257, 258, 259
  mental health services for, 272–276
  mortality rates for, 235, 245
  oppression of, 32–33
  physical health of, 235
  population of, 2–3, 5–6
  psychological testing for, 61, 62, 67
  as psychologists, 284–284
  and psychotherapy, 84–85, 87, 172, 267–268, 272–274, 277
  racism and, 33–34, 111, 140, 187
  schizophrenia among, 45–47
  sex roles among, 175, 182–183
  substance abuse among, 168, 216, 217–218
    treatment for, 224, 225, 227
  suicide rate of, 169
  and traditional healing practices, 152–154, 243
  verbal styles of, 176
    and "Black English," 166, 191
  violence, issue of, 136–137
  and white values, 23–24
  women, 181, 185–186, 187, 189
Afrocentrism, 289
Ageism, 204

Agency for Health Care Policy Research (AHCRP), 311
AIDS (Acquired Immune Deficiency Syndrome), 234–246
  activism, importance of, 242, 245–246
  African Americans and, 236, 237–238, 240–241, 243, 245
  Asian Americans and, 236, 241
  and at-risk activities, 240–241
  bisexuality and, 239, 240
  census data for, 236
  cultural attitudes toward, 237–238
  education about, 239, 242, 244
  ethnic minorities and, 234–236, 237
  family networks and, 241–242
  health care delivery for, 242–244
  homosexuality and, 238–239, 241–242
  women and, 236, 237–238, 239, 240
Al-Anon, 226
Alcohol abuse, 15 (see also Substance abuse)
  among African Americans, 217–218
  among Asian Americans, 223
  among elderly, 209–210
  among Hispanic Americans, 221–222
  and homelessness, 254
  among Native Americans, 219–220
Alcoholics Anonymous (A.A.), 209–210

327